WHAT DEMOCRACY
LOOKS LIKE

WHAT DEMOCRACY LOOKS LIKE

A New Critical Realism for a Post-Seattle World

EDITED BY

Amy Schrager Lang and Cecelia Tichi

RUTGERS UNIVERSITY PRESS

NEW BRUNSWICK, NEW JERSEY, AND LONDON

Library of Congress Cataloging-in-Publication Data
What democracy looks like : a new critical realism for a post-Seattle world / edited by Amy
Schrager Lang and Cecelia Tichi.
    p. cm.
    Includes bibliographical references.
    ISBN-13: 978-0-8135-3716-0 (hardcover: alk. paper)
    ISBN-13: 978-0-8135-3717-7 (pbk.: alk. paper)
    1. Democracy.   2. Anti-globalization movement.   3. Social change.   4. Political development.
I. Lang, Amy Schrager.   II. Tichi, Cecelia, 1942-
    JC423.W448 2006
    321.8—dc22

              2005011644

A British Cataloging-in-Publication record for this book is available from the British Library

To the activists of Seattle

To the next generation
of teachers and scholars
of U.S. culture

CONTENTS

PREFACE

This project originated in despair and optimism: despair at the rapidly failing commitment to social democracy in the United States, and optimism at the rise of a generation determined to imagine new social and economic arrangements and to work to bring them into being. Because of its origins, *What Democracy Looks Like* differs substantially from the customary essay collection. Such collections ordinarily rely for their coherence on their devotion to a literary canon or genre, a single author, a literary movement. All have a built-in, self-evident unity; their essays fall into certain clearly defined categories.

What Democracy Looks Like arrives without the customary long foreground of scholarly dialogue. It intervenes peremptorily in the contemporary historical moment and assigns a new, unfamiliar name to that moment: the name of the first American city to see an outpouring of protest against the catastrophic inequalities that divide nations and persons. The attention that the events in Seattle drew to the growing impact of privatization, corporate globalization, militarism, and political repression on the workplace, the environment, and public life forced us to rethink the relationship between our work and our world.

As part of this rethinking, we appealed to colleagues across a broad range of fields of expertise to join us in imagining how "Seattle" might refocus our teaching and scholarship. Somewhat to our surprise, we confess, these colleagues were not only willing to set aside their own research to meet the breakneck schedule of this collection but were also eager to turn their attention to the quandary of how our work would change were the urgent issues of Seattle to frame it.

The essays that comprise *What Democracy Looks Like* reflect the variety of scholarship now undertaken under the aegis of U.S. literary and cultural studies: work that attends to the physical costs of the new world order, that experiments with the limits of exegesis, that addresses the loss and reclamation of literal and metaphorical common space in a world for sale, and that reflects on the problem of democracy in our times. Several generations of scholars bring their different perspectives and expertise to the shaping of this project. Their insights about what democracy—and contemporary literary study—looks like press us to imagine new critical paradigms.

What Democracy Looks Like differs from other essay collections in another way, too. Its introduction, as readers will discover, provides a short course in the social and political history surrounding Seattle. In its notes, readers will find a bibliography of recent investigations of social issues ranging from the privatization of natural resources and stealth government by multinational corporations to expanding militaries and the decimation of national economies. Alongside the introduction, we include a timeline indicating the extent and range of international public outcry against these developments in recent years.

Novelists, poets, playwrights, and journalists have taken up the issues raised by Seattle more readily than have scholars or teachers. The section of the introduction called "A New Bookshelf" provides an overview of their work, furnishing primary literary resources for scholarship and teaching. These titles, we propose, constitute the beginnings of a new literary canon through which students of U.S. literature and culture can find ways to think and talk about literary interventions in social crises.

"Structural violence" is used by some social scientists to describe the endemic but often invisible damage inflicted on populations by standing social and economic arrangements. Along with the short history of Seattle and the new bookshelf, we offer the concept of structural violence as an analytic tool for a new critical realism.

The editors and contributors to *What Democracy Looks Like* represent something like an affinity group, to use the language of Seattle, a cohort of literary scholars joined by their deep concern with current social and political conditions in the United States and elsewhere. Together, we intend to initiate a new movement in U.S. literary study. *What Democracy Looks Like* is both summons and mandate.

ACKNOWLEDGMENTS

Anyone who has edited a collection knows that the first thanks must go to those who contribute their time, their intellectual energy, and their goodwill to the project. The contributors to this volume have given both their wisdom and new insights into the recalcitrant problem of the relationship between our daily work as scholars and teachers and the catastrophic global conditions that surround us as we undertake that work. Their commitment to the larger purposes of this project was evident in the alacrity with which they agreed to contribute, in their willingness to adapt to an extraordinarily tight publication schedule, in their graciousness throughout—for all of which we are deeply grateful.

Leslie Mitchner of Rutgers University Press supported this project from the very beginning. Her continuing enthusiasm, her practical assistance, and her flexibility have made the creation of this collection possible. Adi Hovav offered us invaluable help through each stage of production, and Margaret Case deftly and swiftly handled the task of copyediting across a range of styles. We also thank Caleb Huntington for help on short notice.

Our respective institutions—Syracuse University and Vanderbilt University—supported us, both materially and as sites of research and planning. To Natalie Baggett of Vanderbilt's English Department, who assumed much of the clerical burden of this project, our heartfelt thanks.

As always, the people with whom we share our lives, Bill Tichi and Julie Abraham, gave us not only their encouragement and their patience but also their invaluable assistance in the making of this book. The experiences of our children—in the university, in the workplace, and on the streets—dramatically heightened our awareness of the conditions this collection addresses. For showing us what democracy now looks like and what worlds are possible, we thank Claire, Daniel, Julia, and Emma.

Narrative is not just story but also action, the telling of a story *by someone to some-one on some occasion for some purpose.*
   —James Phelan

A poem in its own oblique way is deeply telling of the lives of the world we exist in.
   —Homi Bhabha

What do we make of the fact that the rise of political democracy around the world . . . has been accompanied by a global collapse of social democracy: the savaging of the social safety nets, welfare systems and price subsidies, and the global privatization of public lands, public industries, and public services—a new round of enclosures?
   —Michael Denning

We believe if we can say what many already know in such a way as to incite courage, if the image or the word or the act breaches the indifference by which people survive, day to day, enough will protest that by their physical voices alone they will stir the hurricane.
   —Barry Lopez

WHAT DEMOCRACY LOOKS LIKE

A New Critical Realism: Introduction

Amy Schrager Lang and Cecelia Tichi

> The naming of the intolerable is itself hope.
> —John Berger

Retrieving "Seattle"

This volume, true to its title, is meant to inaugurate a new critical realism in U.S. literary studies in a post-"Seattle" world. This world came into being for many Americans following the much-publicized convergence of activists at the Third Ministerial meeting of the World Trade Organization (WTO). The most dramatic objection to corporate globalization the United States has seen, Seattle was the first major expression on U.S. soil of worldwide opposition to the growing disparity between the lives of the rich and the poor, both persons and nations.

To address that world, however, requires that this project first contend with the reframing of history that followed September 11, 2001. Since that day, we have been told again and again that our history and public life are forever transformed: the world as we knew it, our political leaders insist, will never be the same. Institutionalized reminders of "9/11" have marked and reinforced the notion of a nation fundamentally altered. Pundits assert America's lost innocence; coffee table books commemorate the tragedy; terror alerts from the newly organized Department of Homeland Security punctuate our lives. Television footage of the jetliners aimed at the World Trade Center mark each anniversary, as do reruns of the towers' collapse. The numbers "9/11" and the term "Ground Zero" serve to instill the belief in Americans that the United States and the twenty-first century are defined entirely by this singular catastrophic national trauma. Everything before it, the public rhetoric insists, belongs to an irrecoverable past.

Tantamount to a nationalistic version of religious doctrine, the notion of a transformative September 11 allows events of national, or even global, import to be subsumed into the permanent "war on terror" and renders it un-American to suggest that the problem of terrorism is a long-standing international one. The idea of a rupture in history—a temporal as well as a physical Ground Zero—rewrites the national chronology, mapping all events, whatever their social, political, or cultural provenance, in relation to one cataclysmic moment. From that moment forward, every occasion of public life—from the Superbowl to the presidential inauguration, from a train derailment to a biomedical breakthrough, from a power outage to a political protest—can be assimilated to the rhetoric of terror.

To recover Seattle is to restore to legitimacy an event invoked for rhetorical purposes since September 11 to support the permanent "war on terror." The activists of Seattle 1999 have been assigned the title "anarchists," a name long calculated to terrorize Americans, by law enforcement officials and journalists.

The elision of "anarchists"—and by extension all dissenters, protesters, activists—with "terrorists" is used to justify mass preemptive arrest, protest pens of chain link and barbed wire, rubber bullets, pepper spray, and 50,000-volt Taser guns.* Seattle is simultaneously relegated to an irrecoverable past and exploited to historicize and legitimate what some call "the war without end."

Seattle involved not New York's towering symbols of world trade, but rather conference hotel gatherings of the 130-nation organization that formulates trade policy for the planet, thereby affecting hundreds of millions of lives. The WTO and local planners expected the meeting to showcase the triumph of free markets and free trade on the verge of the third millennium and to spotlight a jewel of a U.S. city whose name is synonymous with aircraft manufacture, the computer revolution, and franchised upscale coffee in an era of branded lifestyles.

Instead, three thousand miles from lower Manhattan and some twenty-two months before the September 11 attacks, tens of thousands of activists converged on the WTO meeting. The media's first flippant and erroneous nickname for them, "antiglobalizers," does not begin to encompass the diversity of interests or the range of political positions represented in Seattle, let alone the distances traveled to reach the Pacific Northwest port city. A major television news story for several days, "Seattle" was presented as a sudden, unforeseen, and unforeseeable eruption of street demonstrations and civil disorder, a motley mix of activists, unionists, anarchists, and police, a dark carnival of puppets and pepper spray.

Behind the TV news clips and the sneering nickname—The Battle of Seattle—was an event that cannot be allowed to recede into the mists of public amnesia nor to be appropriated for statist control or fear mongering. A display of outrage at the widening chasm separating the interests of corporate and government elites from those of ordinary citizens in the United States and abroad, it brought activists from across the country face to face with those who broker their fates as workers and as citizens.

Prior to November 1999, Seattle was largely without current political resonance for scholars of U.S. culture, as for most citizens. On the literary-cultural map, it appeared as the city named after the famous Native American leader whose 1855 plea for the sanctity of the natural environment and an amicable accord between pioneer settlers and native peoples graces the pages of the newer anthologies of American literature (despite recent revelations of its dubious au-

---

*The astonishingly and intentionally vague language of the first USA Patriot Act conspicuously conflates terrorists and political activists by stating that "terrorism" includes "acts that violate federal or state law, and are committed with *intent of affecting government policy* and are *potentially* dangerous" (18USC L2331). By this definition, a charge of terrorism could, in theory, be sustained against almost any form of civil disobedience. Citing Seattle in its first paragraph, a front-page article in the *New York Times* ten days before the 2004 Republican National Convention ran under the title "Anarchists Emerge as the Convention's Wild Card" (August 20, 2004, A1). The specter of anarchism is now commonly invoked in the news media whenever demonstrators gather, while "terrorism" accounts, directly or indirectly, for all social ills. See Nancy Chang, *Silencing Political Dissent: How Post-September 11 Anti-Terrorist Measures Threaten Our Civil Liberties* (New York: Seven Stories Press, 2002), and Lewis H. Lapham, *Gag Rule: On the Suppression of Dissent and the Stifling of Democracy* (New York: Penguin, 2004). For historical background, see Jeffory [sic] A. Clymer, *America's Culture of Terrorism: Violence, Capitalism, and the Written Word* (Chapel Hill: University of North Carolina Press, 2003).

thenticity). Or, in another register, as the site of the 1919 general strike and a particular target for the violence of Attorney General A. Mitchell Palmer's raids during the first "red scare." At midcentury, Seattle commanded attention as the site of the 1962 World's Fair, its futuristic Space Needle remaining as a signature landmark of the city skyline. By the late twentieth century, the city had come to be known as the home of Boeing, Microsoft, and Starbucks, of Kurt Cobain and grunge music, and of Judi Bari, the Earth First activist responsible for persuading lumberjacks and environmentalists to join forces to fight Washington State's lumber interests.

If Seattle had no special political resonance for those of us engaged in U.S. literary studies before 1999, so too the World Trade Organization and its global trade policies did not, on the whole, command the interest of scholar/teachers of U.S. literature and culture. The devastating lending practices of the International Monetary Fund (IMF) and the World Bank, now so familiar, were then only barely visible. Absorbed in countering right-wing attacks on the humanities and buffered by the perquisites of our stable academic lives, we failed to read in the local changes on our campuses signs of the far more dramatic global shift toward inequality, privatization, and political and intellectual repression that Seattle would address.

Nonetheless, those signs were everywhere. Cast publicly as a response to the indoctrination of students by "tenured radicals," a 1991 University of Michigan commencement address by George H. W. Bush formally inaugurated the "culture wars" of the 1990s. In that address Bush warned that "political extremists roam the land, abusing the privilege of free speech, [and] setting citizens against each other on the basis of their class or race." [1] Postsecondary education, the political right claimed, had become a wasteland of multiculturalism, "political correctness," and boundless relativism. Pandering to minorities, as the right saw it, the university had abandoned classical truths in a wash of popular culture and French philosophy. [2] But the virulence of the attacks on changes in scholarly and pedagogical practice during the 1970s and 1980s hinted at the real affront to the right. Invoking a putative meritocracy that purportedly reigned in some Arcadian academic past, ultraconservative critics of the "new" university took their stand on the question of affirmative action, the legal strategy that opened higher education to women and African Americans. The real "war," as those on the right were fully aware, was over who would—and who would not—have access to the resources and prestige of the universities.

Not surprisingly, the impact of right-wing opposition to affirmative action quickly became apparent in our classrooms, as well-funded plaintiffs brought suit after suit to the courts to block policies that insured racial diversity in university admissions. These, combined with soaring tuitions, draconian cuts in state funding for pre- and postsecondary education, the increasingly straitened economic circumstances of middle-class families, and the acute curtailment of direct educational lending, have sounded an alarm among educators and scholars.* Increasingly, the composition of our classrooms has come to mirror the

5

*The constriction of the American middle class has meant that many students at public insitutions must extend their years-to-degree to accommodate the demands of part- or full-time work. Others are stalled by the

widening disparity of wealth recorded in U.S. census data and by think tanks across the nation — with elite private colleges now filled with students drawn almost entirely from the upper echelons of society. Anthony W. Marx, president of Amherst College, used his 2004 commencement address to admonish his listeners that "our great colleges and universities have hit a wall of blocked opportunity. . . . Our nation and our colleges are moving toward an inequality not seen since the Great Depression."[3]

Just as our classrooms are shaped by widening economic inequality, so too is the campus workforce. Emulating the corporations, colleges and universities "externalize" their costs, systematically outsourcing as many services as possible, shedding workers and, with them, any accountability for the conditions of work on campus.[4] No longer on the payroll of the college or university, staff have become low-wage McWorkers hired by national or transnational corporations variously to cut grass, shelve books, clean dormitories, repair computers, or police students.* Deprived of whatever benefits attend university employment, they are, for the most part, deprived as well of the advantages of collective bargaining, particularly when the so-called parent company is headquartered far away and the workforce scattered.†

---

dearth of seats in courses required for their majors as schools cope with severe budget cuts. Newspapers report unprecedented requests by hard-pressed middle and upper-middle-income parents for tuition refinancing and call attention to stunning increases in educational debt (see *New York Times*, February 3, 2002, and January 28, 2003, 1A; *Wall Street Journal*, January 8, 2003, D1, D3. In December 2004, the U.S. Department of Education announced that, effective in 2005, the Pell Grants of 1.3 million low-income students will be cut back; an additional 89,000 students will lose their grants entirely. According to the *New York Times*, "The new rules are expected to have a domino effect across every type of financial aid, tightening access to billions of dollars in state and institutional grants and, in turn, increasing the reliance on loans to pay for college." See Greg Winter, "Students Will Bear More of College Cost under Aid Change," *New York Times*, December 23, 2004, A1, A14.

* A 2000 survey by Patricia A. Wood of the Clearinghouse on Higher Education at George Washington University defines outsourcing (or "contracting") as a form of privatization in which a college or university contracts with "an external organization to provide a traditional campus function or service"; the contractor, it continues, "either takes over the employees of the university, paying the group according to its standards, or replaces the university employees with its own staff." Advocates of this practice point to reductions in labor and benefit costs, critics to the degrading of wages and working conditions for campus employees. In addition to campus bookstores and dining services, the survey finds that it is now "a legitimate option" to outsource "additional campus functions, including facilities operation, computer services, security, child care, residence halls, teaching hospitals, remedial classes, and even entire institutions." Wood's survey projects that over one-half of colleges and universities "expect to contract for more services in the coming years" (see ERIC Identifier ED446726; ERIC Clearinghouse on Higher Education Washington DC/BBB32577). A 2004 study, "Outsourcing of Instruction at Community Colleges," directed by Thomas Bailey and James Jacobs of Columbia University Teachers College, reports similar findings for community colleges (see "Executive Summary").

† Intervention on behalf of the lowest-wage campus workers, when it occurs at all, is driven by the conscientious, but unreliable, activism of students and faculty. The most notable instance of such intervention to date is the Harvard Living Wage Campaign, which, after a lengthy battle, forced an increase in the appalling wages

The outsourcing of services is not the only way in which higher education has come to mirror the corporate practices highlighted by Seattle. Just as the corporate world depends on multitier contracts that offer some employees diminished compensation and benefits relative to others, so the university too depends on a multitier employment system. Those at the top reap financial rewards at unprecedented levels: university chancellors' and presidents' compensation packages now mirror those of corporate executives, even as tuitions rise and state higher education budgets are slashed. "These huge salaries feed into the ongoing corporatization of the academy," warns Roger Bowen, the former president of the State University of New York at New Paltz, adding, "we send the wrong message when we transmogrify our campus presidents into C.E.O.'s." Compensation for instructional faculty at the low end of the academic hierarchy, meanwhile, mimics that of contingent corporate workers. Part-time or fee-for-service instructors on whose labor academic departments rely are routinely denied the health care, insurance, and retirement benefits guaranteed to their tenured or tenure-track colleagues who teach fewer sections of the same courses in adjacent classrooms.*

From the menial to the professional, campus work is contracted out; students are recast as "consumers," administrators as CEOs or as "managers"; instructional material is dubbed "courseware" amid questions of who funds, owns, and will profit from the "intellectual property" of faculty. Corporate logos blossom in campus "food courts," bookstores, and gyms,+ while corporation-funded institutes and academic chairs proliferate. Higher education ceases to be a public resource and becomes instead, and increasingly, a perogative of the monied classes; academic freedom ceases to be a given. We confront, that is to say, something like a "structural adjustment" that has brought the shape and practices of the university into accord with the new world order highlighted by Seattle.[5]

As Michael Denning and others have observed, we are, like it or not, "living

---

of workers on the best-endowed campus in the United States. See Greg Halpern, *Harvard Works Because We Do* (New York: W. W. Norton, 2003).

* See Sam Dillon, "Ivory Tower Executive Suite Gets C.E.O.-Level Salaries," *New York Times*, November 15, 2004, A18. The 1990s saw an unrelenting unionization effort by graduate students at institutions, from the University of California, Rutgers University, the University of Illinois, and the University of Michigan to the Ivy League. As of this writing, the Republican-controlled National Labor Relations Board has thwarted union drives by graduate students at private institutions such as Brown University, the University of Chicago, Columbia University, New York University, the University of Pennsylvania, and Yale University.

+ Students are far more attuned to corporate incursions in the university than faculty. Even before Seattle, United Students against Sweatshops were pressuring administrations to cease contracting with suppliers of insignia wear who violate the rights of their workers. See Andrew Ross, ed., *No Sweat: Fashion, Free Trade and the Rights of Garment Workers* (New York: Verso, 1997). Likewise, students on "Coke campuses," where, by contract, all beverages offered in eateries, at campus events, and in vending machines must be provided by Coca Cola, have joined the "Campaign to Stop Killer Coke" directed at ending Coca Cola's human rights abuses in Central America, southern Africa, and India.

in the corporation," or anyway working in it.[6] While the most devastating effects are felt elsewhere and by others, the degradation of the workplace, the disregard for human needs, the pressure to privatize essential goods and services, the repression of dissent — in short, the critical issues raised in Seattle — are no longer distant. It is, then, imperative to retrieve and engage Seattle. In its wake, teachers and scholars of U.S. literature and culture must imagine new ways of looking at the world, at the narrative, the poem, the essay, the drama, commensurate with the social and political order we inhabit.

The Imprint of Seattle

By the end of the week of November 29, 1999, many Americans had come to recognize the presence of profound sociopolitical purposes and energies in the television footage of marches, rallies, and police crackdowns. The moving montage of tens of thousands of labor unionists, environmentalists, indigenous activists, homeless people, students, radical anticapitalists, pure food advocates, academics, consumer groups, welfare rights activists, community organizers, Latin American solidarity groups, farmers, and others provided a lens through which to focus the present — and to see the worst and best prospects for the future. In all their variety, these groups converged on Seattle to call a halt to the WTO meetings in the name of human life, economic justice, and planetary health. No isolated event, the Seattle convergence was planned to coincide with demonstrations worldwide, from Hong Kong and Iceland to France, Turkey, England, and Pakistan; from New Delhi, Amsterdam, Geneva, Buenos Aires, and Mexico City to Brisbane.

Whatever bemusement or skepticism may initially have attended the convergence of protesters in Seattle, the impact of that convergence is undeniable. The steel worker and professor who marched shoulder to shoulder with the Korean farmer and, famously, the environmentalist costumed as a sea turtle asserted irrevocably, as they intended to do, another less tangible convergence. As activists took control of the intersections surrounding Sixth and Union in downtown Seattle, they mapped out for the rest of us the intersecting corporate and governmental interests that impoverish workers, privatize resources, undercut local markets, increase joblessness and degrade work conditions, undermine environmental protections, assault indigenous land rights, and militarize police forces around the globe. Much as the city fathers would like to live down the "Battle of Seattle," the WTO protest marks a mappable, undeniable, embodied convergence of the central issues of our historical moment.

Despite the importance we ascribe to it, Seattle marks a single intermediate point in a still-lengthening history of resistance to rampant corporate globalization. Behind it lies an intercontinental network of resistance dating from the Zapatista uprising in 1994 and encompassing demonstrations, strikes, boycotts, and disruptions in every corner of the globe, from Mexico to France to Turkey to India. (See "A Short World History of Seattle" for this history.)* Nonetheless,

---

* Resistance to neoliberalism and the anticapitalist movement form the subject of a raft of new books, among them. Notes from Nowhere, ed., *We Are Everywhere: The Irresistible Rise of Global Anticapitalism* (London:

Seattle signals the particular point by which the devastating impact of world debt, of demands for "structural adjustment," of international trade policies on the global South — and the opposition prompted by them — became too pressing for even the corporate-controlled U.S. media to ignore. As the *Los Angeles Times* put it, "On the tear-gas shrouded streets of Seattle, the unruly forces of democracy collided with the elite world of trade policy. And when the [WTO] meeting ended in failure . . . the elitists had lost and the debate had changed forever."[7]

The press began to take note of the soaring injury rates and appalling working and living conditions of workers in the *maquiladoras* and the criminal collaboration of U.S. apparel manufacturers and East Asian sweatshops. The decimation of local agriculture from the Caribbean to Africa by subsidized U.S. (and European) agribusinesses and of indigenous industry by the lending terms of the IMF, the "water wars" in Bolivia, and the ever more violent policing of dissent at home and abroad were suddenly newsworthy. The impact of a world in which forty-seven of the one hundred largest economies are nation-states, while fifty-three are multinational corporations, became unavoidable.[8]

What the press was less inclined to notice was the failure of social democracy in the United States. By 2001, the United States had become the most unequal society in the industrialized West, with 40 percent of the nation's wealth held by 1 percent of the population. This, despite the purported ubiquity of the American middle class. The numbers — floating through foundation and government reports, buried in the back pages of the *Wall Street Journal* or the *New York Times*, distilled in a raft of recent book-length exposés — tell a frightening tale. Despite the fact that the United States has the highest per capita income worldwide, "the gap between the top and bottom 10 percent is so large that those at the bottom are considered poorer than the bottom 10 percent in most industrialized countries — the United States ranking nineteenth" among these. Some 37 million Americans live in poverty; 45 million lack health care. The U.S. Census Bureau estimates that 3.7 million American households suffer from hunger, while 9 million additional households have "uncertain" access to food.[9] In 2004, it was reported that a typical U.S. worker needed three times the current hourly minimum wage to afford a two-bedroom apartment, thus excluding one-quarter of the working population from such housing.* Like its analogues abroad, domestic structural adjustment signals the catastrophic abandonment of the needs of people by government.

Verso, 2004); Benjamin Shepard and Ronald Hayduk, *From Act Up to the WTO: Urban Protest and Community Building in the Era of Globalization* (London: Verso, 2002); Tom Martes, ed., *A Movement of Movements: Is Another World Really Possible?* (London: Verso, 2004); Eddie Yuen, Daniel Burton-Ross, and George Katsiaficas, eds., *Confronting Capitalism: Dispatches from a Global Movement* (New York: Soft Skull, 2004); Alexander Cockburn, Jeffrey St. Clair, and Allen Sekula, *5 Days that Shook the World: Seattle and Beyond* (London: Verso, 2000). For one account of the Zapatista rebellion, see Subcommandante Insurgente Marcos, *¡Ya Basta!: Ten Years of the Zapatista Uprising* (Oakland: AK Press, 2004).

* To fully document U.S. domestic degradation is a task beyond our capacity here, but the signs are ominous: infant mortality rates are up; earning power is down; housing costs are ballooning; public schools are crumbling; health care is unaffordable; private pension funds are evaporating; personal bankruptcy and home fore-

The 1999 convergence in Seattle was neither the first nor the last outpouring of public protest against economic globalization. On the contrary, its essential elements have been repeated whenever multinational trade and banking agreements are negotiated behind closed doors — in Prague (2000), Quebec (2001), Genoa (2001), Cancun (2003), Miami (2003), and Santiago (2004). And with each reiteration, the determination to avoid transparency and avert public criticism becomes more conspicuous. When they are not held in remote locations (the 2001 WTO meetings, for example, were held in Doha, Qatar), the meetings of the world's power brokers are, since Seattle, routinely conducted behind barricades. And dissent is met with increasingly militarized police violence.

The fences and walls that now invariably surround the meetings of national and international elites stand as synecdotal evidence of their fundamentally undemocratic nature. A provocation to protesters — a fraction of whom inevitably try to breach them — the walls of concrete, chain link, and barbed wire, like the walls of armed and armored police, have come to symbolize the divide between those who make the policies and those who live with them. Ironically, at least one WTO representative casts this divide as between economic realists and economic theorists. "The protesters are simply too focused on reality, and on facts and figures," insists WTO spokesperson Granwyth Hulatheri. "We have to find a way to convince perhaps not the protesters, but the protester's children, to follow thinkers like Milton Friedman and Darwin," the putative fathers of "free market" economics and "natural" social selection.[10]

---

closure rates—and military expenditures—have reached historic highs. Meanwhile, under the sign of privatization, migratory corporations evade taxes and hold local and state governments hostage; environmental and workplace safeguards are dismantled; public treasuries are depleted; and more than three-fifths of employers offer their workers no ongoing contracts. To see the fuller dimensions of some of these problems, see C.I.A. *World Factbook* (Washington, D.C., January 2004); *Out of Reach* (Washington, D.C.: National Low-Income Housing Coalition, 2004); *Working Hard, Falling Short* (n.p.: Annie E. Casey, Ford, and Rockefeller Foundations, 2004); *Tax Notes* (Arlington, VA, 2004); Noreena Hertz, *The Silent Takeover: Global Capitalism and the Death of Democracy* (New York: Free Press, 2001); Elizabeth Warren and Amelia Tyagi, *The Two-Income Trap: Why Middle-Class Mothers and Fathers Are Going Broke* (New York: Basic Books, 2003); James G. Speth, *Red Sky at Morning: America and the Crisis of the Global Environment: A Citizen's Agenda for Action* (New Haven: Yale University Press, 2004). See also Robert H. Frank and Philip J. Cook, *The Winner-Take-All Society: Why the Few at the Top Get So Much More Than the Rest of Us* (New York: Penguin, 1996); Beth Shulman, *The Betrayal of Work: How Low-Wage Jobs Fail Thirty Million Americans and Their Families* (New York: New Press, 2005); Thomas Frank, *One Market under God: Extreme Capitalism, Market Populism, and the End of Economic Democracy* (New York: Doubleday, 2000); Kevin Phillips, *Wealth and Democracy: A Political History of the American Rich* (New York: Broadway Books, 2002); Lou Dobbs, *Exporting America: Why Corporate Greed Is Shipping American Jobs Overseas* (New York: Warner, 2004); David Cay Johnston, *Perfectly Legal: The Covert Campaign to Rig Our Tax System to Benefit the Super Rich—and Cheat Everybody Else* (New York: Portfolio, 2003); Marcia Angell, M.D., *The Truth about the Drug Companies: How They Deceive Us and What to Do about It* (New York: Random House, 2004); Tara Herival and Paul Wright, eds., *Prison Nation: The Warehousing of America's Poor* (New York: Routledge, 2003); Gerald J. Swanson, *America the Broke: How the Reckless Spending of the White House and Congress Is Bankrupting Our Country and Destroying Our Children's Future* (New York: Doubleday, 2004).

The activists' attention to "reality" sounds the keynote for this volume. It calls us to a new critical realism, a new attention to the material conditions out of which the literature we teach arises. It speaks to the urgent need for what Michael Denning calls a "new kind of 'inter-discipline,' a new way of looking at the world"—and at the text. For scholars and classroom teachers of U.S. literature and culture at the secondary and college/university levels, it mandates new approaches to the books that are fundamental to our work lives.

A New Bookshelf

Seattle changed what we read, how we read, and the nature of our teaching and writing. A palpable sense of social urgency drove this change and began to disrupt the categories that organize our work. New accounts of the literary and cultural impositions of class, of U.S. imperialism, of consumer capitalism across the lines of race, ethnicity, gender, sexuality, region, and religion—and across time—as well as new and closer readings of the documents of U.S. legal, political, and business history, moreover, suggested newly sophisticated ways of understanding literature as a register of changed material conditions, social crisis, and ideological conflict. These question the relation between literary periods, the uses of theory, and status of established literary taxonomies. Moreover, they make compelling the work of contemporary authors who offer, in literary form, new epistemologies, new histories, and new visions of social engagement.

A number of these authors summon teachers and students of literature to a set of texts largely bypassed in criticism and the classroom: narratives of social disclosure or exposé. Better known as investigative journalism or muckraking, these are more precisely termed "civic melodrama."[11] Portraying a social world roiled in stark inequality, rampant corruption, human suffering, and unchecked greed, they promote incentives for socially corrective activism. Employing literary and rhetorical strategies for social diagnosis and remediation, they urge the recognition of common interests and obligations. Alongside the "classics" and the newly recovered works of women, African Americans, ethnic and gay/lesbian/queer writers, the theory and the criticism that furnish our libraries, the bookshelf of a teacher-scholar of U.S. literature might now hold such civic melodramas as Barbara Ehrenreich's *Nickel and Dimed: On (Not) Getting by in America* (2001), whose protagonist narrates the harrowing experience of minimum-wage work in a social milieu that renders the worker desperate and invisible. It might include Eric Schlosser's *Fast Food Nation: The Dark Side of the All-American Meal* (2001), a low-key but devastating exposé of an industrial meat and fast food oligarchy that is as politically powerful as it is dangerous — even lethal — to its workers and consumers. Both are required reading these days on some college campuses. With these, one might find Naomi Klein's *No Logo: Taking Aim at the Brand Bullies* (2000)—the story, told with ironic wit, of global corporate branding, of McJobs, and of the young activists who resist with an array of tactics from lawsuits to street carnivals. Or Laurie Garrett's *Betrayal of Trust: The Collapse of Global Public Health* (2000), a Tolstoyan narrative with vividly realized "settings" from tuberculosis-ridden south-central Los Angeles to the "Alienation Zone" of Chernobyl. Or Joseph T. Hallinan's *Going up the River: Travels in a Prison Nation* (2001), a picaresque journey through a

United States in which the human and monetary cost of the recent prison boom is captured in the image of sunlight on razor wire — a social "fool's gold."[12]

Likewise, the post-Seattle bookshelf might contain a recent American jeremiad, Walter Mosely's *Workin' on the Chain Gang* (2000). In the wake of Seattle, Mosely, author of the popular E. Z. Rawlins detective series, published an extended essay on the deteriorating socioeconomic conditions afflicting Americans of every "group, creed, race, and religion" — poor medical care, job insecurity, inadequate education, and exclusion from the benefits of high productivity.[13] Arguing that heretofore privileged whites now find themselves subject to a share of the social exclusions and subordination experienced by blacks and other minorities throughout American history, the African-American novelist-turned-essayist decries a world in which "decisions are made by governments in concert with corporations that are designed to increase profit and influence, not to advance humanitarian ends" (5). As Cornell West more recently and succintly put it in a dialogue with Toni Morrison: "Now the whole nation is niggerized, and everybody's got to deal with it."[14]

The altered conditions of the nation, the extension of social and economic subordination to which West and Mosely point, and the global effects of a permanent state of war inflect a startling range of contemporary U.S. literature and film. This impact is particularly visible in the new attention and prestige lent documentary film by the work of directors like Michael Moore and Errol Morse and in the broad resurgence of the topical in film more generally. These crises are, moreover, reinforced in recent drama and poetry. The revival of political and documentary drama by a growing cohort of writers, from Anna Deveare Smith and Suzan-Lori Parks to Tony Kushner and others, occupies a crucial place in the new literary landscape.[15] Smith's *Twilight: Los Angeles, 1992* — based on the police beating of African American Rodney King, the trial of the police, and the riots following their exoneration — assembles public and private documents to confront audiences with the hard facts of the new world order. So does Victoria Brittain and Gillian Slovo's *Guantanamo: "Honor Bound to Defend Freedom"* — a scathing and painful portrayal of the illegal detention of alleged Middle Eastern "enemy combatants" by the U.S. militaries. From the one-actor play to Kushner's grand dramas, most notably *Angels in America*, these plays force recognition of a world of escalating violence and increasing social and material inequity.[16]

So too does much recent poetry, from the anthology *Against Forgetting* (2001) to Philip Levine's *What Work Is* (1991), Spencer Reece's *The Clerk's Tale* (2004), and Wesley McNair's *My Brother Running* (1993).[17] *Affrilachia* (2000), the debut collection of the Kentucky-born Frank X. Walker, exposes the cynical exploitation of young black men in "Death by Basketball," in which the NBA, Nike, and the Coca-Cola brand Sprite all cynically manufacture "a dream" that kills "legitimate futures / every night / under street lights / wherever these products / are sold." The late Denise Levertov, in "Roast Potatoes," contrasts the homelessness of the 1960s with that of the 1990s, noticing a lost camaraderie in the Bronx of "old fashioned hobos" and a new census of homeless "throngs," now including women. In "Losing a House," Mary Oliver laments the forced departure of longtime occupants unable to keep their beloved, if ramshackle, shore house in a severely monetized world. The buyers "can sign the papers, / can turn the key" because they, unlike the longtime dwellers who love, know, and understand the house, have "money, money, money."[18]

If the impact of global structural adjustment on the intimate lives of Americans leaves its trace effects on much recent poetry, its impact is bluntly visible in a new body of fiction. Only a portion of this fiction is by or about Americans, but all of it recognizes the central role of the United States in global inequality and international repression. Mosely's American crisis is dramatized in domestic terms in André Dubus III's novel, *House of Sand and Fog* (1999), whose central conflict is the life-or-death struggle for the consummate emblem of American middle-classness: home ownership. As a single woman and a former Iranian air force colonel fight for possession of a modest West Coast house, readers are pressed to the realization that their circumstances mirror those of the imperiled U.S. upper- and lower-middle class. The woman, reduced to living in her car, slips from middle-class life altogether; the colonel, having lost the lavish resources of his past life, hides his menial low-wage jobs from family and friends — just as laid-off corporate executives are urged to do in a recent *Wall Street Journal* advice column.[19]

Whereas Dubus portrays the domestic tragedy of the middle class, Barry Lopez's volume of interlocked stories, *Resistance* (2004), posits a tragedy of national proportions: a United States that has declined into fascism, its citizen-spies complicit with statist instruments of oppression, including a federal Department of Inland Security. Censuring writers and artists for burnishing their reputations instead of exposing "the escalating nerve of corporate institutions," "the connivance of government with business," the collapse of families, neighborhoods, and schools, the extinction of species, and the rise of state repression, the narrator of *Resistance* accuses late-twentieth-century writers of failing to indict "the cowardice of those reporting the news." The world's adolescent nation, the United States of Lopez's fiction wants "no part of its elders' remonstrance or any conversion to their doubt" and is riven by "fundamentalism's rave and cant." *Resistance* mounts a scorching critique of what it calls America's "folklore": "that success is financial achievement, that the future is better, that life is an entertainment."[20]

A growing cohort of recent novelists joins Lopez in portraying current social crises in terms that complement the new civic melodramas of the post-Seattle era. In the science fiction tradition of Orwell, Huxley, and Bradbury — or more proximately, the Octavia Butler of *Parable of the Sower* — Jean-Christophe Rufin's dystopian *Globalia* (2004) imagines first-world Globalians living in bulletproof domes and enjoying privatized lives of awesome longevity under the motto, "Liberty, Security, Prosperity." The statist doublespeak, "Security is Liberty," encourages them to comply with measures that putatively keep them safe from Third-World "nonzones" teeming with impoverished populations. *Globalia*'s author, a French physician formerly serving with Doctors Without Borders, calls his novel "a projection of today's U.S.-dominated world" of "totalitarian democracy."[21]

M. T. Anderson's *Feed* (2002), equally dystopian, presupposes environmental degradation so severe that a privileged Globalian America is doomed even as it cleaves to its consumerist raison d'être. This America favors those who, as new-borns, receive cranial implants enabling data to be streamed directly to the brain. Thought is confined solely to entertainment and consumer choice ("images of Coke falling in rivulets down chiseled mountainsides . . . boys in Gap tees shot from a rocket").[22] Similarly, obsessive consumerism and the quest to "productize" street style undergirds William Gibson's *Pattern Recognition* (2003). The unerring eye of Gibson's American "coolhunter" for future fashion trends, her uncanny "pattern recognition," is worth untold fortunes to corporations prepared to brand and market products based on the design ideas she endorses. *Pattern Recognition* is predicated on a corporatized world whose natural resources and human artifacts alike are of value only insofar as they can be monetized.[23]

Reminding us that the novels profiled here are authored by an international cohort, John Le Carré, whose name is synonymous with Cold War spy novels, now enmeshes his protagonists in the violence of the new corporate power blocs. In *The Constant Gardener* (2001), he dissects the criminality of a multinational pharmaceutical industry that uses Third World Africans in drug trials that prove fatal to their credulous, uninformed subjects.* Following in, and in important ways deviating from, the tradition of Tocqueville, Harriet Martineau, Frances Trollope, Dickens, D. H. Lawrence, de Beauvoir, Baudrillard, Eco, and others, Le Carré, like Rufin and Gibson, offers the "outside" view of a global disaster in the making, over which the United States looms by dint of its disproportionate economic and military power.†

---

*John Le Carré, *The Constant Gardener* (New York: Scribner, 2001). The author's note acknowledges that Le Carré's research for *The Constant Gardener* disclosed far more horrifying industrial practices than those represented in his novel. Other recent suspense fiction predicated on pathological or criminal corporate practices include Donald Westlake's *The Axe* (1998), on the lethal effects of mass layoffs; Sara Paretsky's *Hard Time* (1999), on the private prison industry; and Clive Cussler's bestselling *White Death* (2003), on a sinister multinational corporation with historical links to the Nazis and the Inquisition.

†The conditions that undergird the fictional worlds of *Feed*, *Globalia*, and other titles discussed here have been acknowledged recently by some prominent figures in government, business, international finance, and the academy. Former U.S. secretary of labor Robert B. Reich describes the vast physical, social, and economic distance that now divides the corporate executive from the managers and workers on whom the corporation depends in *Reason: Why Liberals Will Win the Battle for America* (New York: Knopf, 2004). Jeffrey E. Garten, dean of the Yale University School of Management, urges the CEOs of multinational corporations, obsessed with stockholders, customers, and personnel problems, to recognize their responsibility for the world's social problems in *The Mind of the CEO* (New York: Basic Books, 2001). Nobel laureate in economics Joseph E. Stiglitz, in his *Globalization and Its Discontents* (New York: Norton, 2002), like Jeffrey Sachs, director of the Earth Institute at Columbia University, severely criticizes economic globalization under the policies of the WTO, IMF, and World Bank. Sachs, moreover, decries the catastrophic ignorance of U.S. congressmen and women who routinely ignore the global inequalities that threaten not only the stability of the United States but that of the world ("Don't Know, Should Care," *New York Times*, June 5, 2003, A25). See also Jeffrey Sachs, *The End of Poverty: Growing the World's Wealth in an Age of Extremes* (East Rutherford, N.J.: Penguin, 2005). Former World Bank president James Wolfensohn deplores the hundreds of billions wasted on military rather than social investment and denounces as well the U.S. and EU agricultural subsidies that cripple farmers around the

Like their foreign counterparts, certain American novelists also respond to the new global consolidation of corporate, military, and state power by expanding their fictions beyond national borders. In the hands of these writers, the fictional milieu of the "American novel" becomes a carefully selected global site of sociopolitical contestation. While the plots of these novels are linked to Georgia, to Chicago, to Seattle (and "Seattle"), their central action takes place in Africa, in Peru, in Mexico, and London. All explicitly address what the Nobel Prize-winning economist Joseph Stilglitz calls "globalization and its discontents."

Africa, for instance, is the vast terrain of Barbara Kingsolver's *The Poisonwood Bible* (1998), an account of three decades in the history of the patriarchal Price family of south Georgia. Nathan Price's family are evangelical Baptists whose year-long commitment to undertake missionary work in the Belgian Congo in 1959 becomes a thirty-year sojourn through neocolonial U.S. Cold War foreign policy.[24]

An ocean away in South America, Ann Patchett's *Bel Canto* (2001) takes the Lima of 1997 as its setting.[25] Overrun by armed revolutionaries, the official residence of the Peruvian vice president becomes the backdrop for a doomed rapprochment between empoverished indigenous "terrorists" and the high-ranking international businessmen and government officials and their wives who are their hostages. The thoroughly enmeshed power of the state and multinational corporations is the given of this captivity narrative, in which sociopolitical interests clash and the outcome is a wedding and a massacre.

From the Andes, readers criss-cross the Atlantic, transported first to London and then to northeastern Mexico in Robert Newman's *The Fountain at the Center of the World* (2004). Newman's story involves separated twins. One, reared as an educated Englishman, works as a high-level public relations operative for companies that privatize, commodify, and contaminate the planet. His mantra and his company's cynical motto, we are told, is that "It is easier and less costly to change the ways people think about reality than to change reality."[26] The unavoidable reality of life for his long-lost twin is incessant struggle in a once-fertile Mexican river basin turned arid and toxic by the multinational chemical plant that has depleted its water and contaminated its soil. The culminating scenes of *The Fountain at the Center of the World* take place in Seattle in November 1999, and graphically represent the gassing, beating, and mass arrests of activists by the city's police.

Like the fiction of Patchett and Kingsolver, Newman's novel draws its interlocked plots from the growing catalogue of conflict over economic globalization; the "reality" the PR man hopes successfully to spin is, to an informed reader, all too real. Not only does *Fountain* detail the police violence in Seattle,

---

world ("Closing Remarks," Conference on Scaling Up Poverty Reduction: A Global Learning Process, Shanghai, (People's Republic of China, May 25–27, 2004). On U.S. income inequality, see also Ronald Paul Hill, *Surviving in a Material World: The Lived Experience of People in Poverty* (South Bend: University of Notre Dame Press, 2001) or Judith Goode, *The New Poverty Studies: The Ethnography of Power, Politics, and Impoverished People in the United States* (New York: New York University Press, 2001).

it offers a thinly veiled version of the notorious 1990s Metalclad case (dubbed Ethylclad in the novel).*

Patchett's *Bel Canto* likewise recollects an actual Peruvian political crisis. In December 1996, armed members of the Tupac Amaru Revolutionary Movement (MRTA) stormed the residence of the Japanese ambassador during a reception and took some four hundred hostages, including the younger brother of Peru's president, Alberto Fujimori. Denying their characterization as terrorists, the MRTA identified themselves rather as "social fighters" and demanded the release of four hundred of their comrades from Peruvian prisons, claiming their conditions to be intolerable. The standoff continued into the spring of 1997, at which point government forces stormed the residence, killing the fourteen hostage takers.

The Poisonwood Bible, too, relies on geopolitical events widely reported in the press, events whose international repercussions were felt for decades. Set in Congo, Zaire, and Angola, the novel begins with the 1959 Congolese struggle for independence from Belgium. It recalls the CIA-backed assassination — authorized by President Dwight D. Eisenhower — of Patrice Lumumba, the democratically elected president of Congo, and the installation of the pro-U.S. dictator Joseph Mobutu. Moving forward into the mid-1980s as the Price family pulls apart, Kingsolver tracks covert U.S. military intervention and neocolonial policies in Zaire and Angola. Incorporating its sources within its covers, *The Poisonwood Bible* concludes with a bibliography listing not only sources on African history, culture, and biology but also, more pointedly, the report of a 1976 U.S. Senate committee, chaired by Senator Frank Church, which disclosed the Cold War role of the CIA in the murder of Lumumba, and Stephen R. Weissman's 1979 article, "The CIA Covert Action in Zaire and Angola" in *Political Science Quarterly*.[27]

What unifies the eclectic mix of titles on this new bookshelf? Convergent topical issues and thematic concerns, certainly, and the vision, implicit or explicit, of a better order of things. *The Poisonwood Bible* posits an alternative Congolese history under the able leadership of Lumumba. *Bel Canto* imagines an

---

*Pressured by the residents of Guadalcazar, Mexico, to shut down a toxic waste dump long held responsible for birth defects, cancers, and other grave illnesses, the Mexican owners complied. In the early 1990s, however, U.S.-based Metalclad bought the dump site and, despite community objections, a local stop-work order, and its own inexperience in hazardous waste handling, enlarged it for renewed dumping. Faced with a conflict, the U.S. embassy and its then ambassador, James Jones (1993–1997), sided with Metalclad and threatened to "blackball" the state of San Luis Potosí by warning away potential U.S. investors. Metalclad's "grand opening" for investors and stockholders in March 1995 was met with vociferous protest, and political pressures in a democratizing Mexico prompted the governor to declare the area a protected ecological zone. Metalclad successfully sued the state and local Mexican governments for "expropriation" of its investment and took the case to the NAFTA Chapter 11 tribunal, which provides for the constitution of a secret trade court wherein international companies can press lawsuits claiming that their investment agreements have been violated ("expropriated") by national governments. Though the tribunal proceedings are secret, on October 25, 2001, the Mexican government paid Metalclad $16,002,433 dollars. For an account of this and other such cases, see "Trading Democracy: A Bill Moyers Special," *Now*, February 1, 2002.

idyllic space in which art — music — bridges the distance between peasant revolutionary and cosmopolitan elite. The expatriates in Lopez's *Resistance* urge us to share their belief that an antidote to the current iron triangle of corporate-state-military power may be found "within the histories of other, older cultures."[28] Like the nonfiction narratives — the civic melodramas — that now fill entire sections of bookstores, these too, mark out pathways for change, the prospects and the means for the redirection of global resources and the restoration of social democracy.

Despite their generic eclecticism, the titles on the post-Seattle bookshelf address the global arrangements that obstruct social democracy here and elsewhere while fostering chasmic inequality, political repression, environmental degradation, and human suffering. All engage the abysmal conditions of work and employment even as they disclose the racism that exacerbates disregard for economic and social justice. In this sense, they self-evidently constitute a new critical realist canon. It would be a mistake, however, to see this new realism as united primarily by narrow political goals. Like other such movements in the past, the social realism of the post-Seattle world we inhabit aims to shape sensibility, to remap the United States, to reconfigure relationships across the globe, to "stir the hurricane." The cultural work it claims as its own is, in short, nothing less than the reformation of consciousness.

Reading after Seattle

Just as the matter of our reading has changed, so too has the lens through which we view our national literature. Seattle arguably frames our work at the threshold of a new historical period — a second Gilded Age, as some have dubbed it — in which vast disparities of wealth both within and between nations, new imperial adventures, and growing threats to global human rights make a constant claim on our conscience and consciousness. Our role as scholars and teachers is not solely to witness current conditions but also to discover and hone the heuristic tools adequate to this new era, to recognize Seattle not as a rupture but as a bridge connecting texts across and within periods, genres, authors, and traditions. After Seattle, it is no longer possible or responsible to rely on the customary terms by which we routinely bring U.S. literature to students or engage texts in scholarly discussion. Quite simply, Seattle imposes its own critical demands.

The question remains, of course, how to formulate those demands. In this, the new bookshelf offers us assistance. Early in his chilling account of artists accused of terrorism by the agents of a ubiquitous Inland Security apparatus, the narrator whose story introduces Lopez's *Resistance* names their dilemma and profers a remedy. The first is "simple": "we cannot tell our people a story that sticks." It is not, he explains, "that no one believes what we say, that no one knows, that none of our countrymen cares"; rather, "we forget what we want to mean." The remedy for that forgetting lies in "repetition," in the rehearsal of "what many already know in such a way as to incite courage."[29]

In a radically different register, Lopez echoes an argument launched by literary critics some years ago in relation to the fictional forms of the nineteenth century. Writing about the hard social facts of Native American genocide, chattel slavery, and the extinction of self in the modern city as these were negotiated in popular fictions, Philip Fisher proposed that the object of novels like *The Deer-slayer, Uncle Tom's Cabin,* or *Sister Carrie* was the "cultural incorporation" of new social and emotional terrain. The obsessive repetition of motifs, of settings, of stock characters, of moral precepts and structures of feeling across multiple texts provides the means, Fisher argued, "by which the unimaginable becomes, finally, the obvious." [30] Repetition, that is, serves a mnemonic function ensuring that the new way of regarding the world cannot be forgotten. "The radical 'work' done by popular forms" ambitious to "redesign the common world" of the nineteenth century is accomplished, in other words, not by means of estrangement or defamiliarization but by its opposite, by the making familiar of hard facts.*

Such too is the ambition of the works on the new bookshelf which are, in this respect at least, closely allied with a literature of the past. And such, as well, is their strategy. Taken together, these recent works, whatever their genre, rehearse the hard facts of our "common world" in which the vast majority of people, here and elsewhere, now suffer the consequences of structural violence. The term is Johan Galtung's, a Norwegian sociologist who, in the last decades of the last century, drew a crucial distinction between "structural" and "direct" violence — that is, overtly violent acts committed in the name of the state. The former identifies forms of violence endemic to standing social, economic, and political arrangements, attributable, that is, to a "world structure" in which resources are "maldistributed and mismanaged, taken away from those who need them the most and misused to produce unnecessary commodities." [31]

Galtung's formulation has not gone unchallenged, particularly by feminist scholars who argue that it takes insufficient account of the wider "continuum of violence" that attends gender regimes. Structural violence, nonetheless, has been adopted as a broad rubric to name, in Paul Farmer's version, "a host of offensives against human dignity: extreme and relative poverty, social inequalities

---

*The books surveyed above are not the sole engine driving the process of cultural incorporation in the post-Seattle era. The cultural work of the these titles is amplified by modern media, by national book awards, authors' lectures, and radio talk show and TV appearances, as when Naomi Klein debates neoliberal opponents in a public lecture or Barbara Ehrenreich describes low-wage work on a television program titled *Wage Slaves*. This multiplier effect also occurs in the reviews of major metropolitan dailies and monthly magazines (such as those lavished on *Bel Canto*) and in the transposition of book into stage play (*Nickel and Dimed*) or Hollywood film, complete with Oscar nominations and major stars (*House of Sand and Fog*). It occurs as well through the presence of a title, such as *Fast Food Nation*, on the *New York Times* bestseller list, and in the conversion from print to book-on-tape (*Feed*). Amplification occurs, too, in the "certification" of new facts by brand-name authors, like Walter Mosely and John Le Carré, and in book club circulation, especially Oprah's Book Club (*Poisonwood Bible, House of Sand and Fog*).

This amplification is particularly evident in a string of recent films: Michael Moore's satirical documentary *Roger and Me* (1990), indicting General Motors; the searing Canadian dissection of corporate sociopathology, *The Corporation* (2004); Ethan Hawke's *Hamlet* (2000), measuring the shift in cultural focus from Cold War political paranoia to current anxiety about the overweening power of the multinational corporation. *What Democracy Looks Like*, too, is part of this process of "cultural incorporation," of making the unimaginable obvious.

ranging from racism to gender inequality, and the more spectacular forms of violence that are uncontestedly human rights abuses."[32] Nobel Prize-winning economist Amartya Sen is more pointed, linking structural violence and the loss of economic rights — "poor economic opportunities as well as systematic social deprivation, neglect of public facilities as well as intolerance or overactivity of repressive states" — with an inevitable loss of civil rights.[33]

Like other tools adapted from the social sciences for the purposes of literary analysis in recent years, structural violence offers a framework for thinking about American literature in the wake of Seattle — and, indeed, becomes a critical term for literary study. And this is not only because the stories of structural violence are repeated across contemporary genres, from the civic melodramas of muckraking journalists to fiction, poetry, film, and drama, in the hope that they will "stick," but also because structural violence resonates across time and canons. It encourages us to see the insidious regime of violence in which racist elites collaborate in a novel like Frank Webb's 1857 *The Garies and Their Friends* on a continuum with the less visible and dramatic violence that distorts the lives of the millowner's daughter and the millgirl who join forces in Elizabeth Stuart Phelps's *The Silent Partner* (1871). It presses us to scrutinize a text like *Moby-Dick* not only as an exercise in symbolism, a disquisition on democracy and authoritarianism, or an instance of precocious modernism, but also as a systematic inquiry into the conditions of work and brotherhood in a major global industry of the mid-ninteenth century.[34] It makes W.E.B. DuBois's account of the social and economic plight of black sharecroppers as central to our reading of *The Souls of Black Folk* as his more famous account of double consciousness. And it asks us to attend to Allen Ginsberg's depiction, in "A Supermarket in California," of Walt Whitman not only as an avatar of the gay poet but also as a shopper in the modern supermarket whose queer questions "'Who killed the pork chops? What price bananas?'" conjure up the Chicago stockyards and the United Fruit plantation.[35]

Similarly, an engagement with questions of structural violence encourages the repositioning of texts — some to recede from prominence, others to gain new stature — and their recombination in unfamiliar patterns. Titles thought to define whole periods might change, and the essential works in a given oeuvre might likewise be revised. Forms fallen into disregard might recover their value. In teaching the first Gilded Age, one might be led to place Dreiser's *Jennie Gerhardt* alongside *Sister Carrie* or the latter in conjunction with Crane's *Maggie: A Girl of the Streets*. Jane Addams's rendering of the lives of the immigrant families of Halstead Street and her autobiographical account of the struggle of an educated native-born woman to claim place and agency in *Twenty Years at Hull House* might seem more nearly related. A recognition of the social and economic stakes in narratives of racial passing and those of what Eric Shocket calls "class transvestism" might bring these into fruitful relation. So might Edward Bellamy's utopian alternative to industrial capitalism and Mark Twain's diatribe against imperialism in "To the Person Sitting in Darkness" come into relational synergy.

In offering structural violence as a framework within which to consider the scholarly and pedagogical imperatives of Seattle, we are not, then, proposing that we annex or add recent titles to courses already crammed and crowded by the academic calendar. Nor do we mean to call for additional sections in already bulging anthologies, much less for the abandonment of current work. The imperative is, rather, to undertake an interpretive reformulation of the whole table of contents, as it were, in accordance with the insights enabled by the historical pressures of a new period.

That is to say, we are summoned by Seattle to take seriously our responsibilities as scholars and teachers in shaping the culture we inhabit. We are, as Denning has observed, instrumental in determining "which works of art and culture will be preserved, kept in print, taught to young people, and displayed in museums, and which cans of film will be housed, whose manuscripts and letters will be archived and indexed." [36] The struggles to secure space on the syllabus and in the libraries for the words of African Americans, of lesbians, gay men, and queers, of Latino/as and Native Americans, and of working people converge in the now "niggerized" nation. The liberation movements that dramatically reconfigured the literary canon over the past half century fostered the global movement for civil, social, and economic justice for which Seattle stands. And just as these movements demanded what some have called cultural justice, so too does this present one.

Seattle, then, mandates a critical internal audit of the established canons in light of the new conditions imposed by late twentieth- and early twenty-first–century neoliberalism and the militarism that undergirds it. Summoning us to the overt issues on the page, it demands that we recognize that the material conditions of life are integral to textual structure, that under the umbrella of the material all else is set in motion.

Affinity and Convergence

The language of affinity and convergence employed by global activists provides the metaphors for this project, as the Seattle convergence provides its model. Over the past forty years, extraordinary work has been produced under a variety of now familiar rubrics—feminist theory and criticism, race theory/African American studies, ethnic studies, queer theory/lesbian and gay studies, postcolonial and working-class studies. Founded in affinity—intellectual, political, and emotional—these critical movements have reconfigured, even revolutionized, literary scholarship and teaching. Marking out particular territory or a unique vantage point, each has demonstrated the centrality of concerns and insights formerly regarded as at best peripheral in American literature. And intersecting, they have together come to capture the complexity of social experience. With their origin in a liberatory social vision, these critical movements offer a model for the future of literary studies in a post-Seattle world.

For it is, increasingly—necessarily—to a convergence of the full range of our "local knowledges" that scholars, like activists, must turn in speaking to the current global crisis. Like political affinity groups gathering and converging on a central—and now invariably heavily guarded—space, so too scholarly affinity groups are bound together by common intellectual commitments, by shared workplaces, and by a mutual concern for the kind of world we and our students inhabit. These provide a starting point and site of action.

In proposing, as action, a reformulation of American literature, we are impelled by our sense of the jeopardy, and the penalties, to be incurred through a gradual adjudication of the proper name for this period and its dominant concerns. In this era of Seattle, the traditional interval between an epoch and its periodizing rubric is an unaffordable luxury. It is time that we converge — that we set in motion the knowledge generated out of affinity and intersection — and that we claim our "convergence space," the place in which we articulate and from which we deploy what we know.

Notes

1. *New York Times,* May 5, 1991, 32; quoted in Michael Denning, *Culture in the Age of Three Worlds,* (New York: Verso, 2004), 120.

2. The deep history of the ultraconservative campaign to dominate postsecondary education and U.S. political life is outlined in Lewis H. Lapham's "Tentacles of Rage: The Republican Propaganda Mill, A Brief History," *Harper's* 309, 1,852 (September 2004): 31–41. For the more recent history of this campaign, see Ellen Messer-Davidow, "Manufacturing the Attack on Liberalized Higher Education," *Social Text* 36 (Fall 1993), 40–80, and her "Dollars for Scholars: The Real Politics of Humanities Scholarship and Programs," in *The Politics of Research,* edited by George Levine and E. Ann Kaplan (New Brunswick: Rutgers University Press, 1997), 193–233. See also John K. Wilson, *The Myth of Political Correctness* (Durham: Duke University Press, 1995).

3. *New York Times,* June 6, 2004, A28.

4. In business, under the mandate to *externalize* costs, large numbers of full-time employees are laid off; a fraction of these (as in the case of Motorola or Boeing) are rehired as lower-wage temporary, contract, or part-time workers. Classing these now-contingent workers as "independents" or "subcontractors," corporations cast off the cost of long-term salaries and employee benefits. See *The Downsizing of America* (New York: Times Books, 1996) and Jill Andresky Fraser, *White-Collar Sweatshop: The Deterioration of Work and Its Rewards in Corporate America* (New York: Norton, 2001).

5. A spate of books published in 2003 is indicative: Eric Gould, *The University in a Corporate Culture* (New Haven: Yale University Press); Derek Bok, *Universities in the Marketplace: The Commercialization of Higher Education* (Cambridge: Harvard University Press); David R. Kirp, *Shakespeare, Einstein, and the Bottom Line: The Marketing of Higher Education* (Cambridge: Harvard University Press); and Christopher Newfield, *Ivy and Industry: Business and the Making of the University, 1880–1980* (Durham: Duke University Press). These books were authored by two professors, a former dean, and a former university president.

6. Denning, *Culture in The Age of Three Worlds,* 146.

7. Quoted in *We Are Everywhere: The Irresistable Rise of Global Anticapitalism,* edited by *Notes from Nowhere* (London: Verso, 2003), 204–205. See Chalmers Johnson, "Whatever Happened to Globalization?" in *The Sorrows of Empire: Militarism, Secrecy, and the End of the Republic* (New York: Metropolitan Books, 2004), 255–281. For a first-person account of the later twentieth-century multinational corporate and U.S. governmental enmeshment (via the World Bank and IMF), see John Perkins, *Confessions of an Economic Hit Man* (San Francisco: Berrett-Koehler, 2004).

8. See Medard Gabel and Henry Bruner, *Global, Inc.: An Atlas of the Multinational Corporation* (New York: New Press, 2003).

9. Noreena Hertz, *The Silent Takeover: Global Capitalism and the Death of Democracy* (New York: Free Press, 2001), 44, 59.

10. CNBC, "European Marketwrap," July 19, 2003. Quoted in *We Are Everywhere,* 250.

11. For a discussion of the literature of social critique, see Cecelia Tichi, *Exposés and Excess: Muckraking in*

America, 1900/2000 (Philadelphia: University of Pennsylvania Press, 2004). This project deploys the work of Peter Brooks, James Phelan, Hayden White, and others in urging the inclusion of "muckraker" narratives in U.S. literary study. Interviews with the new muckrakers, included in *Exposés and Excess*, disclose these authors' self-conscious writerly efforts to shape political narrative.

12. Barbara Ehrenreich, *Nickel and Dimed: On (Not) Getting by in America* (New York: Holt Metropolitan, 2001); Eric Schlosser, *Fast Food Nation: The Dark Side of the All-American Meal* (New York: Houghton Mifflin, 2001); Naomi Klein, *No Logo: Taking Aim at the Brand Bullies* (New York: Picador, 2000); Laurie Garrett, *Betrayal of Trust: The Collapse of Global Public Health* (New York: Hyperion, 2000); Joseph T. Hallinan, *Going up the River: Travels in a Prison Nation* (New York: Random House, 2001).

    Magazines, too, belong on the new bookshelf. From the *New Yorker* to the *Atlantic Monthly* and the *New York Times Magazine*, one finds the story of the Sisyphean life of the American working poor in the U.S. Northeast or an account of the deepening desperation of those whose jobs repeatedly collapse under them in the Southwest. A magazine journalist taking her readers to the tomato fields of south Florida tells the same story of workers' de facto enslavement as her counterpart investigating working conditions at the opposite end of the country in the strawberry acreage of southern California. See David Shipler, "A Poor Cousin of the Middle Class" (*New York Times Magazine*, January 18, 2004); Katherine Boo, "Letter from South Texas: The Churn" (*New Yorker*, March 29, 2004); John Bowe, "Annals of Labor: Nobodies" (*New Yorker*, April 21 and 28, 2003); Eric Schlosser, "In the Strawberry Fields" (*Atlantic Monthly*, November 1995).

13. See Walter Mosely, *Workin' on the Chain Gang: Shaking off the Dead Hand of History* (New York: Ballantine, 2000), 11.

14. See "Blues, Love, and Politics," *Nation* (May 24, 2004), 18. The French demographer Emmanuel Todd makes something of the same argument, reinforced by demographic data. See *After the Empire: The Breakdown of the American Order*, translated by C. Jon Delogu (New York: Columbia University Press, 2004).

15. We have in mind, for example, Parks's *In the Blood* (New York: Theater Communications Group, 2001) or *Topdog/Underdog* (New York: Theater Communications Group, 2002), or *The Laramie Project* (New York: Random House, 2001), based on the 1998 murder of gay University of Wyoming student Matthew Shepard by homophobic townsmen; or Newcity Chicago's *Exonerated* (n.p.), centered on the death penalty; or *Sin: A Cardinal Deposed* (n.p.), about the child sex-abuse scandal in the Roman Catholic Church.

16. Anna Deveare Smith, *Twilight: Los Angeles* (New York: Random House, 1994); Victoria Brittain and Gillian Slovo, *Guantánamo: Honor Bound to Defend Freedom* (New York: Theater Communications Group, 2004); Tony Kushner, *Angels in America: A Gay Fantasia on National Themes* (New York: Theater Communications Group, 1993).

17. Caroline Forché, ed., *Against Forgetting* (New York: W. W. Norton, 2001); Philip Levine, *What Work Is* (New York: Knopf, 1991); Spencer Reece, *The Clerk's Tale* (Boston: Houghton Mifflin, 2004); Wesley McNair, *My Brother Running* (Boston: D. R. Godine, 1993).

18. See Frank X. Walker, *Affrilachia* (Lexington, ky.: Old Cove Press, 2000), 26; Denise Levertov, *Selected Poems* (New York: New Directions, 2002), 197–198; Mary Oliver, *What Do We Know: Poems and Prose Poems* (New York: Da Capo, 2002), 31.

19. Andre Dubus III *House of Sand and Fog* (New York: Random House, 1999). For recent studies of the downward mobility of the U.S. middle class, see the following: Katherine S. Newman, *Falling from Grace: The Experience of Downward Mobility in the American Middle Class* (New York: Free Press, 1988); *The Downsizing of America*; Elizabeth Warren and Amelia Tyagi, *The Two-Income Trap: Why Middle-Class Mothers and Fathers Are Going Broke* (New York: Basic Books, 2003).

20. Barry Lopez, *Resistance* (New York: Knopf, 2004), 7, 8–9, 10.

21. See Jean Christophe Rufin, *Globalia* (Paris: Editions Gallimard, 2004). See also Alan Riding, "A Doctor Who Also Wields a Pen, Writing of a Brave New World," *New York Times*, May 4, 2004, B8. A U.S. mili-

tary analyst projects a twenty-first–century world similarly bifurcated economically between functional "core" and dysfunctional "gap" zones, both governed by the U.S. military. See Thomas P. M. Barnett, *The Pentagon's New Map: War and Peace in the Twenty-First Century* (New York: Putnam, 2004). For an autobiographical account of the covert U.S. policies that have created a world of haves and have nots from the post–World War II era to the end of the twentieth century, see Perkins, *Confessions of an Economic Hit Man*.

22. See M. T. Anderson, *Feed* (Cambridge, Mass.: Candlewick, 2002), 22.

23. William Gibson, *Pattern Recognition* (New York: Putnam, 2003).

24. Barbara Kingsolver, *The Poisonwood Bible* (New York: HarperCollins, 1998).

25. Ann Patchett, *Bel Canto* (New York: HarperCollins, 2001).

26. Robert Newman, *The Fountain at the Center of the World* (Brooklyn, N.Y.: Soft Skull, 2004), 4.

27. Frank Church, U.S. Congress, *Senate Select Committee to Study Governmental Operations with Respect to Intelligence Activities*, Frank Church, chair, final report of Select Committee, U.S. Senate, *Congressional Record*, 1976; Stephen R. Weissman, "The CIA Covert Action in Zaire and Angola," *Political Science Quarterly* 94, 2 (summer 1979): 243–261; as cited in Kingsolver, *Poisonwood Bible*, 546.

28. Lopez, *Resistance*, 9.

29. Ibid., 10, 12.

30. Philip Fisher, *Hard Facts: Setting and Form in the American Novel* (New York: Oxford University Press, 1985), 8.

31. Johan Galtung, *The True Worlds: A Transnational Perspective* (New York: Free Press, 1980), 23. See also Galtung's *Human Rights in Another Key* (Cambridge, Mass.: Polity Press, 1994) and *Essays in Methodology*, 3 vols. (Copenhagen: Ejlers, 1977–1988). See also Penny Green and Tony Wald, eds., *State Crime: Governments, Violence, and Corruption* (London: Pluto Press, 2004).

32. Paul Farmer, *Pathologies of Power: Health, Human Rights, and the New War on the Poor* (Berkeley: University of California Press, 2003), 8.

33. Quoted ibid., 8.

34. On Webb and Phelps, see Amy Schrager Lang, *The Syntax of Class: Writing Inequality in Nineteenth-Century America* (Princeton: Princeton University Press, 2003). On *Moby-Dick*, see C.L.R. (Cyril Lionel Robert) James's *Mariners, Renegades and Castaways* (New York, 1953). It is significant in the Seattle moment that *Mariners, Renegades and Castaways* was reprinted in 2001.

35. Allen Ginsberg, "A Supermarket in California," in. Alan Trachtenberg and Benjamin DeMott, eds., *American Literature*, vol. 2 (New York: Wiley, 1978), 1,044.

36. Denning, *Culture in the Age of Three Worlds*, 165.

A Short World History of "Seattle":
1994—2005

The timeline that follows is intended to give readers an idea of the extent and scale of global resistance to state and corporate policies responsible for the radical inequities of our world. For reasons of space, we are able to include only a fraction of the acts of resistance of the last decade. A more complete chronology would include protests against rising student fees and declining teacher salaries from Nigeria, Angola, Malawi, Kenya, Ghana, Morocco, South Africa, and the Democratic Republic of the Congo to Columbia, Mexico, and Equador, Iran, Canada, and the United States. So too would it include demonstrations by health care workers from Poland to El Salvador, Bangladesh to the Ukraine. It would, likewise, document the many demonstrations on behalf of immigrant rights occuring over the past ten years in almost every nation of western and central Europe as well as in Canada, the United States, and Australia. It would as well include the founding of the myriad organizations struggling to address debt relief, human and workers' rights, environmental abuse, and the privatization of social services. For a more detailed timeline, see Notes from Nowhere, *We Are Everywhere: The Irresistable Rise of Global Anticapitalism* (London: Verso, 2003) to which we are deeply indebted.

1994
JANUARY 1. The Zapatista Army of National Liberation (EZLN) declares war against Mexico, bringing its struggle for life and humanity to the forefront of political imaginations across the planet. Within twenty four hours, the Mexican army responds, bombing communities and killing at least 145 indigenous people. An outraged Mexican civil society retaliates with massive demonstrations calling for an end to military repression. The date of the uprising marks the implementation of the North American Free Trade Agreement (NAFTA), which condemns millions of indigenous people, peasants, farmers, and workers across North America to poverty, and accelerates environmental destruction and corporate ascendance.

APRIL 5–6. More than 150,000 Indians protest in New Delhi against the soon-to-be-signed General Agreement on Tariffs and Trade (GATT) treaty, which will create the World Trade Organization.

JUNE. A World Bank delegation appraising the Kaeng Sua Ten dam in northeast Thailand is surrounded by 5,000 angry villagers, who demand that the World Bank leave. "There is no need for any more studies, because we oppose the project," they say.

JULY 8–10. The G7 meet in Naples, Italy. Participants in the "Other Economic Summit," which has stalked the G7 summits since 1984, send the G7 a message: "Keep your wealth. Enjoy your consumer civilization. Withdraw completely your interest, companies, investment, tourist resorts, and good humanitarian intentions from our countries. Leave us to confront ourselves. . . ."

JULY 9. Sixty-seven workers at a local McDonald's in a suburb of Paris, France, close the store down during its busiest period, demanding the right to engage in union activity.

JULY 12. Four thousand United Rubber Workers in five states of the United States walk out, beginning a bitter strike against Bridgestone/Firestone, the world's largest tire manufacturer, which leads to a lockout lasting twenty seven months.

JULY 20. One million Turkish workers stage a one-day strike to protest cutbacks ordered by the World Bank and private lending sources. The government threatens arrests, but is overwhelmed by the sheer size of the walkout.

SEPTEMBER 29. A nationwide strike is held in India in protest against the structural adjustment programs (SAP) of the World Bank and the signing of GATT (WTO). The strike affects the functioning of banks, financial institutions, and public sector units across the country, and is the eighth in a series of protests against SAPs during the previous two years.

OCTOBER 2. Bolivian workers fight back against World Bank-ordered "reforms," which require that the country cut wages of public workers and privatize the national phone system. After twenty three days of demonstrations, the government agrees to wage demands and backs down from privatization.

OCTOBER 2–4. Eleven people scale the overhead beams of a conference center in Madrid, Spain, during the opening ceremonies of the IMF/World Bank's fiftieth anniversary meetings and shower thousands of dark-suited delegates below with fake dollar bills that say "50 Years of Destruction". Outside the building a carnivalesque march of 5,000 declares opposition to IMF policies. The 50 Years is Enough network is founded.

OCTOBER 6. One thousand French workers invade the Paris stock exchange, halting the billion-dollar trade in financial futures and options for the entire day, in protest against the partial sale of car maker Renault and all privatizations in France.

OCTOBER 9. Over 100,000 people march in London, against the Criminal Justice Bill, which criminalizes direct action, rave music, and squatting, as well as terminating the right to remain silent under interrogation.

DECEMBER 1. United States Congress approves joining the WTO. Prior to the vote, an offer of a $10,000 donation to the charity of choice is made to any congressperson who has read the entire treaty and can answer ten simple questions about its contents. Only one member of Congress accepts (though only after the vote is delayed), whereupon he changes his vote to a "no."

DECEMBER 2. Hundreds of indigenous people from Chile, Mexico, Peru, and Bolivia march in Temuco, Chile, to protest Chile's joining NAFTA, decrying the ease with which multinational corporations would be able to take their land.

26

DECEMBER 3. Police arrest thousands of people heading for a demonstration in Bhopal, India, on the tenth anniversary of the chemical leak from the Union Carbide plant that resulted in 7,000 deaths.

1995

JANUARY 2. The General Agreement on Tariffs and Trade (GATT) becomes the World Trade Organization (WTO).

APRIL 19. Following a six-week strike against privatization by Bolivian teachers, a general strike is called in solidarity with them and against the neoliberal policies of the Bolivian government. The government imposes a ninety-day state of siege, and over one thousand trade union, student, peasant, and political leaders are arrested.

MAY 1. One and a half million demonstrate in Mexico City, calling for an end to NAFTA and an increase in salaries, and declaring their support for the EZLN.

MAY 3. Declaring "The oil is ours," 50,000 workers at Brazil's government-run oil company, Petroleo Brasileiro, walk off the job over pay cuts and a plan to privatize the company. The strike is reinforced by another involving thousands of rail workers and truckers, as well as tens of thousands of other government workers demanding higher wages and an end to privatization.

AUGUST 8. Nearly 600,000 public workers in Turkey strike against the government's austerity program. Three days earlier, 100,000 workers marched through the capital city, Ankara, calling for an increase in the minimum wage, higher pay, and broader trade union rights.

AUGUST 12. Nearly 1,500 landless peasants try to occupy the National Bank for Housing in Guatemala, demanding the land promised to 2,800 landless and homeless families.

OCTOBER 20. During their annual meetings in Washington, D.C., the IMF/WB are stunned by four days of demonstrations.

NOVEMBER 10. Protests against Shell erupt around the world, as the Nigerian government executes nine environmental activists, including writer Ken Saro-Wiwa, who were imprisoned on fabricated murder charges. The activists had resisted Shell's environmental destruction of Ogoniland, Nigeria. In Ken Saro-Wiwa's closing statement at his trial, he predicts that "the ecological war that [Shell] has waged in the delta will be called to question, and the crimes of that war duly punished."

1996

MARCH 10. The largest gold mine in the world, located in West Papua, a colony of Indonesia, and owned by U.S. company Freeport McMoRan, is closed down for six days by riots. The company has dug out the top of a sacred mountain. More than 90 percent of the mined mountain end up as tailings, poisoning rivers for miles downstream.

MARCH 28. Thousands of people take to the streets in La Paz, Cochabamba, and Santa Cruz, Bolivia, demanding a raise in salaries and denouncing the privatization of Bolivia's oil fields. On the same day, workers in Paraguay initiate a general strike demanding salary increases of 32 percent and calling for a referendum on the rapid privatization of their nation's wealth and resources. Meanwhile, in São Paolo, Brazil, more than 5,000 students are attacked and detained by the police while protesting against tuition fee hikes and other neo-liberal policies on education.

MARCH 29. Thousands of farmers in southern Chile block national highways in protest against Chile's imminent inclusion in the "free" trade agreement, Mercosur, which will result in the unemployment of at least 80,000 Chilean farmers.

JUNE 27–29. The G7 meet in Lyon, France. Eight counter summits take place, and for the first time in the G7's twenty one-year history, 25,000 trade unionists take to the streets, protesting against job cuts, labor deregulation, attacks on public services, and the "sinister impact of the global economy."

JULY 27–AUGUST 3. In Chiapas, Mexico, the Zapatistas organize the first Intercontinental Encuentro for Humanity and against Neoliberalism. Thousands of people representing social movements from all five continents attend.

AUGUST. Enraged mothers organize a march of more than 150,000 campesinos in the provinces of Guaviare, Putumayo, and Caqueta, Columbia, after aerial spraying of Ultra Glyphosate pesticide on 45,000 acres causes convulsive vomiting and hair loss among children. Colombian *federales* diffuse the protest with false compromises, then assassinate march organizers. The United States then insists that Colombia allow it to switch to the far more poisonous tebuthiuron.

AUGUST 8. An estimated 90 percent of all Argentinian workers honor a general strike, decrying President Menem's neoliberal policies and the IMF-imposed structural adjustment, which has privatized virtually everything of value in the country, including highways and zoos.

AUGUST 16. Riots break out in Karak, Jordan, after IMF-imposed subsidy removal results in tripling of the price of bread.

OCTOBER 2. The longest strike in the U.S. steel industry begins against WCI Steel Inc. over diminished job security and deep cuts to pensions. Strikers target banks and financial institutions linked to the corporation.

NOVEMBER 22–25. Mass mobilizations against "free" trade occur throughout the Philippines during the Asia Pacific Economic Cooperation (APEC) summit. The authorities ban certain foreigners (including Archbishop Desmond Tutu and former French first lady Danielle Mitterand) from entering the country, as they might cause "disharmony." Protests include a march of 130,000 as well as a massive blockade of the road connecting Manila to the summit site of Subic Bay.

1997

FEBRUARY 5. IMF restructuring in Ecuador forces overnight price rises of electricity (500 percent), gas (340 percent) and telephone charges (700 percent), among others. A general strike brings over two million people into the streets.

APRIL–MAY. A large white tent is erected in Buenos Aires to host 1,500 teachers conducting a rotating hunger strike for an increase in public education funding and their many thousands of supporters. The White Tent of Dignity becomes a focus for opposition to the government's neoliberal policies, and other white tents spring up around Argentina as protests against unemployment and privatization follow in other towns across the country.

JUNE 14. The European march against unemployment, job insecurity, and social exclusion converges in Amsterdam, arriving from all points in Europe and culminating with a demonstration of 50,000 during the EU summit.

JUNE 19. The McLibel case ends after 314 days and the verdict devastates the corporation. McDonald's had sued two activists for handing out leaflets criticizing the corporation. The judge rules that they exploit children with their advertising, produce misleading advertising, are culpably responsible for cruelty to animals, are antipathetic to unionization, and pay their workers low wages. But the judge also rules that the activists had libeled McDonald's and should pay close to $98,000 damages. They refuse.

JULY. Financial crisis hits Southeast Asia and reverberates across the world's markets. The IMF steps in to rescue the region with a $100 billion restructuring program, generating protests across the region.

AUGUST 22. Earth First! Activists in Humboldt County, California, lock themselves to a gate at Pacific Lumber's main entrance into the Headwaters redwood forest. Three weeks later, 7,000 people converge for the third annual mass rally for Headwaters.

SEPTEMBER. Workers in Ecuador occupy the Paute Power Works in an attempt to prevent privatization of the company during a wave of threats to publicly controlled health care, social security, oil, telecommunications, ports and docks, education, water, and irrigation.

SEPTEMBER. Workers in Hong Kong, protest against a World Bank/IMF meeting there, saying they take inspiration from workers resisting layoffs and privatization in Sichuan, China, and South Korea.

SEPTEMBER 8. An international day of action for dockers fired in Liverpool, for fighting "casualization"—contingent work without contract—results in dockers taking action in twenty one countries spanning five continents. Every port on the West Coast of North America, from Mexico to Alaska, is shut down.

OCTOBER 5. Workers in a Hyundai-affiliated *maquiladora* in Tijuana, Mexico, vote overwhelmingly for an independent union, the first in the vast *maquiladora* system along the U.S. border. Days later, the company fires the pro-union workers, and one month later the election is declared invalid.

OCTOBER 15. Zimbabwe's impoverished farm workers, the largest single group of workers in the country, win a hefty wage increase as a result of their first organized national strike against the country's wealthy, predominantly white, commercial farmers.

NOVEMBER 10. A U.S. coalition of labor, environmental, farm, and other groups block the passage of "fast-track" legislation that would allow the president to negotiate new trade agreements without congressional approval. This defeat is seen as the first major check to the growing power of global trade organizations.

NOVEMBER 16. Over 250 unionists and activists from twenty countries participate in the Western Hemispheric Conference against Privatizations and NAFTA in San Francisco, to hear testimony from across the Americas on the effects of Mercosur, NAFTA, and rampant privatization.

NOVEMBER 25. Canadian students protest against the annual APEC summit in Vancouver and are met with preemptive arrests and an unprecedented attack with pepper spray, leading to a national inquiry known as "Peppergate."

1998

JANUARY 17. The Global March against Child Labor kicks off in Manila with over 10,000 participants, largely children. An allied march continues for fourteen weeks, passing through several Asian countries.

FEBRUARY 23–26. A network called People's Global Action against Free Trade and the WTO is born at a meeting in Geneva of about four hundred people from all continents.

MARCH 23. A battle against a new uranium mine in Australia's Kakadu National Park kicks off when 9,000 people protest in three major cities. Aboriginal land owners and environmental activists vow to prevent development of the mine until the project is abandoned.

APRIL 22. Construction begins illegally on the Maheshwar dam in Madhya Pradesh, India, and over 4,000 people penetrate police barricades to stop it.

MAY 16. The first global day of action is called by People's Global Action to coincide with a G8 meeting in Birmingham, UK, and the second WTO ministerial meeting in Geneva. More than seventy cities take part in the first coordinated worldwide action by grassroots groups calling for the abolition of these multilateral institutions. Faced with over 75,000 demonstrators, the G8 leaders flee Birmingham to hold their meetings in a local manor house. In Geneva, 10,000 march to the WTO headquarters; Prague sees its biggest mobilization since the 1989 Velvet Revolution; on May 20, 50,000 landless peasants, unemployed workers, and trade unionists converge on Brazil's capital, redistributing food from supermarkets as they go.

AUGUST. Fifty children aged between seven and thirteen launch a hunger strike in New Delhi to protest being forced to work as bonded laborers in carpet factories.

AUGUST 5. Ten thousand people take to the streets in Rio de Janeiro, Brazil, protesting against privatization of the nation's largest telecommunications company.

OCTOBER 1. In Peru, following demonstrations against President Fujimori's pro-IMF policies, hundreds storm the presidential palace, looting the storage room of the presidential guard, and painting the walls with graffiti. Thirty people are arrested and marches the following day demand their release.

DECEMBER 7. A unusual coalition of locked-out steelworkers, members of the International Workers of the World, the International Longshore and Warehouse Workers Union, and Earth First! successfully blockade a ship in Tacoma, Washington, belonging to MAXXAM Corporation, whose subsidiaries, Kaiser Aluminum and Pacific Lumber, are responsible for locking out 3,000 steelworkers and logging old growth forests, respectively.

1999

JANUARY 4. To celebrate Ogoni Day, and in solidarity with Nigerian activists, UK activists occupy the offices of Shell's directors, declaring their intent to send a message to Shell and other corporations that 1999 will be a year of increased global protest.

MARCH. Five thousand civilian Zapatistas conduct a week-long program of popular education throughout the country in preparation for a popular referendum, or *consulta*, on indigenous rights and culture. Over three million Mexicans vote that the San Andres Peace accords, guaranteeing indigenous rights and calling for constitutional reform, be implemented.

MARCH 24. Thousands of workers denouncing government austerity measures march through Romanian cities and threaten a general strike unless their demands are met.

MARCH 31. Bahamian telecommunications workers stage a walkout, accusing the government of deceiving them in negotiations over privatization of the state phone company.

APRIL 20. South Korean docks are idle as shipyard workers walk off the job to protest Daewoo Heavy Industry's threats to auction off its shipbuilding division in order to eliminate half of its $49 billion debt and meet the terms of a $58 billion loan being issued them by the IMF.

JUNE 18. The first global day of action to name capitalism as its target is called by various UK groups and then taken up by People's Global Action. Actions take place in forty countries, from Brazil to Zimbabwe. A Carnival against Capital attended by 10,000 turns London's financial district upside down while stock exchanges are disrupted in Madrid, Amsterdam, Vancouver, and New York. Port Harcourt, Nigeria's oil capital, is shut down by 10,000 Ogoni, Ijaw, and other peoples of the region. Mexican diplomatic service Web sites are blockaded with the help of 18,000 people in forty-nine countries in solidarity with Zapatista communities. Banks are symbolically demolished in Lisbon; attacked in Eugene, Oregon; painted pink in Geneva; occupied in Bourdeaux; and picketed in several Spanish cities.

JULY 5. Outraged at IMF-mandated social cuts and massive hikes in food, gas, electricity, diesel, and water costs, thousands of Ecuadorians rise up in protest. At least thirteen people are shot and four hundred are arrested, with the government declaring a state of emergency.

AUGUST 31. Twenty million people from Colombia's labor unions, students, and indigenous groups begin the first day of an indefinite national strike in protest at the government's IMF-backed privatization plans and social-spending cuts. After three days, the government releases all arrested during the strike and agrees to set up a working group to discuss demands.

OCTOBER 22. Eighty thousand Filipino farmers protest against feudal exploitation and globalization in nationally coordinated actions.

NOVEMBER 30–DECEMBER 2. The global day of action to shut down the WTO speeds the collapse of the WTO ministerial meeting in Seattle. More than seven hundred organizations and about 75,000 people obstruct the opening ceremonies, spurring a revolt by African and Caribbean WTO

31

representatives, who refuse to agree to the proposed new round of trade liberalization. Thousands of trade unionists join the blockade. Actions from Hong Kong to Iceland are reported through the newly created Indymedia Web site. Eighty cities in France host demonstrations; Turkish peasants walk 2,000 miles to Ankara, visiting eighteen towns along the way; massive protests sweep India; the electrical mains at the WTO's Geneva headquarters are cut; and 8,000 farmers and supporters take to the streets in Muzafer Ghar, Pakistan. Over the following week, actions in solidarity with the more than six hundred arrested in Seattle take place around the world, most notably in Mexico City, where 10,000 striking students demonstrate outside the U.S. ambassador's residence.

2000

JANUARY 3. The Zapatista Air Force bombards a federal army encampment in Chiapas, Mexico, with paper airplanes.

FEBRUARY 18. One thousand Thai activists march on the UNCTAD conference, burning effigies of IMF director Michel Camdessus and calling for radical changes to the global financial system. Inside the conference, Algerian president Abdelaziz Bouteflika says in a keynote speech that the African continent is being rubbed off the map by the trade policies of richer nations.

MARCH 8. Youth activists of color in San Francisco storm the corporate headquarters of Chevron, Hilton, and Pacific Gas and Electric, who give tens of thousands of dollars to a campaign to put a proposed juvenile "justice" measure (Prop 21) on the ballot. Prop 21 would give prosecutors the power to decide whether children as young as fourteen are to be tried and jailed as adults.

MARCH 12. Over a million people in Spain take part in an unofficial referendum on "Third World" debt. More than 97 percent vote in favor of Spain's cancellation of external debt with poor countries.

MARCH 16. Pressured by the IMF, the Costa Rican government passes a law allowing the privatization of the state telecommunications company. Widespread protests erupt.

APRIL 10. After a fierce and bloody struggle, the people of Cochabamba, Bolivia, regain control of their water supply and evict U.S. corporation Bechtel, which had imposed water rate hikes of 400 percent.

APRIL 15–17. Thirty thousand people converge in Washington, D.C., to protest the World Bank/IMF annual meeting. A total of 678 are arrested and report widespread abuses in prison. Parallel protests are held in several countries including South Africa, Hungary, Turkey, and Kenya.

MAY 6. The Asian Development Bank (ADB) meeting in a luxury hotel in Chiang Mai, Thailand, is blockaded by farmers and students calling for ADB loans to Thailand to be scrapped.

MAY 10. Half of South Africa's workforce honor a general strike across the country, demanding an end to neoliberal policies that have resulted in mass job losses.

MAY 31. Protests against the IMF austerity plan in Argentina, which will raise taxes, reduce social spending, and cut salaries, culminate with 100,000 people taking to the streets of Buenos Aires. Protesters liken the IMF to a financial dictatorship and promise "fiscal disobedience" by refusing to pay taxes, which have jumped from 8 to 22 percent.

JUNE 4–6. The U.S.-Canada border is shut down on the occasion of the meeting of the Organization of American States in Windsor, Canada, preventing thousands from demonstrating against the planning session for the Free Trade Area of the Americas (FTAA). The Canadian Auto Workers join members of U.S. and Canadian steelworkers' unions, service employees, and Ontario public employees in the streets. The meeting is surrounded by a ten-foot-high fence of mesh steel.

JUNE 5. The Nigerian government imposes IMF-mandated cooking fuel price hikes, and in response the country is crippled by the most serious general strikes since the end of military rule. After forty are killed, hundreds injured, and more than 1,000 arrested, the government backs down.

JUNE 9. In continued defiance of the new IMF-prescribed labor laws, Argentina is paralyzed by a twenty-four-hour general strike supported by more than 7.2 million workers.

JUNE 15. Ecuador's new president faces his first general strike, organized by trade unions and church groups, against continued IMF economic reforms. Among those striking are more than 30,000 doctors.

JUNE 15. Rural villagers from Altiplano, Bolivia bring their deformed dead sheep to the city of Oruro to prove the seriousness of a massive oil spill from Enron-Shell's pipeline that contimated 120 miles of rivers and irrigation canals and affected water used by 127 farming communities.

JULY 21–23. The G8 meet in a luxury beach resort on a remote peninsula in Okinawa, Japan, protected by 20,000 heavily armed police, six navy warships, and a mile-and-a-half nautical exclusion zone. Debt campaigners send 200,000 protest emails to the G8, pointing out that the $750 million spent on the summit would have been enough to cancel the servicing of a year's debt by Guyana, Rwanda, Laos, Zambia, Nicaragua, Benin, Cambodia, and Haiti.

AUGUST 3. Over 700,000 Columbian workers go on a twenty-four-hour general strike to protest IMF-imposed austerity measures. The conditions set out in the $2.7 billion IMF loan require Columbia to privatize public companies and cut back spending.

SEPTEMBER 7. Over five million people vote on an independently organized referendum asking if Brazil should discontinue IMF reforms. Organized by the National Council of Bishops and Jubilee 2000, the "unofficial" referendum is a success, with nearly all voters rejecting the IMF presence.

SEPTEMBER 11–13. A week-long Carnival for Global Justice takes place in resistance to the World Economic Forum meeting in Melbourne.

SEPTEMBER 26. World Bank and IMF meetings in Prague end a day early due to protests, despite a "security" force of 11,000. Hundreds of solidarity actions take place around the world, at World Bank offices in Moscow, Ankara, New York, Dhaka, Paris, Calcutta, and Kiev, among other places. One hundred and fifty demonstrations occur in India alone.

SEPTEMBER 29. Palestinians living under Israeli rule begin a new intifada, resisting the decades-long military occupation of the West Bank, Gaza Strip, and East Jerusalem; the denial of refugees' right to return home; and land and water theft.

OCTOBER 19–20. Twenty thousand workers and students erupt onto the streets of Seoul, under a banner reading "We oppose Neoliberalization and Globalization," to protest against the Asia-Europe Meeting.

NOVEMBER 16–18. In Cincinnati, thousands calling for an end to corporate rule protest the meeting of the Trans-Atlantic Business Dialogue.

NOVEMBER 19–22. Fighting the privatization of their water, the Sri Lankan National Alliance for the Protection of Water Rights holds four days of action.

2001

JANUARY 25–30. Over 11,000 activists from social movements in 120 countries declare that "another world is possible" as they converge on Porto Alegre, Brazil, for the first World Social Forum, an alternative gathering to the World Economic Forum meeting in Davos, Switzerland.

FEBRUARY. Members of the grassroots farmers union, the Coalition of Immokalee Workers, join with students across Florida to launch a campaign for fair wages and working conditions, targeting especially Taco Bell, the largest purchaser of tomatoes picked by union members.

FEBRUARY 26–27. The World Economic Forum meets in the resort town of Cancun, Mexico, behind solid metal fencing and lines of riot police.

MARCH 27. Twenty thousand protesters take the streets in demonstrations against the Global Forum Conference on E-government in Naples.

MARCH 21. Thousands of protesters descend on Johannesburg to demonstrate against the privatization of the city's water, sold to the French multinational, Suez Lyonnaise des Eaux.

MARCH 29. South Africans take to the streets of Durban to protest pharmaceutical companies' imposition of patents on essential AIDS medicines. Linking their struggle to that in Brazil, where the drug giant Merck threatens legal action on the same morning, they surround Merck's headquarters and hold a rousing rally.

MARCH 31. Mass demonstrations clog the streets of Istanbul, protesting the financial crisis that began in 2000 and the austere IMF bailout package.

APRIL 20. Resistance to the Sixth Summit of the Americas and the proposed FTAA begins with a demonstration of 10,000 in Buenos Aires on April 7, following a two-week strike against the IMF. The April 20 summit in Quebec City is greeted by many thousands of protesters, including both Canadians and those internationals permitted through the tightened border security. From the Detroit-Windsor tunnel to the Vancouver-Blaine Peace Bridge, U.S. and Canadian demonstrators block border crossings; Mexican and U.S. activists celebrate transnational resistance along the fourteen-mile fence separating San Diego and Tijuana. FTAA-related actions take place in Brazil, Uruguay, and elsewhere in the hemisphere. No FTAA agreement is reached in Quebec.

MAY 8. Harvard University students begin a three-week occupation of the president of the university's office, demanding that the school pay its employees a minimum hourly wage of $10.25. A year later, janitors' and security guards' wages increase and raises for food service workers are negotiated.

JUNE 18. Students and ordinary citizens join striking bus drivers in Jakarta declaring that the proposed removal of fuel subsidies will make it impossible for bus drivers to earn a living wage without raising fares. Local authorities decide that rather than maintaining subsidies, they will increase fares by 30 percent, vastly compromising the ability of poor people to get to work.

JUNE 18. In Zimbabwe, protesters block roads in response to a 70 percent rise in fuel prices.

JUNE 26. Students stage a five-day blockade of university and government buildings in Port Moresby, Papua New Guinea, in protest against World Bank plans to privatize national assets. As the students exit the university, the police fire shotguns and M-16s, killing four and injuring twenty.

JULY 18–19. Argentina's main union calls for a two-day strike following the president's public admission that the country is forced to implement IMF-imposed austerity measures because the country's "sovereignty is limited" due to difficulties in repaying its $128 billion debt.

JULY 19–21. In the largest protest against the G8 to date, 300,000 converge on Genoa. The protests are perhaps the most violent to take place in Europe, with the police beating hundreds, including sleeping activists, and killing one. For a month afterward, Italian embassies and consulates are targeted for demonstrations, blockades, and direct action, from Athens to Oakland, Kiev to Sao Paulo, Buenos Aires to Warsaw.

JULY 25. Ten million Indian state employees go on general strike against privatization plans and call for a halt to IMF, World Bank, and WTO policies.

JULY 31. More than 500 Nepalese protesters denounce a 40 percent electricity price hike by the Nepal Electricity Authority, which succumbed to pressure from the Asian Development Bank and the World Bank to raise prices as a precondition to fresh loans for water resource development.

AUGUST 30–31. All major South African towns and cities are nearly shut down as 4 million people participate in a two-day strike against privatization and layoffs. A union spokesperson says: "We want to broaden the public sphere and limit the space in our society that is dominated by unelected, undemocratic, profit-driven forces."

SEPTEMBER 17. In Cochabamba, Bolivia, the third conference of Peoples' Global Action begins, despite having been described as a meeting of "potential terrorists" by the governor.

SEPTEMBER 17. Activists in Ayvalik-Sarimsakli, Turkey, storm the conference hall where the twelfth Biotechnology Congress is taking place.

OCTOBER 4–13. Massive protests rock the region of occupied Western Sahara and southern Morocco, as demonstrators converge on town halls demanding self-determination and independence for indigenous people, a release of political prisoners, and an end to the repression of the Saharawi people. Meanwhile, the Moroccan government illegally grants concessions for offshore oil exploration along the entire Saharan coast to oil companies from the U.S., UK, South Africa, and France.

DECEMBER 19–21. Argentina's largest and most widespread protests in a decade erupt across the country on December 19. The protests, demanding an end to neoliberal policies, last two days, despite the imposition of a state of emergency banning all demonstrations. Over a million people take to the streets of the capital, with hundreds of thousands more in other cities. The financial minister resigns, as does the president; riot police kill at least thirty protesters and injure countless others. Ten days later, on December 30, another wave of protestors storm the parliament; the new governing coalition collapses and another president resigns.

DECEMBER 25. Protesting against imminent privatization, eight hundred workers occupy the seventeen-story headquarters of Bogota's water, electricity, and telecom company. After a month of occupation, the union wins its demands to keep the company in public hands and maintain low utility prices for the poor.

2002

JANUARY 15. Over 7,000 people in Santa Fe, Argentina, attack banks in protest against the currency devaluation. Similar scenes occur throughout Jujuy province, where government employees, unpaid for six weeks, attack five banks. Others destroy the façade of the provincial energy company, which had raised rates to unpayable levels. A month later, on February 18, hundreds of depositors whose savings had been "structurally adjusted" by the government tour Buenos Aires's financial district, smashing seventeen banks, in full view of the police, and demanding the return of their money.

FEBRUARY 1–4. Defying 10,000 militarized police as well as those who said that protest couldn't happen after September 11, 20,000 people hit the streets of New York City, to protest the World Economic Forum's meeting.

FEBRUARY 1–5. The World Social Forum gathers again in Porto Alegre, Brazil, where 60,000 global activists converge. Meanwhile, regional social forums begin to spring up on every continent.

FEBRUARY 20–25. Indigenous people, farmers, and municipal workers occupy the oil industry infrastructure in northeastern provinces of Ecuador, demanding compensation for ecological damage wrought by a crude oil pipeline. The government eventually concedes and declares that 10 percent of revenues generated by the pipeline will return to local communities affected by it. Opposed to the 10 percent allocation, the IMF withdraws a loan.

MARCH. As China moves toward neoliberalism, it confronts mass demonstrations of workers and farmers across the country, protesting against cuts in benefits and subsidies.

MARCH 15. Despite the closing of borders and a simultaneous football match between Madrid and Barcelona, 400,000 to 500,000 people take to the streets of Barcelona to protest the EU summit.

MARCH 28–29. Backed by a Korean drum group and shouting "The working class has no borders," close to 1,000 people occupy the Los Angeles International Airport in protest against a week of raids by the Immigration and

Naturalization Service and against a state supreme court ruling that denies back pay to undocumented workers fired for union organizing.

MARCH 29. Over 1,000 people assist refugees to escape from Australia's Woomera Detention Center.

APRIL 22. Rejecting the notion that Coca Cola is an acceptable substitute for water, 2,000 indigenous people and Dalits (oppressed castes) gather at the gates of the Hindustan Coca Cola factory in Plachimada, Kerala, India, to protest the mining of groundwater that has dried up wells and contaminated groundwater aquifers. The villages demand restoration of the damaged aquifers and long-term water supply to those affected.

MAY 23. Several hundred Russians burn American flags to denounce President Bush during his summit talks in Moscow. Protesters speak out against the indefinite war on terrorism and the neoliberal policies that have sent their country into economic turmoil.

JUNE 28. The largest strike by city workers in Canada begins with a walkout by 23,500 municipal workers, paralyzing Toronto. Fearful of losing jobs if the city privatizes public services, the workers strike for job security, not money.

JULY 8–18. Women in Ugborodo, Escravos, Nigeria, take control of the Chevron/Texaco oil terminal. The six hundred women, from villages surrounding the terminal, block access to the helipad, airstrip, and docks, demanding that the transnational invest some of its riches in development of the water supply, schools, electricity hookups, and clinics and repair the erosion damage from dredging. After eleven days, the company accedes to their demands, and the occupation ends.

OCTOBER 12. Massive demonstrations throughout the Americas on the 510th anniversary of Columbus's invasion focus on Plan Puebla-Panama, a $20 billion industrial and transportation infrastructure project. The hemispheric day of action called by the Latin American Cry of the Excluded network includes strikes across Central America and blockades of border crossings and the Pan-American highway. Almost all commerce through El Salvador is halted. Indigenous protesters objecting to the FTAA in Santiago, Chile, are joined by hundreds of gay and lesbian activists. Two dozen U.S. cities respond to calls for solidarity.

OCTOBER 24. In the first large protest against capitalist globalization in the nation, a massive crowd of over 15,000 demonstrate in Colombo, Sri Lanka, against the passage by parliament of thirty-six bills expediting the privatization of state institutions and natural resources, believed to be directly legislating IMF structural adjustment demands.

OCTOBER 26. About one million people around the planet demonstrate against the U.S. plans to attack Iraq.

OCTOBER 31–NOVEMBER. Ten thousand mostly indigenous activists converge on Quito to protest the FTAA meetings.

NOVEMBER 14. Thousands take to the streets in Homebush, Sydney, to protest the WTO meeting there and the U.S. war in Iraq, and to highlight the connections between military adventurism and corporate rule.

NOVEMBER 27. In Tbilisi, activists protest outside the office of the Georgian International Oil Company, which has partnered with British Petroleum to construct the Baku-Ceyhan pipeline. The 1,090-mile pipeline would create a two-and-a-half-mile militarized corridor, destablizing the region and degrading the environment.

DECEMBER 9. The government of Zambia makes a surprise announcement that the planned privatization of 51 percent of the national bank would be halted, due to public and union pressure. In immediate retaliation, the IMF declares that Zambia will not receive debt relief. Days later, thousands march in Lusaka in support of the government's decision.

2003

JANUARY 1. 30,000 Zapatistas from across Chaipas converge on San Cristobal de las Casas for the anniversary of the 1994 uprising.

JANUARY 13–24. Mass mobilizations leading up to a general strike sweep Bolivia as coca growers, peasants, workers, students, pensioners, women's groups, antiprivatization groups, and others reject the government's neoliberal economic policies and its cooperation with the IMF.

FEBRUARY 15. Millions demonstrate worldwide against the pending U.S. invasion of Iraq, from Rome (2.5 million), New York (500,000), Sydney (250,000), and Baghdad (100,000) to Mexico City (50,000), São Paolo (30,000), Tokyo (25,000), Calcutta (10,000), Johannesburg (10,000), and research bases in Antarctica (dozens).

FEBRUARY 28. Northern Ontario First Nations communities blockade forestry operations in solidarity with Grassy Narrows First Nation to prevent clearcutting of their land by the Abitibi-Consolidated pulp mill, which makes newsprint for the *Washington Post* and the *New York Times*.

MARCH 1. One hundred thousand peaceful protesters take to the streets of Ankara, forcing parliament to reject a government plan to permit the United States to use Turkey as a base for its planned attack on Iraq. Earlier on the same day, the Anti-War Platform presented parliament with a one-million-signature petition against the war.

MAY 1. The U.S. Navy ends sixty years of bombing tests and military practice on the island of Vieques, Puerto Rico, after years of struggle by residents.

JUNE 11. Over 30,000 public sector workers demonstrate in Brasilia against neoliberal pension reform policies. The Brazilian pension system has a surplus of over $10 billion, most of which is diverted to pay off public debt according to guidelines imposed by the World Bank and the IMF.

SEPTEMBER 9. Residents of the Phiri section of Soweto, South Africa, resist the installation of "prepaid" water meters, which would stop all water supply unless water is paid for in advance. The infrastructure for the device is destroyed, preventing the Johannesburg Water Company from moving forward with the installation.

SEPTEMBER 12. Actions against the American free trade agreement ALCA, including a general strike and a mass demonstration of 100,000 in Bogota, paralyze Columbia during the U.S. trade delegate's visit.

SEPTEMBER 11–15. The WTO ministerial meeting in Cancun, Mexico, collapses as delegates from developing countries take their cue from the thousands in the streets and pull out of the meeting.

SEPTEMBER 30–OCTOBER 17. Protests, strikes, roadblocks, and hunger strikes against the privatization of natural gas resources sweep Bolivia, where a general strike begins September 30. President Sanchez de Lozada resigns on October 17. Dozens are dead, amid reports that the military is executing soldiers who refuse to fire on civilians.

NOVEMBER 12. As part of the International Day against the Wall, 150 activists — Palestinian, Israeli, and international — cut the separation fence near the Palestinian village of Zbube. Demonstrations and rallies take place in dozens of countries.

NOVEMBER 18. Thousands of demonstrators, notably farm workers and day laborers, gather to protest the FTAA negotiations in Miami. Meanwhile, inside the walled-in fortress of downtown Miami, trade negotiators encounter internal resistance that disrupts the week's talks.

DECEMBER 13. The overwhelming majority of Uruguayan voters demand abolition of the law allowing privatization of the national oil company.

2004

JANUARY 19. The Narmada Banchao Andolan occupy an entrance to the State Building of Maharashtra in Mumbai in support of long-standing demands, including an end to big dam construction on the Narmada River and compensation, rehabilitation, and resettlement of tribal peoples displaced by flooding. Over the last fifty years, around 50 million Indians have been flooded out of their villages.

JANUARY 31. Mobilizations called by the European Social Forum take place all over Europe in support of three goals: the closure of detention centers, the regularization of all immigrants in Europe, and recognition of the right to exile. Fifty actions take place in eleven countries.

FEBRUARY 19. Hundreds of Nigerian women leave Chevron/Texaco pumping stations, ending a siege to demand more jobs, business loans, schools, and hospitals for their communities.

MARCH 8. California's Mendecino County approves Measure H, a countywide ban on the "propogation, cultivation, raising and growing of genetically modified organisms," making it the first county in the United States to ban genetically altered crops and animals.

MARCH 20. A demonstration takes place in Baghdad, in tandem with protests around the world, against the violence of the U.S. occupation of Iraq. In a powerful show of unity, Sunni and Shi'a Muslims meet at the bridge joining their neighborhoods and march together.

MAY 19. The Guarani people of Bolivia's Chaco region blockade gas-producing conveyor systems owned by the transnational oil companies Maxus, Repsol, Petrobras, and TGS. Their most important demand is the repeal of the coal hydrocarbon law of 1996, which opened the door to transnational energy exploration.

MAY 22. Thousands of workers march in all the large cities of Columbia during a national strike against the FTAA. Across the country, over 7 million public school children are left without classes when 300,000 teachers join the strike.

JUNE 13. Ten thousand people, including Filipino migrant workers, march to the Shilla Hotel in Seoul, in an attempt to thwart the World Economic Forum's "Asia Strategic Insight Roundtable."

JULY 23. Teamsters in San Diego, California, who produce and distribute Coca Cola products, strike to protest increases in workers' health care costs. Their action follows the World Social Forum's International Day of Action against Coca Cola, launched to bring attention to the murder of Coca Cola trade unionists by company-hired death squads in Columbia.

AUGUST 31–SEPTEMBER 2. Hundreds of thousands participate in marches and direct action targeting the Republican National Convention in New York City.

AUGUST 23–OCTOBER 6. Hundreds of thousands of protesters take to the streets in weekly demonstrations across Europe to resist drastic social cuts. On August 23, 200,000 demonstrate in Liepzig, Berlin, Magdeburg, and elswhere; by September 6, 223 cities in Germany are participating, and similar rallies are held in Paris and Vienna. In late September, 50,000 Berliners demonstrate, and 250,000 more do the same in Amsterdam. Related strikes and road blockades occur in Italy, France, and the United Kingdom.

DECEMBER 10–14. The African Social Forum is held in Lusaka, Zambia, with delegates emphasizing that Africa's poverty, wars, and disease are causally related to a global economic system predicated on the poverty of the many.

2005

JANUARY. Resistance continues to water privatization and evictions in Soweto and other South Africa townships. Issues of water privatization and local autonomy provoke continuing strikes and blockades in Bolivia.

JANUARY 20. Protests in Washington, D.C., and elswhere in the United States and abroad mark George W. Bush's second inauguration as president.

MARCH. Immolakee workers end a four-year boycott of Taco Bell after Yum Brands—owner of Taco Bell as well as KFC, A&W, and Long John Silver restaurants—agrees to increase wages for migrant workers and impose a strict code of conduct on Florida tomato suppliers.

APRIL 2. Activists in eleven countries and dozens of cities participate in the European Action Day for the Freedom of Movement and Right to Stay (Here).

APRIL 10. Frustrated in their effort to stop air and water pollution from neighboring chemical plants after months of peaceful protest, thousands riot in the southeastern Chinese village of Huaxi.

APRIL 13. At Yale and Columbia universities, 82 percent of graduate students vote to strike in an effort to gain voluntary recognition by their institutions of their status as workers and their right to collective bargaining.

MAY 4–6. Demonstrations are anticipated when the Asian Development Bank holds its annual meeting in Istanbul.

JULY 6–8. The G8 nations will meet in Gleneagles, Scotland, where massive resistance is expected throughout the region and beyond.

— to be continued everywhere

PART I: Body Count / Bodies Count

To invoke the material means beginning, of necessity, with the body, on which social and economic inequities are most dramatically recorded. All the essays in this section approach the problem of the body, as experience and representation, drawing the attention to the hard, individual costs of the new world order. Setting side by side the physical vulnerability of class and of war—a vulnerability often shared by the same bodies—these essays highlight the connections between the commonplace systematic violence that attends the everyday lives of workers and the heightened violence of the battlefield. Focusing on the immediacy of social experience, the hard data of the social sciences, or the gendered language of imperialism, they frame in radically different ways the cultural and social consequences of literary representation. Taking up the unbidden conditions of illness and disability and the insidious violence that distorts their representation, they expose widely shared social assumptions about the nature of justice and compassion. Contemplating images of the dissenting body, they ask: What does democracy look like?

The contributors to this section range from scholars of working-class studies to those whose work engages film and photography, from scholars whose work has reconfigured our understanding of literary movements or figures to those in new fields like disability studies and queer studies.

41

CHAPTER 1

Working-Class Actuality: "The Great Unexamined"

Janet Zandy

Teach the children well—I think their experience under [this] President and his administration is probably giving them a lot of unwanted lessons.
  — Carol Tarlen, working-class poet

The intellectuals of America have not yet discovered their relation to the workers.
  — Emma Goldman, "Intellectual Proletarians"

We live in a time of violent clashes, not safe literary contact zones. The repetitive beat of the drums in the documentary *This Is What Democracy Looks Like* takes us, temporarily and vicariously, into the clash between helmeted and bullet-proof vested police and unarmed Seattle demonstrators. We live in a time of theft — of stolen futures, stolen truths, and stolen lives. The thieves appear to have it all — military, political, economic, and propaganda power. We live in a time of fear, uncertainty, and, for some, grief. In the United States, we seem to have few mechanisms to transform our personal fears into mutual and reciprocal awareness. Many can barely acknowledge U.S. military war dead, never mind the bodies of thousands of Iraqis. Some of us who have the safety of our work as teachers, writers, and scholars feel, even know intimately, the weight of these realities which we carry with us like a heavy rock. I am one of those lucky ones to have a safe space to work and live. But I also carry that heavy rock. I know that what I write, publish, speak, and reach for in the classroom will not make a revolution. I am cautious about a too-facile view of cultural or textual work as resistance. And yet, I still believe that books and pedagogical practices matter; those tools are not yet — completely — hijacked.

Out of the fissure of incompatible elements — stubborn hope and creeping despair — I ground my work in the material conditions and lived experiences of working-class people and the cultures they make and shape. This grounding, this rootedness, comes out of my identity as someone born and raised working class, but it is also something larger. It emerges out of a conviction of the importance of class as a shaping force, both positively and negatively, in the process of creating culture. That bland statement has deep implications. It is more than including the poetry, songs, manifestos, stories, jokes, and speeches of working-class people in American literary history and anthologized canons — critical as those polyphonic voices are. Rather, it recognizes another epistemology, foundational ways of knowing, surviving, and creating culture that are situated primarily outside the academy. If class is to be more than a tagged-on category, if class is something to be acknowledged as a force field within the

43

academy, if cultural formation is inseparable from material circumstance and realpolitik, then the Seattle moment announces that it is time to rethink and reimagine the multiple meanings of class.

This renewed commitment to understanding class as a cultural shaping force (as well as an economic relationship) should not be the sole provenance of an intellectual elite, nor should it collapse into abstract discourse among well-intentioned progressives. Acknowledging that proles speak is not enough, they also have to be heard, and space provided for the expression of their intellectuality. To really do so is a radical and unsettling act because it involves shared, even relinquished, power. It requires an expansive, reimagined architecture of cultural and literary studies that includes worker epistemologies. Such a new construction would call for a deeper and more critical assessment of ingrained class assumptions about art, aesthetics, cultural value, and agency, what Roxanne Rimstead identifies as the "bourgeois national imaginary" (2001, 276). It would open the academic field to nonacademic players. This heightened dialogism is not the same as a study of a period, genre, or field, valuable as that work is, but rather it is a more radical interconnection between cultural formations and movements for political and economic justice. Gramsci described it a "struggle for a 'new culture,' and not for a 'new art,'" that is, "for a new moral life that cannot but be intimately connected to a new intuition of life, until it becomes a new way of feeling and seeing reality" (1985, 98). Academic language can be a barrier in this construction because it does not express the interiority of the lived experience of class oppression, deprivation, struggle, camaraderie, and cohesion. On the other hand, the academy can be a site of linkages, offering students access to knowledge and culture located outside bourgeois institutions. One way to make these linkages, I believe, is through representations of the physicality and intellectuality of labor. Rather than view physical work as a deficit of intellectuality, this approach posits a more complex understanding of what Mike Rose calls "the mind at work," how "people tend to seek agency and meaning within the constraints placed on them" (2004, xxviii). It also draws connections between physicality and textuality, recognizing and recovering the materiality and actuality of the human body and its cultural representations. In writing about the meanings embedded in human hands, I am seeking a method for turning theoretical, literary, and pedagogical practices toward very specific, physical, tactile human conditions, such as how the body is worn down by labor, how childhood is stolen, how home — conceptually and literally — is threatened or denied, how motion and stasis (the necessary migration to find work and the stasis of repetitive labor) are inextricably bound, and how the poor and working class are more subject to violence. This alternative praxis includes, perhaps centers, the common ground of struggle — a visceral, material, and psychic state not easily or theoretically translatable (Zandy 2004, 146). In practice, it can be an academic discomfort zone for both students and teachers. It raises complicated questions of representation, objectification, voice, and aesthetics. It illuminates the tensions between the limitations of textual and visual representation, on the one hand, and the actuality of the physicality of labor and quotidian of survival, on the other.

Human Actuality

In the writer James Agee and the photographer Walker Evan's iconic *Let Us Now Praise Famous Men*, we see the complications of cross-class representation. Despite his elite education and his rich lyrical writing gifts, James Agee struggled to find language that would match the reality he and the photographer Walker Evans witnessed when in 1936, on assignment for *Fortune* magazine, they entered the lives of three white tenant farm families in rural Alabama. In his cautious and anxious preface to *Let Us Now Praise Famous Men*, Agee acknowledges both the limitations and aspirations of his project: this is a *book* only by necessity. More seriously, it is an effort in human actuality," in which the reader is no less centrally involved than the authors and those of whom they tell" ([1941] 1980, xvi). Recognizing, actually seeing, the families' daily lives, Agee expresses his dilemma as a writer to "contrive techniques proper to its recording, communication, analysis and defense" (xiv). The final text, with its great power of lyrical, evocative language and its great flaws of grandiose overwriting, is an effort to present his subject as "human beings, living in this world" (12–13).

With its ironic title, *Let Us Now Praise Famous Men* also transcends its own time and documentation by alerting us to the humbling complexities of representation, the risks of objectifying working-class and poor people. Writers face the dilemma of showing absence and presence, shame and dignity, simple rhythms and complex survival strategies. Beyond canon revision and conference papers is the ongoing task of finding new forms, paradigms, or hybrid models that reveal working-class and poor subjects within their own materiality enriched by the particularities of their own subjectivity. This work of writing and engaged reading involves, I believe, a critical self-consciousness about one's own class position. This is not an evocation of privileged-class guilt, but rather an expanded capacity to recognize the class markings (latent and overt) inscribed on judgments about cultural value. I think Agee understood this, and yet notice how little space in the voluminous *Let Us Now Praise Famous Men* is given to the actual voices of the Gudgers, Woods, and Ricketts (pseudonyms), the three families whose lives he and Evans entered with notebook and camera. What did they think of Agee and Evans? One response, then, to Seattle's imperative is to find strategies of expanded and reciprocal visibility and dialogue. On one level, this involves correspondences between cultural workers inside and outside the academy, and on another, perhaps more troubled and difficult level, the cultivation of a (in)common language between professors and workers.

Organic Working-Class Intellectuals

Within the developing field of working-class studies there is a contingent of scholars and teachers who grew up working class and poor and now find themselves in an academic world often at odds with the familiar language, customs, behaviors, and values of their youth. Indeed, writing about straddling two class worlds and juggling double identities is a minor genre within working-class studies.[1] But these working-class experiential narratives are not always welcomed — too much "pathos," I was told once. And even in the most politically progressive intellectual circles, casual jokes and insults about class are uttered in ways that would be unthinkable if the subject were race. This unnamed psychological violence is all too familiar to people of color in the wider culture. That said, what is more relevant is how the experiences of organic working-class intellectuals, their complicated structures of feeling, to use Raymond Williams's language, carry an epistemological and cultural weight. This is not about working-class nobility, purity, or essentialism. What is really at stake is the calculus of knowledge and power. The differences of class language, of parental education, ownership, and wealth matter because they unsettle cultural assumptions and call attention to how class marks the process of cultural formation: how, for example, labor-specific historical references are often catalysts for creativity; how a vernacular of irony, sarcasm, rage, and humor speaks back to class oppression; how originality is dependent on community; and how knowledge and culture are embodied. These constellations of class meanings are not exotic artifacts but rather the ground for mutual recognition despite multiple differences.

In rendering the lives of my deceased working-class parents I also feel connected to Melida Rodas's story ("El olor de cansansio"/The Smell of Fatigue) and her description of her Guatemalan father working in a restaurant kitchen in Bayonne, New Jersey: "He's worked hard ever since his toes were small and wrinkled in the rain because the leather from his shoes had finally surrendered. Life has always been as hard as the soles of my father's feet" (2001, 27). Rodas and I have witnessed the physicality of labor inscribed on the bodies of our parents. We carry that body knowledge with us. That is the intense, interior knowledge I wish to make space for in the academy.

There is also a continuum of a working-class ethos of reading the world that is deeper than nostalgic respect for hard-working parents. Its politics distinguishes organic intellectuals from others who come from the working class and "made it" (and I am thinking particularly of white neoconservative ethnic males) in that they seek alternatives to bourgeois assimilation, and ways to recover and use their tough heritage rather than discard it as dutiful Ragged Dick and Janes are expected to do. Our project is not about individualistic ascent but rather another form of *bildung*, a collective expansion of the boundaries of knowledge and culture. The photographer Hansel Mieth in describing her documentary work offers some insight about intentionality in relation to an ethos of responsibility: "We were born, we have a place in life, and we felt we had a responsibility to give back, to help if we possibly could to move the world a little closer to understanding — one person to the other, against wars and the war industry" (Light 2000, 22). This clarity about responsibility, especially for those of us who have some reprieve from the exigencies of material survival and some cultural tools, offers an imaginary of praxis, multiple ways to struggle and resist the deceitful power of the ruling and owning class.

Lying behind and beneath these powerful literary and personal narratives of class experience is an alternative ground, a reimagined intellectual community that recognizes the inseparability of cultural formation and political and economic struggle. In other words, what is surfacing through working-class studies is a vein of American history and culture that from time to time breaks through the dominant culture and is its own, to draw on Gramsci's language, "historical continuity" (Forgacs 1988, 302). This Seattle moment, I believe, can take us toward new academic, labor, and political affiliations and alliances, a fledgling resistance or counter-hegemony. Working-class studies (composed of workers and scholars, middle class and working class, with multiracial and gendered voices) has the potential to link culture and labor, students and workers, environmentalists and unionists as a parallel academic movement concomitant with anticapitalist globalization and antiwar political movements. We certainly are not there yet. And although I acknowledge and value the conferences, fledging academic organizations, and journals on working-class studies, I have always taken the position that this work would lose purpose if it becomes merely an object of study and not a means of struggle — and the struggle is for economic justice for everyone (Zandy 2001, xv).

A word about "everyone." Working-class studies is not "white" studies, nor is it solely focused on the male industrial proletariat. It is assuredly not in opposition to critical work on race and gender as categories of analysis. It emerges at a political, economic, historical, and technological moment (and I think that technology as a shaping force is undertheorized) of urgency and crisis. It asks, how do we move from well-intentioned gestures of sympathy and beautifully articulated critiques into a fuller Seattle moment that links our cultural work with the actualities of laboring people in the United States and around the world? Systemic, structural inequity can only be answered through a powerful network of multiple forms of resistance. One response, humble as it might be, is to recognize and open up the pipeline of labor through access to the subjectivity of experience in working-class literature.

Working-Class Literary Formations

> Why was the earth he loved—with its tender magnificent beauties, its treasures within and without, its order and change—not a fit place for a full and joyous life? Work, yes, because work itself is no hardship, if done in reason, a reason connected with life. Why should a man wish to leave his body and the earth to reach completion? Had he no respect for himself and for the world? What of the many lifetimes wasted in endurance? Could not these lives moving together change the world?
> —Sonora Babb, 2004, 38–39

In her belatedly published novel, Sonora Babb imagines the ruminations of an old (by 1930s Okie standards) farmer questioning the existential actuality of his life. This story also encapsulates many elements of the intersubjective-interior/exterior worlds of working-class literature: an inherent aesthetic and love of beauty that is fleetingly accessible because of the often crushing needs of survival, a recognition of thwarted human capabilities as well as the articulation of dignity and strength, and a belief in the possibility of a better world through collective action. These threads of absence and presence, dignity and oppression, expression and silence run through working-class literature from its earliest formations to its present articulations.

This descriptive assessment reflects a particular angle of vision, that of seeing the formation and creation of literary expression from the perspective of the

47

least powerful—laboring people. For the past several years Nicholas Coles and I have been engaged in building an anthology of American literature of, by, and about the working classes. "Building," as active verb and as final edifice, aptly describes our slippery construction project. We are not *adding* literature about labor and class to an already recognized American literature canon; instead, we are constructing an alternative foundation, comparable to those in anthologies of women's and African American writing. However, our focus is the unstable, porous, and often-denied category of class.

Rather than acquiescing to the seeming impossibility of defining a stable working class in the United States or utilizing a reductive economic definition based on selling one's labor (tenured professors do not sell their labor under the same conditions as miners or Wal-Mart associates), we are recognizing through the literature threads of class connection (sometimes conscious, sometimes unconscious) and solidarity among laboring people. And within these webs of connection are dynamic sets of relationship that form, to use Bakhtinian language, an "architectonics" of labor.[2] In other words, the architecture or structure of our work is not based on a priori class categorization but rather on gathering elements of commonality and on revealing how parts relate to the whole. That common ground often exposes the physicality and hazards of jobs, and the necessity of worker-to-worker solidarity rather than identification with the boss, manager, or corporate CEO. How this "unconscious socialism," as Eleanor Marx described the potentialities of the American working classes in the 1880s, manifests itself in this Seattle moment is a story yet to be fully told, but perhaps can be imagined as a "historically *immanent* humanity" (Marx 2000, 43), that is, a working class that is still in the process of making/naming/unmasking itself.[3]

Working-class literature is an aperture into a cloaked American labor history and an antidote to the Goliath militarization of the life options of the poor. This process of recovery and uncovering reveals the variegated, complex, and sometimes internally contested elements of the American working classes, historically and presently. We see this anthology as a way of offering a metanarrative that reveals filaments of connection across differences of race, gender, and ethnicity. It is also something more than an alternative thread of American literature. Without condescending to, blaming, or patronizing the working class, it illuminates the obstacles to class agency because of strikebreaking, militias, red-baiting, union thwarting, corporate dominance, media control, fearmongering, and a general political unwillingness (in both dominant parties) to name a class that embodies the majority of Americans—a class that because of the particular history and hegemony of American politics has been denied its own name. And in this time of sketchily visible war, it offers some insight as to how workers' genuine patriotism is used against them.[4]

The depth and range of the writing itself pressed us to be skeptical of preconceived literary genres, periods, and timelines. If one were interested, as one example, in the concept of a "renaissance" of writing by and about the working classes, then the glance should be toward the proletarian literature of the 1930s or the rich multicultural literature of the 1980s, not the canonical writers of the 1850s. But this is not a status game. Our aim is to show a historical continuum of literary expression, moving from the earliest ballad song/poems, memoirs, and narratives of laborers and indentured servants; the sorrow songs, autobiographies, and oral histories of enslaved people; the feisty, angry, thoroughly class-conscious songs and poems of "mechanics" and cordwainers; the voices emerging at critical points in industrial and technological change; the zipper songs and hymn-based calls to action, to the complex interplay of class, ethnicity, sexuality, and race in contemporary writing. Across this continuum, authorship contains a collective sensibility, and many of the texts embody a materiality that is nearly tactile. This writing seeks connection and is intended for audience response, dialogue, and use.

We see our anthology as a parallel construction illuminating and in dialogue with American social and labor history. Along the way we made several critical decisions: to foreground as much as possible the voices of workers themselves, hence raising questions about aesthetics and literary judgments; to include writing *about* the working classes in a context that reveals changes in labor relations; to recognize enslavement and peonage as categories of labor often in tension with (usually white) wage earners; and to juxtapose contemporary writing with earlier writing about a particular labor event or industrial change, that is, to highlight a labor-focused process of literary formation and cultural antecedents. We have included such recognized writers as Herman Melville, John Greenleaf Whittier, Rebecca Harding Davis, Stephen Crane, Upton Sinclair, Jack London, Carl Sandburg, Agnes Smedley, Langston Hughes, Tillie Olsen, Mike Gold, Richard Wright, Meridel Le Sueur, John Steinbeck, Philip Levine, Muriel Rukeyser, Lucille Clifton, Martín Espada, Carolyn Chute, and Jim Daniels (to name a short list) alongside those less known: the anonymous ballads of indentured laborers and transatlantic sailors, the letters of Lowell factory "girls," speeches attesting to the limited choices of educated and free nineteenth-century black workers, Frederick Douglass's assessment of labor stratification, a 1866 ultimatum from the "washerwomen of Jackson, Mississippi" writing in response to the Homestead (1892) and Lawrence strikes (1912), poetry by coal miners and immigrant laborers, songs and cartoons of the Wobblies (Industrial Workers of the World), women's childbearing stories, fiction and poetry about hazardous and dangerous labor, and lesser-known writers coming out of the working class or writing in solidarity with them (often both), such as Morris Rosenfeld, Joe Foley, Sara N. Cleghorn, Lola Ridge, John Beecher, Joseph Kalar, Kenneth Patchen, Jack Conroy, Pietro di Donato, Tom Kromer, Don West, Tom McGrath, Judy Grahn, John Gilgun, Tomas Rivera, Hattie Gossett, Wilma Elizabeth McDaniel, and Carol Tarlen, to cite a few examples. We invite readers to consider writers primarily identified as black or ethnic such as Ann Petry or Leslie Marmon Silko or Hisaye Yamamoto or Maxine Hong Kingston as also writers of the working classes.

To illuminate the importance of events in labor history as catalysts for literary expression and as literary antecedents, we assembled literary "clusters." For example, in response to the Triangle Shirtwaist Company fire of 1911 we include not only poetry written at the time of the fire but also writing by contemporary poets, mostly women, in response to the powerful story of the fire itself and the theft of the lives of the 146 fallen workers, mostly immigrant girls and women. A similar cluster centers around the Dust Bowl farmers of the 1930s, where

Steinbeck's reportage is juxtaposed with the poetry of Wilma Elizabeth Mc-
Daniels, whose family actually migrated from Oklahoma to California (*Primer
for Buford*), and Sonora Babb's *Whose Names Are Unknown*—a literary embodiment of Arthur Rothstein's famous photograph "Fleeing a Dust Storm" (Rodgers
2004, vii) with Woody Guthrie's "Talking Dust Bowl Blues." This approach
heightens attention to and respect for differences of voice — who is speaking for
whom and from what standpoint, and what spaces exist for workers to speak or
represent themselves. Readers/students begin to hear a larger conversation of
multiple voices: the "I" (through oral history or memoir) of workers themselves;
the "they" narratives of witness (often from the better-educated second generation); and the collective "we" that not only includes personal experience and witness but also grasps a larger historical narrative of collective resistance and
struggle. This labor-focused set of literary antecedents and formations deem-
phasizes anxieties of authorship, evoking instead a sense of responsibility to
speak to and for an audience (working class and middle class) whose own labor
history and legacy have been confined to the shadows of American culture.

There Is a River in Me

> The tide pulls. Do not try to
> stop it, Mother. I am
> leaving heaven to you, taking
> space to dive. If I drown,
> I drown.
>   — Carol Tarlen

"Unrecognized depth" could describe the life of the working-class writer Carol
Tarlen. Although she would occasionally steal time to write on company time,
Tarlen was, by necessity — because of chronic health problems she couldn't risk
jobs without benefits — a secretary by day and a writer by night, earning two
college degrees while working full time. She read widely and deeply, and
wrote — about the women she met in jail when she was repeatedly arrested for
feeding the poor, about the survival strategies of mothers, about gang deaths,
about inflation eating into low wages, about working-class solidarity and how
"everyday is an act of resistance." She read to appreciative audiences, published
regularly, edited workers' writing in the zine-like *Working-Classics* and *Real Fiction*, raised children and grandchildren, was active in the San Francisco Labor
Council, and a member of three unions. A Quaker, she "knew about the Diggers,
those English landless peasant communists who during the 1650s went to establish communes on abandoned land."[5] She lived in a three-floor walk up in
North Beach and died too young. Had she economic resources and fewer family
responsibilities, she might have found a presence as a creative writing teacher
as well as a more recognized poet, fiction writer, and editor. When she was
young, her family moved frequently and lived in trailer parks; her truck-driving
father was often out of work, his labor legacy: never cross a picket line. In her
memoir poem, "White Trash," she reclaims the word "trash" from every critic,

writer, or citizen who smugly conflate the material living conditions of the poor with their dignity and worth:

> Our friends were Mexicans, Indians, Okies,
> farmworkers, gas station attendants, taxi drivers,
> carpenters, communists, ex-cons, out of work,
> Red, Brown and White Trash.

In "Today" she counts the imagined rebellions and pleasures of a day off with pay:

> Today I slept until the sun eased
> under my eyelashes. The office phone
> rang and rang. No one answered.
> . . . .
> I sat in a bistro and drank absinthe
> while Cesar Vallejo strolled past,
> his dignity betrayed by the hole
> in his pants, and I waved . . .

Carol Tarlen's life and death embody the contradictions faced by the worker writer — how the power of the writing is in the experience of the life itself and how that life also constricts and limits what might have been. Most important, her writing should not be reduced to only personal, individual anguish, nor should its craft and sophistication be undervalued. She had political consciousness, an imaginary of possibility. In "Believe in My Hands (Which Are Ending)" a working-class credo, she connects the tactile and physical, "the thick, black dirt / that sifts through my closed fist" with the abstract necessity of hope: "the mystery of future / which is always beginning."

In *Silences*, Tillie Olsen famously describes class (economic circumstance) and its relation to works of literature as the "great unexamined" (1979, 264). Let us use this Seattle movement to respond to Olsen *and* Tarlen, and begin a much fuller examination and embrace of the laboring classes within the academy and outside its national borders. That is part of the active struggle for new consciousness that can transform the "hegemony in the fibers of the [American] self" (Williams 1977, 212).[6]

Notes

1. See C. L. Barney Dews and Carolyn Leste Law, eds., *This Fine Place So Far from Home* (Philadelphia: Temple University Press, 1995); Michelle Tokarczyk and Elizabeth Fay, eds., *Working-Class Women in the Academy: Laborers in the Knowledge Factory* (Amherst: University of Massachusetts Press, 1993); Janet Zandy, ed., *Liberating Memory: Our Work and Our Working-Class Consciousness* (New Brunswick: Rutgers University Press, 1995); Kathleen A. Welsch, ed., *Those Winter Sundays: Female Academics and Their Working-Class Parents* (Maryland: University Press of America, 2005). See also Gramsci, "Intellectuals and Education," in Forgacs 1988, 300–311.

2. For Bakhtin's concept of architectonics, see Michael Holquist and Vadim Liapunov, eds., *Art and Answerability: Early Philosophical Essays by M. M. Bakhtin* (Austin: University of Texas Press, 1990).

3. When Eleanor Marx and Edward Aveling toured the United States in 1886 they encountered a lively working-class culture and labor movement that included nearly one hundred prolabor newspapers and journals. That is, they had an audience.

4. Most critics agree that the compelling protagonist of Michael Moore's *Fahrenheit 9/11* is Lisa Lipscomb, the conservative, working-class mother of a son killed in Iraq. Her sense of betrayal, testing her patriotism and trust, her anger and political epiphany are a microcosm of the political turn possible within the working class. But at great cost.

5. From Julia Stein's obituary and tribute to Carol Tarlen, June 29, 2004.

6. With appreciation to Nicholas Coles and Sylvia Gasoi for their careful reading and editorial suggestions.

Works Cited

Agee, James, and Walker Evans. [1941] 1980. *Let Us Now Praise Famous Men.* 1941; Boston: Houghton Mifflin.

Babb, Sonora. 2004. *Whose Names Are Unknown.* Norman: University of Oklahoma Press.

Forgacs, David, ed. 1988. *An Antonio Gramsci Reader.* New York: Schocken Books.

Gramsci, Antonio. 1985. *Selections from Cultural Writings.* Edited by David Forgacs and Geoffrey Nowell-Smith; translated by William Boelhower. Cambridge: Harvard University Press.

Light, Ken. 2000. "Hansel Mieth: The Depression and the Early Days of *Life*." In his *Witness in Our Time: Working Lives of Documentary Photographers,* 15–23. Washington, D.C.: Smithsonian Institution Press.

Marx, Eleanor, and Edward Aveling. 2000. *The Working-Class Movement in America.* 1891. Edited with an introduction by Paul LeBlanc, with essays by Lisa Frank and Kim Moody, Amherst, N.Y.: Humanity Books.

McDaniel, Wilma Elizabeth. 1990. *A Primer for Buford.* Brooklyn: Hanging Loose Press.

Olsen, Tillie. 1979. *Silences.* New York: Dell.

Rimstead, Roxanne. 2001. *Remnants of Nation: On Poverty Narratives by Women.* Toronto: University of Toronto Press.

Rodas, Melida. 2001. "El olor de cansansio (The Smell of Fatigue)." In Janet Zandy, ed., *What We Hold in Common: An Introduction to Working-Class Studies,* 27–29. New York: Feminist Press.

Rodgers, Lawrence R. 2004. "Foreword." *In Whose Names Are Unknown.* Norman: University of Oklahoma Press.

Rose, Mike. 2004. *The Mind at Work: Valuing the Intelligence of the American Worker.* New York: Viking.

Tarlen, Carol. 1990. "White Trash: An Autobiography." In Janet Zandy, ed., *Calling Home: Working-Class Women's Writings,* 37–43. New Brunswick: Rutgers University Press.

Williams, Raymond. 1977. *Marxism and Literature.* New York: Oxford University Press.

Zandy, Janet, ed. 2001. *What We Hold in Common: An Introduction to Working-Class Studies.* New York: Feminist Press.

———. 2004. *Hands: Physical Labor, Class, and Cultural Work.* New Brunswick: Rutgers University Press.

CHAPTER 2

Crane and the Body Count

Cindy Weinstein

Isn't the story, though, bigger than just the simple numbers, with all due respect to the Iraqi civilians who have lost their lives – the story bigger than just the numbers of people who were killed?
  – CNN anchor Daryn Kagan, April 12, 2004

Far in front he thought he could see lighter masses protruding in points from the forest. They were suggestive of unnumbered thousands.
  – Stephen Crane, 1895

I frame this essay about Stephen Crane's representation of the Civil War dead in terms of the question of numbers, to which these two quotations allude, albeit from the perspective of different media, different centuries, and different wars. Although General Tommy Franks of the U.S. Central Command famously claimed in March 2002 that "we don't do body counts," referring to Afghanis killed in the war against Afghanistan and speaking out of the conviction that body counts during the Vietnam War were a powerful mechanism in activating the antiwar movement, many today are doing just that. They're counting.

Not only are people counting the billions of dollars that are going to support the troops in Iraq (in the last few days, another 80 billion dollars has been requested, bringing the total to 280 billion dollars), but they are counting how much money we should give to families when they lose a loved one. As of spring 2005, the government pays $12,000, but some in Congress are demanding that that number go up to $100,000. Of course, people are also counting the number of dead. When that number reached 1,000, the September 9, 2004, edition of the *New York Times* featured what they called the "Roster of 1000 Dead" with photographs of the dead soldiers. Every day, one can go to the Web site iraqbody-count.org to get updated estimates of military and civilian deaths. More recently, the issue of the wounded has gotten much attention as their numbers pass the 10,000 mark. Atul Gawande, professor at the Harvard School of Public Health, has published an article in the *New England Journal of Medicine* that demonstrates how new medical techniques have saved the lives of soldiers who, in other wars, would have died of those very same injuries. He describes the wounds of one soldier who lost both legs, one arm, part of his face, and had serious internal injuries, and remarks, "The cost, however, can be high" (Gawande 2004, 2,473). As the numbers of dead and wounded keep mounting, and the question of numbers keeps coming up in a variety of contexts (for example, does a volunteer draft have enough bodies to fight this war? Are there enough surgeons to care for the wounded?), it is important to ask the following questions: how do we count, who does the counting, and who counts or, to pose the question

53

in a more pointed and ideologically precise way, who matters? It is, for example, impossible to know how many Iraqis are dying every day.

There is, moreover, a profound connection between counting as a method of statistical knowledge and counting as a vehicle of visual precision. Both involve a decision to acquire or elude information. Both are matters of and opportunities for representation. It is no coincidence that the government's disinclination to discuss body counts is accompanied by a Pentagon ban on photographs of the caskets of Americans coming into Dover Air Force Base. About 350 images were released under the Freedom of Information Act in April 2004, courtesy of First Amendment advocate Russ Kick, but in less than a week, the Department of Defense stepped in and put an end to the circulation of images that, quite simply, showed rows of metal coffins covered with American flags. Government officials claimed that these photographs invaded the privacy of the families mourning the loss of loved ones; others argued that these images conveyed the essential fact about the war — death. What might be the affective value and impact of statistical knowledge in contrast, say, to the visual images of photography? Are numbers and photographs ever really just simple?[1]

Stephen Crane's *The Red Badge of Courage* is a text that takes up many of these questions in the context not only of the Civil War but also in relation to the decades that followed it. In the thirty years between the end of the war and the writing of the novel, the war itself was being transformed into mythology. Photographs, memoirs, and military histories combined to rewrite and remember the war, not as something that tore the nation apart but as an heroic act that ultimately brought the nation together. Rather than acceding to this coherent and progressive narrative of the Civil War, Crane produced a different version that inscribes a fundamental illegibility about the war into its reading of the war. In fact, *The Red Badge of Courage* is more about what comes after the war — how the chaos of war is turned into something comprehensible through pictorial and verbal representations — than about the war itself. Indeed, Crane's text is made up of the representational forms that war takes, whether it is the "newspapers [that] printed accounts of a decisive victory" (47) or the "large pictures extravagant in color" that Henry "had longed to see" (46). To be in Henry's consciousness is to experience his compulsion not only to render his experience as something outside of himself to be viewed, related, and lionized but also to textualize it in the form of pictures or words or numbers. "He made ceaseless calculations" (56). He wants to count. And yet as preoccupied as Henry is with "review[ing] the battle pictures he had seen" (154), the novel demonstrates over and again the impossibility of "getting a view of it" (81). The texts are unreliable, the numbers keep changing, and the component parts of the image (especially the people) refuse to remain stable.

Therefore, as much as Crane's text is about Henry's commitment to form, in the shape of tales, photographs, numbers, measurements, and pictures, the text consistently enacts the refusal of war to adhere to the logic of coherent form. The soldiers continually assume the lineaments of that which cannot be demarcated, as in the passage where the "skirmishers" are described as "melting into the scene" (69) or later, when "the rifles [were] . . . fired without apparent aim into the smoke or at one of the blurred and shifting forms" (86). The "fleeting forms" (93) taken by the troops is almost always blurry, as if seen through the haze, smoke, and tears of warfare: "Near [the flag] were the blurred and agitated forms of troops" (78); they were "a mass of blurred shapes" (85). "The men dropped here and there like bundles" (87).[2] One wonders exactly what does a bundle or a "vast hive of men" (137) or "a rush of men" (197) look like? Yes, Henry wants to organize the chaos of his experience by transforming it into spectacle ("he must go close and see it produce corpses" [105]; "he was the picture of an exhausted soldier after a feast of war" [141]), but the narrator refuses this transformation and instead uses Henry's attempts "to observe everything" (69) to engage in an analysis of what we might call the optical illusions and elusiveness of war.

To call attention to the importance of vision in *The Red Badge of Courage* is nothing new; however, to think about what Henry sees in terms of his inability to know what he sees or how many people he sees is different. First, it is illuminating to register the weird defamiliarization caused by Crane's allegorical designation of characters, such as the loud soldier, the tattered soldier, the young soldier, and the blatant soldier. The use of allegorical names rather than proper names is a literary mechanism that has the odd effect of making the individual character seem at once individualized and not. When Crane refers to the tattered man or the tall soldier, he is talking about a particular person, a particular tattered man and a particular tall soldier. And the same applies to the other characters so nominated. The fact is, however, that these very common attributes are shared by many persons (many soldiers can be loud or tall or youthful), not only outside of *The Red Badge of Courage* but even within it. At one point, for example, Henry is described in the following way: "he went tall soldier fashion" (132), but Jim Conklin is "the tall soldier" (111). No sooner are we introduced to Jim, also referred to as the "spectral soldier" (110) than he is described as becoming "the grim, stalking specter of a soldier" (112). Similarly, the "loud soldier" (64) becomes the "loud young soldier" (143), presumably in contrast with "the youth," who "exploded in loud sentences" (157). My contention is that the attributes of characters become the mechanism by which the narrator identifies characters — in the mode of allegory, the attributes function as their names — yet those attributes become disarticulated from the individual, applicable to many, thus obfuscating the reader's ability to individuate the novel's characters.

This, of course, is a key contention of the novel. The war machine does to the individual members in it what the allegorical denotation of personhood does to individual characters.[3] Both produce a fundamental disconnect that renders porous the boundaries between bodies and persons, making it difficult to know how many characters are being represented. We read passages such as "there was but one pair of eyes in the corps" (71), or "the two bodies of troops exchanged blows in the manner of a pair of boxers" (186). The question of whose body and how many bodies permeates the text, and this confusion is written into the text in another important way, not often commented upon, as well. Throughout, we read of "armies," "battalions," "corps," "regiments," "troops," the "cavalcade" (170), the "mass" (122), and the "throng" (80), to take just some of the terms Crane uses to describe groups of persons engaging in battle.

But precisely how many is "a squadron of cavalry" (133)? And what is the difference between a "corps" (135) and a "division" (172)? A "squadron" (133) and "a column" (62)? "Brigades" (61) as opposed to "troops" (78)? "A command" (155) and a "regiment" (54)? An attempt at definition to this last term is provided in chapter 3, when the narrator reports, "the regiment was not yet veteranlike in appearance. Veteran regiments in the army were likely to be very small aggregations of men" (67). Clearly, a "veteran regiment" is veteranlike by virtue of its diminished size relative to a "regiment." That diminution is, of course, a result of the deaths of a certain number of soldiers in the regiment. But we have no numbers to guide us. How many did the regiment have to begin with, and how many have to die before the regiment becomes veteranlike? The passage continues to stage this question of numbers when "some perambulating veterans, noting the length of their column, had accosted them thus: 'Hey, fellers, what brigade is that?' And when the men had replied that they formed a regiment and not a brigade, the older soldiers had laughed, and said, 'O Gawd!'" (67). As often as the narrator deploys the allegedly clarifying discourse of the military to describe not only what is happening but who is involved in the happening, it is the case that this language is proven to be inadequate to the task, as regiments become "a moblike body of men" (79), "a brown swarm" (83), "reluctant groups" (87), "a parcel" (141), "dark waves of men" (130). The presumed clarity of military enumeration falls apart under the pressure of incalculable numbers.

And with good reason. The OED helps to reveal the terminological confusion. A regiment is defined as "a considerable body of troops"; a battalion as "a large body of men in battle array"; a brigade as "a large body or division of troops"; a corps as "a body of troops regularly organized." Military dictionaries attempt to offer more precise definitions of these various groups of fighting men. *A Military Dictionary*, written in 1876, defines a battalion: "a body of infantry of the maximum strength to be efficiently handled and commanded in action by one officer, and considered the tactical unit of infantry" (34), whereas a corps is "any body of forces destined to act together under one commander" (93), and an infantry "is formed into what is commonly called regiments, whether they consist of one or more battalion" (Voyle 1876, 200). Any clarity one might seek regarding the number of soldiers participating in battle quickly disintegrates. One could explain this by noting that different countries have different configurations of how an army should be organized, or one could say that the size of the various fighting units depends upon the specific conflict, or one could even suggest that the imprecision of these organizational units mirrors the chaos and insanity of war. This, I think, would be Crane's position.

Nineteenth-century historians of the Civil War, who tried to assess the human costs of the war, also confronted the profound elusiveness of enumeration. Texts that purported to offer reliable estimates of the numbers of soldiers fighting, dying, and being wounded nevertheless conceded the virtual impossibilities of separating those who died from wounds as opposed to disease, those who died in combat as opposed to those who died while deserting. It is fascinating to read a work such as Thomas L. Livermore's *Numbers and Losses in the Civil War in America: 1861–65* (1900), whose information comes from the Military Historical Society of Massachusetts *War Records* (129 volumes), rosters of troops gathered from the Bureau of Conscription, and several other sources. In an analysis of Union losses, Livermore quotes the *War Records* and adds the following: "as the reports referred to usually give the number of 'men,' and 'muskets,' or rank and file, it is possible that about 3500 should be added for officers; and artillery is probably not included in the numbers above given, and therefore at least 1500 should be added for this arm." These data are reliable compared to the information about Confederate troops, which must be pieced together from the 1860 census, conscription records, and rosters published by Colonel Charles C. Jones of the Confederate army, some of which were "derived in part from papers in private hands and . . . not verified by reference to official records" (Livermore [1900] 1967, 84, 27).

William F. Fox's *Regimental Losses in the American Civil War, 1861–1865* (1889) is similarly absorbing and illuminating, especially when read in relation to Crane. In the introduction, Fox, president of the Society of the Twelfth Army Corps, writes powerfully about the vast numbers of dead and wounded, and concedes that, "as the numbers become great, they convey no different idea, whether they be doubled or trebled." Fox's strategy for dealing with the problem of overwhelming numbers is to give readers a concrete sense of the losses involved by explicating and enumerating specific units of men fighting, such as the regiment, because "it is only when the losses are considered in detail . . . that they can be definitely understood." Fox asks, quite poignantly, "Who were these men who fought so well in defense of their flag? What were the names and numbers of their regiments?"(2). Thus he explains that the First Minnesota Regiment, Harrow's Brigade, Gibbon's Division, Second Corps at Gettysburg "lost 50 killed and 174 wounded, total, 224 casualties" (27). This could not be more different from Crane who, though committed to representing certain especially violent corporeal details of the war, not only refuses this particular kind of numerical detail but won't even name the battle — Chancellorsville — upon which the novel is based. In the absence of their proper names, Fox tries to individualize the soldiers as much as possible (he lists the regiment in which they fought and the battle in which the soldier died or was wounded, and he names the chaplains who died while serving) by distilling or, to invoke Henry's language, "ceaselessly calculating" (56) the enormous numbers of deaths into smaller units and discrete battles.

Like Livermore, however, Fox admits the difficulty of gathering accurate statistics and, in the case of his discussion of the Second Wisconsin regiment, explains why: "In stating the total enrollment of a regiment, the statistician is often in doubt as to what figures may be fairly used. In the Second Wisconsin there were two companies K. The first one remained with the regiment but a few weeks and was then permanently detached. Its place was taken by another company which was recruited in October, 1861. It would, manifestly, be unfair to include both companies in the enrollment, and so the first was not counted." Elsewhere, he observes that "it is impossible to ascertain definitely the number of men engaged" (Fox 1889, 37). What I find so interesting here is that even though Fox and Crane have very different ideas about how best to represent war and the sacrifices it has exacted, their texts, nevertheless, intersect. For example, Fox's images of companies becoming "permanently detached," spectralized ("the first was not counted"), or "doubled or trebled" perfectly encapsulates the kind of images Crane creates, in which to be detached from something outside of oneself, like one's regiment, or oneself, like one's body, is the definitive state of being ("he held the wounded member carefully away from his side" [79]). Similarly, Henry is haunted by an inability to know which specters are alive and which ones are not ("one of the swollen forms would rise and tell him to begone" [105]) and by "a brown mass of troops, interwoven and magnified until they appeared to be thousands" (183–184). Finally, *The Red Badge of Courage* is like *Regimental Losses* and *Numbers and Losses* in that all three texts explicitly are not about why the war was fought, but rather about how many people died in it. But whereas Fox, in particular, endeavors to make those numbers as meaningful as possible by subdividing (and individuating) them into distinct and separate battles and regiments, each with their own name, Crane makes the point that such subdivision is illusory and, far from making the experience of war more meaningful, actually takes away from its true meaning, which is the incalculable enormity of suffering and death. Crane's counting looks like this: "The men had begun to count the miles upon their fingers, and they grew tired" (66).

Lest we imagine that Fox's and Livermore's admitted difficulties with the numbers are the product of a past whose naïve handling of statistics has been fully remedied by up-to-date methodology, the fact is that similar claims can be found in more recent scholarship on the Civil War. "The best estimate of military casualties," according to social science historian, Maris A. Vinovskis, is "about 618,000 Union and Confederate soldiers and sailors," although the footnote accompanying this statement acknowledges that "information about military casualties is limited and often highly unreliable" (1989, 36). That said, the numbers usually given are 360,000 Union and 258,000 Confederate deaths. The estimate of wounded Union men is 275,175. There isn't even an estimate for wounded on the Confederate side. Vinovskis concedes, "the figures on the wounded are even less reliable than those on the dead" (39, n.8). These numbers have been made more meaningful and concrete by analyses that study the pensions of Civil War veterans, the role of disease in the war, and the frequency of desertions on both sides. In addition, statistics such as the following give scholars a more concrete idea of the specific numbers involved: "before the Vietnam conflict, the number of deaths in the Civil War almost equaled the total number killed in all our other wars combined" (36) or "more than one out of every five whites participating died" (40). The fact is, however, that in the face of these enormous and inexact numbers, we are left with, quite simply, a sense of their enormity and imprecision: "a sizable proportion of military-age white males fought" (43); "large numbers of soldiers on both sides deserted" (35); "large numbers of soldiers and sailors were killed in the Civil War" (40). Though the words come from twentieth-century demography, we are, ironically, back to Crane.[4]

If additional evidence were required to prove that "a vast blue demonstration" (50) of men fought in the war, to invoke the figurative language of *The Red Badge of Courage*, one need only glance at photographs taken in the early 1860s of troops readying themselves to do battle. Images such as "Drilling Troops near Washington, D.C." (fig. 2.1) and "Camp of the 50th Pennsylvania Infantry" (fig. 2.2) are astonishing in their ability to communicate, on the one hand,

Figure 2.1: Drilling Troops Near Washington, D.C., (Brady–Handy Collection, Library of Congress)

Figure 2.2: Camp of the 50th Pennsylvania Infantry, Gettysburg, Pa. July, 1865 (William Morris Smith; Library of Congress)

Figure 2.3: Company H, 6th Vermont Infantry, Camp Griffin, Va. (Library of Congress)

a sense of the vast numbers of men participating in the war and, on the other hand, a sense of unknowability about the individuals involved. What are their names? What about their families? Have they joined the military to fight against slavery? How many men are there in the image? These questions are, of course, precisely the ones we might ask of Crane's novel, but his refusal to engage them, let alone answer them, speaks to his sense that in the context of the war machine, they are irrelevant. What matters is the surrender of individual identity in the name of something bigger than oneself. This, I believe, is the narrative of an image like "Company H, 6th Vermont Infantry, Camp Griffin, Virginia" (fig. 2.3), and the many other photographs featuring several men with a flag in the background that identifies their company by a letter — A, B, C, and so on. There is both a process of division and aggregation going on here: The troops are divided into infantries, which are further divided into companies, which are then designated with a single letter which is meant to redefine and reconstitute as a whole the previous acts of division. One is now a Company A man (an allegorical name if ever there were one, which Crane surprisingly doesn't use in *The Red Badge of Courage*). These photographs, though taken of living men, partake of the logic of their deaths: inseparable, unnameable, and uncountable. Indeed, what does count in the experience of war is the psychic and corporeal fact of a having a body and a name that one no longer experiences as one's own, whether because one has been disciplined into a larger aggregate that has become one's primary source of identification; or because one's body part has become "detached"; or because one can't distinguish, because one can't see, where one's body ends and another's begins.[5]

Clearly, the discourse of military enumeration is fundamentally inadequate to the task of description because the forms (and formations) of the soldiers are constantly morphing into formlessness or, as Donald Pease puts it, "what Fleming perceives is not a conventional battle scene but the loss of any framework capable of informing [a] scene with significance" (Pease, 158).[6] To be sure, *The Red Badge of Courage* is preoccupied with seeing, framing, calculating, measuring, "accumulat[ing] information," (52) and deriv[ing] an answer" (56), and yet the novel's numerical and visual confusions are pervasive because whenever Henry "finds leisure in which to look about him" (88), the narrator reminds us that what he sees depends upon how he sees: "he saw their dripping corpses on an imagined field" (127), "he thought he could see" (89), "at times he thought he could see heaving masses of men" (133). Instead of focusing on the blurriness of the vision and the illusions of imagined form, though, recent critics who take up the issue of Crane's visual imagination concentrate on its "calculating" aspects. In one of the most interesting readings of the novel, Bill Brown writes, "the novel as a whole also shares something of photography's fundamental structure. That is to say, *The Red Badge of Courage: An Episode of the American Civil War* (to quote the novel's full title) not only isolates the episode from the battle, and the battle from the war, but also extracts the war (the scene of fighting and the scene of seeing) out of American history" (Brown 1996, 157). Amy Kaplan similarly argues that "draw[ing] attention away from the activity of fighting to the act of seeing . . . has the effect of freezing all motion within a static snapshot-like frame . . . as Crane's spectacles isolate discontinuous moments of vision" (1986, 96). An example of this "snapshot-like frame" would be when Henry confronts the dead man who "was seated with his back against a columnlike tree" (101). This is a photographic moment of the kind captured in some of the most famous images of the Civil War dead, to which, Hemingway reminds us in his introduction to *Men at War*, Crane had access. There is only one body, it is posed, and it is meant to function in the way Timothy Sweet suggests — as an aesthetic object that includes "the pictorial conventions of the established genre of pastoral landscape, [where] the corpses and the terrain harmonize to present a unified image of desolation" (1990, 118). A canonical example of this genre of death as pastoral would be Timothy H. O'Sullivan's 1863 photograph "Home of a Rebel Sharpshooter" (fig. 2.4), where the soldier is nestling, almost as if napping, among the rocks in Gettysburg. His death is individualized, contained and framed by the natural setting. The rifle is carefully placed at a right angle to the soldier's body, signaling that both man and munition are at rest. The photograph provides an experience of closure for the viewer, and a peaceful one at that, in which there is a cessation of fighting, as if the conflict has stopped, even if temporarily, to honor the loss of even just one life. It is clear that when Henry "saw a picture of himself" (12A) and imagines "his dead body lying, torn and gluttering, upon the field" (199), he has a photograph of exactly this kind in mind.

There are, however, photographs from the Civil War archive that present a somewhat different narrative of war: one in which the participants are neither individualized nor reincorporated into the natural scene. They do this most palpably by defying the viewer to individualize the number of dead soldiers. Their proximity to one another and often the physical entanglement of their corpses

Figure 2.4: Dead Confederate Sharpshooter at Foot of Little Roundtop, Gettysburg, Pa., 1863 (Timothy H. O'Sullivan, Library of Congress)

makes it nearly impossible to know how many soldiers one is viewing and to ascertain where one body begins and another ends. One example is the photograph "Dead on Battlefield" (fig. 2.5), taken in September 1862 at Antietam, Maryland. There is simply no way to separate the corpses from each other. Their bodies merge into a pile. Their individual identities are gone, not unlike that "great ruck of men and munitions" that Henry "at times thought he could see" (133). Indeed, I would suggest that images like this represent more accurately the quality of visual experience in *The Red Badge of Courage*, even though what Henry desires are images like the soldier at Gettysburg. Although "swift pictures of himself, apart, yet in himself, came to him" (124) or he "thought of the magnificent pathos of his dead body" (124), chances are greater that his dead body will neither be a picture of himself (rather he will be one among many) nor will his dead body be more magnificently pathetic than anyone else's.

Thus, I would maintain that the novel, time and again, demonstrates the impossibility of precisely this kind of isolation and framing, and it does so by presenting us with images that at their moment of representation are being undermined or unformed. To be sure, Henry desires to make images and spectacles of what he sees, but that desire for form and isolation is constantly being thwarted by a series of mirages. Henry may be searching for that perspective, that "sharper point of view" (99), from which to get an accurate picture or photograph, but it is impossible to do so as episodes, things, time, people, and attributes are seen not as separate forms but rather as forms that continually blur into one another ("he dimly see[s]," 145) or even vanish ("landmarks had

Figure 2.5: Dead on Battlefield, Antietam, Md

vanished," 131). This applies most significantly to Henry, who "failed in an effort to see himself" (52).

Indeed, there are many scenes that self-consciously call attention to the inability to know what the content of a particular image would be — how many people would be in it, what is in the frame and what isn't, where does one body begin and another end? "They grew in numbers until it was seen that the whole command was fleeing" (79). For example, after Henry has fled the battle scene, he meets up with the corporal who says, "We thought we'd lost forty-two men by straight count, but if they keep on a-comin' this way, we'll git th' comp'ny all back by mornin' yit" (139). A few chapters later, a soldier remarks on the casualties of the Confederate army, "Lost a piler men, they did. If an' ol' woman swep' up th' woods she'd git a dustpanful," to which another soldier replies, "Yes, an' if she'll come around ag'in in 'bout an' hour she'll git a pile more" (167). A dustpanful of men, "bundles" (87) of men, "a mass of blurred shapes" (85), men "carried along on the stream like exasperated chips" (80). At one point in the novel, the narrator notes, "far in front he thought he could see lighter masses protruding in points from the forest. They were suggestive of unnumbered thousands" (89). Rather than reproduce a photographic logic of isolation, precision, and atemporality, which many critics argue is the effect of the obsessive visuality of the novel, these images suggest precisely the opposite.

If anything, the photographic logic of the text obsessively calls attention to the ideological structure of vision: "curtains of trees interfered with his ways of vision" (155). Henry's "ways of vision" sometimes produce coherent images, such as when he imagines himself "getting calmly killed on a high place before the eyes of all" (124) or "he was the picture of an exhausted soldier after a feast of war" (141). More often than not, however, the pictures are neither coherent nor calm. He sees "a handful of men splattered" (179) and "bodies twisted into impossible

63

shapes" (200). Even when he begins to "discern forms," they almost immediately "begin to swell in masses" (91), as the forms themselves refuse to conform, won't stay in place, and endlessly change. Whereas Mark Seltzer argues that these images of flow and motion are part of a larger realist project of "flow technology," in which "drilling and training" produce "visible and measurable movements of the body" (1992, 166), the fact is that the flow of the regiment does no such thing. Not only do we never see any drilling or training in *The Red Badge of Courage* but the flows in the novel, that is the "waves of men" (130), "the scurrying mass" (179), have little relation either to visibility or calculation.

Henry's problem, then, is not so much that he fails to see pictures (he sees them all the time), but rather that the pictures he sees are of the wrong kind and content. Their illegibility and unintelligibility frustrate his capacity to understand his experience. When he is "doubtful if he had seen real battle scenes" (104), the doubt stems from the fact that the scenes are not made up of recognizable individuals fighting in a battle, whose participants have been made knowable by texts he has read and to which he can refer his war experience. That, for Henry, would, paradoxically, be a "real battle scene." Instead, what he sees are "smoke-fringed" (105) images, whose separate elements elude him: "Farther off there was a group of four or five corpses" (105). "At nightfall the column broke into regimental pieces, and the fragments went into the fields to camp" (62). The real battle scenes, then, occupy a textual and visual space where the characters of the narrative are pieces and fragments, where the content of the pictures is shifting and unreadable, where the individual elements of the image (and the individuals themselves) cannot be separated one from the other and, as a consequence, cannot be counted. Is it four or five?

The compulsion to count or, as Seltzer observes, "the obsessive return to numbers, counting, and calculation" (106) is of central importance to *The Red Badge of Courage*, although rather than reading the numbers inhabiting the text as evidence of "the realist imperative of making everything, including interior states, visible, legible, and governable" (95), it seems just as accurate to think about the novel's numbers or, more precisely, the many terms that signify numbers that can't be enumerated and individual persons who elude denotation, as illegible and ungovernable. For example, in preparation for an enemy attack, Henry describes the regiment as "display[ing] a feverish desire to have every possible cartridge ready to their hands. . . . it was as if seven hundred new bonnets were being tried on" (82). This simile is very revealing because, on the one hand, Henry gives us an idea of how many men are readying themselves for battle, and the other hand, the simile used is utterly bizarre. Comparing their actions to the trying-on of bonnets has the almost comic effect of making the soldiers' actions incomprehensible, if not emptying the action of meaning. If this is an attempt to "inform a scene with significance," to return to Pease's reading, the attempt completely fails.

As this simile suggests, what is happening to Henry lies beyond the narrative capacity of conventional language, or, in certain cases, of language at all: "they made gestures expressive of the sentence: 'Ah, what more can we do?'" (156). Why it is happening is an even remoter question in the face of all of this death. The answer to this has, of course, to do with slavery, race, economics; that is, the entire historical framework that Crane situates beyond Henry's and the reader's view. The only thing Henry (and we) can really know is, to quote Livermore, that "it is hard to realize the meaning of the figures . . . they are too large" ([1900] 1967, 46). Ultimately, Henry, like the brigades, battalions, and regiments, is "an unknown quantity" (52) capable only of making "vague calculations" (201) because his experiences refuse to remain inside a coherent frame. "His mind took a mechanical but firm impression, so that afterward everything was pictured and explained to him, save why he himself was there" (176). Or perhaps, he is already inside of a camera, having had his photograph taken and now only waiting for it (and himself) to be developed and framed. "He was about to be measured. For a moment he felt in the face of his great trial like a babe, and the flesh over his heart seemed very thin. . . . He was in a moving box" (69).

This image of Henry as photograph, photographer, and bewildered reader of his own experience speaks to Crane's skepticism about making sense of an event that killed more Americans than any war before or after, and, more broadly, about making war subject to the logic of coherent narrative. When one can't tell the difference between who is living and who is dead, between where one's body begins and another's ends because body parts are strewn on the battlefield, between the seemingly mathematical certainty of the numbers four and five, a narrative of cause and effect simply doesn't work, which is why the question of why Henry is there is one that Crane refuses to answer. That this evasion of an overtly political framework is a political liability is to miss the point of Crane's intervention. In focusing on the question and questionableness of representations of the war, *The Red Badge of Courage* is not making the case that there is nothing worth fighting for (for example, the end of slavery), but rather that the experience of battle itself makes those reasons intangible. The only thing that is immediate is the very real possibility that one is going to die. To then reconstruct and romanticize and rationalize that experience is to falsify its psychological complexity and the accompanying narrative chaos, both of which Crane's novel is intent upon demonstrating.

To read *The Red Badge of Courage* as an act of representational subversion is also to return our analysis to the present day. Tommy Franks will not count bodies and Crane will not count them either, but for completely different reasons. One is a refusal to confront the mounting death toll; the other is a claim about the incomprehensibility of the death toll. One is a circumscription of numerical representation in order to minimize and ease the national conscience about the violence being done to others. The other is an attempt to foreground the violence as the number of bodies expands and diminishes, as one has no idea who is alive and who is not. The issues are strangely similar, and yet the way they play out is oddly reversed. Perhaps this is a function of not having those thirty intervening years of representation that Crane could look back on when writing his novel. The fact is, however, that whereas Crane critiques mythic narratives of the Civil War by challenging photography, naming, and numbers, today's critiques of the Iraqi war are a function of photography, naming, and numbers. At least Crane had some photographs against which to argue. In our own context, the problem has not been the photograph but getting the photograph. Photographs of soldiers dying in the Iraqi war have been taken and disseminated in opposition to governmental restrictions. And whereas Crane, by and large, prefers allegorical designations to proper names in order to register the destructiveness of war, the heated debate that erupted when Ted Koppel wanted to honor the U.S. dead in Iraq by reading their names on *Nightline*, without comment, demonstrates how the articulation of the names of dead soldiers was taken as subversive, antiwar, and unpatriotic. The dissemination of names, like the circulation of photographs, like the number of dead and wounded, gives us information that eludes the frame, the television frame to be more precise, in which Iraq gets blown up to the tune of patriotic music. This is a version of Henry's attempt to create form out of chaos: "He thought of the magnificent pathos of his dead body" (124). Today, the pathos of the dead body is increasingly difficult to make narrative sense out of, and the representational forms that Crane had challenged become the instruments of critique.

Notes

1. Ellen Goodman points out the historical nexus of war and photography in her April 29, 2004, *Boston Globe* editorial, "Getting the Picture": "This tension around cameras and combat is as old as the battle of Antietam. When pictures of that bloody day were hung in Matthew Brady's studio, a reviewer wrote, 'If he has not brought bodies and laid them in our door-yards and along streets, he has done something very like it.'" Of course, the issue of numbers is relevant to the situation in Iraq, whether it is American casualties reaching and surpassing the 1,000 mark or the debate about whether or not we had enough troops in Iraq right from the start.

2. The process of forms melting or objects being scrutinized by an individual psyche that undoes representation is a feature not only of *The Red Badge of Courage* but also of other texts of the — broadly speaking — realist school. Objects and persons in Kate Chopin's *The Awakening* (1899), for example, are continually melting beneath the force of Edna Pontellier's gaze. Also see William Dean Howells, *A Hazard of New Fortunes*, and Jacob Riis, *How the Other Half Lives*.

3. Terry Mulcaire examines the relation between the field of scientific management and Crane's view of individual persons becoming an army aggregate. See his article, "Progressive Visions of War in *The Red Badge of Courage* and *The Principles of Scientific Management*," *American Quarterly* 43 (1991): 46–72.

4. I am grateful to J. David Hacker in the Department of History at Binghamton University for advice and assistance. The hermeneutic and ideological relations between literary and numerical representation is a field of inquiry that is beginning to be approached by literary critics, most recently those interested in exploring how literature and the social sciences spoke to and against one another in the postbellum period. See, for example, Martha Banta, *Taylored Lives: Narrative Productions in the Age of Taylor, Veblen and Ford* (Chicago: University of Chicago Press, 1995); Cecelia Tichi, *Exposés and Excess: Muckraking in America, 1900/2000* (Philadelphia: University of Pennsylvania Press, 2003); Howard Horwitz, "*Maggie* and the Sociological Paradigm," in *ALH* 10.4 (1998): 606–638; Susan Mizruchi, *The Science of Sacrifice: American Literature and Modern Social Theory* (Princeton: Princeton University Press, 1998); my discussion of Twain and statistical persons in *The Literature of Labor and the Labors of Literature: Allegory in Nineteenth-Century American Fiction* (Cambridge: Cambridge University Press, 1995); and my article, "How Many Others are There in the Other Half? Jacob Riis and the Tenement Population," *Nineteenth-Century Contexts* 24. 2 (2002): 195–216. There is also a rich vein of British literary studies that takes up this issue. See Francis Ferguson, "Malthus, Godwin, Wordsworth and the Spirit of Solitude" in *Literature and the Body: Essays on Populations and Persons*, ed. Elaine Scarry (Baltimore: Johns Hopkins University Press, 1988), 106–124; Catherine Gallagher, "The Body versus the Social Body in Malthus and Mayhew," *Representations* 14 (1986):

83–106; and Mary Poovey, *A History of the Modern Fact: Problems of Knowledge in the Sciences of Wealth and Society* (Chicago: University of Chicago Press, 1998).

5. I would like to thank Jeff Bridgers in the Photographs and Prints Archive at the Library of Congress for assistance with these images, as well as Jean Ensminger and the Division of Humanities and Social Sciences at Caltech for supporting this research. I am also grateful to Michael Gilmore, John Sutherland, and Cecelia Tichi for their incisive readings of this essay, and to Carolyn Karcher for provocative conversation that helped me formulate ideas about Crane, war, and contemporary politics.

6. For a related discussion of how antebellum literature and photography are capable of "revers[ing] the trajectory of abstraction by reconsidering the process of idealization in light of some of war's particulars," see Franny Nudelman, *John Brown's Body: Slavery, Violence, and the Culture of War* (Chapel Hill: University of North Carolina Press, 2004), 12. Also see James Dawes, *The Language of War: Literature and Culture in the U.S. from the Civil War through World War II* (Cambridge: Harvard University Press, 2002).

Works Cited

Brown, Bill. 1996. *The Material Unconscious: American Amusement, Stephen Crane, and the Economies of Play.* Cambridge: Harvard University Press.

Crane, Stephen. [1895] 1982. *The Red Badge of Courage: An Episode of the American Civil War.* New York: Penguin.

Fox, William F. 1889. *Regimental Losses in the American Civil War, 1861–1865.* Albany, N.Y.: Albany Publishing.

Gawande, Atul. 2004. "Casualties of War — Military Care for the Wounded from Iraq and Afghanistan." *The New England Journal of Medicine* 351. 24 (December 9): 2,471–2,475.

Goodman, Ellen. 2004. "Getting the Picture." *Boston Globe*, April 29.

Kaplan, Amy. 1986. "The Spectacle of War in Crane's Revision of History." In *New Essays on The Red Badge of Courage,* ed. Lee Clark Mitchell, 77–108. New York: Cambridge University Press.

Livermore, Thomas L. [1900] 1967. *Numbers and Losses in the Civil War in America: 1861–65.* Bloomington: Indiana University Press.

Pease, Donald. 1982. "Fear, Rage, and the Mistrials of Representation in *The Red Badge of Courage.*" In *American Realism: New Essays,* ed. Eric J. Sundquist, 155–175. Baltimore: Johns Hopkins University Press.

Seltzer, Mark. 1992. *Bodies and Machines.* New York: Routledge.

Sweet, Timothy. 1990. *Poetry, Photography, and the Crisis of the Union.* Baltimore: Johns Hopkins University Press.

Vinovskis, Maris A. 1989. "Have Social Historians Lost the Civil War? Some Preliminary Demographic Speculations." *Journal of American History* 76. 1: 34–58.

Voyle, George Elliott. 1876. *A Military Dictionary, Comprising Terms Scientific and Otherwise, Connected with the Science of War.* 3rd ed. London: Williams Clowes and Sons.

CHAPTER 3

Conquest and Liberation: Mark Twain on Imperialism

Amy Kaplan

"Why, we have gotten into a mess, a quagmire from which each fresh step renders the difficulty of extrication immensely greater. I'm sure I wish I could see what we were getting out of it, and all it means to us as a nation." Someone could have said this about Iraq today or about Vietnam thirty five years ago. But in fact it was Mark Twain who said it a century ago about the American occupation of the Philippines (Zwick 1992, 3–4). I was reminded of that quote when I heard President Bush's speech before the Philippine Congress in October 2003. He referred to America's history in that country as a "model" for establishing democracy in Iraq. Alluding to the 1898 Spanish-American War, he said, "America is proud of its part in the great story of the Filipino people. Together our soldiers liberated the Philippines from colonial rule" (Bush 2003).

Twain would have laughed with outrage at this stretch of the truth, which obscures a shameful chapter of this story. What Bush called liberation, Twain decried as a bloody campaign against the Philippine struggle for independence, a campaign that would usher in five decades of occupation by the United States. The outspoken vice president of the Anti-Imperialist League, Twain believed that once Spanish rule ended, the Philippines would achieve their independence: "It was not to be a government according to our ideas, but a government that represented the feeling of the majority of the Filipinos, a government according to Filipino ideas" (Zwick 1992, 4).

Instead, the United States annexed the Philippines, which it "purchased" from Spain, in 1899, and waged a brutal war to enforce its rule across the archipelago. Nearly 5,000 American soldiers died, and historians estimate that 250,000 Filipinos perished — 20,000 were killed in combat and the vast majority died from disease and starvation. The U.S. Army burned villages and fields, massacred civilians, and herded the residents of entire provinces into concentration camps. Americans justified this inhumane treatment by calling Filipinos uncivilized and incapable of governing themselves. American soldiers in the Philippines, many of whom had fought Indian wars in the U.S. West, used the racist appellations "gugu" and "gook," which gained notoriety during the Vietnam War.

Many distinguished Americans across the political spectrum joined Twain in protest of this war, including Grover Cleveland, Jane Addams, Samuel Gompers, Andrew Carnegie, William James, and W.E.B. Du Bois. When the Senate conducted hearings in 1902 on atrocities, American soldiers testified about the killing of prisoners and torturing of civilians. Although the war officially ended with the declaration of U.S. sovereignty in 1902, there was ongoing resistance to the occupation. In one incident, U.S. troops massacred at least nine hundred Muslim women, children, and men in 1906 on the southern island of Jolo. Today, U.S. military advisors are being sent to that region, where the Bush administration and that of Philippine President Arroyo see only terrorists, but where residents remember tales of the brutal occupation of a century ago.

Twain's brilliant political satire against imperialism still has much to teach us at a time when supporters of the war in Iraq have pointed to the Philippine-American War as a model for counterinsurgency in the twenty-first century (they don't mention the five-decade occupation).[1] In his most influential and controversial essay on imperialism, "To the Person Sitting in Darkness," Twain imagined a benighted "native" trying to understand how liberation could turn into its opposite. The Person Sitting in Darkness muses, "There must be two Americas: one that sets the captive free, and one that takes a once-captive's new freedom away from him, and picks a quarrel with him with nothing to found it on; then kills him to get his land" (Zwick 1992, 32). In his anti-imperialist writings in the last decade of his life, Twain repeatedly underscored the terrible irony of fighting a war of liberation that ultimately enslaved the liberated.

Twain's interest in imperialism, however, did not start in 1900. The career of this quintessentially American writer was forged in the routes of U.S. empire building since his earliest writing in the aftermath of the Civil War. For Twain, imperialism was not simply a matter of exerting power abroad, but was intimately tied to the legacy of slavery at home, the subject of his major novels in the 1880s and 1890s: *The Adventures of Huckleberry Finn, Pudd'nhead Wilson*, and *A Connecticut Yankee in King Arthur's Court*. In his anti-imperialist writing from his last dark decade, Twain brought lessons to bear from his earliest writing and worldwide travels. As a writer, the power — and limits — of his critique can be found less in a summary of his political ideas than in the way he wielded language as a weapon against injustice.

Twain's career followed the westward expansion of the American empire. After the outbreak of the Civil War ended his career working on the riverboats of the Mississippi, and he escaped his two-week stint in the Confederate army, Twain moved to the western territory of Nevada to seek his fortune in mining and journalism. This journey finally took him to California, where he first made a name for himself as a Western humorist. Yet Mark Twain became a national celebrity only after he traveled to Hawaii in 1866 for six months to report on the sugar industry for a San Francisco newspaper. Nominally an independent kingdom, Hawaii at the time was being colonized by American missionaries and their children, who were developing the plantation system for growing and exporting sugar. Twain viewed the colonization of Hawaii with ambivalence; on the one hand he decried the devastating damage done to native society since the arrival of Captain Cook. On the other, he promoted bringing Hawaii economically into the American orbit. In a theme that would emerge with virulence at the end of his life, he satirized the missionaries' effort to "civilize" the natives, yet he also saw Hawaiians through the gaze of the colonizer as childlike, primitive, and inferior. Nonetheless, his trip to Hawaii catapulted Twain into the national limelight. When he returned to San Francisco, he started to lecture about "Our Fellow Savages." It was the wild success of this lecture, which he delivered over a hundred times, that propelled him eastward and brought him renown as a great American humorist. Twain became an imperialist of sorts as he extracted raw material from his observations of Hawaii to market as a commodity for sale in the literary marketplace.[2]

Hawaii also had a disturbing yet profoundly creative effect on Mark Twain. In the racially stratified culture of the sugar plantation, he found uncanny if unstated parallels between the colonized setting of Hawaii and the slaveholding south of his youth. Whereas the Civil War has been understood by literary critics to have cut off Twain from his past, the loss of which became a repository of memories that would fuel his creativity twenty years later, his trip to Hawaii provided an immediate entry into the memories of the prewar south, both the nostalgia for and nightmare of slavery. He saw similarities between the colonization of Hawaiians and the enslavement of African Americans, while he was wary of freedom for both. He made fun of the Hawaiian parliament in a way that resonated with white Americans' mockery of African Americans during Reconstruction. In Hawaii he found many of his great themes: the intimate relation between freedom and slavery, of his critique of the hypocrisies of civilization, which he satirized in *Huckleberry Finn* as being "sivilized" with an "s."

One of the most disturbing parts of *Huckleberry Finn* comes at the end of the novel, when Tom Sawyer takes the lead from Huck in staging Jim's escape from slavery by subjecting him to the humiliation and pain of being enchained in a rat-infested hut. The terrible irony is that Jim is already legally free. "Why set a free man free?" is the question that underlies the childish antics of Huck and Tom and the novel at large. It shows that liberating another can easily lead to another form of enslavement, that people instead need to liberate themselves. Reenslavement was the dire predicament of African Americans in the post-Reconstruction period of Jim Crow segregation and disfranchisement in the 1880s, when Twain wrote the novel. A source for this scene of Jim's entrapment can be found in one of Twain's letters from Hawaii in 1866: The legacy of American slavery and the colonization of Hawaii come together in a visit to a government prison during his first tour of Honolulu. There he is introduced to

> General George Washington, or, at least, to an aged, limping Negro man, who called himself by that honored name. He was supposed to be seventy years old, and he looked it. He was as crazy as a loon, and sometimes, they say, he grows very violent. He was a Samson in a small way; his arms were corded with muscle, and his legs felt as hard as if they were made of wood. He was in a peaceable mood at present, and strongly manacled. They have a hard time with him occasionally, and some time or other he will get in a lively way and eat up the garrison of that prison, no doubt. The native soldiers who guard the place are afraid of him, and he knows it. (1989, 5)

The history of this man is "a sealed book." He is said to have set off on a ship of black sailors from New England twenty years ago, but he is fond of reminiscing dreamily about the Blue Ridge in Virginia. "I do not think he is the old original General W." concludes Twain.

Twain ends the letter by calling the prison, for its pastoral qualities, a "model for the western world," a model that centers on this chained black man. How do we understand this powerful image of a black man who appears both harmless and dangerous — Samsonlike able to tear down a building — who is both Southern and Northern, free before the war and enslaved after it? Is this part of Twain's rediscovery of the South in Hawaii, that slavery can be reinvented through colonization, that the black man's threatening strength can be rechained? That he can be reconceived as the primitive cannibal? Or is this a countermyth of American origins? A photographic negative of the founding father? Is this chained free man indeed the father of the country? And is the father of the country indeed in chains? Yet as George Washington, this prisoner also represents American power as cannibalistic, in his threat to devour the Hawaiian guards. Like Melville's description of Queequeg as "George Washington cannibalistically developed," this description both acknowledges and at the same time ridicules the desire for independence by nonwhite peoples. Did Twain find imprisoned in Hawaii a consoling reconstitution of plantation society, or a counterimage that destabilizes the meaning of American origins in slavery and colonialism? Or does it hold out a prophetic image of the postwar South, not with the North as an imperial power occupying the South (as Southern rhetoric claimed) but with emancipation as recolonizing the African American. It is difficult not to think of this scene in Hawaii rewritten in *Huckleberry Finn*, as Jim entrapped in the cabin from which Tom and Huck are freeing a free man.

Twain revisited the subject of Hawaii throughout his career, like the return of the repressed. Between completing *Huckleberry Finn* and starting *A Connecticut Yankee in King Arthur's Court*, he tried to write a novel about Hawaii that he never finished and only exists in fragments. Instead, his musings on colonization there directly informed his dystopian fantasy of that novel, an allegory of colonialism gone haywire. In *Connecticut Yankee*, Hank Morgan, a nineteenth-century mechanic, gets hit over the head in a factory dispute and wakes up in King Arthur's Camelot. Using the colonial strategies of Columbus and Cortés to awe the natives, Hank gets the English islanders, who are described as Indians and children, to worship him and dub him "The Boss." With Yankee ingenuity, he proceeds to "modernize" medieval England, replete with telegraphs, patent offices, and newspapers and, of course, a military academy. He enlists the knights of the round table in advertising campaigns for toothpaste and stove polish and gets them to play on baseball teams. Those serfs and slaves who show desire for liberty and change he sends to a "man factory," to manufacture free modern men. This humorous satire criticizes the aristocratic system that relied on slavery and peonage as well as the capitalist system that creates automatons and robber barons. Twain's burlesque also has a dark underside: Every facet of civilization that Hank introduces is in fact founded on violence. And Hank himself worked at an arms manufacturing factory in Connecticut. Hank's victory for science over superstition comes from using hidden explosives to blow up a castle and awe a groveling mass into submission. His victory of enlightenment over tradition lies in using guns to destroy the opposing knights at a jousting match. When the forces of the church and the aristocracy turn against his "civilization," the novel

71

ends in a massacre reminiscent of imperial warfare from the Indian wars in the West to the European conquests in India and North Africa. Hank and his few followers are trapped in a sea of thousands of corpses who have been electrified by his technologically advanced means of warfare. Twain's prescient vision sees that the destruction wrought by the colonizers will engulf them in their own pyrrhic schemes.

Thus a decade before his critique of American imperialism, he had already written an allegory of the destructive basis of the civilizing and modernizing mission of empire. In the time travel of *Connecticut Yankee*, the domestic space of the nation and the foreign space of colonialism are merged. Slavery in King Arthur's England resonates with Twain's attack on Russian serfdom as well as slavery at home. The slave driver was illustrated as a capitalist robber baron. And the name "Yankee" itself was shifting geographically at the time, referring not only to Northerners in relation to Southerners but also to the nation as a whole in the international arena.

Writing *Connecticut Yankee* drove Twain into bankruptcy. He tried to recoup his losses by taking a lecture trip around the world, which meant touring the outposts of the British Empire. He wrote of this journey in a two-volume travelogue, *Following the Equator* (1896). His first stop was Hawaii, which he was sad not to revisit, because it was quarantined due to a cholera outbreak at the time of heightened struggle between annexationists and those who defended Hawaiian sovereignty, three years before it would be annexed by the United States. From Australia to India to South Africa, Twain found hundreds of Hank Morgans in British colonial rule. He lambasted the destructive effect of colonialism on the lives of the colonized, even as he enjoyed the privilege of colonial patronage and indulged his Anglophilia. Throughout his travelogue, he showed that the equator was closer to home than one might imagine; the beating of an Indian servant, for example, brought back a childhood memory of his father beating a black slave.

Thus when Twain turned his pen to American imperialism at the turn of the twentieth century, he brought to bear his half-century journey through the global routes of empire, which linked Hawaii with the American South, and Indian wars in the American West with the European conquest of Asia and Africa. The last decade of his life was marked by Twain's dark, pessimistic, misanthropic turn. Yet texts like *The Mysterious Stranger* represent more than a turn to personal despair and a retreat from history into the imagination. His science fiction stories about nightmarish journeys through time and space explore the dislocations and destruction Twain witnessed firsthand in a world encompassed by and unraveled by the struggles for imperial power.

Twain wrote "To the Person Sitting in Darkness" at the height of this outrage and despair. His language and narrative strategies represent two different approaches to American imperialism in the Philippines. On the one hand, he sees it as part of the global enterprise of what he calls, sardonically the "Blessings-of-Civilizations Trust" and its methods of "conferring our Civilization upon peoples that sit in darkness" (Zwick 1992, 27). In this "Trust" he includes violent corruption on the streets of New York, outrageous reparations demanded by missionaries following the suppression of the Boxer rebellion; the German Kaiser's "mailed fist" policy in China; and the atrocities performed by the British in South Africa and by the United States in the Philippines. Thus he places American imperialism within a global imperial system. On the other hand, he tries to separate a different vision of America as liberator, genuinely committed to setting people free, a vision of what we might call American exceptionalism, in which the true American identity is defined as anti-imperial and essentially different from that of European conquerors. These visions clash and expose both the power and limits of Twain's anti-imperialist vision.

In his powerful assault on the "Blessings-of-Civilization Trust" he uses economic language to expose its self-serving ideology that merely cloaks "offenses against humanity." He exposes righteousness as motivated by profit, and debunks altruistic pretensions by describing it as a game. Twain's most effective rhetorical strategy adopts the voice of the "civilizer" to parody the hollowness and hypocrisy of its high-flown rhetoric. In turn, he adopts the voice of the colonized, the "Person Sitting in Darkness," supposedly lost in ignorance, to speak the truth about empire. He introduces, for example, a newspaper piece written by a Tokyo correspondent and claims satirically that "it has a strange and impudent sound, but the Japanese are but partially civilized as yet. When they become wholly civilized they will not talk so" (Zwick 1992, 27). Then he quotes this "partially civilized" speaker: "religious invasions of Oriental countries by powerful Western organizations are tantamount to filibustering . . . missionary organizations constitute a constant menace to peaceful international relations" (27). In response, Twain asks, "Shall we go on conferring our Civilization upon the peoples that sit in darkness, or shall we give those poor things a rest? Shall we bang ahead in our old-time, loud, pious way, and commit the new century to the game; or should we sober up and sit down and think it over first?" (27–28). He debunks the piety of the civilizing mission by using the language of gamesmanship and business: "Would it not be prudent to get our Civilization tools together and see how much stock is left . . . and balance the books, and arrive at the profit and loss, so that we may intelligently decide whether to continue business or sell out the property?" (28). Twain shows that language serves as much as a weapon in the civilizing mission as guns do. Language perpetuates and veils the underlying violence, what Twain calls "The Actual Thing that the Customer Sitting in Darkness buys with his blood and tears and land and liberty" (29). In contrast, the "pretty" language he lists of "love," "justice," "Christianity," "liberty," "law and order" is "merely an outside cover" which "we reserve for Home Consumption" (29).

Twain then marches through the atrocities committed around the world by the British in South Africa, the Germans in China, the czar in Manchuria, and the French in North Africa, ending with the United States in the Philippines. In each case, he has the "Person Sitting in Darkness" observe and comment: "It is yet *another* Civilized Power, with its banner of the Prince of Peace in one hand and its loot-basket and its butcher knife in the other. Is there no salvation for us but to adopt Civilization and lift ourselves down to its level?" (31–32).

When Twain turns to the United States, he sees two different Americas and has the "Person Sitting in Darkness" say (as quoted above): "There is something curious about this — curious and unaccountable. There must be two Americas: one that sets the captive free, and one that takes a once-captive's new freedom away from him, and picks a quarrel with him with nothing to found it on; then kills him to get his land" (32). These two Americas would resonate with memories of the Civil War at home, when the nation emancipated the slaves and then re-enslaved them through systematic violence against black people, which stripped them of whatever rights they had achieved under Reconstruction. (Twain wrote an unpublished essay called "The United States of Lyncherdom.") Twain here is referring directly to the America that rushed to the aid of Cuban Independence in the war against Spain in 1898, when he believed it was "playing the usual and regular *American* game" (32). The other America annexed the Philippines at the end of that same war and was currently conducting a brutal war against its struggle for independence. Twain saw this America as not acting American at all, but as slavishly imitating the European game of colonial conquest. His powerful condemnation of imperialism works here in part by disavowing its centrality to American politics and identity, by representing imperialism as a foreign activity, an aberration from the genuine national commitment to freeing the captive. Splitting America in two does not acknowledge how the narrative of liberation legitimated the exercise of imperial power. What Twain's anti-imperialism had in common with proimperialist arguments was the representation of U.S. intervention as a narrative of rescue: of Cuba and the Philippines from the tyranny of an old-world empire, on the one hand, and from the anarchy of revolution and self-rule, on the other.

Proponents of imperialism merged Twain's two Americas through an accompanying narrative of liberation; they saw imperial warfare abroad as an opportunity for the American man to rescue himself from the threatening forces of industrialization and feminization at home. In a speech urging the United States to annex the Philippines in 1900, for example, Senator Albert Jeremiah Beveridge asked: "What does all this mean for every one of us?" and then readily answered: "It means opportunity for all the glorious young manhood of the republic — the most virile, ambitious, impatient, militant manhood the world has ever seen" (Beveridge 1989, 390). Without specifying the opportunities for particular actions, Beveridge implied tautologically that the empire offered the arena for American men to become what they already were, to enact their essential manhood before the eyes of a global audience. In subduing the Philippines, asserted another proimperialist, a man could escape the thrall of modern life and be rejuvenated as a "free, glorious man, the real sinews of the republic in the days when too many of us are city bred" (quoted in Hoganson 1998, 151). By fighting abroad, this logic held, an American man could return home to his republic origins.

A similar rescue mission was conducted on the pages of the popular historical romance, where thinly veiled American heroes pursued chivalric adventures in bygone eras. In the opening scene from the 1898 bestseller *When Knighthood Was in Flower*, the heroine declares passionately upon her first sight of the hero fighting a duel: "For once I have found a real live man, full of manliness" (Major 1898, 27). In these novels, mythical kingdoms in historical settings function as the fictional equivalent of the Philippines for Beveridge, as the site where a man can reassert his "militant manhood." In these romances, a woman serves both as the damsel in distress for the hero to rescue and as the eyes of the world for which masculinity is performed. These were the kind of popular novels that *Connecticut Yankee* mocked.

The narrative of liberation can easily slide into a narrative of conquest because it places the liberated in a passive, feminized, dependent role. McKinley justified the war against Filipinos by chastising them for not consenting to play the role of the rescued: "It is not a good time for the liberator to submit important questions concerning liberty and government to the liberated while they are engaged in shooting down their rescuers" (quoted in Hilderbrand 1981, 44–45). The narrative of liberation implies that those in need of rescue are inferior to the heroic liberators. When U.S. Americans imagined that Filipinos and Cubans were dependent on the United States to free them from the evil Spanish Empire, they also assumed that these same people could not fight for their own freedom and were indeed incapable of national independence and of governing themselves. In the buildup to U.S. intervention against Spain in Cuba, the popular press often represented Cubans as damsels in distress waiting for heroic American men to rescue them. This gendered narrative of liberation resonates today with one of the justifications for the recent war in Afghanistan, to rescue Afghani women from the oppression of the Taliban.

Twain's critique of American imperialism at the dawn of the twentieth century has its power — and its limits — that speaks to our understanding of the American Empire in the twenty first century. In criticizing U.S. actions in the Philippines, Twain was challenging America to live up to a better image of itself, as liberator and not conqueror. This powerful critique led many Americans to oppose the war in the Philippines, because it held up a mirror to U.S. violence that seemed "un-American." When they read reports of atrocities again soldiers and civilians, it became hard to uphold the notion that they were the civilizers and the Filipinos the barbarians. Twain quotes a letter that a young American soldier wrote to his mother in Iowa: "WE NEVER LEFT ONE ALIVE. IF ONE WAS WOUNDED, WE WOULD RUN OUR BAYONETS THROUGH HIM" (Zwick 1992, 37). This kind of testimony made it difficult to believe that the United States was bestowing the "Blessings of Civilization" on the Philippines when its soldiers were acting so savagely.

The question of holding up America to its own professed ideas is terribly relevant today, during the ongoing revelations of torture at the Guantánamo Naval Base in Cuba and the Abu Ghraib prison during the U.S. occupation of Iraq. Time and time again across the political spectrum in the United States, we hear outrage about torture expressed as a betrayal of American ideals and moral authority in the world. Sometimes there seems to be more concern about the photographs from Abu Ghraib tarnishing America's image than about the violence and debasement inflicted upon the human beings held as prisoners. As in Twain's "To the Person Sitting in Darkness," the image of two Americas, with one failing its better self, can offer a powerful political critique and a rallying cry for change, but this strategy also has some it limits. It can work to reaffirm the belief in America's essential goodness and to downplay and disavow "the abuse scandal" (as the choice of these words themselves do) as an aberration from the true America. Is the real problem with torture and indefinite detentions that they betray American ideals? Condemning America for failing to live up to its own higher standards may have strategic value in public debates, but this approach can become both provincial and exceptionalist, as it makes the United States the measure of universal values.

Upholding a narrative of a good America that rides to the rescue became increasingly hard for Twain, who came to decry the United States as it played the same global imperial game as the Europeans in violently suppressing the Philippines' fight for independence and in deferring independence for Cuba, as well. Twain may have wished to believe in a dream of American exceptionalism, one that viewed the United States as unique and different from Europe, as a nation that only intervenes in other countries to bring freedom and not conquest, liberation and not occupation. But Twain powerfully showed in his writing how indistinguishable these two Americas can be.

If Mark Twain were alive today, which of these two Americas would he see at work in Iraq?

Notes

1. See Boot 2002, Ignatieff 2003, and Robert Kaplan 2003.
2. For more detailed account of Twain's relation to Hawaii see Amy Kaplan 2002, chapter 2, "The Imperial Routes of Mark Twain."

Works Cited

Beveridge, Albert J. 1989. "Senator Albert J. Beveridge's Salute to Imperialism, 1900." In Thomas Paterson, ed., *Major Problems in American Foreign Policy: Documents and Essays*. 1: 389–391. Lexington, Mass: Heath.

Boot, Max. 2002. *The Savage Wars of Peace: Small Wars and the Rise of American Power*. New York: Basic Books.

Bush, George W. 2003. "Remarks by the President to the Philippine Congress." October 18. http://www .whitehouse.gov/news/releases/2003/10/20031018-12.html.

Hilderbrand, Robert C. 1981. *Power and the People: Executive Management of Public Opinion in Foreign Affairs, 1897–192*. Chapel Hill: University of North Carolina Press.

Hoganson, Kristin. 1998. *Fighting for American Manhood: How Gender Politics Provoked the Spanish-American and Philippine-American Wars*. New Haven: Yale University Press.

Ignatieff, Michael. 2003. "Why Are We in Iraq? (And Liberia? And Afghanistan?)." *New York Times Magazine* September 7.

Kaplan, Amy. 2002. *The Anarchy of Empire in the Making of U.S. Culture*. Cambridge: Harvard University Press.

Kaplan, Robert D. 2003. "Supremacy by Stealth: Ten Rules for Managing the World" *Atlantic Monthly* July–August.

Major, Charles. 1898. *When Knighthood Was in Flower*. Indianapolis: Bowen-Merill.

"Mark Twain, The Greatest American Humorist, Returning Home." *New York World* October 6, 1900 in Zwick 1992, 3–4.

Twain, Mark. [1885] 2002. *The Adventures of Huckleberry Finn*. New York: Penguin.

———. [1890] 2003. *A Connecticut Yankee in King Arthur's Court*. New York: Penguin.

———. [1894] 1986. *Pudd'nhead Wilson: And Those Extraordinary Twins*. New York: Penguin.

———. [1901] 1992. "To the Person Sitting in Darkness." 1901; In Zwick 1992, 22–39.

———. 1903. *Following the Equator: A Journey around the World*. New York: Harpers.

———. 1982. *No. 44. The Mysterious Stranger*. Berkeley: University of California Press.

———. 1989. *Mark Twain's Letters from Hawaii*. Edited by A. Grove Day. Honolulu: University of Hawaii Press.

Zwick, Jim, ed. 1992. *Mark Twain's Weapons of Satire: Anti-Imperialist Writings on the Philippine-American War*. Syracuse: Syracuse University Press.

CHAPTER 4

Welcoming the Unbidden:
The Case for Conserving Human Biodiversity

Rosemarie Garland-Thomson

I want to offer here a bold proposition, one that is even counterintuitive. I will argue that a democratic order's premise of equality should promote and accommodate the widest possible variety of human forms, functions, and behaviors. Stated in the abstract, this proposition does not seem controversial. Indeed, it conforms to the slogans about the value of diversity and inclusion that abound in our current picture of democracy. An avalanche of public images featuring shoulder-to-shoulder groups of smiling, stunningly standard people with a rainbow of skin tones and well policed ethnic variation lulls us into a belief that modern America has become truly integrated. Yet the limits of this eyewash diversity are revealed by widening economic disparities and persisting racism, sexism, homophobia, and classism. Perhaps the most uncontested example of our collective refusal to accommodate, let alone cultivate and embrace, the wide range of human variation that democracy implies is the way we think about disability and treat disabled people.

The human variation we think of as disability is virulently rejected in the modern consumerist democracy that is the United States. That we might decide to welcome rather than reject disability is the counterintuitive part of my argument here. I want to offer a rationale for how and why we might reimagine disability as a form of human variation we want to recognize and accept in a modern democracy. I will do this by enlisting the opposing logics of eugenics and biodiversity, both of which have much cultural currency in our historical moment and place. To focus on a specific example, my contention that we should "welcome the unbidden" centers here on the contrast between two utopian feminist discourses: ecofeminism and eugenic feminism. I will contrast the logic of ecofeminism's call for biodiversity with the logic of eugenic feminism manifest in the recently reclaimed and often taught 1915 utopian novel *Herland* by feminist writer Charlotte Perkins Gilman. My point is that the logic of ecofeminism's call for valuing and conserving biodiversity can serve as a way to rethink the logic of eugenics that informs Gilman's utopia and that persists strongly today in our attitudes and treatment of human variation in general and specifically that which we consider to be disability.

I must say at the outset that I am not offering a presentist feminist progress narrative that simplistically condemns an earlier way of thinking by invidiously comparing it to a contemporary view. The very terms I use, "ecofeminism" and "eugenic," are freighted by history, the first partaking of the ethical and progressive, the second thoroughly discredited and besmirched by a history of forced sterilizations in the United States and elsewhere, and especially by the

Nazi extermination program. Yet the terms are important and precise in re-vealing two distinct ways of understanding and responding to human variation.

The Old and New Eugenics

Let me begin with a brief account of eugenic thinking in the modern West. Eu-genics, meaning good genes, was an optimistic new form of science formulated in 1865 and coined in 1883 by Francis Galton, a statistician and cousin of Darwin. The precursor of modern genetics, eugenics arose from Galton's concept of "nat-ural ability" and quickly gained supporters under the progressive banner of im-proving the race, of augmenting the process of natural selection. Its practical application — often enacted in public policy— took the form of positive eugen-ics, which encouraged the ostensibly "fit" to reproduce, and negative eugenics, which prevented the proliferation of the supposedly "unfit." Positive eugenics gave America utopian rhetoric, Better Baby Contests, and Fitter Family initia-tives. It gave Germany the virulent nationalistic concept of the Aryan *Volk*.

Negative eugenics was a much more robust initiative that yielded a felicitous credence and implementation to already ascendant ideologies such as racial pu-rity, nativism, and white supremacy and provided a new application to older ideas such as perfectionism, millennialism, and social reform. Negative eugen-ics was realized in the United States through legalized forced sterilization between 1907 and 1939 of more than 30,000 people in twenty-nine states ("Deadly Medicine" 2005). It was legitimated by pronouncements such as those of Supreme Court Justice Oliver Wendell Holmes, who declared in the 1927 de-cision in *Buck vs. Bell* that affirmed forced sterilization: "Three generations of imbeciles are enough" (Black 2003, 121). It was institutionalized in the Ameri-can Eugenics Society, founded in 1922 — among whose board of directors were the president of the University of Michigan, the medical director of the Rocke-feller Foundation, and a Harvard sociologist. It was codified in the Eugenics Record Office, dedicated in 1910 to document the desired and the defective Americans lines — the latter of which were estimated to be 10 percent of the population. Negative eugenics thus created a new class of subordinated persons composed of a wide range of people systematically disenfranchised by race, class, gender, or disability under the supposedly biological category of the "fee-bleminded," measuring and registering them variously as "morons," "defec-tives," and "degenerates." Eugenic logic also birthed the idea in the United States of the "lethal chamber" as a final solution to the problem of the unfit. Moving eugenics to euthanasia, the lethal chamber was proposed as early as 1913 by American psychologist Henry Goddard, echoed by other American eu-genicists, and materialized with chilling efficacy by the Third Reich as a way to secure the "Aryan race" against pollution by disabled people, homosexuals, Gypsies, and— of course — Jews.[1]

Eugenics marshaled the authority of science, statistics, positivism, and prog-ress to justify eliminating certain kinds of people in the name of social improve-ment. Such a culling of imagined outsiders and the ostensibly illegitimate as-sured that power remained in the hands of a dominant group defined as superior according to indisputable biological criteria. The Chosen People of eugenics were not the elect of God but rather the elect of Nature itself, revealed not through divine intervention but through the logic of Social Darwinism. The effect of eugenic ideology and practice was and is to reduce human variation in the interest of establishing what the Nazis called a master race, whose ascendancy is naturalized by an appeal to the rationality of objective science and validated as common sense.

Eugenics was not an historical aberration or anomalous excess, as it has often been seen in a post-Holocaust era. Rather it was the logical product of modernity, as Zygmunt Bauman has suggested. The science Galton named "eugenics" in 1883 emerges from the trends we call modernity, growing out of Jeremy Bentham's utilitarian philosophy in 1788, Malthus's instrumental notion of expendable populations in 1798, Darwin's theory of evolution in 1859, and Mendel's theories of inheritance in 1866. The ideology of eugenics is also a product of the standardization of labor and the rise of capitalism in modernity. The body regularized in form and function that is demanded by wage labor, industrialization, and consumer capitalism has become the valued body of modernity, first in the developed world and now globally. The rise of scientific medicalization was fused with industrial and technological development to police human variation in the name of progress and improvement. The idea that we should and can shape the world, our collective and individual fates, and the future — as opposed to accepting a divinely decreed status quo — is the informing principle of the modern secular capitalist subject (Haskell 1985 a and b). This radically new sense of ourselves that arises from historical and material circumstances has been described variously as rationalization, secularism, the disenchantment of the world, consumer capitalism, the control revolution, classification, and the taming of chance.[2]

One way to frame the way we see others and ourselves in our moment of late modernity is as the rationalization of humanity, an ideological and material shift that has increasingly occurred since the mid-nineteenth century in developed capitalist societies. Rationalization evolved as a way for modern societies to control the rapidly growing amount of information, products, processes, and movement that industrialization spawned. The aim of rationalization is to abstract and simplify us within a defining bureaucracy that structures our lives. This technological and institutional network of information is so vast and complex that it must simplify us in order to manage us and our lives. Things and people must fit into preexisting patterns and templates for modern information systems to process them and for material practices associated with industrialization and development to include them. Consumer capitalism reduces human variation by excluding bodies of both producers and consumers that do not fit the standard. This fundamental impulse of modernity saturates and configures the material environment in such instances as check boxes on census forms, Fordism, ready-to-wear clothing, interchangeable parts, wage labor, the military-industrial complex, global outsourcing, and social security numbers. The conventional, unrealistic bodies we see in commercial images are a form of visual rationalization of the body. Such rationalization does not actually reduce human variation; rather it erases our particularities from the record of who we are and how we live. This pervasive smoothing out of human complexity and variation profoundly molds who we take ourselves and others to be.

Both our bodies and the way we imagine them are shaped to conform to a standard model of human form and function that has come to be called *normal* in medical discourses, *average* in consumer capitalism, and *ordinary* in colloquial parlance. The measure of all things human, normal is the central concept governing the status and value of people in late modernity. It is the abstract principle toward which we are all herded by myriad institutional and ideological forces. It is "the centre from which deviation departs" (Hacking 1990s 164).[3] Normalcy, as Lennard Davis tells us, is "enforced" (1995, 1). It is the destination to which we all hasten and the stick used to drive us there. We are obliged to act, feel, look, and be normal — at any cost. And normal does cost. The anxious demand to achieve the right clothes, cars, toys, faces, or bodies creates enormous commercial markets that fuel consumer capitalism.

Normal is the objective of eugenics. Whereas eugenics lost favor after Hitler enacted it in the Holocaust, normal has taken over its mission to relentlessly standardize bodies.[4] The eugenic goal of reducing human diversity by eliminating the "unfit" has now morphed into eliminating the "abnormal," an untainted term for the older idea of improving the race through eugenics. This aim is largely now accomplishable in the developed world through technological and medical interventions that materially rationalize our bodies in the interest of such concepts as progress and improvement. This issue is deflected and obscured by the reductive, popular call for individuality and diversity. Yet, a deeper and seldom challenged project of creating bodily uniformity and eliminating devalued differences marches forward through what Daniel Kevles calls a "new eugenics" that aims to regularize our bodies and that persists in robust but recast forms today (1985, 267). Eschewing the terminology of pre-WW II eugenics such as *racial improvement, undesirables,* and *evolutionary fitness,* this new eugenics is expressed as a matter of technological advancement and individual freedom under banners such as reproductive choice, genetic engineering, enhancement, elective surgery, and physician-assisted suicide.

The goal of both old and new eugenics — including eugenic euthanasia — is to eliminate people imagined as unfit, in the double sense of being unhealthy and of not, or no longer, fitting the bodily or behavioral expectations set for a socially valued human being. Whereas the old eugenics was directly racist, elevating the "white" race to the pinnacle of evolutionary fitness, the new eugenics of normalcy is subtly racist by casting the variations we associate with "nonwhite" races, the disabled, and the underclass as aesthetically or functionally aberrant. The new eugenics of normalcy employs what might be called the positive eugenics of curing, repairing, or improving people and groups. This eugenics of improvement is enacted through practices as diverse as reconstructive and aesthetic surgery, medical and technological treatment, enhancement procedures, gene therapy, and faith healing — all of which aim to make us better. At the same time, the new eugenics supports eliminating supposedly undesirable or inferior human variations in people through practices such as genetic manipulation, selective abortion, reproductive technology, so-called physician-assisted suicide, institutionalization, withholding nourishment, sterilization, surgical normalization, aesthetic standardization procedures, and ideologies of health and fitness.

Eugenic Feminism

Early twentieth-century feminists such as birth-control movement leader Margaret Sanger, radical social justice advocate Emma Goldman, suffragist Victoria Woodhull, and writer Charlotte Perkins Gilman all took up the seductive Progressive mission of eugenics. Gilman, in particular, found empowerment in the idea of eugenic feminism that charged mothers with the responsibility for transforming the social world and achieving gender equality through improving the race. This feminist social progress agenda takes the form of what Dana Seitler calls Gilman's "regeneration narratives," which detail a program of "eugenic motherhood," the best known of which is the 1915 novel *Herland* (Seitler 2003, 64, 82).

Gilman's utopian novel posits a world elsewhere that is inhabited, built, and run exclusively by women and girls who reproduce through a sacred and exalted parthenogenesis; that is, without the biological participation of men. The plot is driven by the incursion of three male scientist-explorers into this realm of communal motherhood. The male outsiders are eventually converted, domesticated, and two of them are happily assimilated through heterosexual marriage. Although Herland has been established by women in a jungle forest away from civilized, man-made society, the women do not renounce what we now call development in favor of a harmonious and symbiotic relation with nature (Hudak 2003). They see the environment as a resource to be appropriated by a perfected human community and shaped to meet their needs. They engineer crops, clear the land, use machines, construct a futuristic transportation system of "perfect roads," and build "rambling palaces" (Gilman 1998, 18, 19). What is banished from Herland is individualistic masculine civilization's aggression and hierarchy. There are no wars, weapons, crime, punishment, poverty, kings, priests, or aristocrats. The femininity of Herlanders retains and celebrates motherhood and communal cooperation, while it refuses "feminine charms" along with constrictive comportment, dress, and ornamentation (59). Although *Herland* rejects men and masculinity, this feminist uplift narrative celebrates rationality, an ethic of efficiency, a trust in science and technology, and a commitment to Western civilization. Like many other white, elite feminists of her time, Gilman focuses on gender inequality alone, ignoring the ways that oppressive systems such as race, class, sexuality, and ability operate in tandem and mutually constitute one another. Thus, Gilman's utopia is a reversal of the modern Western status quo, so that women rather than men are in a position of superiority. Its commitment to development as a form of economic colonization also generates its eugenic ideology.

The eugenic feminism of *Herland* emerges as a faith in what was taken in the early twentieth century as social improvement but was expressed in a way we now understand as racism and ableism. At the root of *Herland*'s utopia is the principle of selective breeding, the oppressive aspects of which are totally absent in the narrative. Although the racism of eugenic feminism has been critically examined, the ableism — that is, the discriminatory attitudes toward the disabled — has gone unremarked. The Herlanders are a perfected strain of "Aryan stock," but they are also all nondisabled (54). Negative eugenics is expressed here not through extermination but through population control, through sacrificial renunciation of motherhood by those who are supposedly unfit. In a chilling precursor of the Nazi *Lebensraum* rationale for murdering Jews, Gilman evokes the "pressures of population" as leading to a "writhing mass of underbred people trying to get ahead of one another — some few on top, temporarily, many constantly crushed out underneath, a hopeless substratum of paupers and degenerates" (68). Here Gilman rejects Malthusian and Social Darwinian logic not because it is unjust but because it produces "degenerates." The utopian aim of Herland is "to breed out, when possible, the lowest types," those with "bad qualities" (82). What is cultivated through "gentle breeding" is "a higher level of active intelligence, and of behavior," "sturdy children," and "smooth and happy" lives (78, 103). What is purged are old age, "degenerates," "the diseases of childhood," "disease and insanity," and "the abnormal" (68, 95, 136). In short, the utopia that is Herland has no disability. Its citizenry — its *Volk* — has been regularized, here by selective breeding, so as to manifest only the forms, functions, behaviors, and heritage that the dominant order values.

Ecofeminism and Biodiversity

Although it is easy now to expose the racism of Gilman's eugenic feminism and to argue for encouraging a racially diverse world, it is much more difficult to argue for a world that has disability in it. However, the bold, counterintuitive proposition I promised at the outset does exactly that. I want to apply a feminist ethic of biodiversity conservation to humans by suggesting a utopian vision that expands rather than reduces human variation in form and function. I am arguing for a world that makes a tenable space for the kinds of bodies variously considered old, abnormal, retarded, crazy, crippled, diseased, blind, deaf, ugly, deformed, or degenerate.

This proposition is counterintuitive because our modern, consumer capitalist society emphatically denies vulnerability, contingency, and mortality as the human condition. Much in modern America tells us that if we buy the right products, cultivate the right habits, pay careful attention, and employ the most sophisticated medical technology, we can banish disability from our lives. Strong disincentives such as social stigma and a sense of somehow having failed to "overcome" or "beat" life's inevitable limitations pressure us not to identify as a person with a disability. Disability is neither a label we are eager to assume nor a situation we want to embrace. We enact often virulent measures to deny, avoid, and eliminate disability and other forms of human variation we do not value. We encourage aborting disabled fetuses and approve of so-called physician-assisted suicide for disabled people. We devalue physical and mental variety and expect medicine to wipe away all disability. As a consequence, when disability does enter our lives, often our only available responses are silence, denial, shame, or determined and desperate vows to "fight it." Seldom do we imagine disability as an aspect of all lives that our society and community should accommodate. Disability — whether manifest in a singularly disabled body or in whole classes of people with disabilities — is imagined to compromise the collective social order. The supposedly hopelessly incurable frustrate modernity's will to change the world; disabled groups ostensibly drain communal resources, prompt suffering, or pollute the social body.

And yet what we think of as disability is integral to being human. Disability studies points out that, in fact, all bodies are shaped by their environments from the moment of conception.[5] We transform constantly in response to our surroundings and incorporate our histories into our bodies. Sometimes we call it growth, sometimes identity, sometimes disability. Our bodies need care; we all need assistance to live. Ability and disability are not so much a matter of the capacities and limitations of bodies as about what we expect from a body at a particular moment and place. Whereas Neil Armstrong breathes easily on earth, he needed a heavy-duty prosthetic suit to breathe on the moon. Some people on earth need respirators to breathe easily. Stairs disable people who need to use wheelchairs to get around, but ramps let them go places freely. Reading the print in a phone book or deciphering the patterns on a computer screen are abilities that our moment demands. So if our minds cannot make sense of the patterns, or our eyes cannot register the print, we become disabled. We are expected, however, to look, act, and move in certain ways so we will literally fit into the built environment. If we do not, we become disabled.

Although modern society presses us to all be the same, the human body varies greatly in its forms and functions. We should cultivate our differences, the rich distinctiveness that makes up human variation. For one thing, our experience of living eventually contradicts our collective fantasy that the body is stable, predictable, or controllable. Disability insists otherwise. What we call disability is unavoidable, even when we rightly mitigate the pain or suffering that often accompanies it. Our conventional response to disability is to change the person through medical or high technology rather than through changing the environment to accommodate the widest possible range of human form and function. Disability in its broadest sense is perhaps the essential characteristic of being human. The body is dynamic, constantly interacting with history and environment. We evolve into disability as we evolve into life. If we live long enough, we will all become disabled in some way.

Ecofeminist theory provides a welcoming understanding of disability and suggests an alternative world to the one offered by eugenic feminism. Biodiversity conservation is a key principle of ecofeminism — which links women's exploitation with the exploitation and domination of the environment. Biodiversity, according to Helen Zweifel, is "the totality of genetic resources, varieties, and ecosystems" and comprises nothing less than "the very foundation of all life on earth" (1997, 110). Because the gendered division of labor in agriculture has traditionally given women the role of custodian of the seed, ecofeminism sees women as the preservers of biodiversity, which in turn is a feminist project. Ecofeminism's utopia offers a sustainable environment that fosters the widest possible biodiversity. This emphasis on a harmonious and mutually supportive relation between humans and their environments contrasts with the drive toward mastery over matter that has produced an environmental and social crisis in modernity that threatens all life. Such an attempt to control the natural world — manifest in the domination of women, who represent nature — also pressures us relentlessly toward standardizing the natural world, from plants, seeds, and food to the appearance, size, and function of human bodies. Ecofeminism asserts that ecological survival and human justice require social transformation that shifts from a masculinist model of domination, exploitation, and hierarchy to a feminist model of cooperation, conservation, and mutuality. The enhancement of life from a biodiversity perspective would preserve and respect variations rather than reducing them through the process of rationalization. Most important, biodiversity is necessary for survival: "Human and ecological survival and justice are linked with nurturing the interdependence of diverse humans" (Howell 1997, 235).

Creating an environment that sustains biodiversity is also the goal of disability rights advocates. A material, built, and attitudinal environment that accommodates the widest rage of human variation encourages the flourishing of human biodiversity (Kafer 2005). An environment that sustains rather than excludes human biodiversity—from curb cuts in sidewalks and ramps into buildings, to inclusive teaching methods in schools, to the structure and demands of the workplace, to health care policies and practices — also helps achieve the social justice democracy promises. Such a sustainable environment, for example, would provide public education for all people in American Sign Language, just as we do now in foreign languages such as Spanish, so that when hearing people age and become deaf or hard of hearing, communication between them and the still-hearing can continue smoothly. Curb cuts in sidewalks would allow baby strollers, cyclists, and skaters — as well as wheelchair users — to pass across curbs without barriers. Implements, from can openers to door handles, and built spaces, from offices and homes to public transit systems, would be universally designed so that they would not become barriers when people develop disabilities. This is environmental sustainability with a low impact on resources. Such a universally designed built environment does not individualize the expenditure of resources on a case-by-case basis, but rather creates a material world that anticipates variation and accommodates it in advance.

The benefit that facilitating such variation provides to everyone is that "[s]ocial and cultural diversity represents different solutions to the problems of surviving in particular environments, and helps society to adapt to changing conditions" (Zweifel 1997, 115). Acquiring or being born with the traits we call disabilities fosters an adaptability and resourcefulness that often is underdeveloped in people whose bodies fit smoothly into the prevailing environment. Moreover, that resourcefulness extends to the nondisabled as they relate to and live with people with disabilities. For example, people born without arms all learn to use their toes to accomplish tasks that those of us with arms never are able to do. Blind people learn to navigate through the world without the aid of light, a skill useful when our sources of artificial light fail. Deaf people indigenously develop modes of communication that are silent. Such adaptability enriches us all.

We should value and accommodate disability as a form of human diversity for several reasons. First, it can help us see disability not as an anomalous but as a significant universal human experience that occurs in every society, every family, and almost every life. Second, it may help us accept that fact. Third, it can serve social justice by better integrating disability into our knowledge of human experience and history and integrating disabled people into our society.

Fourth, it can offer a model of interdependence rather than independence by reminding us that all people rely on one another for life tasks and survival. Fifth, it can produce what Patricia Hill Collins calls "subjugated knowledges" that can yield useful perspectives and skills in adapting to changing and challenging environments (2000, 9). The indigenous knowledge of disabled people is parallel to that of nondeveloped, so-called primitive cultures that ecofeminism seeks to preserve. Sixth, it can offer a model of intrinsic rather than instrumental valuing of human beings, which is the foundational principle of democracy.

Conserving, respecting, and accommodating the wide range of human variations of form, function, and behavior we think of as disability will also promote human ethics — a quality that our history reminds us we need desperately to cultivate. When Gilman's utopian "gentle breeding" does not lead to the "smooth and happy lives" she presents in *Herland*, the eugenic logic at work there can and has led us not just to individual unethical practices but often to communal atrocity as well. Eugenic logic seeks to promote human traits it values (positive eugenics) and eliminate those it devalues (negative eugenics). But when the carrot fails, the stick is quick to compensate. When the supposedly undesirable traits refuse to be eradicated — when the disabled will not be cured or the natives resist assimilation or the queer decline normalization — all too soon the often regrettable but altogether rational solution trumps the less efficient "gentle" tactics. Such a logic has given us Indian removal policies, hate crimes, mercy killing, Jack Kevorkian, capital punishment, the lethal chambers proposed by American scientists and enacted by the Nazi euthanasia program known as T–4, and the Final Solution. Eugenic logic — whether old or new — can never be ethical, just, or democratic, but it can be paraded as progress or pragmatism.[6]

It is difficult for us to imagine welcoming disability. But we might better understand the need to conserve and respect an experience and a way of being in the world that is fundamental to our humanity if we can shift from the dominant eugenic model to a biodiversity framework for understanding the human variation we think of as disability. Two disabled women writers offer thoughtful and complex meditations about living with disability that may help the rest of us conceive of why we might want a world that does not necessarily desire disability but is welcoming to its inevitable presence. Susan Wendell concludes of her life with chronic illness, "I would joyfully accept a cure, but I do not need one" (1996, 84). Accepting disability as a legitimate human experience rather than an anomalous one thus augments what might be considered her quality of life. Nancy Mairs's perspectivally entitled book, *Waist-High in the World*, offers a probing personal account of her own life with multiple sclerosis. Mairs's disability indeed has compromised the function of her body, but it has also informed her sense of self. She offers no narrative here of chastening through suffering, but rather a deep understanding of the human condition and a sharp critique of social justice. Her utopian "task," says Mairs, "is to conceptualize not merely a habitable body but a habitable world: a world that wants me in it" (1996, 63).

Notes

1. See here Black 2003, Galton 1978, Haller 1984, Kevles 1985, Kühl 1994, and Trent 1994.

2. See Horkheimer and Adorno 1987, Beniger 1986, Bowker and Star 1999, and Weber 1998.

3. For discussions of normalcy, see also Baynton 2001 and Canguilhem 1989.

4. There is however a reluctance to compare the logics of the new and old eugenics in the United States. Nazism besmirched and ended any support for the supposedly progressive eugenic movement in the United States. Nazi extermination procedures far exceeded the forced sterilization programs that the United States and the National Socialists had in common. The Holocaust wiped out the language of the old eugenics—including the word itself—and drove its logic underground. It is now generally accepted that eugenic thinking in the United States was a mistaken and generally innocuous undertaking, particularly when contrasted with the excesses of National Socialism. This serves to obscure the commonalities in the rationales underlying mass euthanasia and outmoded and thoroughly discredited eugenic practices such as forced sterilization. Seemingly elective practices such as selective abortion and genetic manipulation cannot comfortably be discussed in terms of eugenics because of the history of National Socialism.

5. See Linton 1998.

6. For an argument for eugenic euthanasia, see Singer and Kushe 1985.

Works Cited

Bauman, Zygmunt. 2000. *Modernity and the Holocaust*. Ithaca: Cornell University Press.

Baynton, Douglas C. 2001. "Disability and the Justification of Inequality in American History." In *The New Disability History: American* Perspectives, *eds. Paul K. Longmore and Lauri Umamsky*, 33–57. New York: New York University Press.

Beniger, James R. 1986. *The Control Revolution*. Cambridge: Harvard University Press.

Black, Edwin. 2003. *War against the Weak: Eugenics and America's Campaign to Create a Master Race*. New York: Four Walls Eight Windows.

Bowker, Geoffrey C., and Susan Leigh Star. 1999. *Sorting Things Out: Classification and Its Consequences*. Cambridge: MIT Press.

Canguilhem, Georges. 1989. *The Normal and the Pathological*. Translated by Carolyn R. Fawcett in collaboration with Robert S. Cohen. New York: Zone Books.

Collins, Patricia Hill. 2000. *Black Feminist Thought*. 2nd ed. New York: Routledge.

Davis, Lennard J. 1995. *Enforcing Normalcy: Disability, Deafness, and the Body*. New York: Verso.

"Deadly Medicine." 2005. U.S. Holocaust Museum, Online Exhibit. 30 January. http://www.ushmm.org/museum/exhibit/online/deadlymedicine/.

Galton, Francis. [1883] 1978. *Hereditary Genius: An Inquiry into Its Laws and Consequences*. Introduction by H. J. Eysenck. New York: St. Martin's.

Gilman, Charlotte Perkins. [1915] 1979. *Herland*. New York: Pantheon Books.

Hacking, Ian. 1990. *The Taming of Chance*. Cambridge: Cambridge University Press.

Haller, Mark H. 1984. *Eugenics: Hereditarian Attitudes in American Thought*. New Brunswick: Rutgers University Press.

Haskell, Thomas L. 1985a. "Capitalism and the Origins of the Humanitarian Sensibility, Part 1." *American History Review* 90.2 (April): 339–361.

———. 1985b. "Capitalism and the Origins of the Humanitarian Sensibility, Part 2." *American History Review* 90.3 (June): 547–566.

Horkheimer, Max, and Theodor Adorno. 1987. *Dialectic of Enlightenment*. Translated by John Cumming. New York: Continuum.

Howell, Nancy R. 1997. "Ecofeminism: What One Needs to Know." *Zygon: Journal of Religion and Science* 32.2 (June): 231–241.

Hudak, Jennifer. 2003. "The 'Social Inventor': Charlotte Perkins Gilman and the (Re) Production of Perfection." *Women's Studies* 32: 455–477.

Kafer, Alison. 2005. "Accessible Futures? Disability, Feminist and Queer Theory, and Progressive Politics." Ph. D. dissertation, Claremont Graduate School.

Kevles, Daniel J. 1985. *In the Name of Eugenics: Genetics and the Uses of Human Heredity.* New York: Knopf.

Kühl, Stefan. 1994. *The Nazi Connection: Eugenics, American Racism, and German National Socialism.* New York: Oxford University Press.

Linton, Simi. 1998. *Claiming Disability: Knowledge and Identity.* New York: New York University Press.

Mairs, Nancy. 1996. *Waist-high in the World: A Life among the Nondisabled.* Boston: Beacon.

Seitler, Dana. 2003. "Unnatural Selection: Mothers, Eugenic Feminism, and Charlotte Perkins Gilman's Regeneration Narratives." *American Quarterly* 55.1: 61–88.

Singer, Peter, and Helga Kuhse. 1985. *Should the Baby Live? The Problems of Handicapped Infants.* New York: Oxford University Press.

Trent, James W. 1994. *Inventing the Feeble Mind: A History of Mental Retardation in the United States.* Berkeley: University of California Press.

Weber, Max. 1998. *The Protestant Ethic and the Spirit of Capitalism.* Translated by T. Parsons; Introduction by R. Collins. Los Angeles: Roxbury.

Wendell, Susan. 1996. *Rejected Bodies: Feminist Philosophical Reflections on Disability.* New York: Routledge.

Zweifel, Helen. 1997. "The Gendered Nature of Biodiversity Conservation." *NWSA Journal* 9.3: 107–123.

CHAPTER 5

The "Face" of AIDS: Commodity Compassion and the Global Pandemic

Roger Hallas

Although it is a phenomenon without an end, an event that many argue is in fact just beginning, AIDS already engenders a complex history of its own. Since the mid-1990s, two discursive tropes have emerged that reconfigure how AIDS is understood in a wide range of contexts, ranging from public policy to activism to media representation. The first of these tropes is "post-AIDS," a First World discourse that frames the development of effective antiretroviral drug therapy against HIV/AIDS as the possible end of the AIDS crisis, in that it could transform the syndrome from being almost inevitably and eventually terminal to chronically manageable. The second trope, "global AIDS," relates to the shift from discussing AIDS in terms of an epidemic or a set of epidemics to nominating it a pandemic. Thus AIDS is now not only globally prevalent but it also constitutes a global crisis, significantly affecting a whole range of international public policy issues, including public health, economic development, and regional security.

Since the beginning of the AIDS crisis, documentary photography, film, and video have been privileged sites for the media representation of the disease, both for the pathologizing tendencies of mainstream journalism and for the interventionist strategies of AIDS-activist videos. Within mainstream documentary representation of AIDS, the trope of the face emerged as one of its most significant organizing metaphors. Throughout the almost quarter century since the discovery of AIDS, recurrent references to "giving a face to AIDS," "the changing face of AIDS," and "the new face of AIDS" have provided a persistent discursive framework of faciality for the documentary representation of AIDS. Such recourse to the human face has been taken up by both the disciplinary gaze of popular media eager to identify and pathologize the deviance of infected bodies and the humanistic gaze of documentary photographers and filmmakers who seek to exploit the human face's presumed ability to address the Other along universal lines (see Crimp 2002).

In this chapter I examine how two recent documentaries about the AIDS pandemic, Robert Bilheimer's *A Closer Walk* (2003) and Rory Kennedy's *Pandemic: Facing AIDS* (2002), utilize such facial discourse as they engage with the temporalizing dynamics of post-AIDS and the spatializing dynamics of global AIDS. However, it is not just questions of textuality that interest me here. It is also vital to investigate the production and reception contexts for these documentaries, especially since they were both conceptualized as global projects, that is to say, with a global set of audiences in mind. Furthermore, in its exploitation of media synergy, *Pandemic* appropriates a central strategy of contemporary globalized media. The project's Web site serves both as source of specific information and as a hypertextual hub linking all the elements of this multimedia project, including several versions of the documentary film, public service announcements, a touring photographic exhibition, a "coffee-table" book, and a set of educational materials.[1] All these materials are given a branded identity through the repeated use of specific documentary images embedded in a distinctive graphic design. Although most theatrically released documentaries are now served by their own promotional Web sites, *Pandemic* marks the arrival of a new synergistic form of documentary media that responds and adapts to ongoing media convergence.

Before we turn to these documentaries however, we should first understand the wider cultural contexts in which post-AIDS and global AIDS have emerged within First World public cultures. Since the mid-1990s, when the success of protease inhibitors in keeping down viral levels of HIV became widely acknowledged, discourses around the "end of AIDS," "post-AIDS" identities, and cultures "after AIDS" have burgeoned in both mainstream and lesbian and gay media in the United States (see Sullivan 1996 and Román 2000). To posit that the AIDS crisis is over in the First World requires a complex set of disavowals and erasures. First, one must ignore the fact that the AIDS pandemic comprises many epidemics in different places, affecting different groups, each with its own temporality, its own historicity. Second, even to declare the "end of AIDS" only in certain epidemics, such as the gay male epidemic in North America, requires one to disavow the differing rates of HIV infection and access to treatment among various groups within those epidemics. Third, protease inhibitors and the new combination therapies they have spawned do not constitute a cure, and the long-term effectiveness of these drugs is still in question.

As David Román has commented, these discourses about the "end of AIDS" consistently imply that "the need to talk about AIDS has ended as well" (2000, 1). In many cultural and political contexts, AIDS and HIV-related issues have become, like the retrovirus itself, almost undetectable. However, one place where people with AIDS have become more culturally visible is in advertising. It is here that we see an agile rock climber standing proudly on the top of a mountain gazing across an open vista (fig. 5.1); or two men and a woman in a golden wheat field holding life-affirming placards (fig. 5.2); or an interracial gay couple in tuxedos exiting a church amid an exuberant flurry of confetti. These are the "new faces of AIDS" that circulate in publications dedicated to particular niche markets, such as gay men and African Americans, and occasionally in mainstream publications like the *New York Times Magazine*. One encounters these images in print advertisements for Zerit, Combivir, and Crixivan, the various antiretroviral drugs used to combat HIV and AIDS. If you overlooked the accompanying text to these images, you might mistake them for ads promoting anything from life insurance to allergy medication. The glossy banality of such images signals the prevailing normalization of AIDS in the current moment in the First World.

After almost two decades in which AIDS representation in the First World has figured the person with AIDS as the Other against which the normative "general public" may be posited — that is to say as victim, pariah, killer, carrier

Figure 5.1: Magazine advertisement for Crixivan, 1997

(and occasionally as hero)— people with AIDS are now invited to join the "general public" as a targeted demographic through the consumer address of such advertising. As Gregg Bordowitz argues, "The figure of the AIDS consumer is merely the latest addition to a growing collection of portraits, hung in the gallery of the Diseased, found in the wing of the Other, exhibited in the Museum of Modern Identity" (1998, 9). In their invocation of an affirmative, well-regimented lifestyle, these figures are barely distinguishable from the normative body of contemporary fitness culture.

Should we thus accept these images of people *living* with AIDS, now understood as a chronic manageable disease, as precisely the kind of affirmative representation that AIDS activists demanded in the late 1980s? Are these the "PWAs who are vibrant, angry, loving, sexy, beautiful, acting up and fighting back" that were called for by ACT UP (AIDS Coalition to Unleash Power) in its critique of Nicholas Nixon's documentary portraits of PWAs on display at the Museum of Modern Art in New York City in 1988? (Crimp 2002, 87). Hardly. Although this iconography certainly undoes some of the phobic aspects to the "spectacle of AIDS," it continues to individualize and privatize the AIDS pandemic. These advertisements offer only images of individuals or couples, never a community of people who are living with AIDS, since the purpose of these advertisements is to stimulate private consumption of pharmaceutical products. Even ads that include groups, such as figure 5.2, frame them as individuals functioning as codified representatives of specific "risk groups" now remodeled as new pharmaceutical niche markets. Furthermore, addressing people with AIDS as consumers affirms only those who can afford the health coverage that provides access to such medications. A great many people with HIV in resource-rich countries have little or no access to these combination drug therapies.

Figure 5.2: Magazine advertisement for Combivir, 2001

Moreover, the number of people similarly disenfranchized elsewhere in the world is infinitely greater.

Over the last decade, the discursive construction of "African AIDS" as the foreign Other to the AIDS epidemics in the First World has been supplanted by global AIDS. As in the case of African AIDS, the dominant iconography of global AIDS continues to revolve around the figure of the impoverished "AIDS victim" who has long been normalized within the existing media representation of the Third World, with its supposedly intractable poverty, its chronic hopelessness, and its recurrent human disasters. A cover story in the *New York Times Magazine* from January 2001 entitled "How to Solve the World AIDS Crisis" demonstrates the continuing reliance on such iconography (Rosenberg 2001). Although the article by Tina Rosenberg provided a well-researched analysis of the economic and geopolitical issues preventing the Third and much of the (former) Second World from gaining affordable access to treatment, the accompanying visual discourse persisted in a singular focus on the person with AIDS as hopeless, poverty-stricken victim. The front cover presented a high-contrast black-and-white photograph of an African man with AIDS close to death, while the first page of the article was accompanied by a photomontage of twenty more

91

emaciated AIDS victims from around the world. In replicating the dominant iconography of global AIDS, this photo spread elides any attempt to visualize the tenacious local AIDS activism and progressive institutional initiatives that the article actually describes.

AIDS subsequently becomes naturalized within the representational space situated "out there" in the Third World, contrasting with its perceived decline "here" in the First World. Such simultaneously temporalizing and spatializing dynamics in the media representation of the pandemic bear out Cindy Patton's argument that there have always been what she calls two competing thought styles shaping the scientific and media construction of AIDS, that of epidemiology and that of its colonial antecedent, tropical medicine (Patton 2002, 34). Epidemiological thinking is driven by a temporal imperative to simulate the progression of pathogens from one vector to another. The location of disease is thus continually on the move, establishing potential new centers with each new infection. Tropical medicine, on the other hand, developed within colonialist ideology. Disease was thus understood to be proper to a place, to a "there," but only to operate as disease when it afflicted people from "here." Tropical thinking is thus driven by a spatial imperative to demarcate the boundaries between the health of the center and the infectious space and bodies of the periphery. Such spatializing and temporalizing dynamics are central to the ways in which *A Closer Walk* and *Pandemic* represent the AIDS pandemic.

Robert Bilheimer began *A Closer Walk* after meeting Jonathan Mann, the architect of the World Health Organization's global AIDS program. The film was shot in over a dozen countries around the world. Bilheimer edited over 100 hours of 16mm footage into a conventional eight-five-minute feature documentary that combines observational footage with interviews and narration by Hollywood celebrities Glenn Close and Will Smith. The $2 million budget, relatively large for a documentary feature, came principally from corporations and foundations, including General Motors, Kodak, and the Bill and Melinda Gates Foundation. A substantial part of this institutional funding went into financing an educational outreach program designed around the film.

After opening on a harrowing scene in which a very emaciated young Ugandan girl is undergoing a medical examination, *A Closer Walk* presents a global montage of people living with and dying from AIDS (figs. 5.3 and 5.4). The editing establishes a rhythm that alternates between almost static portrait shots and observational long shots of social context. Some of these portrait subjects are clearly ill and already bedridden. The aestheticized framing and the stasis of these shots imbues them with the qualities of still photography. In a recent interview, Bilheimer explained the motivation behind the project: "Our fundamental task was to restore or give dignity to the people who have AIDS and are living in poverty" ("AIDS Documentary 2003," 28). Here we encounter the almost ubiquitous ideological trope of "giving AIDS a human face." As I noted earlier, however, this history of giving a face to AIDS has been as much implicated in the disciplinary processes of identification, surveillance, and visual pathology as it has in humanist processes of individuation and intersubjectivity. Bilheimer's documentary subjects are passive, silent victims whose lives are completely spoken by the First World narrators.

Figure 5.3: Frame capture from *A Closer Walk* (Robert Bilheimer, 2003)

Figure 5.4: Frame capture from *A Closer Walk* (Robert Bilheimer, 2003)

Bilheimer has also acknowledged the influence on the film of *The Family of Man*, Edward Steichen's famous international project in humanist photojournalism. He comments, "The texture of that photography was very influential. . . . The humanity of the subjects comes through. In our film, we want audiences to connect on their own with the subjects, so how they are presented is crucial" ("AIDS Documentary 2003," 28). Steichen's 1955 exhibition at the Museum of Modern Art in New York and subsequent book publication became a landmark popular and intellectual event for Cold War culture in the United States. Consisting of 503 photographs made by 273 photographers from 68 countries, *The Family of Man* appropriated photo-design principles from news

93

Figure 5.5: Frame capture from *A Closer Walk* (Robert Bilheimer, 2003)

magazines to arrange its social documentary photography from around the world in a way that suggested that all peoples' goals and problems were fundamentally similar. Roland Barthes's well-known critique of the exhibition could equally be applied to Bilheimer's film: "Everything, the content and appeal of the pictures, the discourse which justifies them, aims to suppress the determining weight of History: we are held back at the surface of an identity, prevented precisely by sentimentality from penetrating into this ulterior zone of human behaviour where historical alienation introduces some 'differences' which we shall here quite simply call 'injustices'" (Barthes 1972, 101).

In the voiceover's claim to narrate "the way the world is," *A Closer Walk* actually naturalizes rather than historicizes the suffering it depicts. The film's conception of the world and its responsibility for the global trauma of the AIDS pandemic never develops beyond a generalized notion of humanity. Although *A Closer Walk* opens on the activist claim that the pandemic is both preventable and treatable, the film never explains the historical conditions that inhibit effective global programs for HIV prevention and treatment. Third World poverty and disease are presented as a tragic structuring determinant of particular places in our world rather than a historical situation sustained by global capitalism. In classic humanist fashion, the film's concern for the Other folds up into a contemplation of the self: "AIDS in the world is a story about ourselves. What kind of people are we?" The two shots accompanying these voiceover lines shift from an image of two African children (who appear to signify "AIDS in the world") to the image of a white man strolling contemplatively through a natural landscape (who presumably embodies "ourselves") (fig. 5.5). One could hardly imagine a more quintessentially Romantic trope of the Western bourgeois subject. The opening sequence ends like many of the film's sequences: with a series of epidemiological statistics. This rhetorical strategy temporalizes the pandemic without actually historicizing it. Presenting epidemiological statistics in terms of frequency is a strategy that the film appropriates from AIDS activist discourse, but *A Closer Walk* fails to counter such dramatic information with either historical explanations of causation or explicit policy demands, which are precisely what made the graphic publicity of ACT UP so effective.

A brief look at the film's reception further illuminates the ways in which *A Closer Walk* depoliticizes and dehistoricizes the pandemic. Although the film's high-powered foundation and corporate benefactors ensured exhibition opportunities in a range of state, corporate, educational, and nongovernmental contexts around the world, the widest audience for the documentary came when excerpts were internationally broadcast on the Oprah Winfrey Show on December 1, 2003, World AIDS Day. The show was structured around South Africa as a site for real and imagined therapeutic tourism, or as the show put it, "A Country That Touches the Soul." A section on the documentary, which highlighted its coverage of AIDS in South Africa and Uganda, joined features on celebrities discussing Alan Paton's *Cry the Beloved Country* in Oprah's Book Club and competition winners' "trip of a lifetime" to "live the magic of South Africa." With its characteristic brand of what I would like to call "commodity compassion," the Oprah Winfrey Show provided the perfect global showcase for *A Closer Walk*, described on the DVD's jewel case as "a beautifully crafted film." Commodity compassion reframes the viewer's ethical relation to the suffering of others in terms of prepackaged aesthetic experiences available for consumption. The demand of ethical and political responsibility is subsequently displaced by the pleasure of aesthetic connoisseurship.

Although Rory Kennedy's *Pandemic: Facing AIDS* doesn't explicitly lay claim to aesthetic value in its marketing, the film does bear strong rhetorical similarities to *A Closer Walk* in its mix of talking-head interviews, humanistic storytelling, and epidemiological statistics. As you can see from the title itself, the discursive trope of the face is even more emphatic. The Web site notes that "*Pandemic: Facing AIDS* aims to aid the fight against the epidemic by *putting a human face* on the overwhelming statistics surrounding the disease and opening channels for people all over the world to become involved in stopping its further spread" ("About the Project"; emphasis added). Kennedy pursues this humanization of the mathematical sublime engendered by AIDS statistics through the narration of five individual stories from different countries: "Lek" in Thailand, "James and Jessica" in Uganda, "Nagaraj and Bhanu" in India, "Sergei and Lena" in Russia, and "Alex" in Brazil. Each half-hour episode follows an individual story from one of the five countries. These individual stories are framed as global in the way that each emphasizes a set of social, political, and medical issues around AIDS that cut across national and local specificities. The sex industry is addressed in the Thailand episode, AIDS orphans in the Uganda episode, mother-to-child transmission in the Indian episode, harm reduction in the Russian episode, and treatment access in the Brazilian episode.

Accompanied by an original score by Philip Glass (in its initial broadcast on HBO), the title sequence of *Pandemic* uses a sophisticated digital fusion of maps and faces to visualize the concept of "global AIDS." Digital animation gradually reveals the world as seen from space. Just as the simulated camera tilt stops, the

Figure 5.6: Frame capture from *Pandemic: Facing AIDS* (Rory Kennedy, 2002)

subtitle "Thailand" appears to identify the land mass at the center of the frame. The simulated camera movement changes to a swift zoom in. As our vision approaches the land mass, the topographic features of Thailand dissolve into a mosaic of human faces (fig. 5.6). One woman's face is fully centered in the frame and slightly larger than the others. Very shortly we learn that this is Lek, a Thai woman living and eventually dying from AIDS, whose story we follow in the episode. As we watch each episode of *Pandemic*, it becomes clear that the map of human faces is made up of the documentary subjects from all five countries. Such digital special effects thus locate AIDS simultaneously in individual bodies and in specific places. The map frames AIDS within the nation, while the global mosaic of human faces invokes both individual and global parameters for understanding AIDS. This title sequence thus succinctly visualizes the organizing logic of the whole documentary.

Elton John's voiceover in *Pandemic* shares some of the rhetorical moves employed by *A Closer Walk*, particularly the first person plural address: "Their tragedy is our tragedy. And so are their stories." Yet his voiceover narration remains minimal throughout the documentary, offering introductory exposition of the national contexts and occasionally providing narrative information that cannot be visualized. The establishing shots of the Lopburi Temple in Thailand direct our gaze to a specific place. Lek is not only given a face but also a voice as she speaks directly to the camera in classical talking-head interviews and indirectly as she shows the filmmaker where she lives (fig. 5.7). The only narrational device framing her in the postcredit sequence is the subtitle that names her.

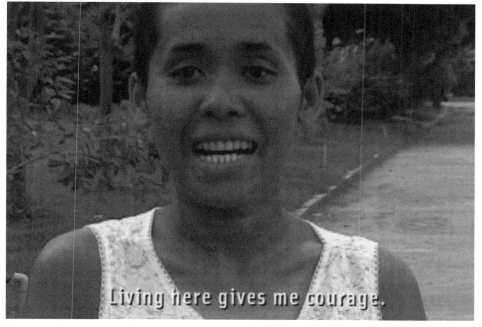

Figure 5.7: Frame capture from *Pandemic: Facing AIDS* (Rory Kennedy, 2002)

Using only a first name to identify the protagonist is a long-standing convention of social documentary. It potentially frames the viewer's encounter with the documentary subject in the more intimate discursive register of the familiar, but at a price. The talking heads of expert witnesses require their full names and titles for their discourse to be considered credible. Their credentials must be situated in history, whereas the credentials of a protagonist like Lek are located precisely outside of history, in that assumed domain of our shared "intimate" humanity. How Kennedy shoots and edits *Pandemic* definitely distinguishes it from the voyeuristic, contemplative gaze of *A Closer Walk*. The documentary continually shifts between its predominant observational mode and interactive moments when Lek addresses the camera or the filmmaker directly. Combined with the documentary's frequent hand-held camerawork, these strategies simulate for the viewer a stronger sense of feeling present in the world "out there." Although this strategy has its own ideological pitfalls, such as displaying the genealogical traces of colonial exploration and travel, it does resist the distanciating visual aestheticism of *A Closer Walk*.

The most significant limitation to *Pandemic*, however, derives from its very reluctance to engage in the expository mode, to explain the way the world is and why. What subsequently falls out of the documentary is an analysis of the role played by global capitalism in the AIDS pandemic. The Thailand episode provides very little analysis of how capitalism maintains the structural violence of the international sex industry there. Similarly, the lack of treatment options in Thailand are explained by Elton John's voiceover solely through the rubric of social stigma. One of the principal problems here lies in the structural nature of global capitalism. Its material, lived effects on people are certainly available to

97

visual documentation, but the structures that maintain it are not so easily accessible to the observational camera. Without exposition or analysis of the larger material conditions and economic structures that obstruct the development of effective prevention and treatment programs, what use is the consciousness-raising function of such documentary projects? This problem becomes conspicuously clear in the Brazil episode. *Pandemic* rightly showcases Brazil's incredible successes in pursuing an aggressive integration of prevention and treatment. Brazil achieved this feat by establishing a medical state of emergency, allowing the government to circumvent international patents for certain antiretroviral drugs. Brazil thus began producing their own generic versions domestically at a price that the national healthcare system could afford, so as to provide them for anyone who needed them. *Pandemic* demonstrates the success of the program, but neglects to explain how and why it has worked.

In response to this critique leveled at the documentary by a number of AIDS activists, Nan Richardson, one of the project's coproducers, counters that the synergistic component of the project allows the individualizing humanistic aspects of the documentary to be complemented by larger contextual frameworks provided on the Web site and in the educational materials (Ryan 2003, N3). But even when you look at the educational workbook, which includes rubrics for class activities in secondary education, the space for any discussion of the political economy of the AIDS pandemic is framed in very narrow and limiting ways. Similarly, the Web links to organizations that *Pandemic* encourages its viewers and readers to join conspicuously omit any activist organization at the forefront of the struggle for the Third World to develop its own commercial infrastructure for supplying affordable drug treatment. The explanation for such serious silences and omissions in *Pandemic* is to be found, I would argue, in the institutional funding that enabled Rory Kennedy to generate such a large-scale globally conceived project. It would be too easy, I think, to single out the Pfizer Foundation as the principal culprit amongst the project funders responsible for suppressing such political dimensions to *Pandemic*. I would argue rather that it is the larger institutional culture of nonprofit foundations that filters out any real political potential for mobilizing viewers of such documentary projects. We are left with a Faustian contract. To fund the kind of project that could mobilize on a global level, one must submit to a framework that weakens the potential to actually mobilize people.

I would like to conclude by taking a brief look at Gregg Bordowitz's video documentary *Habit* (2001) as a means of exploring how the articulation of difference potentially offers more effective opportunities for mobilization around the AIDS pandemic than the kind of humanistic appeal to universality found in *A Closer Walk* and *Pandemic*. Bordowitz is a United States-based AIDS activist and videomaker who has been living with AIDS for well over a decade. *Habit* serves as a sequel to his 1993 autobiographical video *Fast Trip, Long Drop*, which was made at a particularly bleak period in the AIDS pandemic, when the direct action of ACT UP and its culture of individual and collective empowerment was in crisis, and the treatment options for people living with AIDS were fast drying up. Conceived as potentially his final work, *Fast Trip* burns with anger, black humor, self-mockery, and despair. Bordowitz seeks to articulate

Figure 5.8: Frame capture from *Habit* (Gregg Bordowitz, 2001). Courtesy Video Data Bank, Chicago

everything that has become personally and collectively unspeakable within AIDS activist culture at that historical moment. Made almost a decade later, as Bordowitz lives a more stable life on antiretroviral drug therapy, *Habit* reworks many of the scenes and strategies from *Fast Trip* through the optic of his supposedly normalized existence. Not only does Bordowitz problematize the First World discourse of normalization "after" the AIDS crisis, he also situates his current everyday life in relation to the contemporary struggle for treatment access by South Africans living with AIDS. *Habit* shifts back and forth between Bordowitz's life in Chicago and footage taken in South Africa during the 2000 International AIDS Conference in Durban, including interviews with activists Zackie Achmat and Promise Mthembu from the Treatment Action Campaign, South Africa's most effective AIDS activist organization.

The video opens on an image of serenity: a woman, whom we later learn is Bordowitz's partner, Claire Pentecost, sits in a living room in the lotus position (fig. 5.8). The subsequent shots depict the everyday rhythms of domestic routine: Gregg waking up, Claire doing yoga, Gregg making coffee. It is the voiceover conversation between Claire and Gregg that radically qualifies this image of domestic normality, since they discuss the ramifications of his until-recently imminent sense of mortality. Reworking a scene from *Fast Trip*, in which Bordowitz's subjectivity in crisis is visualized in the split image of his face in the doors of a medicine cabinet (fig. 5.9), *Habit* returns Bordowitz to the bathroom, but this time he looks pensively in the mirror, scrutinizing his face as he smiles broadly, almost sarcastically. He pulls back the skin on his slightly gaunt face in a mock face lift (fig. 5.10). We have here returned to the trope of giving

99

Figure 5.9: Frame capture from *Fast Trip, Long Drop* (Gregg Bordowitz, 1993). Courtesy Video Data Bank, Chicago

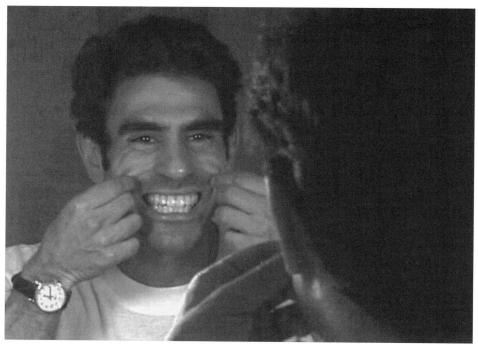

Figure 5.10: Frame capture from *Habit* (Gregg Bordowitz, 2001). Courtesy Video Data Bank, Chicago

AIDS a face, but it is a deeply self-reflexive moment in which the person living with AIDS represents himself in the process of self-scrutiny, a telling metonym for Bordowitz's modus operandi. Moreover, one of the most important aspects of *Habit*, and what differentiates it so radically from *A Closer Walk* and *Pandemic*, is how situated its articulation is, both historically and culturally. It speaks from a specific subject position. It both reflects upon that position and provides a space in which it listens to and allows us to listen to testimony from subject positions radically different from its own. Although the video is emphatically structured around both spatial and temporal difference, it refuses to frame those dynamics around the ideological assumption that South African AIDS activists are now where ACT UP was in the 1980s (and would thus do well to learn from U.S. activists like Bordowitz). *Habit* never tries to resolve the gaping difference between Bordowitz's experience of AIDS in Chicago and that of Zackie Achmat or Promise Mthembu in South Africa. Rather than posit that relationship in terms of a shared humanity, Bordowitz leaves open that glaring discontinuity as an implied ethical question: What historical conditions are responsible for this inequity? In its presentation of activist arguments from South Africa and other parts of the world about the political and economic determinants of treatment access, *Habit* provides its viewers with the knowledge to begin facing the question. *Habit* demonstrates that the ethical imperative to face AIDS in the world cannot be pursued from an omniscient, humanist position outside of history, outside of a consideration of the structural violence wrought by global capitalism.

Note

1. The original Web site for the project (www.pandemicfacingaids.org) closed down in 2004. Its short lifespan points to the often ephemeral nature of such synergistic multimedia strategies. Although HBO's Web site continues to dedicate pages to the project, the amount of material is considerably less than on the original site (www.hbo.com/docs/programs/pandemic/).

Works Cited

"About the Project." *Pandemic* Web site. http://www.pandemicfacingaids.org/en/about/.

"AIDS Documentary Captures Humanity on Film." 2003. *InCamera*, January, 28.

Barthes, Roland. 1972. "The Great Family of Man." In *Mythologies*, translated by Annette Lavers, 100–102. New York: Hill and Wang.

Bordowitz, Gregg. 1998. "Guest List for a Cocktail Party." *Camerawork* 25. 1 (Spring/Summer): 4–9.

Crimp, Douglas. 2002. "Portraits of People with AIDS." In *Melancholia and Moralism: Essays on AIDS and Queer Politics*, 83–107. Cambridge: MIT Press.

Patton, Cindy. 2002. *Globalizing AIDS*. Minneapolis: University of Minnesota Press.

Román, David. 2000. "Not-about-AIDS." *GLQ: A Journal of Lesbian and Gay Studies* 6. 1:1–28.

Rosenberg, Tina. 2001. "How to Solve the World AIDS Crisis." *New York Times Magazine*, January 28, 26–31, 52, 58–63.

Ryan, Suzanne C. 2003. "HBO Series Looks into the Faces of AIDS Epidemic Filmed in Five Countries." *Boston Globe*, June 15, N3.

Sullivan, Andrew. 1996. "When Plagues End: Notes on the Twilight of an Epidemic." *New York Times Magazine*, November 10, 52–62, 76–77, 84.

PART II: Experiments in Reality

The essays that follow constitute a set of exegetical experiments. Their common ground lies in the authors' various responses to the question: What happens to the way we read, what we read — and by extension, how we teach — when the issues of "Seattle" are brought to bear on literary works, both familiar and unfamiliar? These essays test the usefulness of our current critical tools, in all their variety, from narrative theory to social history. Each foregrounds an individual text or author; in some cases, the subject is a text or author of long-standing importance in the classic canon of U.S. literature. In others, the subject in question is commonly understood to belong in one of the 'alternative' canons, or heretofore presumed to be of little interest to the literary scholar, or to be of such recent origin that it does not yet command our attention. The contributors find in these texts, variously, the illumination of current ethical and political life, a way to focus our thinking about the inequities of our world, and a literary rendering of the conditions that surround us.

The expertise of the writers of these essays ranges widely across literary modes and across disciplines, from narrative theory and rhetoric to literary and social history.

CHAPTER 6

"There is evil in the world an I'm going to do something about it": William Faulkner as Political Resource

Joseph R. Urgo

> Just to hate evil is not enough.
> You—somebody—has got to do something about it.
> —Faulkner, *The Mansion*

William Faulkner is the one author to have emerged from United States literary culture to command sustained international attention that shows little sign of abatement. The volume of critical writing on Faulkner is second in the English speaking world only to that on Shakespeare. There are Faulkner foundations or research institutes in France, Japan, and China, and significant levels of research and postsecondary teaching activity on Faulkner are ongoing throughout Europe, Africa, Asia, the Middle East, and South America. Serious international interest in Faulkner as an intellectual resource preceded such recognition in the United Sates. During the Second World War, Faulkner was reputedly among the more popular authors read by members of the French underground—Faulkner's unofficial and undocumented critical genealogy descends from French existentialism. Faulkner was first championed in 1939 as a serious intellectual force by Jean Paul Sartre, whose essay, "Time in Faulkner: *The Sound and the Fury*" remains a landmark study in Faulkner criticism and was highly influential with American critics. Less well known but equally significant is the identification of Faulkner's aesthetics by Hannah Arendt in 1963 as "highly 'political'" because of his employment of "guideposts for future reference and remembrance [that] arise out of this incessant talk" ([1963] 1965, 320n) which characterizes his writing.

Faulkner as political resource, however, is not a characterization that many American critics would find familiar. Early on in the critical history, Faulkner was identified as "apolitical" by such influential voices as Robert Penn Warren (1966, 17), and his novels were understood by his initial American readers to lack any example or representation of "political 'space' within which collective, public action can be taken seriously" (R. King 1982, 156). At the time, however, in the era of the New Criticism, the argument that Faulkner was apolitical was also a way to distinguish his work from inferior novelists — politicized fiction has often, in American criticism, been judged a lesser art. But it is doubtful that Faulkner considered his work to be politically neutral, or unengaged, or that he himself was uninterested in political praxis. It is true that Faulkner responded

105

to a request for assistance from the Spanish Loyalists in 1939 by contributing the manuscript of *Absalom, Absalom!* (Blotner 1974, 1030) to the cause. We have many comments from those outside America attesting to the highly political effect of reading Faulkner, such as that by the Turkish novelist, Yashir Kemal, who told Paul Theroux on the Orient Express that "the greatest Marxist writer was William Faulkner," in his opinion (Kerr 1979, 236). Over the past seventy years, since making his initial mark in the literary world in the 1930s, Faulkner has been called a Communist, a social realist, a naturalist, a sensationalist, a stoic, a Christian humanist, a segregationist, an integrationist, a misogynist, a feminist — and in the past decade, has been examined for his representations of blacks, whites, homosexuals, the indigent, the homeless, the incarcerated — and categorized among Creole writers in the Americas. As hard as critics have argued for an apolitical Faulkner, it seems his work remains a litmus test for every public issue that sweeps through the academy. This chapter, however, is not the place to review the depoliticization of Faulkner by the first wave of American critics, the continued pigeonholing of Faulkner by American critics into the nationally resonant (but internationally suspect) category of "Southern writer," or the seemingly endless debates on whether Faulkner is or is not current, or correct on matters of United States civil rights, especially regarding race and gender. Rather, I seek to establish Faulkner as an intellectual resource for those who consider the encouragement of political engagement to be the responsibility of teaching and research in the humanities.

The political importance of Faulkner's writing, especially in the novels written in his first major period, is found not so much in the content as in the form — in the "incessant voices" identified by Hannah Arendt, the highly political processes by which reality is defined in novels such as *As I Lay Dying* (1930) and *Absalom, Absalom!* (1936).[1] The action in the former novel, for example, is the result of a series of finely wrought narrative maneuvers by various members of the Bundren family in relation to a series of neighbors, certified agents, and townspeople, all of whom possess a great deal more power and influence than this indigent family. The Bundrens manage, nonetheless, to wrest the resources they need to survive away from those who control them, although the costs are quite high, including the loss of one family member to the state. Nonetheless, the family emerges triumphant, richer in the end with the addition of various consumer goods to the household, and with the incorporation of a stepmother to care for them all. In *Absalom, Absalom!*, Faulkner evokes challenges to the historical bases of truth-claims that will culminate later in his career, in *A Fable* (1954), his most radical novel. In the 1936 novel, through the narrative creations of Quentin and Shreve, Faulkner implicitly rejects the idea that meaning or truth may be traced in the return to intention, or origin, or historical beginnings. Rather, the novel supports what Karen L. King identifies as the Gnostic challenge to contemporary historical culture: "History is not about truth but about power relations of domination" (2003, 234). In *Absalom, Absalom!*, knowledge comes to narrators almost like revelation, and their sense of the world is dramatically altered by what they envision as truth. The result, as Jay Watson has argued, "is not so much epistemological as practical, ethical: not who did it or why he did it but how to live with the terrible knowledge you have gleaned, how to put that knowledge to best use" (1998, 70). The question that lingers, in other words, is: What will you do, now that you know? Book titles such as *Absalom, Absalom!, Go Down, Moses* (1942), and *If I Forget Thee, Jerusalem* (1939),[2] wrest these texts away from their historical time and place and suggest an ahistorical, almost mystical challenge to our ideas about the relationship between chronology and truth-claims, freeing a tremendously malleable dimension of space within which to act, seeking to be unencumbered by the weight of historical precedent. Indeed, the "Chronology" appended to *Absalom, Absalom!* literally mocks the idea that the historical record is a reliable source of meaning and understanding in the polis. Throughout his novels, Faulkner's emphasis is on the potential power of the living generation to remake its circumstances, including the transcendence of its historical legacy, a responsibility that can be performed only in the present.

In *Light in August* (1934), the politics of racial identity are inextricable from received and contested notions about God's intent for human beings. Setting that book down, the reader is convinced of nothing so much as the necessity to choose; the world of *Light in August* is one of contending authorities, competing ideas about self, self-worth, and the consequences of both action and inaction. In *Go Down, Moses*, the history of race relations and the legacy of slavery are intertwined with ontological speculations, particularly in the climactic sections of the novel located in "The Bear." And in this complex novel, nothing seems so clear as the need to understand the roots of American power and politics in the context of property relations — property in land, people, and ideas. *The Sound and the Fury* (1929), equating the demise of the Compson family with the decline of southern cavalier society in general, is set on Easter weekend, with its various narrative energies culminating in a resurrection sermon set in an AME church. Deeply concerned about the interior lives of his characters, Faulkner's work is marked by an exploration of the activist spirituality that informs all significant human activity. This Faulknerian sensibility may be best summed up by the Reverend Goodyhay, in *The Mansion* (1959), who runs a public assistance program in the Mississippi Delta, and whose signature prayer, used for grace as easily as for public gatherings and funerals, is "Save us, Christ, the poor sons of bitches" (1999, 574). Goodyhay is an activist, however, fulfilling an insistence that runs throughout Faulkner's work, that people do something with the knowledge they possess. Among Faulkner's greatest or most resonant representations of failure are characters who do not so much commit evil acts as fail to decide, or fail to act at all, even after recognizing the source or manifestation of evil. In 1955, in Japan, Faulkner responded to a question about the representation of evil in his work by asserting, characteristically, "that injustice must exist and you can't just accept it, you got to do something about it" (1968, 125). The character Gavin Stevens in *The Mansion* picks up the thread in its most succinct version: "Just to hate evil is not enough," he says. "You — somebody — has got to do something about it" (1999, 606).

It is no surprise, then, that Faulkner's most overtly political book should also be his most challenging book spiritually; *A Fable* is an act of authorial audacity, in conception, in execution, and in its in-your-face ontological and ideological speculations. Faulkner worked on the novel for ten years. The initial idea for the book, acknowledged in a preface to the text, may be traced to a Hollywood story meeting in the early 1940s, when Faulkner was working for Warner Brothers. Originally, the story of the return of Christ as a soldier in the French army in World War I, buried in the tomb of the unknown soldier, was to have been a movie. When the film project was abandoned, Faulkner kept working on the idea, casting the Christ figure as a rebellious corporal, the son of the Supreme Commander of the Allied Forces in Europe. The corporal is executed for mutiny. His crime was that he led a band of twelve conspirators who influenced soldiers on both sides of no-man's land, bringing the war to a halt and fomenting a crisis within the military hierarchies, both Allied and German. A summit meeting of the warring generals is called to plan the resumption of the war and the execution of the rebellious regiment. A quick summary cannot encompass the novel's numerous subplots and narrative turns, including deep meditations on the genealogy of political and military hierarchies, traced to the medieval church structure and informed by parallel faith demands; the substitution of financial speculation and market expansion for devotion and prayer as determinants of fate and objects of worship; the function of offices and bureaucratic procedures as shapers of identity and personality. My students, consistently over the years, have found the novel tremendously challenging, and identify it as the most disturbing of all Faulkner's novels as they think about vocation, relations to structures of power, and their actual, consequential beliefs, distinguished (as the novel distinguishes them) from those beliefs that have been relegated to gesture and ritual.

And yet there are Faulkner scholars who find the book unreadable, Faulknerians who claim it to be irrelevant, who feel confident making encompassing statements about Faulkner and politics, Faulkner and ideology, while bracketing *A Fable* out of their working bibliography of referenced texts. One reason, perhaps, is that although *A Fable* claims to be allegorical — and it is, as far as the Christ parallels are concerned — its politics are not in the least masked, a least not by fabula. Instead, the novel is perfectly clear (and this may be the problem) in its foregrounding of political activism — including acts of terror. A tendency arose in the novels of Faulkner's second major phase toward narratives of deeply disturbing praxis. In *Requiem for a Nun* (1952), for example, a black maid suffocates the child of her white employer in order to call attention to the inevitable consequences of the employer's intention to abandon her family; in *The Mansion*, the stepdaughter of the notorious capitalist Flem Snopes enlists the assistance of a local agent of the county (the prosecuting attorney, no less) to have released from prison a man who has vowed to kill Flem; the murder is accomplished, and the conspirators remain at large. Flem may have been a strict father and may have done things that his stepdaughter did not like; nonetheless, it is difficult to comprehend a cold-blooded execution that seems entirely condoned by the text. Such acts are not explained away easily; in the context of their narratives, they are acts of terror: premeditated criminality designed to compel a response, or to confront readers with the consequences of seemingly "apolitical" actions. These texts have only become more relevant in the present as the line between political and criminal activity becomes increasingly elusive.

The critical establishment, since the 1960s, has downplayed the importance of these texts in the presentation, packaging, and teaching of William Faulkner in favor of the earlier novels, and in favor of the more comfortable topics of race and gender, where we all agree and can pat each other (and William Faulkner) on the back for being so up to date in recognizing the victims of injustice. The later novels seem to endorse violent encounters with power, and for the most part critics have seen this as a "decline." In *A Fable*, an effort is made to realign Christian faith and symbols with rebellion against war makers, to expose as genuine evil the definition of human cultures according to strategic military alliances — and, for the most part, critics judge this as a grandiose failure, some even blaming it on mental illness or emotional breakdown. *A Fable* is an epic demonstration of global humanism rooted in the capacity of men and women to envision alternatives to oppression. Its form is tremendously demanding; its intended reader, as is the case in most of Faulkner, is the intellectually complacent; and its requirement is deep thought, as the text itself testifies plainly: "To think: not that dreamy hoping and wishing and believing (but mainly just waiting) that we would think is thinking, but some fierce and rigid concentration that at any time — tomorrow, today, next moment, this one — will change the shape of the earth" (1994, 933).

Faulkner worked closely with Random House editor Saxe Commins to prepare the final manuscript of *A Fable* for press (Commins 1978, 194–215). When the two men were preparing book-jacket copy, Faulkner typed a two-page preface or synopsis of the novel "as a favor to Saxe and to Random House," according to Dorothy Commins; it was composed in Princeton, New Jersey, at the Commins's home and on Saxe Commins's typewriter.[3] Here is what Faulkner wished to appear on the book jacket of *A Fable*:

This is not a pacifist book. On the contrary, this writer holds almost as short a brief for pacifism as for war itself, for the reason that pacifism does not work, cannot cope with the forces that produce the wars. In fact, if this book had any aim or moral (which it did not have, I mean deliberately, in its conception, since as far as I knew or intended, it was simply an attempt to show man, human beings, in conflict with their own hearts and compulsions and beliefs and the hard and durable insentient earth-stage on which their griefs and hopes must anguish), it was to show by poetic analogy, allegory, that pacifism does not work; that to put an end to war, man must either find or invent something more powerful than war and man's aptitude for belligerence and his thirst for power at any cost, or use the fire itself to fight and destroy the fire with; that man may finally have to mobilize himself and arm himself with the implements of war to put an end to war; that the mistake we have consistently made is setting nation against nation or political ideology against ideology to stop war; that the men who do not want war may have to arm themselves as for war, and defeat by the methods of war the alliances of power which hold to the obsolete belief in the validity of war: who (the above alliances) must be taught to abhor war not for moral or economic reasons, or even for simple shame, but because they are afraid of it, dare not risk it since they know that in war they themselves — not as nations or governments or ideologies, but as simple human beings vulnerable to death and injury — will be the first to be destroyed.

Three of these characters represent the trinity of man's conscience — Levine, the young English pilot, who symbolizes the nihilistic third; the old French Quartermaster General, who symbolizes the passive third; the British battalion runner, who symbolizes the active third — Levine, who sees evil and refuses to accept it by destroying himself; who says, "Between nothing and evil, I will take nothing"; who, in effect, to destroy evil, destroys the world too, i.e., the world which is his, himself——the old Quartermaster General who says in the last scene, "I am not laughing. What you see are tears"; i.e., there is evil in the world; I will bear both, the evil and the world too, and grieve for them——the battalion runner, the living scar, who in the last scene says, "That's right; tremble. I'm not going to die — never"; i.e., there is evil in the world an I'm going to do something about it.

One might imagine what Faulkner would mean to a generation of students who were introduced to him through this statement, or whose American literature survey included *A Fable*, or whose upper-division or graduate seminar on Faulkner included the novel. However, from what I know of Faulkner scholars, the vast majority do not teach the novel, and there have been books and dissertations establishing expertise on the author without mentioning this book. As a result, a viable American political resource is suppressed, the material observations about power and consequence dismissed as a falling off of literary intensity.

A Fable assumes that reaching for power over others compromises integrity, as in the exercise of petty authority by a military sergeant, equivalent to having "sold his birthright in the race of man" (1994, 675). The novel challenges the powerful, as it does the Supreme Commander, "who no longer believed in anything but his disillusion and his intelligence and his limitless power" (678). The novel challenges the powerless equally, especially those who substitute optimism for action, "the baseless hoping which is the diet of weaklings" (686) or "that sort of masturbation about the human race people call hoping" (722). In the world of *A Fable*, a primary function of those in power is to provide hope to weaklings, to pacify men and women of good intent with the illusion that something is about to be done in their interest while keeping from them at all cost the knowledge that they have the power to effect change, or to bring down those in power. "They may even stop wars, as they have done before and will do again," explains one officer; "ours merely to guard them from the knowledge that it was actually they who accomplished that act" (715). One way this safeguard is accomplished is to keep the population eternally distracted, to keep men and women from joining together in purposeful action by filling their world with noise and visions of hope, because "neither in lust nor appetite nor greed lay wombed the potency of his threat, but in silence and meditation" (839). Silence, and thought, are the eternal enemies of oppressive structures; in *A Fable* elaborate machineries of distraction are described to have been created in order that "silence and meditation" be scarce commodities.

A Fable assumes that Western nations have been financially structured in such a way as to transform these democracies into bureaucracies that culminate systemically in warfare, served by mass-media personnel trained above all to cast human affairs as a series of conflicts resolvable only by death — "all that vast powerful terror-inspiring representation which, running all democracy's affairs in peace, come indeed into their own in war, finding their true apotheosis then" (881). The world of *A Fable* is one where those in power on opposite sides of a conflict have more in common with each other than with those over whom they command; where the common ideology of those in such positions of power is cynicism (the General claims to possess a faith in "man within his capacities and limitations" [987]); and where war makers are described as "bellowing at each other polysyllabic and verbless patriotic nonsense" (994).

Is these interpretable, symbolic rhetoric? How is the teacher positioned in relation to a text which positions itself so provocatively by challenging instructor and student alike: Do you merely hope for better things? Do you confuse the quest for truth with the quest for authority? Do you see how your actions and ideas contribute to the deaths of others, and do you see how your prosperity depends upon such elimination? This is not the Faulkner carefully constructed by the first wave of American critics to fall under the readerly spell of that awesome prose. To see the evils of racism, of misogyny, and to feel bolstered by the ability to see Faulkner on our side, on the side of the good guys, feels good, and seems like accomplishment. This more familiar Faulkner has been the teachable author who says he does not hate the South (well, neither do we); who creates the tragic figure in a racially defined society as one who does not know his racial background (well, sure); who creates sons of slave owners who anguish over their inheritance (we anguish with them) and attempt to find a place in the present untainted by the legacy of injustice (we are still looking). These are powerful narratives, but they allow the reader some place to stand: in sympathy, in outrage, among the enlightened.

A Fable leaves its reader without moorings. Faulkner's aborted jacket-liner notes advocated readers take to the streets, to make their leaders fear war by making war on the war makers. How interpretable is the statement that war makers "must be taught to abhor war not for moral or economic reasons, or even for simple shame, but because they are afraid of it, dare not risk it since they know that in war they themselves — not as nations or governments or ideologies, but as simple human beings vulnerable to death and injury — will be the first to be destroyed"? There are no symbols and allegories here: the next time one is called to war, he "may finally have to mobilize himself and arm himself with the implements of war to put an end to war" by turning the weapons on those who command. The statement was suppressed in 1954, when Faulkner's editor decided against using it on the book jacket (the second paragraph, on the "trinity of conscience," was used as publicity for the novel); the statement was as indigestible intellectually in 1954 as it is today, in 2005. Does William Faulkner really suggest mutiny? Taking to the streets? Bringing down those in power through the display of massed humanity, in common purpose? And short of that, does he see no other avenue for change?

And perhaps the most radical of all aspects of *A Fable*: It is, essentially, a world abandoned by God. This is the great paradox of the text, a contradiction woven throughout the dense prose of its insistent allegory. The corporal is Christlike: His father is Supreme, he has twelve close followers, one of whom betrays him — in fact, the close parallels to the story of Jesus Christ contributes, no doubt, to the alienation of Faulkner's most sophisticated readers. But there is no Christ, no God, no ultimate authority come down from the sky in the novel; there is only the paradigmatic structure of secrecy, insurrection, sacrifice, and delusion, the thirteen soldiers referred to at one point as "keeping pace with, holding their own still within the fringe of a fading fairy-tale" (976). Human beings are abandoned, in *A Fable*, unable to blame or credit God with their predicament; their predicament, on the contrary, repeatedly (and relentlessly, in some of Faulkner's most elaborate prose) traced to human origins, continually explained as the doings of *this man* or *that interest* or traced to *that place*. It as if Faulkner suggests that power lacks mystery: we can see it, we have access to information, and we know when we are being deceived. What is mysterious is the absence of will to do something about it. In the presidential election of 2000 there is evidence of significant voter fraud in Florida. Rather than risk a constitutional crisis, the losing party advocated dropping the matter, lacking the will to do something about it. In Iraq, in 2003, there were no weapons of mass destruction; the grounds for war, dubious even if true, were specious. We know this, we have been told this over and over, but Americans from presidential candidates to college professors appear to lack the will to do something about it.

Cocooned in the pleasures of the text, the mass-mediated thinking, the climate-controlled home, the smooth-talking automobile, we watch the heavens for some sign authorizing us to act. *A Fable* suggests otherwise, that authorization arises from within human beings, if they are able to think their way past the structures of thought that have them looking elsewhere. Intellectually challenging at any time, reading *A Fable* in times of war compels a perspective on a democracy's insatiable and destructive need for solvency and on the organized, systematic elimination of human life from positions of interference with financial or hierarchal aggrandizement. While its faith is with the potential of human communities to remake their world, the bleakness of the plot (the war is resumed, the rebels transformed into martyrs, objects of hope and futility) has only been confirmed by the relegation of the text to relative obscurity. There are indications, in recent years, that a new generation of Faulkner readers will find the book and revisit Faulkner's intellectual presence. Perhaps, in the wake of Seattle, we will find in Faulkner the political resource we need to overcome the fear that leaves us unable to act, but only to hope. We may then hear the words of the condemned corporal, whose response to his pending death informs the meaning of his mutinous politics: "Dont be afraid. . . . There's nothing to be afraid of. Nothing worth it" (992).

Notes

1. Faulkner's career may be divided into three stages: 1. early writing, juvenilia, and three early, relatively less powerful novels (*Soldiers' Pay*, *Mosquitoes*, and *Sartoris*); 2. the first major phase, 1929–1942, including

novels such as *The Sound and the Fury, As I Lay Dying, Absalom, Absalom!,* and *Go Down, Moses*); 3. the second major phase, the main concern of this essay, the later writing, often highly politicized, including *Intruder in the Dust, Requiem for a Nun, A Fable,* and the last two books of the Snopes trilogy.

2. This is the original title to the 1939 novel, which was published in Faulkner's lifetime as *The Wild Palms.* Faulkner's title was rejected by the publisher out of fears that it would arouse anti-Semitic feelings among readers.

3. Mrs. Commins's hand-written note accompanying Faulkner's original typescript may be examined at the University of Mississippi Special Collections. The preface is reprinted in Blotner 1974, 1493–1495, and in Meriwether 1974, 162–163.

Works Cited

Arendt, Hannah. [1963] 1965. *On Revolution.* New York: Viking.

Blotner, Joseph. 1974. *Faulkner: A Biography.* New York: Random House.

Commins, Dorothy. 1978. *What Is an Editor? Saxe Commins at Work.* Chicago: University of Chicago Press.

Faulkner, William. 1968. *Lion in the Garden: Interviews with William Faulkner, 1926–1962,* edited by James B. Meriwether and Michael Millgate. Lincoln: University of Nebraska Press.

——— 1994. *A Fable.* In *Faulkner: Novels 1942–1954.* New York: Library of America.

——— 1999. *The Mansion.* In *William Faulkner: Novels 1957–1962.* New York: Library of America.

Kerr, Elizabeth. 1979. *William Faulkner's Gothic Domain.* Port Washington, N.Y.: Kennikat Press.

King, Karen L. 2003. *What Is Gnosticism?* Cambridge: Harvard University Press.

King, Richard. 1982. "Memory and Tradition." In *Faulkner and the Southern* Renaissance, edited by Doreen Fowler and Ann J. Abadie. Jackson: University Press of Mississippi.

Meriwether, James B., ed. 1974. *A Faulkner Miscellany.* Jackson: University Press of Mississippi.

Sartre, John Paul. 1960. "Time in Faulkner: *The Sound and the Fury."* In *William Faulkner: Three Decades of Criticism,* edited by Frederick J. Hoffman and Olga W. Vickery, 225–232. New York: Harcourt, Brace and World. Originally published as "Le Bruit et la Fureur," *La Nouvelle Revue Francaise,* June and July 1939.

Warren, Robert Penn. 1966. "Introduction: Faulkner Past and Present." In *Faulkner: A Collection of Critical Essays,* edited by Robert Penn Warren. Englewood Cliffs, N.J.: Prentice Hall.

Watson, Jay. 1998. "And Now What's To Do: Faulkner, Reading, Praxis." *Faulkner Journal* 14.1: 67–74.

CHAPTER 7

Rhetoric, Politics, and Ethics in Sandra Cisneros's *Caramelo*

James Phelan

My purpose in this chapter is to demonstrate the interconnections of rhetoric, politics, and ethics in narrative communication. My focus will be on Sandra Cisneros's remarkable novel about the immigrant experience, *Caramelo*. I shall start with an analysis of the rhetorical dynamics of the communication, then consider the consequences of those dynamics for its political dimensions, and, finally, relate rhetoric and politics to ethics. By rhetorical dynamics, I mean Cisneros's use of the formal elements of narrative—particularly character, event, and technique—and their consequences for her multilayered communication to her authorial audience, one that has designs on our emotions as well as our intellects. By "politics," I mean her focus on the identity and social status of her characters, on their location within and relations to American and Mexican culture. By "ethics," I mean the values underlying the narrative performances of Cisneros and her character narrator Celaya as well as the way in which we readers engage with those values.

Because Cisneros clearly has both aesthetic and political aims in *Caramelo*, the novel presents both a good fit and a good challenge for my investigation. On the one hand, her dual aims encourage me to believe that I am reading with the grain of her project; on the other hand, those aims consistently raise the question of whether the analysis does justice to her practice. In Celaya Reyes, Cisneros creates a child narrator in the great tradition of American vernacular narrators, and she uses both footnotes and an idiosyncratic "chronology" of Mexican history to link Celaya's story of three generations of her family to larger political issues about Chicano/a identity and the literal and figurative place of the Chicano/a in American culture.

I also focus on Cisneros's work because she has eloquently described her own evolving awareness of the connection between form and politics. In the introduction to the 1994 edition of *The House on Mango Street*, Cisneros reveals that she developed the voice of her character narrator Esperanza as a rebellion against the kinds of voices she was hearing—and more generally, the kinds of fiction and theory she was asked to value—at the Iowa Writer's Workshop in the late 1970s. She describes Esperanza as having an "antiacademic voice—a child's voice, a girl's voice, a poor girl's voice, a spoken voice, the voice of an American-Mexican. It's in this rebellious realm of antipoetics that I tried to create a poetic text with the most unofficial language I could find. I did it neither ingenuously nor naturally. It was as clear to me as if I were tossing a Molotov cocktail" (xv). This description with its reference to both "voice" and "Molotov cocktail" shows that the Cisneros of 1994 sees the aesthetic and the political as deeply intertwined.

Yet Cisneros goes on to indicate that as she was writing the novel in the early 1980s she did not think about the potential political effects of her rebellion on her readers, because she was so focused on the formal issues: "I had never been trained to think of poems or stories as something that could change someone's life. I had been trained to think about where a line ended or how best to work a metaphor. It was always the 'how' and not the 'what' that we talked about in class. Even while I was teaching in the Chicago community, the two halves of my life were at odds with each other—the half that wanted to roll up my sleeves and do something for my community and the half that wanted to retreat to my kitchen. I still believed that my writing couldn't save anyone's life but my own" (xviii). But when she received "letters from readers of all ages and colors" (xviii) saying that Esperanza's story is their story, she realized that her attention to the "how" had major consequences for the "what," and that through her writing she could do something for others both in her Chicano/a community and in the larger community of her readers.

Cisneros's comments about *Caramelo* show that, as she was writing, she remained very conscious of both the formal and the political. She explains why the book took her nine years to write by reference to its experimental nature: "I really wanted to expand and push myself and do something that I didn't have a model for. I didn't even know how to make what I wanted. I just knew that I could see it in my mind's eye for a flash of a second and then I was in the dark. So I was mainly in the dark, experimenting with this book" (Birnbaum 2002). She also discusses the way in which the narrative exfoliated once she made some initial decisions about its direction and the kinds of demands that exfoliation placed on her composition: "in telling my father's story, I had to place him in time and history, and then I had to go back and look at how he became who he was. So I had to invent my grandmother's story and how she became who she was, so next thing I knew, there was a lot of tributaries from my main story, and footnotes, chronologies, and things like that, that I didn't anticipate when I began" (Suarez). In addition, Cisneros overtly comments on some of the political consequences of her formal choices: "I never saw an upholsterer in American literature" (quoted in Navarro 2002, 1); "[t]hat was what was so much fun for me. To hold up mirrors: for the Mexicans to see themselves from the point of view of the Mexican-Americans, Mexican-Americans to see themselves from the point of view of the Mexicans, Americans as seen by Mexicans, all those mirrors that get refracted" (Birnbaum 2002).

As Cisneros's descriptions of *Caramelo* indicate, it is a more ambitious novel than *The House on Mango Street*, and, indeed, Celaya's narration of three generations of the Reyes family as they live in three different locations—Chicago, Mexico City, and San Antonio—gives it a far greater scope. Cisneros explores, among other things, several salient features of the Chicano/a family: the attachment of sons to their mothers and the corresponding tension between their mothers and their wives; the effects of living in two cultures; the cross-generational bonds of the Reyes family; the importance of storytelling for individuals, families, and cultures; and the refracted mirroring she describes above. Her use of Celaya, the only daughter in the third generation of the Reyes family, is itself a tour de force, a performance that invites comparisons and contrasts with both Melville's use of

Ishmael and Twain's use of Huckleberry Finn. At times Cisneros restricts Celaya's vision and voice to those appropriate for her age and character, but at other times, she lets Celaya burst those boundaries and report on matters that she did not witness or engage in commentary that shows a wisdom far beyond her years. Indeed, it is not possible to do justice in a single essay to the connections between rhetoric, politics, and ethics throughout the novel; consequently, I will focus on a single chapter as a quasi-representative sample: chapter 79, "Halfway between Here and There, In the Middle of Nowhere."

Father comes home with the news, and the words cause my heart to freeze.—We're going home.

Father had a big fight with Marcelio Ordóñez of Mars Tacos To Went that ended with Father cursing his old friend Mars of long ago, cursing all Chicanos for acting like Chicanos and giving Mexico a bad name, cursing the borrowed fifty dollars, the Second World War, the savage border, this rinky-dink stinky *calcetín* of a Texas town, then heaving into a flash flood of tears at the memory of his mother.

—I curse you and the mother who bore you, Father said. Well, not exactly. What he really said was a little stronger, but, since he *is* my father, I can't repeat it without some disrespect.

I curse you and the mother who bore you. At the word "mother," Father remembers the wheeze in his heart.—*¡Ay!, madrecita*, if you'd lived to be a thousand years, it would not be enough! And it's as if at that very moment his mother is putting a pin through his heart to see if he's still alive, as if his mother is holding him again in her soft, fleshy arms. Mother her smell of food fried in lard, and that smell the smell of home and comfort and safety.

Mars raised the rent on Father's shop again.

—I'm losing money. Building needs repairs. See that crack? Whole damn foundation's about to buckle, I kid you not. And the roof is leaking. And taxes. What else can I do? Ain't rich, you know.

Father picks on a tack on the bottom of his shoe. A whole lot of nothing, Father thinks, to explain who knows what.

—You it was who called la Migra!

—What'chu talking about, man?

—You it was. You called la Migra. Explain. How is it the Immigration came only to my shop that day, and not yours, eh?

—Man, *estás zafado*. You shitty *chilangos* always think you know everything!

—*Baboso*. Can't even speak your mother tongue!

—I can speak my mother tongue all right, but you can bet it ain't Spanish.

The words turn from bad to worse until how it ends is this.

Father has to move.

We pack up the compressor, the sawhorses, the pegboard of hammers and scissors and tack strippers and clamps, the rolls of cotton batting and bolts of fabric, the webbing, coil springs, Italian twine, yardsticks, chalk, staples, and tacks, disassemble the homemade cutting tables and shelves, the slouched books of fabric samples in ring binders, the prize Singer one-eleven W fifty-five.

When the shop is almost empty, Father tugs at his mustache and looks out at the street, past the red and yellow letters of KING UPHOLSTERY, to something beyond that we can't see.

Estoy cansado. Sick and tired, Father mutters in his funny English. —Make me sick.

Nogalitos. Old Highway 90. Father remembers too clearly the route south, and it's like a tide that tugs and pulls him when the dust rises and the cedar pollen makes him sneeze and regret he moved us all to San Antonio, halfway between here and there, in the middle of nowhere.

That terrible ache and nostalgia for home when home is gone, and this isn't it. And the sun so white like an onion. And who the hell thought of placing a city here with no large body of water anyway! In less than three hours we could be at the border, but where's the border to the past, I ask you, where?

—Home. I want to go home already, Father says.

—Home. Where's that? North? South? Mexico? San Antonio? Chicago? Where, Father?

—All I want is my kids, Father says.—That's the only country I need. (379–380)

I start with Cisneros's use of Celaya as character narrator, specifically with the range of narrational power Cisneros grants her. Celaya begins the chapter with an abstract of the events she is about to narrate and then moves on to give the rest of the story. For some of the chapter she is the observer narrator, reporting what she witnesses. But she also reports events she does not witness, such as the blow-by-blow account of the argument between her father and his old friend and landlord, Marcelino Ordóñez, a.k.a. Mars. Even more strikingly, Cisneros gives Celaya the power to report her father's thoughts via free indirect discourse, as she does in the passage that begins "it's like a tide that tugs and pulls him." In *Living to Tell about It*, I argue that authors use character narrators to perform two main functions: first, to communicate directly and plausibly with their narratees (this communication constitutes their *narrator functions*); and second, to communicate indirectly with the authorial audience, to be the conduit for everything the author needs or wants the audience to know (this communication constitutes their *disclosure functions*). Authors will typically have the character narrator perform both functions simultaneously, but sometimes the purposes of their narratives are better served by having the disclosure functions trump the narrator functions. Such trumping goes on in this stretch of the chapter, and, indeed, is crucial to the effect. Cisneros needs directly to show us Inocencio's feeling of being caught between Mexico and the United States, of having made a drastic mistake in moving his family from Chicago to San Antonio, and of no longer knowing whether he has any place that he can rightly call home. The best way for her to do that is to give Celaya the power to convey Inocencio's thoughts.

At the same time, Celaya the character is affected by Cisneros's choice: Celaya does not passively report Inocencio's thoughts and feelings but she sym-

117

pathetically understands them. That is why Cisneros has her begin by saying that her father's words "We're going home" cause her heart to freeze. She, too, is no longer sure where home is. It's her voice—and perhaps those of her siblings in San Antonio, Toto, Memo, and Lolo—that asks, "Home? Where's that? . . . Where, Father?"

The interplay between Celaya the narrator's freedom from the normal restriction of her character's perspective and Celaya the character's understanding of and sympathy for her father is even more powerfully, though more subtly, conveyed in the free indirect discourse: "That terrible ache and nostalgia for home when home is gone, and this isn't it." Since the technique involves the blending of character's voice (Inocencio's) and narrator's voice (Celaya's), it effectively shows that Celaya shares her father's sense of dislocation. But Cisneros creates an even more powerful effect by shifting the technique from free indirect discourse to the report of direct thought in the last sentence: "In less than three hours we could be at the border, but where's the border to the past, I ask you, where?" In other words, Cisneros has Celaya move to the side in order to let Inocencio give full voice to his poignant longing, a longing brilliantly but quietly conveyed by the rhetorical question that simultaneously erases and insists upon the distinction between space and time: "where's the border to the past?" We can't help but be moved by Inocencio's sense of loss and dislocation.

These rhetorical dynamics are tightly connected to Cisneros's political concerns. Indeed, the chapter is a demonstration of the affective power of the concrete particulars of narrative: it is one thing to say that an immigrant from Mexico such as Inocencio is inevitably going to feel "halfway between here and there, in the middle of nowhere." It is another thing to write a narrative that invites its audience to see that condition from the inside, as characters whom we care about experience it both literally and figuratively. In this respect, Cisneros's use of Celaya is crucial to both the rhetorical and political dimensions of the chapter: because she is our guide to the whole narrative and the character whose fate has the greatest influence on our affective responses, her role as both participant in and observer of her father's longing for home maximizes its force. Cisneros often makes Celaya's narration seem so natural as to be artless, but that narration is part of Cisneros's extremely artful design.

Cisneros's use of what Bakhtin has taught us to call heteroglossia and Anzaldua *mestiza* discourse provides another example of this design. In these passages where utterances involve either single words inflected with multiple social meanings or successive words drawn from different types of discourse, Celaya's dual functions work seamlessly together: her direct reports to the narratee function as indirect communications to Cisneros's audience, communications whose import Celaya is not fully cognizant of. Cisneros uses the opening of the chapter to call attention to the link between word and ideology in Celaya's apparently unconscious double use of *home:* "Father comes home with the news. . . . We're going home." If the home to which Father comes is not the home to which they are going, where is that home? If the home to which Father comes is not that home, then what exactly is this place in which they are living? The chapter title answers the second question—this place is the middle of nowhere—while the end of the chapter underlines the force of the first question, in part because it initially does not provide an answer.

But the answer that comes in the chapter's last line gives yet another meaning—and another ideological dimension—to the word. Inocencio substitutes "country" for "home" and defines it not as a place but as a relation: "All I want is my kids. . . . That is the only country I need." Because of the substitution, "home" and "country" borrow meanings from each other: home takes on a greater political implication and country a greater personal, affective one. At the same time, the substitution allows Cisneros both to retain the powerful sense of Inocencio's dislocation and to show him finding some consolation. The consolation comes because he believes it possible to locate this country, but the sense of dislocation remains because Inocencio is aware that his three oldest sons are not with him but in Chicago. At the same time, Inocencio's new definition allows Cisneros to generalize from his particular situation to a conclusion that is broadly applicable across political locations: one can be a parent in any culture and endorse Inocencio's idea of home and country.

Another significant instance of heteroglossia occurs in the dialogue between Inocencio and Mars. Here the heteroglossia is not in the hybridization of a single word but rather in the juxtaposition of different discourses. Mars, Celaya has informed us earlier, is from West Texas, and his native language is English, while Inocencio was born in Mexico and his native language is Spanish. Celaya tells us that Inocencio's English is "odd to American ears" (208). Here Mars speaks in the idiomatic vernacular of a Texas working class man: "Whole damn foundation's about to buckle, I kid you not," and "What'chu taking about man?" Inocencio by contrast speaks his unidiomatic English that often mixes in Spanish: "You it was who called la Migra!" The differences in their speech suggest that what is keeping them apart is some cultural difference. Cisneros further underlines this conclusion by marking the increasing hostility between them by means of their insults about each other's language. Inocencio contemptuously asserts, "*Baboso.* Can't even speak your mother tongue!" Mars's reply simultaneously defends himself and gives offense: "I can speak my mother tongue all right, but you can bet it ain't Spanish." Cisneros herself nicely describes one political consequence of this heteroglossia in her remark about holding up mirrors so Mexican Americans can see how they are regarded by American Mexicans and vice versa.

We can identify a second link between the rhetoric of the heteroglossia and its political dimensions by looking at the bottom line. For the bottom line of the split between Inocencio and Mars is, well, the bottom line. Mars and Inocencio first became friends when Mars helped Inocencio out after he had been robbed of his life savings and was stranded in New Orleans. Mars explained that he thought nothing of being generous because "we're *raza* . . . Because we're *familia*. And *familia*, like it or not, for richer or poorer, *familia* always gots to stick together" (281). But now money overpowers those ties: Mars the landlord from West Texas decides that he can no longer afford to have Inocencio, the tenant from Mexico City, because Inocencio won't be able to afford the higher rent Mars wants to charge. Cisneros shows whose side she takes in the argument by structuring the dialogue to support Inocencio's accusation about Mars's use of the Immigration and Naturalization Service. Rather than refuting the accusation, Mars goes on the offensive, attacking Inocencio's character. Mars's greater allegiance to money than to friendship not only underlines the difference between the Mexican American and the American Mexican but further underlines Inocencio's sense of dislocation.

A third and related significant instance of heteroglossia is found in the sign that Inocencio looks past: "KING UPHOLSTERY." Originally Inocencio had the sign read TAPACERIA REYES, but he changed it when money became tight, explaining that "This way they [the white Americans in San Antonio] think Mr. King is the boss, and I just work for him" (352). In other words, what appears to be a straightforward translation is actually a radical shift in meaning, a shift that is deeply rooted in the relative political status of the English word "king" and its Spanish counterpart "reyes." Cisneros calls attention to the sign in this chapter in order to emphasize how much Inocencio has sacrificed for his family and how little that sacrifice means to his Mexican American landlord.

This instance of heteroglossia also sheds light on Celaya's narration of the long list of things the Reyes family packs up, starting with "the compressor" and ending with "the prize Singer one-eleven W fifty-five." Fond of lists, Ciseneros uses all manner of them throughout *Caramelo*, but she uses them for different effects. This list, because it follows the simple report, "Father has to move," builds a strong metonymic relation between Inocencio and the tools of his trade. This metonymy in turn invites us to make the links among these tools, the labor and pride Inocencio has invested in them, and his love of his family. In addition, the list underlines the gap between Mars the landlord wanting more income from his tenant and Inocencio the laborer trying to provide for his family. Reading the list in this light, we get a new understanding of the political implications of Cisneros's statement that before *Caramelo*, "I never saw an upholsterer in American literature."

These rhetorical and political dimensions of Cisneros's communication are also related to its ethical dimension. The key construct in my approach to ethics is what I call ethical position, a concept that combines being placed in and acting from an ethical location. At any given point in a narrative, our ethical position results from the dynamic interaction of four ethical situations:

1. that of the characters within the story world, especially how they behave toward each other in light of the circumstances in which they find themselves;
2. that of the narrator in relation to the telling, the told, and the multiple audiences of the narration—unreliable narration, for example, constitutes a different ethical position from reliable narration;
3. that of the implied author in relation to the narrator, the telling, the told, and the authorial audience—the implied author's choices to adopt one narrative strategy rather than another will affect the audience's ethical response to the characters; each choice will also convey the author's attitudes toward the audience; and
4. that of the flesh-and-blood reader in relation to the set of values, beliefs, and locations operating in situations 1–3.

For my purposes here, the most significant situations are 2 and 3. Celaya uses a range of tones in her treatment of Inocencio—from the mixture of amusement and respect in her confession that she cannot report his curse exactly to the full sympathy of her narration in the final paragraphs. The underlying values of her presentation are admirable: she maintains an appropriate distance from her father's excesses but consistently conveys her love and respect. The ethical dimension of the free indirect discourse is especially admirable: Celaya's participation in her father's feelings of dislocation, as we have seen, is a remarkable act of empathy, one that is crucial for our own affective response. At the same time, Celaya does not overtly condemn Mars or otherwise diminish him in order to make her father look better. Instead, she simply reports his speech and lets the uncharacterized narratee draw the appropriate inferences.

This treatment of Mars also indicates that she treats the narratee with care and respect. Celaya builds the chapter on the foundation of the initial abstract and three short reports: "Father comes home with the news." "Mars raised the rent on Father's shop again." "Father has to move." As she fills in the rest of the story, she nicely balances reporting and commenting on what she reports, consistently indicating her own angle of vision but also leaving the narratee room to fill in gaps and reach his or her own conclusions.

The ethics of Cisneros's telling are even more impressive. Although, as we have seen, Cisneros often uses Celaya's narration for effects Celaya is not herself aware of, Cisneros's treatment of Celaya ends up enhancing our estimation of her as both narrator and character. Cisneros's endowing her with unusual powers, as in the passage of free indirect discourse, similarly increases Celaya's ethical force as both narrator and character. Furthermore, Cisneros's treatment of Inocencio reflects back positively on her own values: she not only shares Celaya's distance from his excesses and sympathy for his plight but she demonstrates an even keener insight into him. At the same time, because Cisneros is so skillful in constructing her apparently artless but extremely artful narration, she treats her audience with considerable respect. She trusts us—and compliments us with that trust—to recognize the many inferences her artful narration invites us to make.

Cisneros's ethics are also revealed through her political commitments because those commitments are undergirded by her values. Cisneros both celebrates cultural differences between the groups she holds the mirror up to and insists that some of those differences—such as the ones between Mars and Inocencio in chapter 79—have deleterious consequences for the less powerful groups. Underneath these political stances are her ethical commitments to equality and justice. Similarly, the political choice to write a novel about an upholsterer is built on her valuing honest labor, regardless of the price it brings in the American economy. The political choice to write a multigenerational novel rests on what is arguably Cisneros's chief ethical value in this novel: the importance of family. Cisneros does not value family in a sentimental way—she gives us lots of reason to endorse Celaya's calling Inocencio's mother the Awful Grandmother—but in a way that recognizes its potential as the greatest source of both comfort and of pain in one's life because it is the site of the greatest love. Furthermore, as chapter 79 indicates, Cisneros consistently shows that what happens in and to the family is related to the prevailing cultural politics.

121

In sum, this chapter offers a brief demonstration of a criticism that seeks to identify the interconnections among literature's rhetorical, political, and ethical communications. One measure of its success is the extent to which it persuades you that *Caramelo* has much more to teach us about those interconnections.

Works Cited

Anzaldua, Gloria. 1987. *Borderlands/La Frontera: The New Mestiza*. San Francisco: Spinsters/Aunt Lute Press.

Bakhtin, Mikhail. 1981. "Discourse in the Novel." *The Dialogic Imagination: Four Essays*, ed. Michael Holquist; trans. Caryl Emerson and Michael Holquist. Austin: University of Texas Press.

Birnbaum, Robert. Interview with Sandra Cisneros, December 4, 2002. http://www.identitytheory.com/people/birnbaum6.html.

Cisneros, Sandra. 1994. "Introduction." *The House on Mango Street*. New York: Knopf.

———. 2002. *Caramelo*. New York: Knopf.

Navarro, Mireya. 2002. "Telling a Tale of Immigrants Whose Stories Go Untold." *New York Times*, November 12, E.1.

Phelan, James. 2005. *Living to Tell about It: A Rhetoric and Ethics of Character Narration*. Ithaca: Cornell University Press.

Suarez, Ray. 2002. "Online News Hour Conversation: Cisneros." On October 15, 2002. http://www.pbs.org/newshour/conversation/july-dec02/cisneros_10-15.html.

CHAPTER 8

Fear and Loathing in Globalization

Fredric Jameson

Has the author of *Neuromancer* really "changed his style"? Has he even "stopped" writing Science Fiction, as some old-fashioned critics have put it, thinking thereby to pay him a compliment? Maybe, on the contrary, he is moving closer to the "cyberpunk" with which he is often associated, but which seems more characteristically developed in the work of his sometime collaborator Bruce Sterling. In any case, the representational apparatus of Science Fiction, having gone through innumerable generations of technological development and well-nigh viral mutation since the onset of that movement, is sending back more reliable information about the contemporary world than an exhausted realism (or an exhausted modernism either).

William Gibson, now the author of *Pattern Recognition,* has certainly more often illustrated that other coinage, "cyberspace," and its inner network of global communication and information, than the object world of late commodification through which the latest novel carefully gropes its way.[1] To be sure, Sterling celebrated the hackers, the heroic pirates of cyberspace, but without Gibson's tragic intensity—portraying them as the oddballs and marginals of the new frontiers to come. The rush and exhilaration of his books, rather alien to the cooler Gibson, has always seemed to me to derive as much from global entrepreneurship, and the excitement of the money to be made, as from paranoia.

But that excitement also expresses the truth of emergent globalization, and Sterling deserves more than a mere paragraph or parenthesis here. The novels are often episodic, but stories like those collected in *A Good Old-Fashioned Future* are authentic artifacts of postmodernity and little masterpieces in their own right, offering a Cook's tour of the new global way-stations and the piquant dissonances between picturesque travellers and the future cities they suddenly find themselves in. Tokyo, to be sure (Tokyo now and forever!), in which a Japanese-American federal prosecutor from Providence, Rhode Island, finds herself entangled in a conspiracy waged through ceramic cats; but also the California of misfit inventors, in which a new process for manufacturing artificial (and aerial) jellyfish threatens to convert all the oil left in the ground in Texas into so much worthless *Urschleim.* Finland then offers an unsurprisingly happy hunting ground for meetings between 60s-style terrorists and the former KGB, along with ruthless young ecological nationalists, veteran industrial spies and an aged Finnish writer of children's books immensely popular in Japan.[2]

Meanwhile, Bollywood actors in flight from the Indian tax system have the luck to happen on the biggest mass grave in history, in Bolton, in an England decimated by the plague and now good only for making cheap movies on location; while, in Germany, in Düsseldorf, the new institution of the *Wende* is explored, in which — observed by a "spex" salesman from Chattanooga — all the destructive collective movements of the time, from football hooligans to anti-modern moral majorities, periodically coincide in a ritual "turbulence." Indeed, it is Chattanooga, its burnt-out downtown future megastructure now a rat's nest of squatters, which serves as the stage for a more complex and characteristic encounter: between a de-sexed bicycle repairman (new gender movements have proliferated in this future, including that of Sexual Deliberation, which artificially eradicates the sex drive) and the private police of a long-serving and now senile congressional stalwart, whose artificial identity replacement (the so-called mook) risks being unmasked by an unwanted package in the mail. Finally, classic Science Fiction returns with the discovery in a Central Asian desert, by twenty-first century bounty-hunters, of an enormous artificial underground cavern, in which the Zone (the latest future form of the old East Asian Co-Prosperity Sphere, now run by China) has housed three world-sized human communities as an experiment in testing the viability of 400-year-long space flights. I have only incidentally mentioned some of the wacky SF technology taken for granted in these tales: more significant are the priorities of global cyberpunk, in which technological speculation and fantasy of the old Toffler sort takes second place to the more historically original literary vocation of a mapping of the new geopolitical Imaginary.

Paperback Seismographs

This is why such Hunter-Thompsonian global tourism has real epistemological value: cyberpunk constitutes a kind of laboratory experiment in which the geographic-cultural light spectrum and bandwidths of the new system are registered. It is a literature of the stereotypes thrown up by a system in full expansion, which, like the explosion of a nova, sends out a variety of uncharted signals and signs of nascent communities and new and artificially differentiated ethnies. Stereotypes are pre-eminently the vehicle through which we relate to other collectivities; no one has ever confronted another grouping without their mediation. They are allegorical cartoons that no longer convey the racist contempt of the older imperialism and which can often (as Žižek has observed of the ethnic jokes popular in the old Yugoslavia) function as affectionate forms of inclusion and of solidarity.

Indeed, an inspection of this literature already provides a first crude inventory of the new world system: the immense role — and manifest in Gibson's evocations, all the way down to *Pattern Recognition* itself — of Japan as the monitory semiotic combination of First-World science-and-technology with a properly Third-World population explosion. Russia now also looms large, but above all in the form of its various Mafias (from all the former Republics), which remind us of the anarchy and violent crime, as well as of the conspiratorial networks and jobless futures, that lurk just beneath the surface of capitalism. It also offers the more contemporary drama of the breakneck deterioration of a country that had already reached parity with the First World. Europe's image ambiguity — kind of elegant museum or tourist playground which is also an evolutionary and economic dead end — is instructive; and the absence of Islam is a welcome relief, in a moment in which it is reality, rather than culture or literature, that is acting on the basis of that particular stereotype.

This new geopolitical material marks a significant historical difference between these commercial adventure stories and the equally cynical gonzo journalism of an earlier period; indeed, the affinities and distinctions between the cultural products of the 60s and 70s and those of the 90s and 00s would be well worth exploring further. Equally significant is that these protagonists — busy as they are in locating rare products, securing secret new inventions, outsmarting rivals and trading with the natives — do not particularly need the stimulus of drugs (still a preponderant, one may even say a metaphysical, presence in so recent a world-historical expression as David Foster Wallace's 1996 *Infinite Jest*).

eBay Imaginary

But it is by way of its style that we can best measure the new literature on some kind of time-continuum; and here we may finally return to the distinctiveness of *Pattern Recognition*, where this style has reached a kind of classical perfection. I will define it as a kind of hyped-up name-dropping, and the description of the clothes selected by the protagonist (Cayce Pollard) for her first day in London is a reliable indicator:

> a fresh Fruit T-shirt, her black Buzz Rickson's MA-I, anonymous black skirt from a Tulsa thrift, the black leggings she'd worn for Pilates, black Harajuku schoolgirl shoes. Her purse-analog is an envelope of black East German laminate, purchased on eBay — if not actual Stasi-issue then well in the ballpark.

I have no idea whether all these items actually exist but eBay is certainly the right word for our current collective unconscious, and it is clear that the references "work," whether or not you know that the product is real or has been made up by Gibson. What is also clear is that the names being dropped are brand names, whose very dynamic conveys both instant obsolescence and the global provenance and the neo-exoticism of the world market today in time and space.

A further point is that, little by little in the current universe, everything is slowly being named; nor does this have anything to do with the older Aristotelian universals in which the idea of a chair subsumes all its individual manifestations. Here the "high-backed workstation chair" is almost of a different species to the seat in the BA 747 "that makes her think of a little boat, a coracle of Mexcel and teak-finish laminate." But there are also exercise chairs, called or named "reformers": "a very long, very low, vaguely ominous and Weimar-looking piece of spring-loaded furniture," which can also be translated into another language, where it becomes "a faux-classical Japanese interpretation in black-lacquered wood, upholstered with something that looks like shark-skin." Each of these items is on its way to the ultimate destination of a name of its own, but not the kind we are familiar with when we speak of a "Mies chair" or a "Barcelona chair." Not the origin, but rather the named image is at stake, so that an "Andy Warhol electric chair" might be a better reference.

In this postmodern nominalism, however, the name must also express the new, and fashion: what is worn-out, old-fashioned, is only useful as a cultural marker: "empty chrome stools of the soda-fountain spinaround kind, but very low, fronting on an equally low bar," where it is the "low," the "very low" that connotes Japan. And in Moscow the table "flanked by two enormous, empty wingback armchairs" only stands for backwardness. This is probably why Gibson's Russian episode is less interesting: he brings a residual Cold War mentality to this built space, "as though everything was designed by someone who'd been looking at a picture of a Western hotel room from the eighties, but without ever having seen even one example of the original." Current Soviet and Central European nostalgia art (*Ostalgie* in German) is far more vibrant and exciting than this, reflecting on an alternate universe in which a complete set of mass-produced industrial products, from toilet seats to window panes, from shower heads to automobiles, had been invented from scratch, altogether different from the actually existing Western inventory. It is as though the Aztecs had beaten Cortéz and survived to invent their own Aztec radio and television, power-vehicles, film genres and popular culture.

At any rate, the premise here is that Russia has nothing new to offer us in this field (the Sterling aesthetic offers much better chances of appreciating what is genuinely new, world-historically innovative, in Eastern nostalgia art); and the conclusion to be drawn is that name-dropping is also a matter of knowledge, and an encyclopaedic familiarity with the fashions of world space as those flow back into the boutiques or flea markets of the West. What I have called name-dropping is therefore also to be grasped as in-group style: the brand names function as a wink of familiarity to the reader in the know. Even the cynicism (taking the word in Sloterdijk's, rather than in its post-Watergate sense) is a joyous badge of group adherence, the snicker as a form of hearty laughter, class status as a matter of knowing the score rather than of having money and power. In-group style was, I believe, the invention — or better still, the discovery— of Thomas Pynchon, as early as *V* (1963), even though Ian Fleming deserves a reference ("Thank you, Commander Bond," murmurs Cayce, as she pastes a hair across the outside apartment door). But just as we no longer need drugs, so we no longer need Pynchon's staples of paranoia and conspiracy to wrap it all up for us, since global capitalism is there to do it more efficiently; or so we are told.

Birth of an Aesthetic?
Nonetheless, *The Crying of Lot 49* remains a fundamental paradigm and, as with Hunter Thompson, the differences are historically very instructive indeed. For the post-horns and the other tell-tale graffiti have here been replaced by something like a "work of art": the clues point, not to some unimaginable reality in the social world, but to an (as yet) unimaginable aesthetic. It is a question of an unidentified film of some kind which has come to be known, among insiders, as "the footage," and which shows up in stills and clips in the most unlikely places (billboards, television ads, magazines, the internet), in "one hundred and thirty-four previously discovered fragments . . . endlessly collated, broken down, re-assembled, by whole armies of the most fanatical investigators." Indeed, as one might expect, a whole new in-group has formed around the mysteries of the footage; we are experiencing, one of the characters observes, the "birth of a new subculture." A worldwide confraternity comes into being, committed to this

new object and passionately exchanging and arguing contradictory theories about it. The footage thus makes *Pattern Recognition* over into something like Bloch's conception of the novel of the artist, which carries the unknown unrealized work of art inside itself like a black hole, a future indeterminacy suddenly shimmering in the present, the absent Utopian sublime suddenly opening up like a wormhole within the empty everyday.

> Light and shadow. Lovers' cheekbones in the prelude to embrace.
> Cayce shivers.
> So long now, and they have not been seen to touch.
> Around them the absolute blackness is alleviated by texture. Concrete?
> They are dressed as they have always been dressed, in clothing Cayce has posted on extensively, fascinated by its timelessness, something she knows and understands. The difficulty of that. Hairstyles too.
> He might be a sailor, stepping onto a submarine in 1914, or a jazz musician entering a club in 1957. There is a lack of evidence, an absence of stylistic cues, that Cayce understands to be utterly masterful. His black coat is usually read as leather, though it might be dull vinyl, or rubber. He has a way of wearing its collar up.
> The girl wears a longer coat, equally dark but seemingly of fabric, its shoulder-padding the subject of hundreds of posts. The architecture of padding in a woman's coat should yield possible periods, particular decades, but there has been no agreement, only controversy.
> She is hatless, which has been taken either as the clearest of signs that this is not a period piece, or simply as an indication that she is a free spirit, untrammeled even by the most basic conventions of her day. Her hair has been the subject of similar scrutiny, but nothing has ever been definitively agreed upon.

The problem, for the group forming around this artifact, as indeed for all group formation, is that of the contradiction between universality — in this case the universality of taste as such — and the particularity of this unique value that sets us off from all the others and defines us in our collective specificity. A political sect (as we now seem to call these things) wishes simultaneously to affirm the universal relevance of its strategy and its ultimate aims, and at one and the same time to keep them for itself, to exclude the outsiders and the late-comers and those who can be suspected of insufficient commitment, passion and belief. The deeper anxiety of the practitioners of the footage website and chatroom is, in other words, simply that it will go public: that CNN will get wind of this interesting development; that the footage, or the completed film, the identified and reconstructed work of art, will become, as they say, the patrimony of mankind, or in other words just another commodity. As it turns out, this fear is only too justified, but I omit the details, as I hate people who tell you the ending; except to express my mixed feeling that Pynchon's solution was perhaps the better one, namely to break off *Lot 49* on the threshold of the revelation to come, as Oedipa is on the point of entering the auction room.

After all this, it may come as something of a surprise to learn that the footage is not the central issue of this novel, even though it supplies the narrative framework. Yet it ought already to have been clear that there is a striking and dramatic contradiction between the style, as we have described it, and the footage itself, whose "absence of stylistic cues" suggests a veritable Barthesian "white writing." Indeed, it is rather this very contradiction which is the deeper subject of *Pattern Recognition*, which projects the Utopian anticipation of a new art premised on "semiotic neutrality," and on the systematic effacement of names, dates, fashions and history itself, within a context irremediably corrupted by all those things. The name-dropping, in-group language of the novel thus revels in everything the footage seeks to neutralize: the work becomes a kind of quicksand, miring us ever more deeply in what we struggle to escape. Yet this is not merely an abstract interpretation, nor even an aesthetic; it is also the existential reality of the protagonist herself, and the source of the "gift" that informs her profession.

Commodity Bulimia

Cayce Pollard's talent, lying as it does halfway between telepathy and old-fashioned aesthetic sensibility, is in fact what suspends Gibson's novel between Science Fiction and realism and lends it its extraordinary resonance. To put it simply (as she does), Cayce's business is to "hunt 'cool'"; or in other words, to wander through the masses of now and future consumers, through the youth crowds, the "Children's Crusade" that jams Camden High Street on weekends, the teeming multitudes of Roppongi and Shinjuku, the big-city agglomerations of every description all over the world, in order mentally to detect the first stirrings of anything likely to become a trend or a new fashion. She has in fact racked up some impressive achievements, of which my favourite, mildly redolent of DeLillo, is the identification of the first person in the world to wear a baseball cap backwards (he is a Mexican). But these "futures" are very much a business proposition, and Cayce is something like an industrial spy of times to come. "I consult on design. . . . Manufacturers use me to keep track of street fashion"; these modest formulas are a little too dry, and underplay the sheer physicality of this gift, which allows her to identify a "pattern" and then to "point a commodifier at it."

There is here, no doubt, something of the specialized training of the authenticator of paintings and the collector of antique furniture; but its uncanny temporal direction condemns Cayce irredeemably, and despite her systematically black and styleless outfit, to the larger category of fortune-tellers and soothsayers — and occasionally puts her in real physical danger. This new *métier* thus draws our world insensibly into some Science Fictional future one, at least on the borders, where details fail to coincide. The job of one character is to start rumours; to drop the names of products and cultural items enthusiastically in bars and nightclubs, in order to set in motion what would in Pynchon have been a conspiracy, but here is just another fad or craze. But Cayce's gift is drawn back into our real (or realistic) world by the body itself; she must pay for it by the nauseas and anxiety attacks, the commodity bulimia which is the inevitable price of her premonitory sensibility — no doubt nourished by obscure traumas, of which the latest is her father's mysterious disappearance in Manhattan on the morning of 9/11. It is as if the other face of the "coming attraction," its reification and the dead-end product of what was once an active process of consumption and desire itself, were none other than the logo. The mediation between these two extremes of *energeia* and *ergon*, of process and product, lies no doubt in the name itself. I have argued that in the commercial nominalism of the postmodern, everything unique and interesting tends towards the proper name. Indeed, within the brand name the whole contradictory dialectic of universality and particularity is played out as a tug of war between visual recognition and what we may call the work of consumption (as Freud spoke of the work of mourning). And yet, to paraphrase Empson, the name remains, the name remains and kills; and the logo into which the brand name gradually hardens soaks up its toxicity and retains the poison.

Cayce's whole body is a resonator for these omnipresent logos, which are nonetheless louder and more oppressive in certain spaces (and places) than in others. To search for an unusual item in Harvey Nichols, for instance, is a peculiarly perilous activity:

> Down here, next to a display of Tommy Hilfiger, it's all started to go sideways on her, the trademark thing. Less warning aura than usual. Some people ingest a single peanut and their head swells like a basketball. When it happens to Cayce, it's her psyche. Tommy Hilfiger does it every time, though she'd thought she was safe now. They said he'd peaked, in New York. Like Benetton, the name would be around, but the real poison, for her, would have been drawn. . . . his stuff is simulacra of simulacra of simulacra. A diluted tincture of Ralph Lauren, who had himself diluted the glory days of Brooks Brothers, who themselves had stepped on the product of Jermyn Street and Savile Row, flavouring their ready-to-wear with liberal lashings of polo knit and regimental stripes. But Tommy surely is the null point, the black hole. There must be some Tommy Hilfiger event horizon, beyond which it is impossible to be more derivative, more removed from the source, more devoid of soul.

These nauseas are part of Cayce's navigational apparatus, and they stretch back to some of the oldest logos still extant, such as her worst nightmare, Bibendum, the Michelin Man, which is like that crack through which the Lacanian Real makes its catastrophic appearance. "National icons," on the other hand, "are always neutral for her, with the exception of Nazi Germany's . . . a scary excess of design talent."

Now it is a little easier to see the deeper meaning of the footage for Cayce: its utter lack of style is an ontological relief, like black-and-white film after the conventional orgies of bad technicolour, like the silence of solitude for the telepath whose mind is jammed with noisy voices all day long. The footage is an epoch of rest, an escape from the noisy commodities themselves, which turn out, as Marx always thought they would, to be living entities preying on the humans who have to coexist with them. Unlike the footage, however, Gibson's novel gives us homeopathy rather than antidote.

It does not seem anticlimactic to return to the future and to everything also auto-referential about this novel, whose main character's name is homonymous with that of the central figure in *Neuromancer*. Indeed, the gender change suggests all kinds of other stereotypical shifts of register, from active to passive for example (from male hacker to female future-shopper). Is it possible, however, that Cayce's premonitions of future novelty can also stand as the allegory of some emergent "new Gibson novel"? *Pattern Recognition* does seem to constitute a kind of pattern recognition for Gibson, as indeed for Science Fiction generally.

Notes

1. William Gibson, *Pattern Recognition* (New York: Putnam, 2003).
2. Bruce Sterling, *A Good Old-Fashioned Future* (New York: Bantam, 1999).

CHAPTER 9

Hawthorne and Class

Teresa A. Goddu

"Ethan Brand" (1850), one of Hawthorne's late tales, concludes with the image of Ethan Brand's body "burnt into perfect, snow-white lime" (102). The scene of Brand's snow-white skeleton lying in repose in the kiln is seemingly an image of redemption and purification: Ethan Brand, the seeker of the unpardonable sin, is burnt clean undergoing a Christlike resurrection in the limekiln that has been burning for three days. Given the kiln's association not just with hell in the story but also with the imagination — Brand "fancied pictures among the coals" (94) — the snow-white image it produces, like the "snow-images" that issue from the magic moonshine in "The Custom House" (36), distills the essence of Brand's sin: his sterile intellect and cold spirituality, figured by his calcified, marble heart, lack any moral empathy for his brother-man. Brand, like many of Hawthorne's artist figures, is a "cold observer," a "fiend" who transforms men and women into "his puppets" and pulls "wires that moved them to such degrees of crime as were demanded for his study" (99). The artist, in Hawthorne's moral lexicon, commits a crime when he violates the sanctity of the human soul, turning its subjects into objects that operate according to his will.

The final image of Brand's snow-white heart, however, renders his moral sin visible in specific material terms: the metaphorical enslavement of the heart and soul is converted into the economic slavery of the laborer. Instead of pondering the perplexity of the marble heart he discovers, Bartram, another lime-burner and the tale's man-of-business, argues that it "looks like special good lime" and calculates that "my kiln is half a bushel the richer for him" (102). The last line of the story reads: "So saying, the rude lime-burner lifted his pole, and letting it fall upon the skeleton, the relics of Ethan Brand were crumbled into fragments" (102). In reducing the sanctity of Brand's body to lime, converting it from a relic into a commodity, the end reorients our reading from religious allegory to economic reality: like the slave, Brand's body rather than his labor is consumed. The kiln, with its "oven-mouth" large enough to admit a man in a stooping posture" (84), as Leo Marx has pointed out (1956, 37), is an image of the emerging industrial order that literally devours laborers alive. Brand's body is reduced "after long toil" (102) by the kiln into a commodity; he is turned into the raw material of the trade he used to practice. His fragmented bones crumbled into lime represent the dehumanized and disindividuated aspects of the industrial laborer. Brand's name further underscores the laborer's position as a commodity. A brand refers not only to a piece of wood burning in the kiln (Bartram stirs the "immense brands with a long pole," 85) but also to the trademark that claims ownership. Given the association of branding with slavery in this time period, Brand's name also figures the working-class laborer as a slave.[1]

Like the corrosive effects of the lime itself, then, the tale's final line dissolves the romancer's spiritual symbol of Brand's marble heart and converts it back into the material realities of the marketplace. "Ethan Brand," however, presents an examination of the material conditions of industrial capitalism not simply to critique that order but rather to locate a place for the artist within it. The tale's composition — it was written in 1848 while Hawthorne served as surveyor of Salem's custom house and broke the "spell" of his two-year hiatus from writing — reveals the origins of this connection (Newman 1979, 96). Serving as a wage laborer as surveyor — he derides himself in "The Custom-House" for having bartered his imaginative abilities for a pittance of public gold, stating "Go, then, and earn your wages!" (34) — Hawthorne uses that marketplace throughout "The Custom-House" as a foil against and through which to project his professional success as an artist. Using the same images he previously deployed in "Ethan Brand," Hawthorne figures the Custom House as dampening the heat he could kindle at his "intellectual forge" and turning his characters into rigid, dead corpses (34). Brand's calcified body, then, also represents Hawthorne's anxiety about how industrial capitalism might deaden his art. Moreover, in revealing that the artist's value lies not in what he can create but in how much his body as/of work is worth, "Ethan Brand" also underscores Hawthorne's anxious understanding that the artist is finally only another wage worker — paid by the page — and his art another commodity for sale.

In this chapter, I will read two of Hawthorne's tales, one early, "Mr. Higginbotham's Catastrophe" (1834), and one late, "Ethan Brand" (1850), to trace the connections between Hawthorne's figuration of the economics of authorship, wage labor, and industrial capitalism. Both tales, I argue, indict the emerging industrial capitalist economy. They make clear the costs of wage labor. Yet they also work to disidentify the author/artist figure from the position of wage worker. This dual move of identification/disidentification is performed through the specter of race and by resurrecting industrial capitalism's shadow economy, slavery.[2] The revelation of both stories is that the artist is not only a commodity but also a capitalist. Hawthorne's tales may critique the costs of capitalism but they ultimately align the author with that power structure.

Although "Ethan Brand" and many of Hawthorne's later works, which are more fully invested in the capital of Hawthorne's authorship, work ultimately to mystify the commercial dependencies of his art and authorship, Hawthorne's early tales, which don't have as much capital to lose, are clearer — and less guilty — about the artist's allegiance with capitalism. One of Hawthorne's earliest tales, "Mr. Higginbotham's Catastrophe," figures capitalism not as a crime but as an order that the artist must defend and protect in order to profit in the emerging economy. Although the story is adept at critiquing the aggression of the emerging capitalist order and in disclosing the racial formations that fuel class affiliation, it makes clear the confederation between the artist and the capitalist. A tale of class warfare, "Higginbotham's" narrative of social crisis is violently contained by the tale's author-figure in order to turn him a profit.

First published anonymously in *The New-England Magazine* (December 1834), under the title "The Storyteller. No. II. The Village Theatre," and later collected in Hawthorne's first volume of stories, *Twice-Told Tales* (1837), "Mr. Higginbotham's Catastrophe" was originally projected as part of Hawthorne's never-published collection, *The Story Teller*. In its serialized form, the tale is embedded in the section of *The Story Teller*'s frame tale called "The Village Theatre," where the wandering storyteller performs the tale before an enthusiastic audience. The frame tale, to which I will return, forecasts the dilemmas of professional authorship. In doing so, it both foregrounds and flees from the revelations of its embedded story. The basic plot of that story, "Mr. Higginbotham's Catastrophe," is as follows: Dominicus Pike, a traveling tobacco salesman who also trades in gossip, meets a man who tells him that Mr. Higginbotham "was murdered in his orchard, at eight o'clock last night, by an Irishman and a nigger. They strung him up to the branch of a St. Michael's pear-tree" (107). He spreads this news only to be discredited by a farmer who drank a glass of bitters with Mr. Higginbotham that morning. Pike then meets a mulatto, who when questioned about the rumor states: "There was no colored man! It was an Irishman that hanged him last night, at eight o'clock" (111). This story also gets discredited first by a lawyer and then by Mr. Higginbotham's niece. Finally on the third night, Pike decides to go see for himself if Mr. Higginbotham is dead or alive. He discovers an Irishman about to hang Mr. Higginbotham in the tree and steal his money. Pike uses the "butt-end of his whip" (119) to prostrate the Irishman and save Mr. Higginbotham. The story discloses its riddle at the end: "Three men had plotted the robbery and murder of Mr. Higginbotham; two of them, successively lost their courage and fled, each delaying the crime one night, by their disappearance" (119). Mr. Higginbotham rewards Pike by allowing him to marry his niece and live off the interest of the property he settles on their children. The story concludes with Pike using the proceeds of Mr. Higginbotham's largesse to establish "a large tobacco manufactory" (120).

The story of Mr. Higginbotham's murder is a tale of class antagonism. Mr. Higginbotham is the town's capitalist: he is part owner in the town's slitting-mill and "a considerable stockholder" in its three "cotton-factories" (112); he is "so absorbed in worldly business" that he is imagined "to continue to transact it, even after his death" (114). Fully invested in cotton, the commodity that joins northern industrialism to southern plantation economics, the industrial capitalist also profits from wage slavery. He is "an object of abhorrence at Parker's Falls" (115). Higginbotham's clerk "manifested but little grief" (109) at the news of his employer's death and the shopkeepers, the mill men, and the factory girls celebrate the news, their loquaciousness compensating for the "silence of the cotton-machines" (112). Their excessive wrath at the news of his resurrection registers the class antagonisms of the town. This antagonism, however, is displaced onto the Irishman and his attempted murder of Higginbotham. Mr. Higginbotham hires the "Irishman of doubtful character" on the "score of the economy" (117), valuing cheap labor over character. Although Mr. Higginbotham's own character, his miserliness, gets impugned in this relationship, the Irishman carries the burden of blame. Structurally, the Irishman and other blackened representatives of the working class enact the class resentment of the oppressed white shopkeepers, mill men, and factory girls.

As David Roediger and others have shown, the Irish were discursively blackened in the antebellum period (1991, 133–134). Eric Lott argues that the "immigrant Irish, whom antebellum whites widely equated with blacks as an alien, subhuman, and brutal species," were an "extreme instance" of working-class blackening (1994, 186). In the tale, the "sturdy Irishman" is associated with two other would-be murderers: the first man, who is of an unidentified race but who is "ill-looking" (107), and the second, who has a "deep tinge of negro blood" (110) and is described as a "yellow man" (111) and a mulatto (112). While the allegiance between the Irishman and the mulatto is made clear from the first — it was "an Irishman and a nigger" (107) who murdered Mr. Higginbotham — the one blackening the other, the first murderer, who is not marked by race and hence read as white, is also blackened. In being described by Pike as carrying "a bundle over his shoulder on the end of a stick" (110), a phrase that is reiterated in the description of the mulatto, the tale deploys the conventional printer's image of the slave used in runaway slave advertisements. All three potential murderers, then, are associated with "blackness." The threat of white labor revolting against capital is recast as a racial division. When Pike prostrates the Irishman with the "butt-end of his whip" (119), he is pictured more as a master putting down a slave insurrection than as a peddler involved in class warfare.

The tale's rewriting of class anxiety as racial antagonism becomes strikingly visible when it is compared to the source that Hawthorne used for this tale. According to Lea Newman, "Mr. Higginbotham's Catastrophe" was composed in 1832 (1979, 209). In 1830, a sensational murder was committed in Salem: Captain Joseph White, a successful East India merchant, was bludgeoned to death in his bed and then stabbed by two brothers from a merchant family, the Crowninshields, acting as hired guns for yet another pair of merchant brothers, the Knapps, who believed one of their wives would inherit a fortune if White died without a will, which the Crowninshield brothers were also hired to destroy. The trial was covered by the Boston and Salem papers and prosecuted by Daniel Webster (Murphy n.d., 18). "Mr. Higginbotham's Catastrophe" parodies the sensationalistic newspaper accounts of White's death in its account of the *Parker's Falls Gazette*'s "column of double pica, emphasized with capitals, and headed HORRID MURDER OF MR. HIGGINBOTHAM!" (112). More important, in rewriting a violent antagonism that occurred within the merchant class as one between classes and then between races, it twice displaces the real rivalry of the story. The merchant class's extreme aggression against itself gets projected as an external threat that can be stigmatized by being blackened and contained. The class solidarity present in the two pairs of brothers working together is transmuted in the tale into a story of racial animosity: the tactical alliance among different races and ethnicities of the working class — white, mulatto, and Irish — more easily comes undone as they turn on each other in order to exonerate themselves. Blackness may be deeply threatening but it placates an even greater danger: intraclass warfare.

The rumor of Higginbotham's death, like all rumors, discloses unspoken aspects of its society. On one level, the rumor divulges the wish fulfillment of the white working class: to see, as the newspaper falsely reports, the capitalist lynched, hanging from a tree "with his pockets inside out" (112). Here the capitalist is not only reduced to poverty but also "blackened," put into the position of slave rather than master. Pike makes this connection clear when he imagines "hanging the nigger" but decides against it since it "wouldn't unhang Mr. Higginbotham" (111). The tale further allies Mr. Higginbotham with the mulatto, the Ethiopian who "appeared to change his skin, its yellow hue becoming a ghastly white" (110), when it describes Higginbotham before he is resurrected from the dead as looking like a ghost, "yellow and thin" (118). The racial fluidity of these images registers the deeper fear of the tale: that class position is also uncertain. The blackened working-class figures, if successful in their aggression, can become white; the capitalist is vulnerable to becoming a slave.

The story may read at points as a gothic tale that registers the insecurities and hostilities that attend class stratification (Mr. Higginbotham at one point is described as Washington Irving's headless horseman) but it ultimately resolves itself into a romance. At the end, Dominicus Pike is described as a champion "blindly obeying the call of fate, like the heroes of old romance" (120). The romance ending of the story projects a fantasy of upward mobility rather than the gothic horror of class instability. Pike begins the tale as a peddler of tobacco and ends it as an owner of a tobacco manufactory. As the storyteller of the tale, Pike emblematizes the class transformation that Hawthorne hopes to make through the agency of his own authorship. Becoming the actor/hero of his own story, Pike enacts his own wish fulfillment: by violently protecting the capitalist order against lower-class intruders, he is rewarded with the wealth that they can only aspire to through crime. "Higginbotham's" sunny ending, however, like the newspaper's sentimental account of the niece's fainting fits in reaction to the news of her uncle's death, remains suspect: some "shrewd fellows had doubted, all along, whether a young lady would be quite so desperate at the hanging of a rich old uncle" (115). The final transfer of wealth would seem nonviolent: Mr. Higginbotham "capped the climax of his favors, by dying a Christian death, in bed" (120). However, given the way that Captain White's brutal murder in bed shadows Higginbotham's Christian death, and given the violent associations of Pike's name (a pike is a weapon) and given Pike's wish throughout the story that Higginbotham would remain dead — "It's a sin, I know; but I should hate to have him come to life a second time, and give me the lie!" (111)— Pike can be read as the real criminal of the tale. Pike pits his life as well as his credit against Higginbotham's: "May I be hanged myself . . . if I'll believe old Higginbotham is unhanged," he states (117); moreover, his account is read by others as "maliciously contrived to injure Mr. Higginbotham's credit" (114). Higginbotham must be dead for Pike's story to gain its full credit.

Pike's investment in the story of Higginbotham's death — despite its sin — reveals that the storyteller is fully vested in the capitalist structure. This investment is emphasized by the alliance between storytelling and tobacco. The peddler trades in both tobacco and stories, each feeding the other: he invites the first would-be murderer to "smoke a Spanish cigar and relate all the particulars" (108), and he tells the story at "every tavern and country-store along the road, expending a whole bunch of Spanish-wrappers among at least twenty horrified audiences" (108). Stories circulate both with and as commodities; moreover, they create the conditions under which Pike's trade flourishes. He may state that he tells the "news for the public good," but in doing so he also drives "bargains for his own" (109). Allied with tobacco, a blackened, southern commodity, the story helps to create an industrialist capitalist order—pictured in Pike's to-bacco manufactory as an "affair of smoke" (1974c, 410)—that produces and profits from wage slavery. Pike's tobacco manufactory, which is decorated with a "splendid image of an Indian chief in front" (1974c, 410), is just a larger, more fully invested version, of the tobacco peddler's "neat little cart" (106) which has "a box of cigars depicted on each side-panel, and an Indian chief, holding a pipe and a golden tobacco-stalk, on the rear" (106). The cart, like the story he circu-lates about "the Irishman and the nigger" (107), trades in racial stereotype to gain interest from its audience.[3] By absorbing the racial other into commodity culture—turning the vanishing Indian into a consumer of pipe tobacco—the cart, like the story that circulates with it, produces a narrative by which the threat of the racial other is consumed by the emerging capitalist order and, hence, neutralized and made to turn a profit.

Tobacco also becomes a sign of class. Pike lights "one of his prime cigars" (109) as he tells his story to a room full of people; the farmer who challenges his story smokes "the vilest tobacco smoke the pedler had ever smelt" (109). The quality of his storytelling, like the grade of his tobacco, earns Pike capital as well as status. In peddling the popular image of slave and Irish uprising, the storyteller gains interest: he fills up the outline of the story until it "became quite a *respectable* narrative" (108, emphasis added). Later when he mounts the town pump to announce himself the author of the story of Higginbotham's death, he becomes "the great man of the moment" (113). He must, however, compete with other professions and their modes of verification—first a farmer, who takes an oath, and then a lawyer, who presents an affidavit—in order to claim full credit for the tale. When his tale is discredited, he loses class status and becomes blackened. After the first time, he dreams of "hanging on the St. Michael's pear-tree" (110); after the second, a mob contemplates tarring and feathering him, but he ends up being pelted by school boys with mud balls, one slapping him in his mouth. His ability to achieve capital—and the respect that accompanies it—relies upon his ability to compete against other forms of truth telling and to appeal to and manage a fickle and often hostile audience.

The peddler must also deal with the unstable conditions of an emerging print marketplace where stories circulate unauthorized and without attribution. When he arrives at Parker's Falls, he tells his story but hesitates, having been proven wrong once before, to "relate it on his own authority" (112); instead he presents it as a "report generally diffused" (112). The story then runs "through the town like fire . . . and became so much the universal talk, that nobody could tell whence it had originated" (112). This image of the story's universal circu-lation that erases its origination is figured by the newspaper, which embellishes the story just as it enhances its headline with capital letters "HORRID MURDER OF MR. HIGGINBOTHAM!" (112) and which circulates its story nationally and transatlantically through reprinting: "the paragraph in the Parker's Falls Ga-zette would be re-printed from Maine to Florida, and perhaps form an item in the London newspapers" (116). Like rumor or gossip, print circulates unauthorized and without the attribution of authorship. Besides being a tale of class warfare, "Higginbotham" is also a meditation on the overlapping transition from oral to print culture that attends industrial capitalism.

Pike's optimism — he is described as a "funny rogue" (116) — like the story's use of humor ultimately obscures these complexities in favor of a romance ending where Pike gets the girl, the money, and the last laugh. In entering into the story he has been telling by reenacting the murder, but with a twist — he prostrates the Irishman instead of Mr. Higginbotham — Pike seems to give the audience what they want, a sensational ending, but with a particular cultural logic: the working-class laborer will only succeed in becoming a capitalist through the subordination of other laborers. The white working class violently subordinates other laborers by blackening them in order to get ahead. The white entrepreneur, it turns out, is the true hero of this romance.

The appeal of this cultural narrative to the white working class is made clear by the tavern audience's enthusiastic reception of the story, "Mr. Higginbotham's Catastrophe," in the frame tale. The frame tale, collected in the 1854 edition of *Mosses from an Old Manse* as "Passages from a Relinquished Work," however, makes clear that the audience is both blind to its own self-interest — even when the benches break beneath them they continue their applause — and manipulated by a print culture that dictates to them the terms of their own reception. The play bills announcing the storyteller "in the hugest type that the printing-office could supply" (417) circulate the story of the tale's success before it has ever been told: they falsely advertise that it had "been received with rapturous applause, by audiences in all the principal cities" (418). The frame tale, like the tale itself, discloses how instrumental print culture and storytelling are in selling cultural narratives to an audience — or in the frame tale's words, its "customers" (419). The newspaper sells the story of Higginbotham's death in sensationalistic and sentimental terms: it gives the dreadful details and repackages them as pathos in the form of the niece's fainting fits. The "village poet" is also implicated, since he "likewise commemorated the young lady's grief, in seventeen stanzas of a ballad" (112). Like the handbills that the selectmen issue that offer a reward for apprehending the murderers and Higginbotham's stolen property, the newspaper and the ballad circulate as part of a print culture that upholds the capitalist order. A story is a commodity that is produced for sale in order to stabilize and enhance capital.

While the tale embraces this revelation in the form of Pike's ascendancy to capital, the frame tale remains much more ambivalent. The storyteller runs away, "untempted by the liberal offers of the manager" (421). Unlike Pike, whose professional movement is dramatic and clear, the storyteller continues to wander, neither embracing nor giving up his profession. This ambivalence toward success at the start of an authorial career — both the storyteller's and by implication Hawthorne's — is striking. If the tale focuses on the peddler's ascension to ownership, the frame tale is more concerned with the storyteller's reduction to property. Allied with actors and the theater, the storyteller is turned into a character without agency by the print market. Unauthorized by him, playbills announce him as an "Unprecedented Attraction!!" (417). He is literally turned into his tale when one of the actors attaches a "stiff queue of horse-hair" to his collar (420). He is depicted as having less control of his story than the audience whose reception of the tale/tail force him to respond with less legitimate strokes of humor: "the story . . . afforded good scope for mimicry and buffoonery; neither of which to my shame, did I spare" (420). The fantasy of pure publicity that print offers — its ability to create a reality — is coupled with the horror of its ability to commodify and cheapen the storyteller, turning him into an ass, the butt of others' jokes. As commodity rather than capitalist, the storyteller becomes a slave to his audience and to the proprietors of print.[4]

The frame tale, then, is less optimistic about the storyteller's position in the emerging economy. Unsure how to negotiate the conundrum of celebrity-as-commodity, the storyteller rejects his fame — calling it humbug — as well as his guardian's call to return to a more proper profession, in order to continue his journey with his companion, an itinerant preacher who tries to "convince [him] of the guilt and madness of [his] life" (421). Although the frame tale recognizes that the storyteller is fully enmeshed in the capitalist order — even the representative of religious culture performs for an audience and his pocket bible invokes the remarkable way the Evangelical movement exploited capitalist print culture — it still flees from its own revelation that he is fully commodified by it. The frame tale understands that stories are like machines — they are "manufactured" and have "mechanisms" — yet it also wants to project a class hierarchy for art: the best stories have "a unity, a wholeness, and a separate character" (417). The storyteller may be allied with and in competition with the showman's cart and the theater, but he also imagines his entrance into his profession as a mystical rainbow, produced by sunshine and morning mist, a mere "unpainted frame-work," "white and ghost-like" (411). This visionary projection of pure professional possibility, however ironized through references to the storyteller as a Don Quixote figure, emblematizes the mist and mystification Hawthorne will employ in his later works to veil and soften the full force of "Higginbotham's" revelations: that the author is both a commodity and a person who commodifies others in order to gain capital.

Throughout his career, Hawthorne obsessively returned to the dilemma he outlines in "The Storyteller": how an author can enter the marketplace and profit from it without being commodified by it. While Hawthorne's author figures project guilt about using others to gain capital, the deep anxiety of his fictions lies in the author's own commodification. Like the image of the dog chasing his tail in "Ethan Brand," Hawthorne chases the same issues in his later tale as he did in his earlier one. Written after two decades of tale writing and before his breakthrough success with *The Scarlet Letter*, "Ethan Brand" is deeply pessimistic about the artist's ability to escape the "blackness" of industrial capitalism or to transform himself, as Pike did, into a capitalist. Instead of ascending to capital, Brand literalizes the fall — when he throws himself into the kiln — back into the position of commodity. Brand's suicide may appear a romantic attempt to transcend the body of the laborer, to dissolve it into perfect whiteness, but it also points to the harsh revelation that all bodies — no matter their race—are ultimately commodities. The only compensation for the economic realities of the industrial marketplace, the story argues, is cultural capital in the form of class status.

If Hawthorne cannot conceptualize authorship without thinking about class, he cannot think about class without invoking race. As Amy Lang argues more generally about nineteenth-century literature, race mediates, displaces, and manages class during the period (2003, 6). The image of the "snow-white lime" and Brand's "snow-white" skeleton (102) highlights the broader racial imagery of the tale and points to the limits of Hawthorne's sympathies with the laborer, both wage and slave. It is the white aspiring middle-class worker that concerns Hawthorne. As the racial politics of "Ethan Brand" make clear, "blackness" may help to identify the problems of industrial capitalism but it must finally be disassociated from them. The full horror of Brand's death lies in the defiling of his "whiteness" by the representative of industrial capitalism, the blackened lime-burner, Bartram. "Blackness" not only allows for a differentiation between slave and free, but also, as David Anthony has shown, forges a distinction between the white working and white middle class (1999, 250–251).

Throughout "Ethan Brand"—and indeed throughout Hawthorne's fictions more generally—"blackness," as Paul Gilmore and I have argued, becomes a sign of a market economy that turns people into property (Goddu 2001, 61; Gilmore 2001, 126). The kiln is the most obvious example. Its massive "iron door" and smoke that turns its tender into a "coal-begrimed" figure (85) associates the "hollow prison-house" (89) of industrialism with blackness. This "blackness" is specifically racialized and tied to the economy of slavery in the description of the German Jew's diorama, the tale's image of the commodification of art, whose pictures are blackened by tobacco smoke. Tobacco also appears in the description of two of the working-class persons that the story use as a foil to Brand: the stage agent is described as "wilted and smoke-dried" (91), puffing on the same cigar he lit twenty years ago; the doctor has an "everlasting pipe in his mouth . . . it was always alight with hell-fire" (91). The tobacco here not only serves to blacken these working-class figures but also to ally blackness with the evil nature of the industrial kiln; the pipe, like the kiln that houses the Devil, is alight with hellfire. Tobacco, one of slavery's commodities, simultaneously exposes the fiendishness of industrial capitalism that steals workers' souls and denigrates those workers as unworthy of anything else. This move occurs by focusing on the workers as consumers rather than laborers. The stage agent whose entire person, ideas, and expression are "impregnated" by tobacco smoke (91) literally becomes the commodity he consumes: wilted and smoke-dried, he resembles a leaf of tobacco. The worker as consumer—the pipe is always lit, the cigar is always in his mouth—rather than as laborer also dominates the image of these (un)"worthies'" consumption of alcohol: they offer Brand to partake of their "black bottle" (92), only to hear him reject it by saying "ye brute beasts, that have made yourselves so, shriveling up your souls with fiery liquors! I have done with you" (93). Alcohol, also blackened, turns these formerly productive professionals (stage agent, lawyer, doctor) into lazy, brute beasts. In so doing, the tale trades on the stereotype of the slave as lazy and subhuman. As the complexity of the tobacco imagery of the tale demonstrates, "blackness" is a sign not only of industrial capitalism's alliance with slavery but also of its Protestant logic of self-improvement. In failing to discipline themselves like a machine, workers turn themselves into slaves: imbibing alcohol, they turn their bodies into a kiln. Violently rejected by Brand, the worker rather than capitalism is blamed for his enslavement.

The tale rejects its own critique of the conditions of wage labor in favor of the middle-class ethics of Protestant capitalism. The violence of its rejection emblematizes the violent forms of dispossession that are required to sustain the emerging capitalist economy and one's place in it. The tale is ultimately about class competition. Bartram's "rough welcome" (85) of Brand to his "own fire-side" (85) makes this clear: seeing Brand return after eighteen years to the kiln that Bartram has now claimed, Bartram threatens to fling a "chunk of marble at [his] head" (85). He thinks "the sooner I drive him away, the better" (86), and that dead people have more right to this spot. Finally, Bartram imagines "toss-ing him into the furnace!" (102). While Bartram is concerned with protecting his capital, Brand's interest lies in solidifying his class status. Brand rejects the working-class worthies in order to differentiate his intellectual labor from their bodily labor and claim his cultural capital. He does not want to be mistaken, as Bartram does when Brand first appears in the story, as some "drunken man" (83). While Bartram and Brand are described as doubles throughout the story, they are also strongly differentiated. Bartram is "a rough, heavy-looking man, begrimed with charcoal"(83); he is repeatedly called "obtuse" (83). Brand, on the other hand, has a "rugged, thoughtful visage" (86). His blackness comes from the dark thoughts he projects into the furnace, while Bartram's comes from his labor at the kiln. Whereas Brand calls the labor he once practiced at the kiln a "craft" (87), Bartram sees it as a "business" (86). Moving out of the position of "unlettered laborer" (99) into the role of intellectual pilgrim, Brand may have committed a crime of "indistinct blackness" (88), but he is no longer a man in blackface.[5] In insisting on Brand's difference from the other workers, the tale encapsulates the racial ideology that attended class stratification. As Eric Lott writes, "Sandwiched between the bourgeoisie above and black below, respect-able artisans feared they were becoming 'blacker' with every increment of industrial advance, and countered with the language and violence of white su-premacy" (1994, 185). Hawthorne, who as Michael Newbury notes, chose craft labor to represent his intellectual work in order to differentiate his authorship from mass-produced or unskilled labor (1997, 36), invokes this discourse of white supremacy in the tale.[6] Brand may ultimately be reduced to a commodity in the kiln, but he achieves a perfect whiteness.

Race, "Ethan Brand" shows, is the ultimate compensatory wage. As David Roediger has argued in his study, *Wages of Whiteness*, antebellum working-class affiliation rested ultimately upon differentiating the worker from the slave: "chat-tel slavery provided white workers with a touchstone against which to weigh their fears and a yardstick to measure their reassurance" (1991, 66). By fashion-ing identities as "not slaves" (13), the working class moved away from a critique of "wage slavery" toward a defense of "free labor" (87). "Whiteness" rather than capital became the worker's wage. For Hawthorne, who was still aspiring to become a middle-class author as he wrote "Ethan Brand," race also played a key function. Writing to Sophia while serving his term as surveyor in the Boston Custom House, Hawthorne states, "your husband has been engaged in a very black business — as black as coal" (1984, 413). He also pictures himself as a "captive" who "feels the iron of his chain" and who desires to be freed from this "very grievous thralldom" (ibid., 445, 428, 422). Blackened by the material he trades in, coal, Hawthorne pictures himself as a slave to the market economy. Although he can never successfully project himself out of the industrializing marketplace even as an artist, given the author's increasingly commercialized status in the antebellum period, he can make claim to a compensatory wage: the cultural prestige of whiteness. While his fictions constantly expose the ways that his authorship and art operate in a commercial economy figured as black and often allied with slavery, they also work to deflect that connection. Unlike the scribbling women, blackened and made detestable by their being "ink-stained," (1987, 161), Hawthorne mystifies authorship as a genteel rather than commercial profession. At the end of "The Custom-House," when he dreams of leaving it behind, he pictures himself as a "gentleman who writes from beyond the grave" (44). The white moonbeams of "The Custom-House" may need the coal fire to warm their cold spirituality, just as the fire is needed to transform the marble into snow-white lime, or ink is needed to mark the white page, but Hawthorne's fictions also indulge in the fantasy of perfect whiteness. In the volume he published immediately after successfully establishing his authorial identity with *The Scarlet Letter*, Hawthorne reifies his art as white: *The Snow-Image*. "Ethan Brand," first published with Hawthorne's authorization in this volume, projects a vision of art — even as it converted into a commodity from the sculptor's marble to the industrialist's lime — as snow white.

If "Ethan Brand" purifies art's status as a commodity, it also excuses the artist's black crimes as a capitalist. The crime of indistinct blackness that overshadows Ethan Brand is the crime of turning people into commodities. In making Esther the subject of his psychological experiment, he "wasted, absorbed, and perhaps annihilated her soul" with "cold, and remorseless purpose" (94). Running off to become a circus performer, Esther represents the end point of Brand's experiment: she has lost her position as daughter to her "white-haired" (93) father and become a painted lady identified with the mass cultural setting of the circus. As an artist who plays people like puppets, Brand commits a crime by turning people into his property. However, the tale also exonerates the crime. Brand remains unrepentant for his sin. Admitting that he "sacrificed everything to its own mighty claims," Brand states: "Freely, were it to do again, would I incur the guilt. Unshrinkingly, I accept the retribution" (90). The tale may disclose the artist's investment in the contaminated property relations of the marketplace, and his sense of being tortured by it, but in whitening Brand, and in emphasizing his freedom to commit this crime, it does not so much damn him for his sins as justify and purify them. The artist, as Hawthorne's prefaces to his romances reiterate, may commit the crime of the capitalist — stealing others' labor or work as his own — but he does so "freely": in *The Marble Faun*, for instance, he depicts himself as a robber with "felonious hands" who steals other artists' designs by allowing himself "a quite unwarrantable freedom" (4). Authorship, for Hawthorne, as I have argued elsewhere, resembles a type of privileged piracy (Goddu 2001, 57–58). The romancer, like the entrepreneur, remains above the law.

In trying to move himself out of the position of unlettered labor into that of lettered author, from a manufacturer of tales and edited books to an author who could gain capital, Hawthorne leveraged his role as author by purifying his art's status as a commodity. Investing in cultural capital — especially the assets of whiteness and the class status that accompanied them — was the way he earned economic capital. In negotiating the emerging market of print capitalism as an author, then, Hawthorne becomes first and foremost a writer of class. His fictions record the unevenness and uneasiness of class transformation in the antebellum period: the competition and hostility, the culpability and uncertainty, the allegiances and rewards. Hawthorne's fictions may work to expose the cultural logic of an emerging capitalist order, a logic that understands race to be a class category; however, they also — often violently — enact that logic in an effort to secure their author status and wealth. As "Mr. Higginbotham's Catastrophe" attests, Hawthorne understood early in his career that he could earn interest by telling stories of social crisis and capital by containing them.

Notes

1. Hawthorne uses these images of branding throughout *The Scarlet Letter.* In "The Custom-House" he describes his name as surveyor being imprinted on dutiable merchandise (27), and in the novel he describes Hester as a slave, standing in the marketplace before a public who would "put the brand of a hot iron" on her forehead (51).

2. There have been a number of excellent essays, to which I am indebted, that discuss the interrelationship between racial and class formation in Hawthorne's fictions. They, however, focus exclusively on *The House of the Seven Gables.* See Amy Lang's *The Syntax of Class,* which calls our attention to the crisis in classification that attends class and the ways in which class distinction gets displaced onto racial and gender difference. See Gilmore, *The Genuine Article,* for a reading of how mass cultural figurations of race mark the dangers of market society for Hawthorne, and Anthony, "Class, Culture, and the Trouble with White Skin," for a discussion of how an aesthetics of race mediate and manage class conflict in the novel.

3. See Monica Elbert, "Nathaniel Hawthorne," for a reading of how the tale plays to anti-Irish sentiment.

4. See Michael Newbury, *Figuring Authorship* (77–118) on the cultural conflation between slavery and celebrity in antebellum America.

5. If Brand's story is about rising in class status, the lawyer's story registers the precarious hold white professionals had on their class position. Drink causes the lawyer to "slide from intellectual, to various kinds and degrees of bodily labor, till, at last . . . he slid into a soap-vat" (91).

6. Also see Nicholas Bromell, *By the Sweat of the Brow* (100–113), on Hawthorne's distinction between writing and manual labor.

Works Cited

Anthony, David. 1999. "Class, Culture, and the Trouble with White Skin in Hawthorne's *The House of the Seven Gables." Yale Journal of Criticism* 12: 249–268.

Bromell, Nicholas K. 1993. *By the Sweat of the Brow: Literature and Labor in Antebellum America.* Chicago: University of Chicago Press.

Elbert, Monica. 1994. "Nathaniel Hawthorne, *The Concord Freeman*, and the Irish 'Other.'" *Eire-Ireland* 29.3: 60–73.

Gilmore, Paul. 2001. *The Genuine Article: Race, Mass Culture, and American Literary Manhood.* Durham: Duke University Press.

Goddu, Teresa A. 2001. "Letters Turned to Gold: Hawthorne, Authorship, and Slavery." *Studies in American Fiction* 29: 49–76.

Nathaniel Hawthorne. 1962. *The Scarlet Letter.* Edited by William Charvat et al. *The Centenary Edition of the Works of Nathaniel Hawthorne*, volume 1. Columbus: Ohio State University Press.

———. 1968. *The Marble Faun.* Edited by William Charvat et al. *The Centenary Edition of the Works of Nathaniel Hawthorne*, volume 4. Columbus: Ohio State University Press.

———. 1974a. "Ethan Brand." In *The Snow-Image*, edited by William Charvat et al. *The Centenary Edition of the Works of Nathaniel Hawthorne*, volume 11. Columbus: Ohio State University Press.

———. 1974b. "Mr. Higginbotham's Catastrophe." In *Twice-Told Tales*, edited by William Charvat et al. *The Centenary Edition of the Works of Nathaniel Hawthorne*, volume 9. Columbus: Ohio State University Press.

———. 1974c. "Passages from a Relinquished Work." In *Mosses from an Old Manse*, edited by William Charvat et al. *The Centenary Edition of the Works of Nathaniel Hawthorne*, volume 10. Columbus: Ohio State University Press.

———. 1984. *Letters 1813–43.* Edited by William Charvat et al. *The Centenary Edition of the Works of Nathaniel Hawthorne*, volume 15. Columbus: Ohio State University Press.

———. 1987. *Letters 1853–56.* Edited by William Charvat et al. *The Centenary Edition of the Works of Nathaniel Hawthorne*, volume 17. Columbus: Ohio State University Press.

Lang, Amy Schrager. 2003. *The Syntax of Class: Writing Inequality in Nineteenth-Century America.* Princeton: Princeton University Press.

Lott, Eric. 1994. "White Kids and No Kids at All: Languages of Race in Antebellum U.S. Working-Class Culture." In *Rethinking Class: Literary Studies and Social Formations*, ed. Wai Chee Dimock and Michael T. Gilmore, 175–211. New York: Columbia University Press.

Marx, Leo. 1956. "The Machine in the Garden." *New-England Quarterly* 29.1: 27–42.

Murphy, Emily. n.d. "Nathaniel Hawthorne's Salem." Pamphlet produced by the National Park Service and the Salem Maritime National Historic Site.

Newbury, Michael. 1997. *Figuring Authorship in Antebellum America.* Stanford: Stanford University Press.

Newman, Lea Bertani Vozar. 1979. *A Reader's Guide to the Short Stories of Nathaniel Hawthorne.* Boston: G. K. Hall.

Roediger, David R. 1991. *The Wages of Whiteness: Race and the Making of the American Working Class.* London: Verso.

10

Experiments in Reality: Wyckoff's *Workers*

Jonathan Prude

A little more than a century ago, in the warm July of 1891, a young man named Walter Wyckoff—the son of Protestant missionaries and by all indications thoroughly middle class, a recent college graduate and current student at Princeton Theological Seminary—put on an "old suit," bid a cordial dawn farewell to the butler of a Connecticut home he was visiting, and set forth to explore first-hand the situation of low-ranking unskilled workers or (as he termed it in commencing his investigation) "the labor problem" of late-nineteenth-century America (Wyckoff 1897, 2–4). Over the next year and a half he crossed the United States in his rough workingman's costume. Picking up jobs as he could, traveling mostly by foot, he moved steadily westward, traversing southern New York, crossing Pennsylvania, pausing in Chicago, and then continuing all the way on to California, finishing up in San Francisco in February 1893. He then shed his disguise and, after more traveling (this time abroad), returned east, undertook more studies (this time in secular subjects), and in the late 1890s joined the Princeton faculty in political economy. But he also took steps to craft a written record of his trek through the Republic. Articles in *Scribners* were followed by books, with a small collection of reminiscences appearing in 1901. By that point, however, he had already turned out the major statement he would make on his odyssey: the richly detailed, and amply illustrated, two-volume sequence entitled, respectively, *The Workers: An Experiment in Reality—The East* (1897) and *The Workers: An Experiment in Reality—The West* (1898).[1]

Attracting plentiful reviews upon their publication, the twinned installments of *The Workers* have been cited through the years by scholars who have gratefully mined their pages for informative vignettes of fin de siècle laboring sorts. And taken together, such initial and subsequent attention has assured Wyckoff (who died prematurely in 1908 at the age of forty-two) a modest yet firm place in the historical record. But that much noted, there may now be reason to take a fresh look at what Walter Wyckoff wrote about what he experienced. At this moment of heightened concern and debate over the "labor problem" of our own day—both the difficulties roiling America's domestic political economy and the reverberations of the nation's socioeconomic policies for working people throughout the world—at this post-"Seattle" moment, it may make sense to consider *The Workers* anew. Why? Not because what Wyckoff said about America of his era provides specific blueprints for coping with the here and now. Rather, it is because pondering the here and now properly includes considering *how* to do such pondering, and because this kind of self-reflecting perspective can benefit from reviewing earlier surveys of American society—including Wyckoff's "experiment" in surveying-through-immersion.

But if Wyckoff's present-day relevance frames this discussion, my central goal in what follows is to probe Wyckoff's text itself, to account for his account of his journey. And in the space available, this entails focusing on three topics: first, the context surrounding his expedition; second, the way he represents his project, his relations to workers, and his own persona in the pages of his chronicle; and third, the extent to which he actually confronts and responds to "the labor problem" he aimed to illuminate by his walk across the land.

So, to begin, what were the precedents and contemporary developments that provided context for Wyckoff's down-dressed tour?

He may have had several inspirations. Cast as the story of a lengthy trip, Wyckoff could have drawn on the tradition of travel narratives published in and about the nineteenth-century United States. Then too, the "experiment" label lodged in the subtitle of *The Workers* could have been responsive to prior instances of Americans implementing (or at least asserting) plans to revise their lives: Thoreau's sojourn at Walden Pond, for example, or the campaign Franklin announces in his *Autobiography* to attain perfection.

Bearing more directly on Wyckoff's venture, however, were certain long-standing undertakings to observe and deal with laboring people from positions more or less outside their ranks. In their antebellum versions, such undertakings included efforts to supervise chattel slaves, to oversee waged "hands" of early industrial workplaces, and to monitor the often lower-ranked inmates of various asylums. But especially after 1820, and especially in the North, outside-in interactions with working sorts began to involve other kinds of dealings with some of the most hard-pressed members of America's free laboring population in settings where they lived and worked: with employees in the early sweat shops, say, or with inhabitants of the protoslums, like New York's notorious Five Points district, beginning to surface in the pre-1861 Republic. Those pursuing these further engagements with the working poor ranged from tourists seeking only the frisson of coming face to face with misery to policemen striving to control the wayward behavior misery supposedly fostered. But no less frequently, these encounters with the free needy in streets and garrets recruited journalists who (joined by some tourists) sought to understand the poor and to broadcast their plight to respectable members of society. Or again, those choosing to interact with the lower strata of laboring folk in situ included members of assorted, often religiously energized reform and charity societies — individuals who might staff settlements among the poor, whose writings about the destitute were often cast as morality tales infused with "spiritual" rather than empirical truth, but who in any event were committed to aiding and uplifting the unfortunate.[2]

But washing over many of these post-1820 initiatives, and supplementing the motives driving them, were two other reasons for dealing with less well-off antebellum laboring folk. First, attending to the poor permitted better-off types, perhaps above all members of the emergent northern middle class, to forge clarifying comparisons: to affirm who they were by confronting who they were not. Second, dealing with the working poor allowed respectable folk (and again probably the emergent northern middle class in particular) to offset gathering anxieties about the hollowness of America and Americans. At a time of advancing (albeit unevenly distributed) urbanization, immigration, industrialization, and commercialization, and at a time, too, of rising calls for individuals to remake themselves in the service of upward social mobility—amid such circumstances, there arose concern that the Republic might be nothing *but* transformation and ambiguous transiency, and that its citizens might be only transient husks, insincere confidence men lacking any stable core. These worries were not all-controlling. Richard Henry Dana's well-known sojourn before the mast demonstrates real-life antebellum willingness to "pass" among the lesser orders. So also, tropes of disguise and mistaken identity pegged at various degrees of acceptability (or at least amusement) remained present in both highbrow and middlebrow literature; and they ran as well through folk customs and developing structures of cheap commercialized entertainment, from fiction to theatrics (including minstrelsy), appealing heavily (though not exclusively) to lower-ranked audiences. Still, numbers of antebellum nonworking folk did worry about hollowness. And for them dealing with the poor offered respite. For notwithstanding the disturbing scenes they might come upon, those trolling through Five Points could take satisfaction from having peeked behind the glitter of Broadway and discovering what they could declare to be the real underlying truth of New York. And (if they did some investigating) they could draw comparable satisfaction from laying bare this or that pauper's core character. Every bit as important, antebellum regarders of the poor could strike blows against insincerity by avoiding masquerading as the lowly. They could, that is, demonstrate their own firm and legible interiority by presenting themselves as every bit the middle and upper-class figures they truly were.[3]

Wyckoff was heir to all this. But he was also affected by the swirl of dealings in his own postbellum time between working and nonworking people. The growth of national markets and styles of mass consumption meant that laboring folk were now increasingly remarked and targeted by manufacturers, retailers, and advertisers aiming to produce and sell "stuff," from ready-made clothing to movies, to plebeian customers. From appreciably different angles, the frequently unsettling reverberations generated by new infusions of women, immigrants, and former slaves into the wage labor force, together with mounting acknowledgments of slums, harsh workplaces, and increasingly frequent and violent confrontations between employees and employers — in sum, the ramifying stirrings of the post-Civil War "labor problem"—produced their own interactions with working people. Tourists continued to frequent poor neighborhoods (and, indeed, now proceeded to visit newly established exhibitions of "model" worker homes and laboring sites). But equally notable, companies and unions put forward newly elaborated and competing views of workers, even as police, overseers, and company guards mobilized to establish strengthened watch over militant workers. What is more, journalists launched amplified investigations of the "other half," building on earlier treatments to generate newly dense bundles of sensationalist inquiries. At the same time, social workers, becoming more typically female and conjoining religiosity with increasing professionalization, multiplied their connections with the poor (not least by raising the number of slum-sited settlement houses). And emergent, purportedly scientific, and — not incidentally — typically male social researchers offered widening streams of increasingly systematic analyses of marginal American workers and (doubtless influenced by vanguard anthropological studies) these workers' alien ways. So too, there were the experiments by Jacob Riis and Lewis Hine to take cameras into tenements and workplaces. And there were the provocative decisions by certain fiction writers, joined by certain painters and printmakers, to reach for freshly articulated realism by engaging the lowest rungs of America's postbellum inhabitants.[4]

All in all, and leaving aside the unions' presentations, the late nineteenth and early twentieth centuries witnessed burgeoning and multitracked undertakings (actually evident in Europe as well as the United States) of society's better sorts to encounter those below. And one can detect running through these encounters amplified projects in exploring and publicizing the plight of lesser ranks, in comforting and relieving the needy, and — significantly — in upper-ranked self-definition. For now more complexly and extensively than ever, nonworking folk sought to define themselves — their class, gender, racial, and at times (through notions of erotically exotic poor folk) even sexual identities — by interacting with lower ranks.[5]

But with these crescendos came a change. For post-1865 top-down engagements with working people were accented by substantial shifts in earlier programs of offsetting hollowness. Doubtless due to the era's expanded marketeering, the producerist values of making and saving hitherto foregrounded in American culture had begun giving way to consumerist priorities of spending, leisure, and self-fulfillment. Which in turn led certain groups, especially among the educated and well-off, to feel (or at least to adopt rhetorics of feeling) that they, personally, were rooted less in production than in purchased accessories and hence that they, in practice, *were* hollow: that they were less expressions of firm centers than gestures of the moment, sequences of masks. And there arose a corollary belief that reality itself was growing elusive. Important social knowledge might still turn on stripping back surfaces to discover undergirding truths. But insofar as truth might well seem, like onion skins, to peel endlessly down to nothing, it was reckoned the real had to be grasped as much as deduced, asserted and experienced as much as derived from data.[6]

Admittedly, the novelty of this recalibration was softened by the way it progressed alongside ongoing evocations of mis-appearances and ambiguity in art and entertainment. Conversely, the force of the change was dampened by the fact that imputations of hollowness still stung. It may have been more common to regard masks and onion skins as intrinsic to modern life, but it was also the case, not least among the sophisticated and better-off of America's citizenry, that lacking stable reality and firm personal centers were disquieting propositions. If hollowness was inevitable, it nonetheless had to be dealt with, navigated around.

Still, the net result was that within the nonworkers' post-1865 involvements with lesser sorts, acts of passing had substantially greater currency. At one level (evident even before Wyckoff's journey), police and company operatives were more prone to go undercover to spy out troublesome workers. It likewise grew more common for journalists to travel "incognito" into slums to secure sensational scoops and (what sometimes overlapped such journalism) for fiction writers mining inspiration from the lowly — Jack London and Stephen Crane, for example — to pose as poor. But at a level more immediately relevant to *The Workers*, people of Wyckoff's stripe — middle- and upper-class educated types — felt newly emboldened to use masks in mounting distinctive "experiments": plumbings into American society that were about learning (not spying), were sober (not journalistically sensationalist), and factual (not explicitly fictional); but nonetheless plumbings that allowed them to combat the wispiness of reality by actively seizing "life." Reflecting the abiding discomfort of hollowness, disguises and adventurous experiences were billed as merely temporary interludes in an investigator's career. Still, in the years following Wyckoff's journey, in fact from the 1890s up through the 1920s, scores of men and women, the bulk of them with college diplomas and of comfortable or prosperous standing, donned one or another species of "old suit," undertook stressful (occasionally risky) stints among workers, including poor workers, and then resurfaced to offer pronouncements. Enclosing disparate interpretations, the expositions of these actor-observers shared the common denominator of real-life role-playing.[7]

Wyckoff, in other words, helped trigger a particular and significant cohort of social commentators. As much as anyone, he led the way for a sizable band of pretend domestic servants and waitresses, temporary steelworkers, miners, and hoboes. And Wyckoff's *Workers* thus emerges as a launching installment in a varied but identifiable literature. As much as any text, it spawned a genre that reverberated strongly for some three decades: a mode of inquiry that, though fading after 1930, has enjoyed compelling after-echoes in works like George Orwell's *Down and Out in Paris and London* (1933), John Howard Griffin's *Black Like Me* (1960) and, the most recent articulation of so-called down-and-out writing, Barbara Ehrenreich's current bestseller *Nickel and Dimed: On (Not) Getting By in America* (2001).

Thus the context surrounding *The Workers*, the contours of Wyckoff's historical niche. But what are the contours of what he wrote? How does the substance of *The Workers* mesh with or diverge from these framing influences? And indeed what, given these adherences and divergences, *is* the substance of this work? How (to move to move to the second topic in our review) does Wyckoff represent his undertaking, his associations with laboring people, and himself in his text?

In some respects, his characterization of his project is predictable. Endorsing the trope of disguise, he also endorsed the eagerness among many of his peers to seize life by the throat — in his case by sharing the often hand-to-mouth lives of low-tiered casual unskilled workers. Hence he presents his venture as an effort to confront "social questions" not through "slender, book-learned lore" but through an "intimate familiarity with practical affairs," through the manly ordeal (as he generally labels it) of securing "vital knowledge" anchored in "the truth of actual experience." In designating his project along these lines, however, Wyckoff situates his perspective in other ways as well. He is clear about wanting to learn about laboring folk. And inasmuch as he digs into the

American social structure to bring his readers (by all signs as nonworking-class as himself) accounts of people largely unknown to them, Wyckoff simultaneously retains the possibility of educating his audience and the notion of knowing-by-uncovering. But his generally calm voice and his insistence on the factual basis of his investigation illustrate how he also separates *The Workers* (and sets the precedent for distinguishing most subsequent down-and-out narratives) from hyperventilating journalistic exposés and from both earlier moralizing tracts and the tales of authors like Crane and London. Then too, though "eager for a place among original investigators," he concedes he has little in common with the budding corps of rigorous researchers. For better or worse, his are the essentially spontaneous reflections of a young naif drawn into the thick of things by his "interest in life." In fact, part of why he repeatedly insists on the manliness of his trek is probably that, declining in join the brotherhood of social scientists, and (it might have been thought) coming perilously close to the musings of female social workers, he must prove his virility through the effortfulness of his inquiry (Wyckoff 1897, vii–ix; 1898, 83; 1901, Preface [n.p.]).

As he represents himself enmeshed in "vital knowledge," so he often depicts his contacts with workers as vigorously empathetic. Wyckoff's narrative rings with insistence that his brushes with laboring folk are intensely personal. As such, he sharply distinguishes his expedition from the ongoing sightseeing tours through poor districts by gawking visitors and from comparably disengaged sessions with carefully modeled demonstrations of lower-ranked life. A powerful passage in *Workers* captures the resentment Wyckoff feels when he and other workers are made objects of such spectating. "[A]s they stood there," Wyckoff writes of the well-heeled onlookers, "eying at leisure, as though it were exhibited for their diversion, this company of homeless, ragged, needful men, there was to my mind a deliberate insult . . . sharper than the sting of a blow in the face" (Wyckoff 1898, 87). In contrast to such distancing, Wyckoff asserts proximity. Certainly he asserts accumulating awareness of ethnic fissures among workers, of divisions between tramps and other laborers, of divides separating unskilled and skilled laborers, and of the trenchant contrast between generally benign situations of workers in labor-scarce rural areas and the tougher prospects facing unskilled workers in crowded urban labor markets. And while, for Wyckoff, this deepened knowledge carries no hint of sexual contact, it frequently implies comradeship. He takes up companions on the road and to share hardships. He lodges with working farmers and befriends several. He is proud of doing physical labor, intermittently sheds his nonworker name (becoming "John" and "Major"), writes "we" in describing workers' attitudes, and includes illustrations showing him grafted seamlessly among fellow laborers (see fig. 10.1). He punches a factory porter mistreating a laborer and, trading on the manliness he ascribes to his journey, claims that upon meeting Pennsylvania loggers he "[i]nstinctively . . . [knows] these men for men." He declines to acknowledge nonworker friends he spots and, at the end of the trail, upon reaching California, concedes "a vague unwillingness" to discard his disguise (Wyckoff 1897, 38–39, 156–157, 60, 36, 241, 66, 200, 77; 1898, 263, 1, 366–373, 40–85, 288, 134–135, 376).

Figure 10.1: Wyckoff (far right foreground) appears as one among many day laborers (their ethnic diversity punctuated by the presence of an African American) trudging back from work, in this illustration of his stint at West Point, New York

Yet Wyckoff also reveals limits to his connections with working people. To start with, the laborers Wyckoff encounters are overwhelmingly white male Christians. Blacks are almost completely absent from *Workers*, Jews go largely unmentioned, and, except for chance contacts with Chicago prostitutes, women appear only as wives and boardinghouse matrons. Just as important, Wyckoff is frequently put off by the rough and (to him) immoral behavior of laborers: their chronic swearing especially distresses him. By the same token, and supplementing his inclination to delve below surfaces, he applies antebellum notions of physiognomy and phrenology (accented by postbellum belief in the special legibility of criminal temperament) to link distaste for plebeian physical appearances with inferences of unsavory interiors. In truth, he is now and again disgusted by the species-level differentness he detects. "[T]heir hideous ugliness of face, [is] unreclaimed by marks of inner strength and force, but reveal[s] rather . . . a deepening in the lines of weakness. . . . [H]ow widely severed from all things human is the prevailing type!" Yet neither is Wyckoff always eager to surrender his own "otherness." He succumbs to binge reading at a library and is occasionally irritated that his inner qualities (and education) are not recognized through his disguise. He makes prearranged stops to fetch letters from home, takes breaks to write, and steps out of character long enough to attend the National Republican Convention in Minneapolis (Wyckoff 1897, 213–214, 140–141, 123–124; 1898, 38, 291).

150

At some points in *The Workers*, these signals of separateness come so thick and fast it is tempting to follow recent scholarship and conclude that, within the assorted self-definings attending upper-ranked dealings with lesser sorts in this period, a major goal of down-and-out writers, at least, was to establish apartness: that not unlike many slum-visiting better sorts of antebellum times, post–Civil War figures like Wyckoff tilted toward setting themselves in contrast to those below.[8] But actually what Wyckoff demonstrates is that the act of passing, at least as he experiences it, entails a persistent melding of closeness and distance, a continuing inclination both to embrace unskilled workers and keep them at arm's length — a finely balanced dance of alignment and disengagement that powerfully flavors *The Workers* and, in the event, rounds out how Wyckoff's text fits within its context.

Thus, from one side, inasmuch as his narrative departs from "scientific" and rigorous social science commentaries, so his identification with unskilled workers are too intense to allow his devolving into anything like policing or spying. From the other side, however, he concedes that his very ability to return at any time to Princeton means he can never be totally one with his workmates or totally comprehend their situation. For "between me and the actual workers was the infinite difference of necessity," and what he learns can consequently at best total only "the slenderest knowledge of their lives." Indeed, Wyckoff reports that the acceptance he usually meets from laboring folk comes despite their usually quick realization (from his speech, from his soft hands and clumsiness) that he is not fully their kind. Now and then Wyckoff finds this unbridgeable differentiation from the lower ranks, and the resulting imprecision of his findings, highly frustrating — even to the point of tempting him to call off his trip before reaching the Pacific. Yet he keeps going. And as he does so, the separateness he feels effectively protects him from the danger sometimes voiced about better sorts living among lesser ranks: the risk of going native (Wyckoff 1898, 82–84, 149, 376; 1897, 21, 73; 1901, 51–52).[9]

But ultimately it is exactly his bifurcated position, his constant interweaving of attachment and disjuncture, that pays the largest dividends. For as he sets about within *The Workers* (as in effect he does) to show how nonworkers might face lower ranks with properly calculated sympathy (how they might alloy empathy with corrective distance and distance with modulating empathy),[10] Wyckoff strengthens his ability to participate relatively comfortably in contemporary conjurings with masks and onion skins. Put more concretely, he makes himself into someone who shares the growing acceptance among educated nonworkers of transient identities and fluid reality and yet, coincidentally, into someone who acknowledges, and steers through, the discomfort that often came from grapplings with these features of postbellum culture. Who, in the final analysis, *is* Walter Wyckoff inside his writings? He is a figure who willingly uses the opportunity to change shapes and willingly endorses the presumption that knowing what's real can involve doing real things. But he is likewise a figure who concedes the temporary and often weird "unreality" of the game he is playing as well as the limited information it yields. More than that, Wyckoff inside *The Workers* is a figure who, just because he does stand among and yet aloof from working people, can claim the solid persona of *being* a writer who self-consciously "experiments" with masks and with assembling fragmented personal experiences into glimpses of how things really are. Indeed, he is a figure whose very slipperiness marks his true position and class power. Because he is a writer whose place in the social order is of someone who can get away with putting on disguises and adopting multilayered attitudes through willful grabbings of reality (Wyckoff 1898, 90–91, 194; 1901, 45).[11]

Such, then, is how Wyckoff presents his undertaking, his links to laboring people, and himself, in *The Workers*. But building on this, what is his message about what he saw? What does he end up saying about the "labor problem" he voyaged out to explore?

Although scarcely mentioning economic downturns, Wyckoff unquestionably recognizes burdens that weighed upon unskilled workers. Thus, while rationalizing the joblessness he found in Chicago as simply the result of an overstocked urban labor market governed by supply and demand (and while concluding that laborers should help themselves by staying out of cities), Wyckoff acknowledges that the force of abstract economic laws in daily life gives lower ranks little reason to trust employers and little protection from facing "human adjustments . . . beyond all calculation." At times, moreover, he refers unhesitatingly to the enervating bleakness of much manual toil (from which "there seems to have been eliminated every element which constitutes the nobility of labor"). Even in the comparatively hospitable countryside, and even amid the fellowship of loggers, he hears the sour note in an old man's quip: "We don't have to work; we can starve." And a raw scene in Chicago (framed in an arrestingly dramatic illustration; see fig.10.2) captures the relentless pressure generated by low wages spawned by too few jobs. "What time have we to keep clean," Wyckoff reports a garment worker shouting at a health inspector, "when it's all we can do to get bread? Don't talk to us about disease; it's *bread* we're after, *bread*!" (Wyckoff 1897, 61–67, 261; 1901, 46; 1898, 246 [emphasis in original]).

This much Wyckoff documents. But it's all left undeveloped. And much the same holds true for the remedies he advances. Early on he proposes a loose blending of self-motivated work groups, semi-Darwinian natural selection, quasi-militaristic hierarchy, and proto-Progressive expert-driven order. Industry, he suggests, should be organized into bonus-rewarded gangs or, better, into units administered by those "fittest to lead" and devoted to the common good, with the expectation those "fit to follow" would respond by laboring in "manly . . . obedience." But this is not taken very far. Nor for that matter, despite mingling with socialists, anarchists, and union members, does Wyckoff show enthusiasm for challenging, or even tweaking, extant institutions of private property, business structures, or government. And here and there he extends this reluctance to middle and upper classes overall, surmising these Americans would do more to aid the working poor if—but only if—they are shown charity congruent with "their practical business sense of things" (Wyckoff 1897, 67–76; 1898, 210–236).

Wyckoff, it seems clear, had only limited interest in directly promoting change. In fact, a further way he locates himself amid the other responses to laboring sorts billowing around him and again sets a precedent for many later down-and-out authors, was to *not* associate himself with social workers, charity advocates, or radical groups. Yet Wyckoff was a sensitive soul. And if he chooses to avoid wrestling head-on with the harsher dimensions of what he re-

Figure 10.2: Depiciting the terrible anguish of Chicago garment workers, this print is among the more explicitly stark graphics Wyckoff included in *The Workers*

ports, he does try to soften their impact. One strategy is to suggest that bad news is really not so bad. Thus his contention that urban deprivation is offset by rural plenitude. Thus too, the glimpses he passes along of individual kindnesses cushioning even brutal city streets (of policemen, for example, aiding the poor and wayward). And thus his summary vision that infelicities of production have largely given way to the "subtler," and surely solvable, difficulties of distribution: that while problems of poverty, bloated wealth, and undigested foreigners comprise "awful sores upon the body politic," the wounds are not lethal and "the sun never shone" upon a nation more primed to succeed. Another strategy for blunting bad tidings is to affirm the possibility of economic and characterological advancement. He insists that with pluck and determination most workers (even lowly tramps) can ascend the occupational ladder. And he maintains that no matter how wretched or morally degraded they might be, virtually all laborers possess "the vital power of [moral] return" and the ability to regain wholesome lives (Wyckoff 1898, 91, 377, 320; 1901, 37, 191; 1897, 245).

But we need to remark another ingredient playing into Wyckoff's response to what he witnessed: his residual Christianity. Having left seminary life, he does not commit himself to a single denomination or to constant preaching. Still, he repeatedly attends (and every so often leads) church services; and he regularly embarks on a kind of religious outreach at least roughly parallel to other strands of Christian activism in his time he feels broadly stirred to alert "fellow-workers" to enough of God's teachings to ease their distress. What mainly resulted from Wyckoff's preserve of spirituality, however, is his strengthened belief in the diffusion of admirable human attributes. Wyckoff's abiding faith fuels confidence that practically everyone, including unskilled workers, shares

abiding threads of integrity, dignity, and hope. It is because they foster awareness of this virtuous commonality, this "deepening sense of brotherhood," that
churches appeal to Wyckoff, just as it is through their support of such leavening
camaraderie that Socialists acquire "their greatest strength and charm." And
once posited, of course, this faith in pervasive marrows of virtue gives Wyckoff
an added way to cope with hollowness. For it lets him share in the utility of disguise and the excitement of catching reality on the run while remaining convinced people possess at least elements of a fundamental core: indications, at
least, of a dependable center congruent with a Truth altogether enveloping, en-
during, and real.

Yet overall, the most substantial effect of Wyckoff's belief in meritorious interiors is precisely to soften the harsher portions of what he reports. After all,
the praiseworthy qualities he finds within these individuals are qualities bound
to support their efforts to advance. But the presence of these qualities also suggests that, even absent upward socioeconomic advancement, the lowliest of
Americans possess luminous potential. In this way he can simultaneously register and evade the stern reality of class in postbellum America. And he can go
further in squaring the circle between his countervailing sense of distance from
and proximity to lower ranks. Because if the outer "ugliness" of workers can be
read as phrenologically coding their separation "from all things human," it can
also disclose what Wyckoff presumably admires and identifies with: the "beauty
of . . . strong lines" redolent of "honest work faithfully done and . . . pain and sorrow bravely born!" Or again: Just as the apparent obesity of a vagrant turns out
to arise from layers of apparel, so might both this man's offputting "filthy outer
covering" and his inner clothing together be reckoned to encrust "a human being, . . . a man, a living soul created by the Almighty" (Wyckoff 1897, 219–220,
264–268; 1898, 210, 112, 131, 88–89).

Wyckoff signals his pious confidence in underpinning moral vitality throughout *The Workers*. But his position on this front builds as his journey progresses.
As Wyckoff moves west — as he moves, that is, closer to the invigorating echoes
of the Frontier — he increasingly stresses the country's splendid promise. He
becomes more persuaded that the Civil War has inspired a unified commitment
toward becoming a great and just society and that all Americans, immigrants
included, are joined into this magnificent errand. Hence, the final reason he can
place himself both near and apart from working people is that he can balance
apartness against prideful claims that he and laborers share residence in the Republic. And the final reason he can forgo advancing formal reformist solutions
to the problems he notices is that he can rely on the country's inbuilt trajectory
toward higher and better prospects.

Blithely ignoring issues of citizenship and naturalization, he becomes ever
more certain as the Pacific heaves into sight that to live in America is to be American, and that to be American means sharing glorious possibilities. It means joining a basically fair society in which "rewards" do mostly go to "energy and thrift
and perseverance and ability." It means joining "a growing, intelligent, industrious, God-fearing people . . . slowly working out great ends in industrial achievement and personal character and in national life." Indeed, although *The Workers*
never enters the category of morality tracts, his coda does take on characteris-

tics of a spiritually colored patriotic parable recited, reassuringly, back to his readers; a mission, one might almost say, to the middle class. For at the end of the day, the Christian-touched spirit of "brotherhood" Wyckoff perceives underlying people across the nation is pretty much the spirit of Americans coming "year by year to a fuller consciousness of national life and of the glorious mission of high destiny." To dwell in America—whether as disguised traveler or unskilled worker—is to hear a "summons to live worthy of the name and calling of an American" (Wyckoff 1898, 376–378, 319–321).

How should we assess *The Workers*? There is no neat answer. Even in his own time, Wyckoff's lack of social science rigor provoked criticism.[12] In fact, this critique signaled a divide between knowing by experience and knowing by more "objective" methodologies, which may actually have prolonged uncertainty about what was real and how to know it. And it was also this critique that probably caused investigations by fake workers to tail off after the 1920s, while causing such inquiries of this sort as were launched after 1830 to be viewed more as belles lettres than as reliable social research. Nor are we today immune from dissatisfactions. Wyckoff's drumbeat emphasis on manliness can grow tedious, while his stress on the good news embedded in America, and particularly his city-on-the-hill conclusion, can strike modern readers as curiously at odds with the destitution he himself discovered along the way. So too, Wyckoff's failure ever to consider the propriety of even trying to fool laborers with an "old suit," or for that matter his unwillingness to probe more deeply into what workers thought of him, into the byways of their discontent, or into whether they themselves may have utilized disguises — all this can leave current readers hungry for a George Orwell or a Babara Ehrenreich, writers whose approach might lack systematically marshaled data but whose prose features antiseptic self-irony and capacious curiosity.

On the other hand, we have Wyckoff's role in initiating the post-1890 brigade of commentators in camouflage. And we have his useful details of postbellum laboring life. What is also true, and what returns us here at the end to the framing links between Wyckoff and the present, is that reading *The Workers* does help us think about how to think about current events. Certainly it helps us understand that the "globalization" we presently hear so much about is not so much new as newly inflected. Because although it is plain that twenty-first–century America relies on blends of immigrant labor and industrial workers stationed abroad, Wyckoff's narrative makes it clear that the economy of his own time required a national workforce heavily supplemented by laborers recruited literally from around the world.

But the deepest lesson Wyckoff offers for considering how to consider our Seattle-shadowed moment is simply the example of his exposition. In this regard, the very distance we may feel from his text can clarify our relation to our own milieu. Yet it is hardly less important that Wyckoff's *Workers* models the importance of facing the world with a "realism" that ultimately turns less on an "old suit" than on being at least open to gauging the weight even (?) liberal capitalistic democracies impose on those toiling for their benefit.

Notes

1. Wyckoff [1901] 1971. Biographical information on Wyckoff is from the *Dictionary of American Biography* (1928–36). Since the 1901 volume was based on the same 1891–93 trek as underlay *The Workers*, I have generally treated *Day with a Tramp* as part of *The Workers* text. And as another procedural convenience, I am using the separate copyright dates of *The Workers'* two volumes (rather than their shared formal publication date of 1898) to facilitate distinguishing between them in the citations that follow.

2. See Blumin 1990; Boyer 1978, chs. 1–7; and Stansell 1986, esp. 30–37, 63–75.

3. Halttunen 1982, esp. chs. 1–2; Blumin 1989. Dana [1840] 1964; Roediger 1991, ch. 6. Stansell 1986, 63–75.

4. For glimpses into the large literature on these assorted interactions with post-Civil War working people see Boyer 1978, chs. 8–20; Ginzberg 1990; Greenwald and Anderson 1996; Nord 1983; Pittenger 1997; Tone 1997; Walkowitz 1999; Zurier, Snyder, and Mecklenburg 1995.

5. See Kovan 2004.

6. This paragraph distills (and simplifies) arguments advanced in Lears 1983, esp. 3–17.

7. See Crane's "Experiment in Misery" and "Experiment in Luxury" (both originally published in 1894 and both further possible sources for Wyckoff's subtitle), in Gullason 1963. Jack London, "South of the Slot," from *The Strength of the Strong* (1914). See, too, London's nonfiction *People of the Abyss* (1903); and the supposedly nonfictional work of racial "passing," Johnson 1912. Other representative titles from this literature are found in citations in Pittenger 1997.

8. This is the central argument of Pittenger 1997.

9. Ibid., 43.

10. In fact, concern over how properly to balance the separating and attracting forces of "sympathy" go back to the eighteenth and early nineteenth centuries. See Halttunen 1995.

11. In a sense, Wyckoff's demonstration of his superiority by temporarily mimicking inferior figures may be seen as transporting to another stage latent but well-grooved innuendoes of blackface minstrelsy. For minstrelsy (which, we should bear in mind, continued into postbellum years) was not just about disguises. Considering its full cultural imprint, it was also a mechanism by which, notwithstanding never-stilled concern about false appearance, the authority of white Americans was paradoxically vested precisely in their capacity to put on and take off blackness, and in the ability to cross boundaries and announce racial ambivalences, which such skin-alterings proclaimed. See generally Lott 1993.

12. See Day 1899.

Works Cited

Blumin, Stuart M. 1989, *The Emergence of the Middle Class: Social Experience in the American City, 1790–1900*. New York: Cambridge University Press.

———, ed. 1990. *New York by Gas-Light and Other Urban Sketches by George G. Foster*. Berkeley: University of California Press.

Boyer, Paul S. 1978. *Urban Masses and Moral Order in America: 1820–1920* Cambridge: Harvard University Press.

Dana, Richard Henry Jr. [1840] 1964. *Two Years before the Mast: A Personal Narrative of Life at Sea*. Los Angeles: Ward Ritchie Press.

Day, A. M. 1899. "Reviews." In *Political Science Quarterly* 14 December: 699–703.

Ginzberg, Lori D. 1990. *Women and the Work of Benevolence: Morality, Politics, and Class in the Nineteenth-Century United States*. New Haven: Yale University Press.

Gullason, Thomas A., ed. 1963. *The Complete Short Stories and Sketches of Stephen Crane*. Garden City, N.Y.: Doubleday.

Greenwald, Maurine W., and Margo Anderson, eds. 1996. *Pittsburgh Surveyed: Social Science and Social Reform in the Early Twentieth Century*. Pittsburgh: University of Pittsburgh Press.

Halttunen, Karen, 1982. *Confidence Men and Painted Women: A Study of Middle-Class Culture in America, 1830–1870*. New Haven: Yale University Press.

———, 1995. "Humanitarianism and the Pornography of Pain in Anglo-American Culture." *American Historical Review* 100 (April): 303–334.

Johnson, James Weldon, 1912. *The Autobiography of an Ex-Colored Man*. Boston: Sherman French & Co.

Koven, Seth. 2004. *Slumming: Sexual and Social Politics in Victorian London*. Princeton: Princeton University Press.

Lears, T. J. Jackson. 1983. "From Salvation to Self-Realization: Advertising and the Therapeutic Roots of the Consumer Culture, 1880–1950." In Richard Wrightman Fox and T. J. Jackson Lears, eds., *The Culture of Consumption: Critical Essays in American History, 1880–1980*, 3–38. New York: Pantheon.

London, Jack. 1903. *People of the Abyss*. London: Macmillan.

———. 1914. *The Strength of the Strong*. New York: Macmillan.

Lott, Eric. 1993. *Love and Theft: Blackface Minstrelsy and the American Working Class*. New York: Oxford University Press.

Nord, Deborah Epstein, 1983. "The Social Explorer as Anthropologist: Victorian Travellers Among the Urban Poor." In William Sharpe and Leonard Wallock, eds., *Visions of the Modern City*, 118–130. New York: Columbia University, Heyman Center for the Humanities.

Pittenger, Mark. 1997. "A World of Difference: Constructing the 'Underclass' in Progressive America." *American Quarterly* 49 (March): 26–65.

Roediger, David R. 1991. *The Wages of Whiteness: Race and the Making of the American Working Class*. New York: Verso.

Stansell, Christine. 1986. *City of Women: Sex and Class in New York, 1789–1860*. New York: Knorf.

Tone, Andrea. 1997. *The Business of Benevolence: Industrial Paternalism in Progressive America*. Ithaca: Cornell University Press.

Walkowitz, Daniel. 1999. *Working with Class: Social Workers and the Politics of Middle-Class Identity*. Chapel Hill: University of North Carolina Press.

Wyckoff, Walter A. 1897. *The Workers: An Experiment in Reality — The East*. New York: Charles Scribner's Sons.

———, 1898. *The Workers: An Experiment in Reality — The West*. New York: Charles Scribner's Sons.

———. [1901] 1971. *A Day with a Tramp: And Other Days*. New York: Benjamin Blom.

Zurier, Rebecah, Robert W. Snyder, and Virginia M. Mecklenburg. 1995. *Metropolitan Lives: The Ashcan Artists and Their New York*. Washington, D.C.: National Museum of American Art; New York: Norton.

PART III: The Commons

These essays address the loss and the reclamation of literal and metaphorical common space in a "world for sale" — an issue of special importance to those historically excluded from the "public." Not surprisingly, then, they range in their focus from the "empty" land of the new republic to the "borderlands" of the Southwest to the contested space of schoolroom and city. Addressing the politics of possession, they present, in a variety of forms, conflicts between local and expansionist histories; they raise questions of "legitimate" ownership and query the legal and social assumptions by which these are adjudicated. Moreover, they scrutinize the American past and present to elucidate the shifting boundary between the public and the private, the citizen and the stranger, the owner and the interloper.

These discussions draw their critical frameworks from ecocriticism, from pedagogy, from scholarship on law and literature as well as from African American studies and the indigenous rights movement.

Photo by Bill Tichi and design by Tina Schrager

159

CHAPTER 11

Cooper and the Tragedy of the Commons

Dana D. Nelson

Waking Up with Seattle

No longer willing to wait passively for the increasingly negative results of corporate privatization, people across the world are demanding public input into the policies behind global economic change. To organize their resistance, they have increasingly taken up a term that has been deployed by social and environmental scientists along with corporate researchers, policy makers, and NGO activists: the commons.[1] Bollier usefully sumarizes the emerging concept of "the commons" as "the many resources we collectively own that are being mismanaged by government or siphoned away by corporations. Some commons are physical assets, such as the global atmosphere, ecosystems, clean water, wildlife and the human genome. Some commons are public institutions such as libraries, museums, schools and government agencies. Still other commons are social communities, such as the 'gift economies' of people who contribute their time and expertise to create valuable resources" (2004, 17). His definition highlights the scope of the human and natural commons — not just what we share in nonhuman nature but also what we build together as part of self-governing, democratic, learning communities. Free market capitalism's drive to fence, own, and patent for private profit ever more of the natural world extracts a huge value for corporations, and comes at a great cost to the environment, to human rights, and democratic possibility.

This drive to enclose is not unique to late twentieth-century capitalism. Economist Michael Perelman argues that the privatization or state management of what used to be locally or communally allocated resources is the founding strategy of capitalism — what Marx termed "primitive accumulation."[2] Perelman traces what he terms "the brutal process of separating people from their means of providing for themselves" (2000, 13) — the coercive impact game laws and enclosure had on seventeenth- and eighteenth-century peasants who traditionally had supplied a majority of their own household needs through hunting, farming, and foraging on the commons. He argues that classical political economists "actively advocated measures to deprive people of their traditional means of support" (2), noting that the small sector of society benefiting from this historical reorganization gained both from the wealth and privileges of the enclosed land they now kept for their own enrichment and pleasure and from the labor of the people who, no longer able to provision themselves, were driven to sell their time for wages.

Perelman brackets "primitive" to highlight how the term misleads by locating the practice "before." Emphasizing the centrality of such coercion to the ongoing accumulation and concentration of capital, he suggests that we might usefully consider it a mainstay of, not a precondition to, capitalist practice.

Studying today's corporate globalization, it is hard to ignore how well the concept captures fundamental tendencies in this new wave of "globalization": its enormous expansion and concentration of wealth in the hands of a tiny elite, its massive immiserization of many, many more.[3]

The American Colonies and Enclosure's Legacies

Some argue that modern capitalism would not have emerged without the expansion of wealth entailed by European colonization. This is another aspect of "primitive" accumulation with human costs for millions of indigenous Americans who were expropriated and subjugated, and millions of Africans who were imported to labor as slaves. Oddly, though, the British American colonies have traditionally been viewed as an exception to the coercive effects of poverty that characterized England during this period. Abundant with land and game, America was, as this story goes, the land of the "common man," where Western European peoples at least could claim life and land ownership unafflicted by poverty and want. Although this mythology has been prevalent since the early years of the colonies, historians since the 1960s have challenged it, turning attention toward the paupers and criminals forcibly brought under indenture to the colonies, the growing disparities of wealth that intensified during the eighteenth century, the emerging racism that intensified black enslavement and resulted in the western ghettoization of Native Americans, and the various class conflicts among whites that emerged around issues concerning access to land, title, debt systems and cash shortages, and taxation that drove the country toward revolution in ways the Founders did not favor.[4]

Acknowledging the environmental abundance of the Americas that allowed more Europeans access to some kind of land title, such historians highlight commonalities in North America with the kinds of pressures created by game laws and enclosure in England on the laboring and nonpropertied classes in the British American colonies and early United States. Their attention to questions about the commons both historically and today can help us learn in new ways from literature of the early nation, helping us consider struggles concerning the commons that precede our own.

For instance, James Fenimore Cooper's *Pioneers* (1823), which is analyzed by the myth/symbol critics as an account of the conflict between "nature and civilization" and by environmental critics as a depiction of man's inherent greed and wastefulness, becomes something more nuanced and complex when read with questions of the commons in mind. From the perspective of a critical (as opposed to celebratory) political economy, Cooper's novel, written in the 1820s and set in the 1790s, appears less simply timeless or mythic and more a carefully historicized account of how people constructed communal economies — for good and ill — on the frontier, and how they reacted to the imposition of more systematized ("modern") economies through the combined force of federal government and private capital. In this sense, the novel plots the formation of white capitalism as it moves across the frontiers of European empire.

Cooper's novel shows us commons traditions encountering forces of modernization: capital, federal government, and systematic management. The novel does not project alternatives to the modernization sweeping the eastern states in the early nation; in this sense Cooper may arguably echo biologist Garrett Hardin's controversial notion that the fate of the natural commons tends inevitably toward tragedy.[5] But he importantly does not share Hardin's sense that people are naturally selfish and acquisitive. Nor does he seem to agree with Hardin's hypothesis that systematized management and a system of laws will be the most beneficial way to allocate the natural and human/civic commons. The alternative traditions he sketches are, as we will see, ethically and politically problematic. But Cooper's novel does provide us with an account that at least argues, if it does not conclude, against the inevitability formulated by Hardin and gives us an important window into a functioning if imperfect local commons. This vision can provide some leverage against the idea that the only plan for averting "tragedy" is management from above, a surrendering of our right to self-governance.

Cooper on Community and the Commons

Cooper's first Leatherstocking novel begins with the problem of the commons: how the community negotiates individual access to limited natural resources. It's Christmas Eve. Judge Oliver Temple, owner of most of the land featured as the setting of the novel, has shot at a deer, hoping to supply his family with prized venison for dinner.[6] The deer comes down, but as two men emerge from the woods with smoking rifles, it is clear there is going to be a dispute. Deer may still be abundant in the late eighteenth-century New York, but it takes skill to bring one down. Of course, all the men who shot want to claim the skill. And Temple is tempted to claim ownership with or without skill: It is his land after all, it is Christmas Eve, and his pretty young daughter Elizabeth has just come home from boarding school. If ever a gentleman should be able to take privileges accorded to rank, it should be now.[7] So when the aged, ratty Natty Bumppo and the stranger, Oliver Edwards, argue that Temple's double barrel in all likelihood did not contribute to killing the deer, the Judge proceeds undaunted to act the part of the gentleman: He will pay for the privilege of the deer, graciously taking his cake by affording his social/economic inferiors to buy bread.

This makes Natty, a seventy-year-old trapper, a little cranky. He invokes his "lawful dues in a free country," grumbling against the idea that "might often makes right here, as well as in the old country" (20). When the Judge reminds him that it is only by his grace that Natty hunts here in the first place, Natty fires back: "There's them living who say, that Nathaniel Bumppo's right to shoot on these hills, is of older date than Marmaduke Temple's right to forbid him" (23). For Natty, the question of who gets the deer goes to a deeper issue, of alternative forms of "ownership" and the new forms marked by enclosure with its impact on a whole way of life: "The game is becoming hard to find indeed, Judge, with your clearings and betterments," he grumps.[8] Edwards likewise connects the deer to questions of land and ownership as he reveals that the some of the Judge's shot has lodged in his shoulder: "The injury is but slight and the bullet has missed the bones; but I believe, sir, you will now admit my *title* to the venison" (23, emphasis added).

The Judge — who comes from a mercantile Quaker and not an aristocratic background — continues insisting that aristocratic privileges come with his ownership of the vast tracts of land. Refusing to relinquish the deer, he makes an aristocrat's offer: Along with one hundred dollars in compensation for the deer, Temple promises Edwards that "I here give thee a right to shoot deer, or bears, or any thing thou pleasest in my woods forever. Leather-stocking is the only other man that I have granted the same privilege to; and the time is coming when it will be of value" (23). It will be of value because the land is being developed — cleared, fenced, and settled — and thus hunting grounds, hunting rights, and game are all becoming more scarce and, therefore, more valuable.

Here Judge Temple invokes what the staff of *The Ecologist* summarizes as the "race between growth and scarcity that growth creates" (1998, 5/7). This is a race propelled by the Judge himself, who, the narrator informs readers in the next chapter, has turned from mercantile enterprise to land acquisition and development after the Revolution. He's good at it, too: "his property increased in a tenfold ratio, and he was already ranked among the most wealthy and important of his countrymen" (35). Like many other land speculators, then, Temple has literally everything to gain from securing tenants and developing his town and county. His sidekick cousin, the indefatigable planner and Sheriff Richard Jones, administrates the developments, as he breathlessly recounts to Elizabeth the next day: "Everything depends on system, girl. I shall sit down this afternoon and systematize the county" (182).[9]

Natty's is the strongest voice of opposition to these managerial plans. When the Judge and the Sheriff appeal to the "dignity" of their laws as established tradition to fortify their own aims and interests (see, for example, 160), Natty objects to their rhetorical trick: "'Game is game, and he who finds may kill; that has been the law in these mountains for forty years, to my sartain knowledge; and I think one old law is worth two new ones . . . your titles and your farms are all new together,' cried Natty; 'but laws should be equal and not more for one than the other'" (160–161). This is an important moment in the novel. Critics have habitually figured Natty as taking a stand against society. Either they figure him as an iconic individual opposed to civilization or as representative of the Lockean State of Nature where individuals operate intuitively on their own divine sense of fairness until the pressures of property accumulation drive them to form a social contract and enter the State of Civilization, where they agree to be governed by civil law.

But Natty's comments here do not support such a reading. Specifically, his invocation of prior laws — ones to which he is willing to subscribe — counters these habitual readings of his opposition to society and law. Natty's comments about the Judge replacing one prior set of laws with another suggests that there is no such antecedent, a lawless vacuum the Judge's civil law fills. Rather, he suggests that the Judge's laws replace by fiat one vision of lawful community with another. His objection to the Judge is not a prepolitical objection, as many critics have assumed. It is fully invested in the question of *who* governs. Natty is questioning where good governance comes from: formal federal or state laws influenced by lawmakers with major propertied interests, or those communally negotiated by the residents of a particular community.

Judge Temple wants to replace Natty's political challenge with the finality of a legal decision. His subsequent judgment on Natty in court depicts the latter as having behaved lawlessly, as being, therefore, against the law. His cousin the Sheriff has already declared him an "out-law" (360). Critics have generally, if regretfully, followed the Judge's and Sheriff's perspective in their reading of the novel. From myth/symbol critics and ecocritics to Brook Thomas's brilliant legal reading of the novel, critics concur, despite other significant differences, that the novel exemplifies "the conflict between the individual and the law that so many Americans have felt" (1984, 87), a conflict, as Thomas terms it later in this essay, between "Natty and society" that Cooper is "unable to resolve" (1984, 110).[10] Thomas and I share a critical project of exploring literature for the ways it might help us expand our sense of democratic possibility today. My argument with him turns on a minor detail, supporting his project: Cooper shows that Natty does not reject the laws he participates in helping to create — the laws-in-common negotiated by the residents of the world he lives in before the arrival of intensive capitalist speculation, real estate development, and federal order as imposed by Judge Temple.[11] It is that arrival *The Pioneers* narrates. Critics influenced by the myth/symbol school's insistence on the conflict between "man" and "civilization," or by Lockean contract theory, have oriented too many readers away from noticing that Natty is not asking to live outside the law. He rather seems to be questioning whose laws he has to abide with: the laws he gets to participate in creating, or the laws imposed by wealthy elites of state and nation.[12]

Thus, to return to the novel's opening scene: its importance develops in contrast to the formalized legal scene that comes later in the novel, when Natty is hauled to court and judged by Temple for shooting another deer — out of season. Here in this opening scene, the immediate actors argue before the eyes of their community (Elizabeth and Aggie) the disposition of the deer.[13] They do so without recourse to the formal rules of British common or U.S. statute law. Rather, they negotiate the fate of one particular common resource face to face, invoking competing traditions (like the coin flip of chance) and settling the dispute informally. The novel will repeatedly demonstrate that the results of these face-to-face, case-by-case adjudications are as morally and environmentally sound as judgments reached by the rules of formal law. But the novel also shows how local self-governance is losing out to newer rules of property and management principles. As much as the vanishing deer, common lands, Indians, and white frontiersmen, then, the right of residents to navigate and allocate their immediate resources among themselves is also a vanishing resource.

Laws-in-Common versus Common Law

The novel's focus from the outset is on local negotiation of resources and questions of fairness in the face of the global/national systematizing changes entailed by the political economy of the late colonies and early nation. Chapter 2 situates these changes by tracing the history between Effingham and Temple, one that maps familiar sociopolitical transitions of the West from feudalism into capitalism in the colonies. The son of a self-made Quaker who married up, Temple's mother's fortune allowed him to attend a better school than people of his class could typically afford. Marmaduke used this schooling to his advantage: He forms a friendship. This "fortunate connexion . . . paved the way to most of his future elevation in life" (29). His friend, Edward Effingham, underwrites

Marmaduke's entry into commercial enterprise, allowing him to build his fortune as a merchant. Then the revolution divides the friends. Just before the Battle of Lexington, Loyalist Effingham gives Temple his titles for safekeeping and leaves the colony. As the war progresses, communication between the two friends ceases, and Patriot Temple, occupied with civil service to his country, "never," the narrator comments, "seemed to lose sight of his own interests" (34). He snaps up the confiscated estates of the Royalists, including Effingham's, at bargain prices. And so we learn, it is Effingham's former holdings, now Temple's, that are the setting for the novel.[14]

Temple's post-Revolutionary activities—his development of "Temple's or Effingham's Patent" and his increasing command of labor earns him the position of judge. The courtroom scene where the Judge must set aside his fatherly partiality—his gratefulness to Natty for saving Elizabeth from a deadly panther—and impartially condemn Natty for killing a deer out of season and resisting arrest, develops its emotional resonance by contrast with the novel's other informal economies of justice: The Judge's impartial ruling feels painful to readers after they have witnessed the ability of a variety of residents to negotiate fair outcomes on their own.

For example, the turkey-shoot scene provides a comic and instructive setting to sketch the differences between communal law and procedural or formal law. Cooper idealizes neither, depicting the turkey shoot as a practice that takes everyone back to the days of the frontier—and, we might add, the days of the commons, when all were still free to take game: "It was connected with the daily practices of a people, who often laid aside the axe or the sithe [sic], to seize the rifle, as the deer glided through the forests they were felling, or the bear entered their rough meadows" (189). Three friendly rivals—Billy Kirby, Oliver Edwards, and Natty Bumppo—compete before the community to kill a turkey. A debate emerges when Natty's flint doesn't spark in his first attempt to fire. The free black citizen Abraham Freeborn ("Brom"), who owns the turkey, insists that Natty has fired and must pay again in order to shoot again. In response, Natty threatens to assault Freeborn.

This is a telling moment for the man who earlier had complained against Temple's use of superior might to win his point.[15] Natty's maneuver here, as well as the white crowd's ritualistic exclusion of Brom, who, as Doolen notes, can appeal to their "democratic sentiments" only by "debasing himself," has seldom tempered critics' enthusiasm for Natty's representation of natural law (145). It certainly highlights how locally negotiated self-governance can produce racist practices and unfair outcomes, and should caution us against overromanticizing or overgeneralizing about self-governance practices. Recognizing the racism and other forms of majoritarian exclusions that can result in local self-governance—and appreciating, for instance, U.S. federal intervention in those exclusionary practices—should not, however, prevent us from examining the value of local practices to expand our sense of a commons-like participatory democracy, and questioning the inevitability of its replacement with systems of top-down management.

In the end, Natty bags the turkey, Elizabeth pays Freeborn for it, and all but the Sheriff seem roughly satisfied. He sniffs: "there is an uncertainty about the rules of this sport, that it is proper I should remove. — If you will appoint a committee, gentlemen, to wait on me this morning, I will draw up, in writing, a set of regulations" (199). Jones muses that such activities should be banned by statute law; that perhaps they already are "indictable at common law" (200). The Sheriff wants to fix the game by banishing its self-managed informality — what I have called laws-in-common.

A less comic version of this conflict comes when Natty shoots a deer out of season. One morning, Natty's hounds chase up a buck that plunges into the lake. Unable to resist the physical and mental sport of spearing the buck as it swims, Natty disregards Edward's warnings against killing the buck. Working as a team, Chingachgook and Natty succeed: "So much for Marmaduke Temple's law" exalts Natty. He counters Temple's law with his own sense of the laws-in-common: "I know many that will relish the creater's steaks, for all the betterments in the land!" (302).

Natty still imagines he can negotiate within the terms of the laws-in-common, as we see when the troops attempt to bring Natty to "justice." Billy Kirby, deputized before he knew his mission, had scoffed at the idea that Natty would mount an armed resistance, and declared "he has as good a right to kill deer as any on the Patent" (337). Nevertheless, he agreed to present Natty with the warrant to search his cabin. This ups the stakes for Natty, who is helping Oliver's scheme to get his father's land back by hiding his grandfather in his cabin. He feels honor-bound to prevent the men from finding Major Effingham inside, and so comes to the door with his rifle. Startled, Kirby initiates a friendly negotiation, clearly assuming there is room to navigate in the "law" that Squire Doolittle declares unbending "for all" (337). In this negotiation, Natty offers to forego claiming the bounty for two panthers he has killed in saving Temple's daughter Elizabeth. "Well that's fair," Kirby proclaims, "he forgives the county his demand and the county should forgive him the fine; it's what I call and even trade and should be concluded on the spot" (339–340).

Billy Kirby's sense of fairness has been widely noted. It's also important that he and Natty assume throughout that they have a right to help make the law, and not just be judged by it. Later, when Kirby is sent to bring Natty in for escaping from jail, he will respond similarly to Natty's gambit to negotiate: "That's fair; and what's fair is right." His comment highlights how the Judge's formal law is not in fact inevitably fair or right, as the narrative underlines by associating it with Jones, Doolitle, and Jotham, who are deluded — and discredited — by a variety of ambitions. Natty repeatedly castigates this formal law for its "wasty ways," as when Kirby first shows him the warrant for his arrest: "Well, well," he says of Judge Temple, "that man loves the new ways and his betterments and his lands, afore his own flesh and blood" (339).

Tragedy of the Commons? or of Privatization?

The Pioneers is perhaps most famous for its scenes of overhunting: the pigeon hunt and the net fishing. Cooper balances these scenes with alternative philosophies, forwarding Natty, the novel's most "natural" white man, as a compelling conservationist who speaks at every opportunity against the greed that has emerged among casual hunters and market-oriented farmers. His commitment to subsistence leads Natty to denounce indiscriminate logging, clearing, and overhunting and fishing.

In biologist Garritt Hardin's famous thesis, it is man's competitive "nature" that leads to overuse and depletion of the commons. Cooper does not present these events as timeless (as Hardin would) but as rooted in a specific history. For instance, the novel presents peoples' behavior in the pigeon shoot through a range of historical discourses, frames, from colonialist violence and proletariat/agrarian recreation to aristocratic privilege. These historically specific registers suggest the scene's implication in the chain of events capably summarized by Alan Kulikoff (and worth quoting at length):

> The first migrants to our shores — *husbandmen* (a term for all those who worked the land, whether as tenants or owners), former husbandmen, and urban workers — had lived through the birth of English capitalism. Although feudal lords had coerced peasants into making extraeconomic payments, in return, peasants had controlled most of England's lands. During the sixteenth and seventeenth centuries, capitalist landlords had expropriated the lands of these peasants, renting the land to improving tenants. Forced into agricultural labor or into the urban work force, these new proletarians protested regularly, tearing down the hedges that enclosed common lands, flooding drained swamplands, rioting for a fair price for bread. In the revolution of the 1640s, they supported the radical democrats. Believing wage labor to be debased, they dreamed of regaining land they or their parents had lost.
>
> When they left England behind, the first white Americans of the seventeenth century carried with them a craving for independence from lordship and an ardor for secure control over land. These goals were difficult to achieve. (84–85)

Cooper's novel registers a keen awareness of the competing desires — the complexly different desires emerging from the same historical process — for private property that drove various classes of settlers in the colonies and early nation. *The Pioneers* shows the collision of these forces in scenes like the pigeon shoot, where settlers overreact to the prospect of scarcity that their own settlement will create. Soon to be banned, by law and by physical scarcity, from open taking, these settlers reactively over-take in an orgy of common privilege — while it lasts.

Natty's opening denunciation, "This comes of settling a country!" has for many suggested simple inevitability, but his later comments on wise use indicate that there could be alternatives within the logic of settlement, not just against it: "Put an ind, Judge, to your clearings. An't the woods his work as well as the pigeons? Use, but don't waste" (248–250). The Judge's regret for the carnage — of trees, pigeons, and bass, if not Native or African Americans — often makes him seem allied with Natty's wise-use principles. As he says of the fish netting: "like all other treasures of the wilderness, they already begin to disappear, before the wasteful extravagance of man" (262). Both men calculate the cost of this natural abundance against the customs of overuse. But they speak, as it were, from opposite sides of the fence, the Judge from the side of private accumulation, and Natty from the side of use-in-common. Sheriff Jones summarizes this neatly when he complains against Temple's expressed regret for the fish kill: "But this is always the way with you, Marmaduke; first it's the trees, then it's the deer, after that it's the maple sugar, and so on to the end of the chapter. One day you talk of canals, through a country where there's a river or a lake every half-mile, just because the water won't run the way you wish it to go; and the next you say something about mines of coal" (262).[16]

The Judge's laws tie his interest in capitalist speculation and development firmly to his commitments to "justice." The novel's happy ending, where Temple can bequeath on Effingham his father's estate and his own daughter, pulls in two directions. It effaces all the tensions suggested by Oliver's antagonism toward Temple, questions hovering around Oliver's alleged Indian heritage and the politics of Anglo-Colonial title in the colonies, as it glosses the question of who gets access to ownership and power in the early nation, through the heteroromantic solution of marriage. But it also glues — and glues solidly — questions of personal interest to the "just" posture of "disinterest." In this condensed moment, what the novel asks of its readers parallels what the Judge asks of Oliver: to acquiesce romantically to the justice of unfettered private development the United States.

This romance between law and capitalist privatization and expansion, historically well documented in the early nation,[17] does not just go to bed with the honeymooners: the novel's critique moves on with Natty. Natty's voice as an environmental conservationist has been applauded. What has been less remarked on is the connection the novel draws between common natural resources and communal self-governance. "Wasty ways" is Natty's term for the double-pronged enclosure of natural and civic commons. He applies the term equally to behaviors fostered under civil law's support of corporate/possessive individualism (such as overtaking of resources) and to civil law's denial that communities can negotiate the allocation of their own local resources. This linkage suggests that in losing control of commons, people lose rights to local self-governance.

In this way, the novel outlines (without really explicating) the forces unleashed by capitalist enclosure. It highlights the guardian logic of privatization, which in both the colonies and early nation put the elite in severe tension with underclass aspirants whose ideals for self-governing — that is, independence — needed to be disciplined and preferably self-disciplined, as we can see in the final episode where Kirby urges Natty to give himself up to the law to continue his punishment for resisting arrest: "So be civil" (437). Kirby, who throughout the novel has stood for the right of residents independently to negotiate fairness, here suggests that surrendering to the law will document Natty's good manners.

Natty's mannerly departure from Templetown has fueled a critical tradition that insists on ineluctable conflict between the individual and society as if there is only one option, one trajectory, for "civilization." Critics have maintained this reading by isolating Natty from not just "society" and "civilization" but from the possibility of *community*. This reading is — as Brook Thomas suggests — a symptom of our own imaginative lack, of the enclosures that limit our own civic imaginations. What is useful about the novel then is how it can help us see this

169

process — the enclosure of the civic commons and the consequences of this enclosure that we are still facing today — historically in progress. The tragedy, as Cooper frames it, does not belong to the commons but to capitalist modernity's desire to eliminate them by fencing everyone but "qualified owners" out and asking everyone to "be civil" about it.

Notes

1. As the staff of *The Ecologist* summarizes in an essay for *Whole Earth:* "Despite its ubiquity, the commons is hard to define. It provides sustenance, security and independence, yet (in what many Westerners feel to be a paradox) typically does not produce commodities. Unlike most things in modern industrial society, moreover, it is neither private nor public: neither commercial farm nor communist collective, neither business firm nor state utility, neither jealously guarded private plot nor national nor city park. Nor is it usually open to all. The local community typically decides who uses it and how" (Staff of *The Ecologist* 1998, 9–10).

2. Susan George's analysis of this new round is chilling: " 'Exclusion,' rather than 'exploitation' " is the key word, for capital excludes more people than it needs to include in the process of extracting surplus values, more commonly known as profit. This new situation helps to explain why capital seeks to incorporate the commons on a grand scale, and why now. It has absolutely no use for the people who live by and from these natural (and sometimes urban) resources but it wants their material base. The Enclosure Act in Britain threw farmers off the lands to make way for sheep, yes, but also to transform the ex-farmers into workers and thereby supply the mushrooming factories of the Industrial Revolution. The Contemporary Enclosure Movement which is attempting massive appropriation of common resources seeks only control over the resources and has no such secondary goals (1998, x).

3. For instance, as I revise this essay, National Public Radio is reporting the growth of the ranks of the poor in the United States by 1.4 million in the past year — this in the face of an "improving" economy.

4. See, for example, Young 1976, 1993; Boulton 2000; Cornell 1999; Holton 1999; Kars 2002.

5. Hardin cast "the tragedy of the commons" in 1968 as a problem emerging between population pressure and man's naturally individualist, acquisitive nature, arguing that the only remedy was severe limits on human freedoms. Governmental, World Bank, and independent planners have since used Hardin's principle as a rationale to take over management of natural resources. Hardin's arguments have come under strong critique from social scientists such as Elinor Ostrum and philosophers such as Stephen Gardiner who argue that Hardin's model for human behavior is insufficiently knowledgeable of group behavioral models, and that it incorrectly describes as man's "nature" the values that capitalism makes it necessary to develop.

6. Although venison was less prized than in England because of its abundance, it had a strong association with aristocratic privilege thanks to Britain's game laws, which for centuries had dictated that only men of wealth were privileged to hunt deer.

7. The Judge's insistence on his own landed privilege to control the game on his property is probably extralegal: as Lundt outlines it, in the American colonies, had "American lawmakers considered game to be the property of the owner of the land on which it was found, landowner interests might have impeded the development of legal doctrines that facilitated free taking. Instead, each of the preemptive rights of landowners was rejected in favor of free taking" (1980, 20–21). The Judge himself acknowledges as much in the discussion at the Bold Dragoon, where he proclaims his hope to "live to see the day, when a man's rights in his game shall be as much respected as his title to his farm" (161). Even today, landowners must post signs forbidding hunting if they do not intend to "share" the game on their land with common hunters.

8. Clearing and bettering was a fundamental feature of converting woodlands to agriculture, and also, by English common law, one way to establish title to land. The "betterment" planned by the Judge and Sheriff includes modern transportation networks, and the kind of land privatization and management that will end squatting and "primitive" or alternative economies once and for all.

9. His plan for improvement runs from streets laid out "by the compass," in disregard of "trees, hills, ponds stumps," to turnpikes and canals, and a grid for law enforcement (see 180–182, 262).

10. Thomas outlines early national alternatives to the legal order represented by the Judge and pithily summarizes: "Too often lovers of democracy, who are convinced by works like Cooper's that the loss of freedom is the cost of civilization, have a tendency to neglect the possibility of increasing human freedom within civilization." . . . If Cooper admits a disparity between what the law stands for and its execution, that disparity is more tolerable once we believe that pure freedom can exist only outside society" (1984, 110).

11. Laws-in-common would be distinguished from British common law by the same analogy that political theorist Antonio Negri (1999) distinguishes "constituent power" from constitutional power — in his argument, the former is governed democratically by the people, the latter is imposed by leadership as an attack or a control on democratic power.

12. In this sense, Natty's political battle echoes that of many of the "lower orders" in the late colonies and early nation, like the North Carolina Regulators, the western farmers involved in Whiskey Rebellion, Fries Rebellion, and in other local rebellions and actions related to protests against government policies. See Slaughter 1986, Holton 1999, Kars 2002, Boulton 2000, and McConville 1999, for example.

13. The Judge even tries invoking British common law to discredit this community's potential opinion: "I am out-voted — over-ruled, as we say on the bench. There is Aggy, he can't vote, being a slave; and Bess is a minor — so I must make the best of it" (22).

14. The narrator documents that this question is open for the residents of Temple's estate as he explains their usage of the term "patent" to his readers: "This term, 'Patent,' which we have already used, and for which we may have further occasion, meant the district of the country that had been originally granted to old Major Effingham, by the 'King's letters patent,' and which had now become, by purchase under the act of confiscation, the property of Marmaduke Temple. It was a term in common use throughout the new parts of the state, and was usually annexed to the landlord's name, as 'Temple's or Effingham's Patent'" (96).

15. Doolen's (2001) explication of the novel's treatment of black characters is worth reading in its entirety. For a fascinating reading of the normalization of violence in local and federal U.S. law and culture, see Lockard 1995.

16. Nancy Shour argues that Natty and the Judge also view history from opposite sides of this fence (1998, 21–23).

17. See Sellers 1991 and Horowitz 1977.

Works Cited

Ahn, T. K., Elinor Ostrom, and James M. Walker. 2003. "Heterogeneous Preferences and Collective Action." *Public Choice* 117: 295–314.

Bollier, David. 2004. "Who Owns the Sky? Reviving the Commons." *In These Times* (March 29): 16–17, 28.

Boulton, Terry. 2000. "The Road Closed: Rural Insurgency in Post-Independence Pennsylvania." *Journal of American History* 87.3 (December): 855–887.

Cooper, James Fenimore. 1985. *The Pioneers.* In *James Fenimore Cooper: The Leatherstocking Tales*, vol. 1. New York: Library of America.

Cornell, Saul. 1999. *The Other Founders: Anti-Federalism and the Dissenting Tradition in America, 1788–1828.* Chapel Hill: University of North Carolina Press.

Doolen, Andy. 2001. "'Snug Stored Below': The Politics of Race in James Fenimore Cooper's The Pioneers." *Studies in American Fiction* 29.2 (Autumn): 131–158.

Gardiner, Stephen M. 2001. "The Real Tragedy of the Commons." *Philosophy and Public Affairs* 30.4: 387–416.

George, Susan. 1998. "Preface." In *Privatizing Nature: Political Struggles for the Global Commons*, ed. Michael Goldman, ix–xiv. New Brunswick: Rutgers University Press.

Hardin, Garrett. 1968. "The Tragedy of the Commons." *Science* new series 162 (December 13): 1,243–1,248.

———. 1998. "Extensions of 'The Tragedy of the Commons.'" *Science* 280 (May, 1): 682–683.

Holton, Woody. 1999. *Forced Founders: Indians, Debtors, Slaves and the Making of the American Revolution*. Chapel Hill: University of North Carolina Press.

Horowitz, Morton. 1997. *The Transformation of American Law, 1780–1860*. Cambridge: Harvard University Press.

Kars, Marjoleine. 2002. *Breaking Loose Together: The Regulator Rebellion in Pre-Revolutionary North Carolina*. Chapel Hill: University of North Carolina Press.

Kulikoff, Alan. 1993. "The Revolution, Capitalism, and the Formation of Yeoman Classes." In *Beyond the American Revolution: Explorations in the History of American Radicalism*, ed. Alfred E. Young, 80–119. De Kalb: Northern Illinois University Press.

Lockard, Joe. 1995. "Talking Guns, Talking Turkey: Racial Violence in Early Amrican Laws and James Fenimore Cooper." In *Making America, Making American Literature: Franklin to Cooper*, eds. W. M. Verhoeven and Robert Lee, 313–336. Amsterdam: Rodopi Editions.

Lund, Thomas A. 1980. *American Wildlife Law*. Berkeley: University of California Press.

MacDougall, Hugh C. 1995. "*The Pioneers* and New York Game Laws." *James Fenimore Cooper Society Newsletter* 3.17: 5–8.

McConville, Brendan. 1999. *Those Daring Disturbers of the Public Peace: The Struggle for Property and Power in Early New Jersey*. Ithaca: Cornell University Press.

Negri, Antonio. 1999. *Insurgencies: Constituent Power and the Modern State*. Minneapolis: University of Minnesota Press.

Ostrom, Elinor. 2000. "Crowding out Citizenship." *Scandinavian Political Studies* 23.1 (March): 3–16.

Perelman, Michael. 2000. *The Invention of Capitalism: Classical Political Economy and the Secret History of Primitive Accumulation*. Durham: Duke University Press.

Sellers, Charles. 1991. *Market Revolution: Jacksonian America, 1815–1846*. New York: Oxford University Press.

Shour, Nancy C. 1998. "'Heirs to the Wild and Distant Past': Landscape and Historiography in James Fenimore Cooper's *The Pioneers*." *James Fenimore Cooper Society Miscellaneous Papers* 10 (August): 17–23.

Slaughter, Thomas. 1986. *The Whiskey Rebellion: Frontier Epilogue to the American Revolution*. New York: Oxford University Press.

Staff of *The Ecologist*. 1998. "The Commons of Small Geographic Places." *Whole Earth* 94 (Fall): 8–13.

Thomas, Brook. 1984. "The Pioneers, or the Sources of American Legal History: A Critical Tale." *American Quarterly* 36.1 (Spring): 86–111.

Young, Alfred. 1976. *The American Revolution: Explorations in the History of American Radicalism*. De Kalb: Northern Illinois University Press.

———. 1993. *Beyond the American Revolution: Explorations in the History of American Radicalism*. De Kalb: Northern Illinois University Press.

CHAPTER 12

Looks the Same to Me:
Post Seattle, Post Sealth

Paula Gunn Allen

> When the last Red Man shall have perished, and the memory of my tribe shall have become a myth among the white men, these shores will swarm with the invisible dead of my tribe, and when your children's children think themselves alone in the field, the store, the shop, or in the silence of the pathless woods, they will not be alone. . . . At night when the streets of your cities and villages are silent and you think them deserted, they will throng with the returning hosts that once filled them and still love this beautiful land.
> —Sealth, S'quamish/D'wamish.

On the one hand we have an America based on the marriage of almighty God and almighty dollar. When combined they yield some monstrous concept of Almighty family, which is code for American Empire, in God we trust.

On the other hand, there is an America based on a liberal strain begun and nourished by Indian thought and civilization prior to, during, and continuing now. This strain keeps on keeping on among Indians and non-Indians on this continent and abroad. The more clothes the Westerners shed, the more they tattoo and pierce, the more they seek ways to enter the Great Dream via herbs, hallucinogenics, meditation, sacred dancing, the more the old way becomes the new.

Ladies and Gentlemen of the world, we are at war. And that war is not between Arab-Moslem/theocratic and European/American Christian, secular. It is not between godless communism and Western christianity. The Cold War is over, because the heat has been turned up. By whom? For what purpose? It is a war that has been going on a long, long time. At this point in time there is no saying which way this conflict will go. Perhaps there are some indicators that can shed some clarity on the snarl.

Long ago so far, as they say or used to say at Laguna, there was a world in which people sought dream-visions that would keep the people in harmony with the Mystery that surrounded them. It moved through them as through all that is on earth and in the sky above. It moved them and all that is. That power, known as *powa* and *manito* (little mysteries) or even *mannitt* when its fullest, most encompassing form was signified, constituted the axis around which their philosophy, social contracts, and spiritual enterprise flowed. *Powa:* of the implicate order. *Apowa:* my dream-vision (my merging in consciousness with the implicate order). *Powhatan:* we dream together (together we move in consciousness with the implicate order). Mundane consciousness, also known as "reality" by moderns, has been designated the explicate order by David Bohm and other quantum physicists. Americans believe intensely, intently, exclusively in explicate organizations. Americans don't like mysteries, unless they are in novels, on television, at the movies. Unless they are confined to places designated "imaginary." "Fiction." "Tall story." Or worst, "Myth."

That world, let's call it Turtle Island, was vast. It extended from what is now Alberta, Canada, to the North Atlantic coast, from the Great Lakes along the Ohio and Mississippi rivers down and across to what is called South Carolina at the moment, which the English dubbed the small portion they first encountered of "Powhatan's Impire," revealing the invaders' idea of dream, their own idea of vision, by which they meant the intentions of management, desire of monarch, goal of nations.

In the terms of the people who were (and are) living there, that particular portion of Greater Algonquia was *tsenecommacah*, community and territory of those tribes allied with and formed into the People of the Dream, Powhatan Alliance. Tsenecommacah extended from the Potomac to the Rappahannock on a north-south axis and from the Piedmont just below the first east coastal mountain range to the great bay known then and now as Chesapeake. The Chesapeake were also Algonquin. And the word that signified them and their homeland, *chesapeake*, meant "lots and lots of clams."

Today in the dawning of the twenty-first century, Christian time, there are at least eleven — ELEVEN — military bases ringing that bay.

For the most part, the central river of the tsenecommacah, from the point of view of the invaders who set up their fort, thus making their intentions perfectly clear, was the river they knew as Powhatan. Renamed the James River by the English (there is a creek on the isthmus/island where they built their Fort James now known as Powhatan Creek), the battle was joined. It's been going on since, and that's nearly 400 years, will be 400 years in December 2007, Christian time.

What time would that be, Powhatan time? Transformation time, final stage.

When your dream is only an intention it can never be true. It must fail because it is only made of muscle and bone, and they rot rather quickly. When your dream is the dream of the manito, of the Mystery, of the All-that-is'ing, well, that's another matter indeed. As it doesn't depend on humans or any of their doings, it lasts a long time. Perhaps as long as the earth herself, which, as even the Christian Bible points out, is forever. Now, that's what one must call "true dreaming."

The idea of implicate order and explicate order comes from the quantum physicist David Bohm. He decided that there is a lot that goes on under the surface of "things," that matter as we know it arises from a configuration or constellation of submatter. Envisioning this constellation as a field, he laid the foundations of a theory that reconnects the gap between the physical and the metaphysical, a connection that has been severed in Western thought for a few hundred years. As I understand it, the world we perceive — three dimensional, moving in time — he denoted "the explicate order." The field that gives shape and movement — and perhaps meaning — to the explicate order he denoted "the implicate order."

His concept of dialogue, and its connection to what he called the implicate order, arose from an observation of Native people's community problem solving, to which he applied concepts derived from quantum mechanics. He noted that they employed a system of communication that depended only partially on physical cues. The verbal event was a conversation among a gathering of members of the Native community he was visiting. A number of community members had met to address an issue of concern to them. As he described it, several people spoke, voicing their thoughts on the matter at whatever length they chose. Then, with no resolution arrived at, they separated, returning to their day-to-day lives. Some time later they met again and the resolution they each arrived at, each independent of the others, matched. Thus consensual agreement was reached and the procedures they needed to take were clear. Bohm was struck by the nonverbal dimensions of the transaction he observed, and combining linguistic concepts with his own discipline, he theorized that information is transferred from one location to another as a property of the field below matter, even that of the quantum variety. Thus, resolution of conflict by the Native community relied on implicate understandings, just as the physical universe relies on an order that he dubbed implicate. However arrived at, Bohm hit on a means of grasping—or at least coming to an understanding of—Native thought and suggesting how it might underlie useful transactions among humans in a process he called dialogue. He believed that thought includes the nonphysical, such as ideas or emotions, as well as the physical, as in action or senses, and that it is from thought that communication proceeds. His description of the relation between the implicate order and the explicate constituted a startling theory of the "between," a mathematical concept that has found its way into Western thinking over the past century or so.

The speaker for the combined S'quamish and D'wamish peoples of the Pacific Northwest, Sealth, made the point in terms perhaps more comprehensible than Bohm's theory to modern readers. Speaking at a gathering called by the government of the United States at which the local native nations and their citizens were compelled to agree that their lands were no longer theirs, he let us know the difference between truth and falsehood, love and lie.

"To us the ashes of our ancestors are sacred and their resting place is hallowed ground," he said. "You wander far from the graves of your ancestors and seemingly without regret." More: with relief to be quit of the lands and ancestors that gave rise to their being. Which he didn't say, perhaps because he didn't know they came here "shaking the dust of their homelands sod from their feet," to paraphrase the poet Alice Duer Miller. "Your religion was written on tables of stone by the iron finger of your God so that you could not forget," written by iron as Turtle Island was bisected by iron, as it was carved up and divided by iron. "Our religion is the traditions of our ancestors . . . and the visions of our dreamers, and is written in the hearts of our people."

I can imagine Americans objecting that the traditions of Anglo-European ancestors form their own religion (although that is actually not the case), and that the words of God are written upon the hearts of the American people, but to think of one's heart being run through a printing press makes that metaphor — and protest — a bit gory.

Do you remember the Puritan preacher Jonathon Edwards's sermon, "Sinners in the Hands of an Angry God"? Perhaps their God was so angry he thought nothing of writing with his iron finger on human hearts. In Edwards's eyes, God thought little of shoving whoever he pleased into a fire that would burn them forever. Right and just in the eyes of those on one side of the conflict; horrifying and malevolent in the eyes of others. I can't say I know which side has the right of it. I can say which side I'm on.

The speaker continues in his analysis of the American character: "Your dead cease to love you and the land of their nativity as soon as they pass the portals of the tomb and wander away beyond the stars." What do the S'quamish and D'wamish dead do? Where do they go? Nowhere. They remain as the earth remains. Their tie to the living, and their obligations to their descendents, all that is of the earth and the Spirit realm, aren't ended with dying. At Laguna they say that the dead come back with the clouds (they ARE the clouds, *shiwanna*) and bring rain. When there is a drought, as there is now, it is because the negative energy from the humans prevents their return. My mother's soul flew back to the pueblo just as we buried her in Albuquerque. My children and I followed her path, although we had to drive, followed her all the way to the door of the old Atseye part of the pueblo where we said "so long." I guess she isn't doing such a good job. Maybe they are all playing the slots in the lands of Sipap^u, telling jokes and forgetting their duty. Maybe the horrors of these years since she died prevents their return as rain. Hard to say.

Sealth, whose name morphs into Seattle and whose being morphs into megapolis, continues, talking about the Americans' dead, who, as he says, "are soon forgotten and never return." He contrasts the modern way with the traditional way of his people, saying that "Our dead never forget the beautiful world that gave them being."

One thing for sure: The earth is not an object. It is not dead matter, just put there for humans to make use of. Nor is it, she, a victim by definition. Indeed, when it comes to a battle between human and earth, my money's on earth. Mother, daughter, matron, crone, the old girl's more than able to give as good as she gets, and then some. BUT. She is more likely to be kindly disposed to humans when humans give back more than they take. When they recognize that the power isn't theirs to wield. When they listen to the songs the earth, the land, sings, the various songs, symphonies, sacred dances, drums pounding heart beat heart beat on and on. The running hoofs of the creatures, the cries and moans, beating wings, buzzing flight, the many voices of the various winds, the surf, trees, the grasses, the snow, the rain. There's so much music. So much our dear Naya Earth has to say. Only we don't listen. We turn on the television, radio, get the news, the weather, as if. We get stupider and stupider. Listen less and less. Care not a bit because we are off line and unable to care unless we hear it on the radio, see it on television, read it in a monograph, in a book, hear it at a rally so noise-saturated that the songs of the earth, that four-fisted woman, cannot be heard. Oh, we weep, we cry, we organize, we wave placards, write papers, give speeches, send money. But never in all the ruckus do we, can we, listen.

There is a country, a bit of earth, lauded by poets for centuries. They tell of its powa, unable to find words, but able to find rhythms, deeper meanings of "this blessed plot, this earth, this realm, this England" (*King Richard II*, ii. 1). The Scots have done the same, and the Irish, and the Welsh. I remember a song learned in grade school about Ireland, "beauty wanders every land, footsteps leaves on many strands, but her home is surely there." Or as the Diné know, all is *hozho.*

The English, Scots, Welsh, Cornish, and Irish love their land. Have loved it since forever. However many wars, however plague and famine and the games people play have been visited on her and them, the love between the two is undying. And so the song. This part of North America called the United States was a land that once sang. Originally known as Virginia, in honor of a dead and bloodthirsty unmarried Queen, now partially recognized by the names of those who "governed" them and oversaw the beginnings of their great destruction. These included De la Warre, Penn, George-ia (for King George) and Carolina (for King Charles).

What's the difference between loving and using? Caring for and stealing from? Renewing and murdering? One thing the old ones used to advise: that you give back more than you take from the earth. This admonition was about restoring, replenishing, enriching the land from which all we have and all we are and can ever hope to be derives, including ourselves. Like all creatures, humans *are* the land. Whatever we do to her, we do to ourselves, Thus, fellows and gals, I can see little difference between the situation Sealth outlined and the situation we face now. From what I can tell, the Americans live in the Dead Zone and fight about how to preserve the corpse best. Chemicals are out. Organics are in. We must save the trees. Save the whales. Save the Tibetans. Save the wilderness.

We must save ourselves, which is not something we can do.

Where I come from they say that we are all parts of the dream St'sitsi'nako, She Who Thinks Creation and All Its Changes, is dreaming. I think that while we argue, while the battle rages, while the score is still unsettled, she continues to dream. I have never been able to imagine just what she needs us in her dream for. Maybe comic relief. Maybe tension because she's trying out conflict-centered plotting devices. Maybe we are to balance the cockroaches. Or the ants — of whom there are enough that they at the could cover the entire surface of the earth should they all surface at the same time.

The sickness of the land is a direct result of modern humans' lack of awareness of and consciousness connection with the living earth. This doesn't mean reading — or writing about — Gaia as a theory; it does not mean going back to nature — which evicts a few more wilderness people. What is needed is the old ritual traditions of the people who have learned from the land and spirits how to negotiate relationships among us; how to provide them with what they need in ways that the ancestors recognized and learned to enact. What is required is the ability to work ceremonially with the planet in all her multitudes of life forms, consciousness capsules, to advocate strenuously in every locale. What is needed is for no gathering to take place, no enterprise to be undertaken, no institutions established or operated without the blessings from Native people in a sacred way that belongs to them.

This means the local Native people must be invited, honored, and provided with whatever is necessary so that they can do their jobs. It means getting white institutions out of their hair, off their backs, and out of their way so that the earth and all her being can reenter conversation as it was before the death culture came our way.

It doesn't mean taking sides in local Indian disputes, for instance that between the Hopi and Diné. Political activism that pits one group of Indians against another is the opposite of what is needed. There is no kind of activism that is in the traditional way of any native nation. Activism is a European phenomena, imported to Turtle Island along with all sorts of other European ideas and institutions. Our way is prayer, peaceful hearts, taking care of day-to-day life, and keeping the ceremonial calendar in terms that are suited to the locale.

What non-Indians can do to help is at once simple and much more difficult than rallies and marches. When organizing any public gathering, secure the presence of a local Indian spokesperson and ask that the venue be blessed in traditional way before the event opens. Give the first event to the local Native people to use: they might lead the gathered in prayer. They might address the gathering. Maybe they'll send a drum. They might not show up at all. Whatever, make sure that you mention the local Native communities. I travel all over the country and immediately ask my driver/hosts where the nearest reservation or Indian center is located. They seldom know, unless the event was sponsored by Native groups.

The other task that can be undertaken immediately is make it your business to know who the local Indian people are. Make sure you know something about their history and customs. Don't assume anything, and it's best not to ask directly. Just hang out when you can, and check the local libraries. Ask your local community leaders — town council, mayor's office, school board — to invite local Native participants to every meeting. Ask that a local representative from the Native community be a paid consultant on Indian affairs to the city or school system. Find out how many Native people are in prison near you, and why. You'd be surprised how many Natives are jailed on spurious charges and without legal representation. We can learn to walk in balance and we can teach our children and grandchildren, our students and friends to value harmony and to honor the Native people around them. We can learn about and teach others about the massive contributions that First Nations civilizations have made to global society.

Disharmony cannot be transformed into harmony through lack of awareness of the REALNESS of the Spirits. Those who have long honored the particular nonphysical beings — and those in physical form as well — are the port of entry. They know how to walk in balance, in harmony. They can lead us all into a better world, where the earth's living being can be part of our lives.

As to the implicate and explicate orders, consider a few items regarding the ceremonial traditions of Indian America — alive and kicking today. There is a commonly held misconception of the meaning of symbol in explicate America and the other Western nations: that a symbol is that which represents something else. The assumption here is that a symbol is not in itself real. Rather it suggests, or implies, something else that is real. Thus literary critics, ethnologists, antiquarians, and a host of other academics hold that people use symbols to artfully refer to whatever. For example, criticism that means to tell us the meaning of a poem by the late eighteenth-century Romantic poet William Blake holds that when he mentions "a thousand thousand angels dancing on the sun" in a poem about sunrise, he means that he feels exalted. According to this point of view the poet is referring to angels on the sun so we will have a graphic image of his emotions. While they acknowledge that Blake was a mystic, they overlook the meaning of mystic as one who sees the implicate reality behind the explicate. Blake wasn't commenting on his emotional state; he was describing what he saw, using explicate language in poetic form (poetics being the language form in which implicate events are told in Western tradition), thus bridging, connecting, the two orders. Similarly, of course, that's what Sealth was doing in his address to the American officials. He, like Blake, wasn't being "metaphorical." He was saying the simple, perceivable, and verifiable facts of the matter. Surely the dead of the S'quamish, D'wamish, and the other First Nations were swarming the streets of Seattle those nights of the protests, as every other. "When your children's children think themselves alone . . . , they will not be alone."

Too bad the protesters were unaware of their presence. Maybe, had they been able to see the spirits of those who loved and still love this land thronging the streets of Seattle, they would have recognized the connection between the two orders of reality. Had they done so, assuredly the results would have been very different.

For a few moments I want to get out of the analytic mode and move to a storytelling mode. In this way you can better grasp the underlying meaning in what I've said. The stories are always more true that any analysis can be. They engage our whole being, whereas analysis addresses left-brain linear processing alone.

Twenty-some years ago when I was teaching at San Francisco State, I had occasion to visit one of our classes in American Indian studies. The professor had invited the Pomo dreamer and weaver Mabel McCabe to her art class to address the students, and I attended in order to hear her. Mrs. McCabe told us about how she became a basketmaker: not through learning how to make them at the side of mother or grandmother. Indeed, she informed us, since the adults knew she would be a Dreamer when she reached the proper age (sometime in her forties, I think it was) they were careful *not* to teach her. It was the task of the tradition to do that, she told us, and recounted how late one night while sitting in her parlor she was startled to see a man sitting across from her. No one had entered the room; he was just there, appearing on the couch as though he had been there all along. He told her that she was a Dreamer and that her period of instruction began that night. He told her about the right plants, making the strips, all the technical details, and instructed her to set about gathering what was needed the next day. What I particularly remember was the way she used the word "tradition." She didn't see it as an institutionally or socially recognized procedure or custom. Rather it was the supernatural being who instructed her. The Dream baskets, she told us, were woven in patterns from the Dream that her gift allowed her access to. No Dream baskets were ever made for sale; although many Pomo made baskets for their own use and to sell, none who did so were Dreamers.

The point I want to make clear is that Mrs. McCabe used the word "tradition" to mean a real person, albeit a supernatural one, a spirit being if you will, because he would instruct her in the old Dreamer way. The being in her living room was not an archetype. He was not part of her unconscious. She did not "go within," to find him; if she had she would have missed him, because he was waiting for her *outside* herself.

179

You know, the planetary beings, humans included along with all the other "kingdoms," as biologists like to refer to terran flora and fauna, are spirits. I am aware that because of our 3D sensibilities we think spirit is not matter. But consider this. As we look through finer and finer microscopes we discover what the Ancients worldwide have been saying: There's nobody, there's nothing there. Perhaps when we locate our perceptions in more dimensions than three — perhaps five or more — we will see what is: matter is spirit.

Thus my larger point: there's nothing about the present post-Seattle, post-9/11, postinvasion, postconquest situation that was not present in the first moments the Spanish and English and other Europeans came to this side of the pond. They were busy casting off all relation to spirit beings, supplanting that experience with flat-line awareness of God, invisible, scary, vengeful, and bloodthirsty; a God who would murder his own son; a God who wants to see all-that-is damned to hell. What other kind of world would people with that mind-set create?

There is a ceremony that some North Coast Native people, the Makah, engage in, and that's a ritual death dance with the great whales. For the most part, Americans view this event as "cultural," like ethnic smorgasbords at some malls, causing many to side with the Makah. Many oppose them on the grounds that, whales being endangered, killing them is wrong. Period. After all, didn't the Hate God admonish us Thou shalt not kill? (Unless the target is those opposed to the One True Vision.)

But suppose, as the Makah do, that the whale people and the human people have a covenant about engaging in a life-to-death transformation, renewal of life, dance. Suppose the whales are disappearing because no one honors them or the agreements made between them and humans in time immemorial, an agreement honored until the last century? Suppose the same can be said for all the life forms said to be dying. As "there is no death," one has to ask where they have gone. To ask how we come to believe that we live in a charnal-house-in-process.[1]

Where I come from the idea is to walk in balance; that means to live as is correct, proper, for humans, as the connection between implicate and explicate orders. We by our natures are doorways, thresholds, liminal beings. We are composed of implicate and explicate folded in together to become all but inseparable. If that seems abstract, think of chiffon cake. Make one for the experience of how balance interweaves this and that and who knows what all. Watch the patterns that occur when you "fold the beaten egg white into the batter." Imagine that process going on forever, ever folding and unfolding. This is not charnal house: it's a dance.

The song, the dance, is in your brain, coming through your ears, your eyes, your nose, your skin. It's not a figment of your imagination, heartfelt or otherwise. As they said in the 1960s, leave your mind and come to your SENSES. Unless and until we do, it will all look the same to me.

What democracy could look like is a social system that demonstrably, visibly and experientially grows out of the assumption, general and thoroughgoing, that spirits walk this land, always have and always will; that they know as much or more than statisticians, social engineers, or bodies of data ever can. Humans are part of a vast community of people, where "All things are connected" and where we know for certain, in our bones, that "Whatever befalls the earth befalls the children of the earth," as Sealth said.[2]

Notes

1. The charnal house paradigm of earthly existence is not universally held among Christians. It was the primary belief of the Puritans and of their born-again descendents.

2. I am aware that some have said that Sealth did not say any of those things, that the soldier or translator wrote them and ascribed them to him. However, it seems pretty unlikely to me that a man out there at the time could have written such ideas. Further, I know that in Indian country there are as many opinions about most issues as there are Indians. It's our kind of democracy.

CHAPTER 13

Agriculture, Empire, and Ecology: Re-farming the New World Order

Scott Hicks

In a positive review of William Conlogue's *Working the Garden: American Writers and the Industrialization of Agriculture* (2001), an ecocritically informed study of representations of farm labor and technology in twentieth-century American literature, Andrew Hoberek praises Conlogue for theorizing what other scholars have not: intersections of agriculture and culture in literature. Lamenting scholars' inattention to the importance of agriculture in human culture and society, Hoberek calls on teachers and scholars to be as attentive to the problems of agriculture as the people directly employed in farming: "[F]or a growing number of people both in the U.S. and abroad — World Trade Organization protesters, new Latino immigrants to the Midwest and their advocates, rice farmers who now find their crop patented — farming is both self-evidently political and intricately intertwined with other aspects of culture" (Hoberek 2002, 106). Hoberek's review not only underscores the importance of further analyses like Conlogue's, analyses that cross disciplinary borders and thus propose more complex and nuanced understandings of the intersections of diverse cultures, sciences, and politics. His review also points to the multi- and transnational character of modern agriculture: an industry fattened by domestic trade subsidies that ravage the economies of developing nations, in the service of a handful of agribusiness conglomerates that seek to export genetically modified, patented seeds and chemicals across the world. The consequence of this brand of global agriculture is a world made over in the developed world's image, culturally, socially, and ecologically.

As Hoberek suggests, the logics of empire and agriculture are basic to making sense of the early twenty-first–century world order. Empire, according to Michael Hardt and Antonio Negri, encapsulates "a new logic and structure of rule — in short, a new form of sovereignty. Empire is the political subject that effectively regulates these global exchanges, the sovereign power that governs the world" (2000, xi). The codes of "empire" are simultaneously the cause and effect of global agriculture: its voracious appetite — for food and fiber, and for human and animal bodies to sacrifice to produce them — causes it to remake and colonize new spaces to supply its needs, while its reinterpretation and redeployment of these newly occupied spaces and peoples effect its coronation as the "sovereign power that governs the world." First World economic, cultural, and political power depends on Third World weakness — that is, its potential to be subordinated and employed within the developed world's industrial-agricultural machine. The developing world's weakness — its malnourished and exiled bodies — paradoxically becomes its power, authenticated in the power of those bodies to provide labor for the empire's profit.

But it is not enough to theorize agriculture's relation merely to empire, though Hardt and Negri's book has spurred much-needed dialogue (including Paul A. Passavant and Jodi Dean's *Empire's New Clothes: Reading Hardt and Negri*, 2004, dedicated entirely to a critique of *Empire*). Indeed, we must add a third term to our discussion: ecology. Because modern farming depends on chemical fertilizers, pesticides, herbicides, and gas-powered machinery—to the extent that "food is oil" (Manning 2004b, 42)—it bears responsibility for widespread environmental damage. As Richard Manning notes, "the long list of problems that inevitably stem from agriculture" includes "[l]oss of biodiversity, pesticide pollution, nitrogen pollution, soil depletion, erosion, siltation, eutrophication, desertification, salinization" (2004a, 99). Agriculture's environmental offenses coalesce with its rapacious reliance on oil (for machinery and for chemicals) to implicate it inextricably in geopolitical policymaking—including the maintenance of military power and the prosecution of war. Because developing nations provide the hope of arable land, and because much of the planet's oil lies underneath the developing nations, agriculture's role in sustaining global inequality—and thus imperial power—is incalculable. "The common assumption these days is that we muster our weapons to secure oil, not food," Manning writes. "There's a little joke in this" (2004b, 42). Not only does agriculture have the power to direct foreign affairs; it also has the capacity to colonize and recolonize native ecologies and cultures in service of the empire.

Through exploitation of developing nations' cultures and ecologies, "developed nations" have engorged and enriched themselves, all the while destroying ecologies both local and global. That nations and peoples practice such atrocities while fouling their own and others' nests confirms farmer-philosopher Wendell Berry's proposition that compartmentalization and specialization confound holistic, meaningful understanding—with dire consequences. He writes:

> What happens under the rule of specialization is that, though society becomes more and more intricate, it has less and less structure. It becomes more and more organized, but less and less orderly. The community disintegrates because it loses the necessary understandings, forms, and enactments of the relations among materials and processes, principles and actions, ideals and realities, past and present, present and future, men and women, body and spirit, city and country, civilization and wilderness, growth and decay, life and death—just as the individual character loses the sense of a responsible involvement in these relations. (1977, 21)

Part of "the rule of specialization" is a constructed alienation from, a fanciful ignorance of, the natural world, the ecology of planet earth, to the extent that human beings no longer have a language for thinking otherwise: "The good of the whole of Creation, the world and all its creatures together, is never a consideration because it is never thought of; our culture now simply lacks the means for thinking of it" (1977, 22). Although the battle is uphill, ecocriticism—"the study of the relationship between literature and the physical and environment" founded on "the fundamental premise that human culture is connected to the physical world, affecting it and affected by it" (Glotfelty and Fromm 1996,

183

xviii–xix)—seeks to theorize a method of analysis that deconstructs binaries between nature and culture and to repair culture by offering a grammar that reintegrates human subjects into their ecology.[1]

My insistence on triangulating agriculture, empire, and ecology grows out of a convergence of "crisis" moments in conceptions of agriculture, the nation, and literary studies, a convergence that guides the theoretical and methodological paradigms of my analysis. To begin at home, as it were, is to begin in my home base, my occupational headquarters—the English Department, where scholars are debating the place and value of theory in literary studies. Terry Eagleton writes that "[t]he golden age of cultural theory is long past" in *After Theory* (2003, 1), finding an encouraging sign of theory's future in "the anti-capitalist movement [that] is seeking to sketch out new relations between globality and locality, diversity and solidarity" (22). Such critical work represents a reimagined political agency, and not just in the texts critics study and the interpretations they produce. University-based scholars, rather than fight just for symbols, now recognize that they must stand against an across-the-board sellout of their universities to corporate interests, as Naomi Klein reports in *No Logo: Taking Aim at the Brand Bullies* (1999). Theory provides an indispensable intellectual and symbolic framework for delineating and approaching a problem; ecocriticism (like new historicism, structuralism, psychoanalysis, and so on) offers a provisional center—in its case, the premise of ecology—as a starting point for engaged cultural analysis. In bell hooks's estimation, such a coupling of theory and practice is critical for the work of cultural and intellectual liberation: "When our lived experience of theorizing is fundamentally linked to processes of self-recovery, of collective liberation, no gap exists between theory and practice" (1994, 61). As Hoberek points out, cultural analysis that is inclusive of the "lived experience" of groups heretofore excluded—"World Trade Organization protesters, new Latino immigrants . . . , rice farmers who now find their crop patented" (2002, 106)—effects a different trajectory of theory and practice, a distinctive set of conclusions.

Just as inhabitants of the ivory tower have begun to recognize the corporatization and privatization of their universities, many Americans are beginning to rethink the received story of American farming. In many respects, the story of agriculture in twentieth-century America has been the rise of technology and the ensuing death of the "family farm," that mythic Jeffersonian image of a nation of yeomen farmers who cultivated the soil, husbanded their livestock, and thus provided for their families and communities. But such a narrative—pastoralizing in its mythic and nostalgic functioning—elides and suppresses competing narratives that always already undermine its bucolic ideology. In many ways, Fox Television's "reality" show *The Simple Life* (2003) puts these issues in clear perspective: the power of wealth and whiteness, symbolized by the paradoxically underfed figure of hotel heiress Paris Hilton, exiled to a farm in rural Arkansas. Inasmuch as the show's success depends on depicting the farm family and community as quaint, backwards, and simple, it gestures toward the "real world" of the farm: high-tech, mechanized agribusiness operations punctuated by low-wage work at local fast-food restaurants and social outings to Wal-Mart. Two years before, and 300 miles away from *The Simple Life*'s Altus,

Arkansas, about 250 black farmers and their advocates from a dozen states took over a U.S. Department of Agriculture service center in Brownsville, Tennessee, protesting continued racial discrimination that denied them federal farm programs and loans (Youngman 2002).[2] In late 2003, fears of "mad cow disease" struck the United States and Canada, prompting in-depth coverage in the nations' major media, with the shocking "news" that the vast majority of cattle in the developed world no longer graze only the open plains — but instead are fattened on a diet that includes the ground bones of cattle, pigs, and poultry.[3] Finally, with World Trade Organization talks in Cancun, Mexico, in September 2003 as a backdrop, the *New York Times* reported and editorialized on the United States' refusal to do away with agricultural subsidies that hurt farmers in the developing world while enriching American agribusiness companies. *Times* writer James Brooke paints a haunting image of South Korean farm union leader Lee Kyung Hae, 55, who "scaled a barricade outside a meeting of the World Trade Organization and then fatally plunged his old Swiss Army knife into his heart. . . . [I]n rural communities like [Jangsu] in southern South Korea, Mr. Lee, a three-time member of the provincial assembly, was seen as a heroic figure, a defender of debt-ridden farmers struggling to maintain an age-old agrarian tradition in a fast-developing country where manufacturing is king" (Brooke 2003). Faced with the pressures of international economic and cultural change — change that is manifested on the farm, in a farming community — the local becomes global.

Protesters of the WTO's Cancun meetings will have to wait and see whether August 2004 negotiations — wherein rich countries would reduce subsidies, while poor nations would trim tariffs — will improve farmers' conditions across the globe.[4] Whatever the result, these difficult WTO discussions not only expose a crisis in agricultural practice and policy but also reiterate a tenuous conceptualization of nationhood in a globalizing world. While U.S. policymakers have refused to cease $12.9 billion in subsidies to American cotton growers — a move that farmers in Brazil and Burkina Faso, for instance, would have hailed ("Harvesting Poverty" 2003) — they have stood by as corporation after corporation moved their accounts to tax shelters overseas and their jobs to Asia and Latin America. No longer do American corporations make things, Klein writes in *No Logo*; they make brands. At the same time that companies export hundreds of thousands of jobs, President George W. Bush proposed an amnesty program for illegal workers in the United States. Assailed by both the political right and left, the debate on immigration centers on whether it makes good political, economic, and social sense to import workers yet export jobs. These economic wars take place alongside real wars in Afghanistan and Iraq — wars waged, ostensibly, to protect the "American way of life" — while the Democratic Party's presidential candidate of 2004 criticized the president's foreign policy as ineffective, arrogant, and imperial. In other words, at the same time that the United States denationalizes itself — that is, becomes a brand, and not a thing, by exporting labor and importing laborers en masse — it nonetheless seeks to withdraw back into the protective shield of nationhood: "America will never seek a permission slip to defend the security of our people," Bush proclaimed in his 2004 State of the Union address. In dissent, Berry (calling agriculture "the economic activity most clearly and directly related to national security — if one grants that we all must eat") condemns Bush's national security policy, on the grounds that it exacerbates national, agricultural, and ecological *in*security:

> It does not address any agricultural problem as such, and it ignores the vulnerability of our present food system dependent as it is on genetically impoverished monocultures, cheap petroleum, cheap long-distance transportation, and cheap farm labor to many kinds of disruption by "the embittered few," who, in the event of such disruption, would quickly become the embittered many. On eroding, ecologically degraded, increasingly toxic landscapes, worked by failing or subsidy-dependent farmers and by the cheap labor of migrants, we have erected the tottering tower of "agribusiness," which prospers and "feeds the world" (incompletely and temporarily) by undermining its own foundations. (Berry 2003)

For Berry, "agribusiness" functions as shorthand for the conflation of empire and agriculture, farming and environmental degradation. His handling of the term thus instantiates the potential to bring together two camps — the agrarian conservative and the anticorporate progressive — a marriage conventional wisdom would never imagine, but one on which the whole of his thought depends.

These malleable tropes of nation and agriculture contest the conventional trajectory of literary study. For starters, American literary study has yet to move fully beyond benighted, romantic visions of nature, though an environmental ethos has been crucial to the formation and perpetuation of American literature as a meaningful category.[5] Today's ecocritical scholars are working to remedy that blunder. But they have yet to grapple with Jefferson's utopic, agrarian vision whose enormity has foreclosed other visions. Berry, for instance, has made a watertight case for profound connections between agriculture and culture, and agriculture and nation, but the thrust of literary studies has been to ignore the farm or — perhaps worse — to romanticize it. Besides Conlogue's *Working the Garden*, Stephanie L. Sarver's *Uneven Land: Nature and Agriculture in American Writing* (1999), and Timothy Sweet's *American Georgics: Economy and Environment in Early American Literature* (2002), few book-length studies of intersections of farming and American literature exist. Conlogue does not blame poets and novelists for this sorry state of affairs; rather, he reproaches his fellow fieldworkers' prevailing tendency to "read American literature through a pastoral prism . . . offer[ing] only an incomplete understanding of American farm literature. At once idealizing and devaluing rural life, pastoral readings divert attention away from the ways in which farm literature grapples with industrial farming and the host of issues that it raises" (2001, 6). The problem lies with critics, he contends, for they are more likely to endow texts about farming with "nostalgia and pastoral assumptions . . . [an] imagining or reworking [of] the agrarian myth, with its self-sufficient family farmer or his country cousin, the preindustrial commercial farmer" (4–5). Such finger-pointing, though, fails to address why such alleged misreadings preponderate in a wide array of intellectual, social, and ecological frameworks.

Critical to righting that critical wrong is an attention to bioregion and environmentalism, in that these categories contest prevailing assumptions of the farm as always already in harmony with pure nature. Such an analysis scrutinizes the contestation of agriculture as both "natural" (thus desirable) and "artificial" (thus problematic). As Max Oelschlaeger explains in *The Idea of Wilderness: From Prehistory to the Age of Ecology*:

> The agriculturist necessarily defines "fields" (areas cleared of natural vegetation), "weeds" (undesirable plants intruding upon fields), and "crops" (desirable plants suited to human purposes). In contrast, the hunter-gatherer lives on what is conceptually the "fruit of the earth" or Magna Mater's manna—fields, weeds, and crops simply do not exist. Furthermore, whereas the hunter-gatherer is at home anywhere in nature, the farmer creates a human settlement that is "home" as distinct from the "wilderness"; and "nature" or the "naturally existing" harbors threats to "home" and "field" as in the predations of "barbarians" or "wild men" who roam about nature, "wild animals" such as wolves and cats that prey on desirable domesticated animals such as sheep and goats, and "wild insects" such as locusts that eat grain. And, finally, the product of the agriculturist is no longer conceived as the fruit of the earth but rather won, at least in part, from nature through sweat and toil. (1991, 28)

As Oelschlaeger describes, the practice and discipline of agriculture requires a grammar that conceptualizes human relationships to nonhuman ecologies as extractive and oppositional. Such conceptualizations serve to make "other" and thus subjugate entities that seek to challenge human dominance; this analysis of the idiom of agriculture contrasts with pastoral interpretations of agriculture in the main body of literary critical study. The problem before us, then, is to rethink the structures of pastoralism in light of the grammars and idioms of ecology and cultural studies. We now must ask how the practice and discipline of agriculture, refracted by a "green consciousness" that posits agricultural practice as degrading and toxic, has shaped American literature—and how that influence unsettles not just culture but literary study as well.

The problem of the treatment of agriculture and ecology in cultural analysis seems to be a dilemma of divided consciousness. That is, the problem is an absence of synthesis; lacking is a grand narrative that coalesces, rather than partitions, these connected concerns. Contemporary literary study seems decadent in a heyday of science and technology; the exponential encroachment of suburbia into "rural" landscapes drives farmland farther and farther out of sight; the hyperindustrialization of agriculture sanitizes it of wildness and intersubjectivity; environmentalism appears to concern a wilderness somewhere else rather than the sport-utility vehicle one drives to work or the many pounds of trash one throws away. Though they are intricately and inextricably connected, the tropes of agriculture, nation, and narrative are driven apart in service of ideology and praxis.

Though it has yet to be used in a sustained way to correct such myopias, ecocriticism nonetheless stands ready. In many ways, its application to the ethics and practices of agriculture could tend toward clearing a long-standing critical logjam in ecocritical discourse. On the one hand, some ecocritics oppose methodologies and approaches that treat nonhuman ecologies as human constructs. Albeit an overstatement of ecocriticism's relationship to other literary theoretical paradigms such as psychoanalysis and new historicism, Laurence Coupe's conceptualization of ecocriticism conveys some critics' commitment to affirming the integrity and autonomy of entities outside human consciousness and existence. Railing at the notion "that because mountains and waters are human at the point of delivery, they exist only as signified within human culture," Coupe militates for "the larger question of justice, of the rights of our fellow-creatures, of forests and rivers, and ultimately of the biosphere itself" (2000, 2, 4). On the other hand, some critics oppose such an adherence to realism, arguing that the position dismisses the productive insights of postmodern inquiry. They advocate instead the power of cultural and intellectual shifts to protect and preserve the environment. William Cronon's work in *Uncommon Ground: Rethinking the Human Place in Nature* serves as ground zero for such a postmodern critique: '[N]ature is not nearly so natural as it seems. Instead, it is a profoundly human construction. This is not to say that the nonhuman world is somehow unreal . . . far from it. But the way we describe and understand that world is so entangled with our own values and assumptions that the two can never be fully separated" (1995, 25). As Lawrence Buell argues, accepting mediations and negotiations — as well as the sanctity of the environment — is vital both to preserving the health of the earth and to theorizing it: "Monist, dualist, and technocultural constructionist theories or myths are likely to prove less convincing than a myth of mutual constructionism: of physical environment (both natural and human-built) shaping in some measure the cultures that in some measure continually refashion it" (2001, 6). If these camps agree on anything, it is the necessity of continued, multifaceted, and engaged explorations of the interpenetrations of human and nonhuman ecologies.[6]

Contemporary agriculture, more than almost any aspect of human endeavor and ecological phenomena, demands close scrutiny of such interpenetrations. Part of the reason for ecocriticism's undertheorization of agriculture, I think, lies in the elemental assumption underlying Coupe's rejections of human constructionist readings of environmental literature: their privileging of "wilderness" as the prime expression of nature. And inasmuch as Cronon and others emphasize the interrogation of the human construction of nature, they do so in an inquiry by and large shaped by the equation of nature with wilderness. To reimagine ecocriticism in the face of modern agriculture and empire, then, stipulates a sustained interrogation of all sorts of physical environments, natural and synthetic, coupled with an intersectional analysis of race, class, and gender.

Intersectionality, articulated by Valerie Smith in 1998, values the interplay of local cultures, lays bare the effects of consumption and production on human and nonhuman registers, and critiques problems that disproportionately affect the poor and peoples of color — groups that by and large do not have access to environments of ecological health and agricultural sustainability. Such an approach holds the promise of fulfilling Patricia Yaeger's important call in *The Geography of Identity* (1996) for a "new self-consciousness about the relation of place and narration . . . a site for investigating the metaphors and narrative strategies that we use to talk about space" (5). The consequences of constructions of race, class, and gender inscribe, and are inscribed by, nonhuman ecologies. Thus agriculture represents both a literal and theoretical site for revisioning "the metaphors and narrative strategies" deployed in the discursive formation of the "environmental imagination" (an appellation of Buell's). Seen through a lens of "green" consciousness, farming in cultural artifacts resists the pastoralizing tendencies of literary study and argues instead for a renewed attention to problems of racism, classism, and sexism in human interactions with other humans, with other species, and within their environment—a new globalization that is not only transnational and transdisciplinary but transsubjective as well.

To read against the grain of the pastoral and the georgic can be a painful experience. The farm communities of Berry's fictional Port Royal or Frost's New England, for example, or the sugarcane plantation of James Grainger's georgic *The Sugar-Cane* (1764) become exponentially more complex when one considers how commercial agricultural-industrial policy influences how farmers work their land, what they produce, and where they distribute their products. No longer does the "farm" represent the "local"; rather, the agricultural production and environmental practice of one farmer shapes the cultural habit and environmental quality of countless other human beings. To take unreflective refuge in Berry's, Frost's, or Grainger's imaginations perpetuates frames of mind that elide the political, ecological, and cultural modes of imperialism.

For an exemplar of an integrated consciousness, of creating and sustaining reflective refuge, however, consider Barbara Kingsolver's culturally, ecologically, and politically sensitive novel *Prodigal Summer* (2000): it juxtaposes chemical agriculture with organic agriculture, celebrates locally responsible production that produces for an urban, non-Western (Islamic) market, and explores the permeable borders between wilderness and agriculture. Her recent decision to become an organic farmer in rural Kentucky represents the enactment of new ways of living agriculture, ecology, and empire, in that her story (featured in Norman Wirzba's *The Essential Agrarian Reader*, 2003) demonstrates and reflects on the paradox of mitigating the problems of the global through a reinvigorated sense of the local. Indeed, the *country*—the rural landscape of human inhabitations dispersed among rolling farmlands and woods—is the *nation*.

Put simply, we need more books like Conlogue's and more reviews like Hoberek's, texts that question "pastoral assumptions," for they call attention to the binaries of "wild" and "domestic," agricultural and pastoral, that shape environmentalist theory and praxis today. An ecocritical study of agriculture is as pressing today as continued interrogations of culture, nature, and empire. Indeed, agriculture is at the heart of intersections of nature and culture, plants and animals, living things and nonliving things. And if some theorists of agriculture have it right—that human beings have already domesticated the entire planet—then agriculture is the sole ideology of human existence, the ecological enactment of empire (a sobering thought, given the current and future state of the environment and world affairs). For it is only by reading against the grain that we might assess fully our responsibility to our global community, both human and nonhuman.

Notes

1. Although William Rueckert coined the term "ecocritical" in 1978, the 1980s witnessed the crystallization of ecocriticism as an academic field. Many literary scholars were writing ecologically informed essays from the 1970s on, but they often were not aware others doing similar work. During the 1980s and 1990s, key texts were published and key organizations were founded. In 1985, Frederick O. Waage edited *Teaching Environmental Literature: Materials, Methods, Resources*, followed by the launch in 1989 of *The American Nature Writing Newsletter*. A year after the University of Nevada, Reno, created the first academic position in literature and the environment in 1990, the first special session on ecocriticism was organized at the Modern Language Association's annual convention. Perhaps the capstone of these important moves toward collaboration and consolidation was the founding of the Association for the Study of Literature and Environment in 1992 and, a year later, the launch of *ISLE: Interdisciplinary Studies in Literature and Environment*, a journal dedicated to ecocriticism (Glotfelty and Fromm 1996, xvi–xviii).

2. The federal government settled with the farmers in 1999. But the Environmental Working Group charged in July 2004 that most had not received compensation, prompting the *New York Times* to call for Congressional intervention: "Again and again, these farmers have run up against procedural hurdles that have effectively blocked most of them from receiving payments that were supposed to be automatic. Because of poor record-keeping, the U.S.D.A. seriously underestimated the number of farmers who had been discriminated against. It also did a terrible job of seeking out farmers who might qualify for payments. And it did nothing to help them get the documents needed to demonstrate the loan and subsidy support that neighboring white farmers had received" ("Restitution for Black Farmers" 2004).

3. Eric Schlosser detailed these practices in his 2001 bestseller, *Fast Food Nation: The Dark Side of the All-American Meal*, while media coverage of a mad cow epidemic in Europe in the winter of 2001 — in which the testing of cows for bovine spongiform encephalopathy revealed dozens of cases and resulted in the slaughter of thousands of animals — should have been fresh in Americans' memories.

4. According to the *Washington Post*, "wealthy nations would cut their subsidies to farmers, especially payments that tend to lead to overproduction and gluts in supply on world markets. Such subsidies have been widely condemned for depressing global crop prices and robbing farmers in poor nations of their livelihoods. In return, developing nations would cut the steep tariffs that many of them maintain on agricultural and industrial goods, expanding market opportunities for rich-country exporters." These concessions are far from set in stone, though: "[W]hether those cuts will be deep or shallow, immediate or gradual depends on how far negotiators are willing to go in making concessions as the Doha Round progresses. [The August 1, 2004] deal leaves a huge amount of detail to be negotiated later, and negotiators here fought hard to keep many of their commitments as vague as possible to maintain their flexibility in the future talks" (Blustein 2004). As Neil King Jr. puts it, "Ministers from all 147 WTO countries now must tiptoe past dozens of land mines on the way to an actual agreement" (2004, A2). The *New York Times* praised the compromise as "a welcome breakthrough" and called on U.S. leaders to follow through on their promises ("Breakthrough on Trade" 2004), while social justice and environmentalist groups such as Oxfam International, Greenpeace, and Friends of the Earth International condemned the compromises: "'The deal is not a victory for multilateralism, but a dangerous fudge,' said Daniel Mittler, Greenpeace International Trade and Policy Advisor. '. . . The WTO does not seem capable or willing to deliver equitable and sustainable development for all.'" (Lobe 2004).

5. As David Mazel argues, this "environmental ethos" has been central to American literature as an object of study, beginning in the 1920s with U.S. literary scholars who argued that Americans' relationship to the frontier and "New World" nature distinguished American literature from British (2001, 5). A major work of the period was Norman Foerster's *Nature in American Literature: Studies in the Modern View of Nature* (1923). Nearly twenty years later, F. O. Matthiessen was instrumental in the canonization of the nineteenth-century writers Dickinson, Hawthorne, Emerson, Melville, and Whitman, in whose works he

traced the theme of nature in his *American Renaissance: Art and Expression in the Age of Emerson and Whitman* (1941). Likewise, the discipline of American studies owes its existence to ecologically informed readings of literature and culture, evidenced by seminal works such as Henry Nash Smith's *Virgin Land: The American West as Symbol and Myth* (1950) and Leo Marx's *The Machine in the Garden: Technology and the Pastoral Ideal in America* (1964) (Mazel 2001, 6–7), and perpetuated by signal contributions such as Annette Kolodny's *The Lay of the Land: Metaphor as Experience and History in American Life and Letters* (1975).

6. Thanks to its encompassing, accretive predisposition, contemporary ecocriticism has the tools to facilitate and conduct such explorations. This is not to say, however, that it is without its imperfections or limitations. John Elder and others have argued that ecocriticism must work toward greater racial and ethnic inclusivity to broaden the definitions and categories of nature writing, for example, while Karla Armbruster and Kathleen R. Wallace, among others, have underscored the magnitude of reforming "standards for 'great literature' [that are] biased toward representations of the disembodied mind and of various cultural and aesthetic issues and away from representations that clearly speak to human relationships with nature" (2001, 8). For a thoroughgoing critique of ecocriticism, consult Dana Phillips's *The Truth of Ecology: Nature, Culture, and Literature in America* (2003).

Works Cited

Armbruster, Karla, and Kathleen R. Wallace. 2001. *Beyond Nature Writing: Rethinking the Boundaries of Ecocriticism.* Charlottesville: University Press of Virginia.

Berry, Wendell. 1977. *The Unsettling of America: Culture and Agriculture.* 2004. San Francisco: Sierra Club Books.

———. 2003. "A Citizen's Response to the National Security Strategy of the United States of America." *Orion* March–April. http://www.oriononline.org/pages/om/03-2om/Berry.html.

Blustein, Paul. 2004. "Accord Reached on Global Trade." *Washington Post*, July 31, August 1. http://www.washingtonpost.com/wp-dyn/articles/A30619-2004Jul31.html.

"Breakthrough on Trade." 2004. Editorial. *New York Times*, August 3. http://www.nytimes.com/2004/08/03/opinion.

Brooke, James. 2003. "Farming Is Korean's Life and He Ends It in Despair." *New York Times*, September 16. http://www.nytimes.com/2003/09/16/international/asia.

Buell, Lawrence. 1995. *The Environmental Imagination: Thoreau, Nature Writing, and the Formation of American Culture.* Cambridge: Belknap Press of Harvard University Press.

———. 2001. *Writing for an Endangered World: Literature, Culture, and Environment in the U.S. and Beyond.* Cambridge: Belknap Press of Harvard University Press.

Conlogue, William. 2001. *Working the Garden: American Writers and the Industrialization of Agriculture.* Chapel Hill: University of North Carolina Press.

Coupe, Laurence. 2000. *The Green Studies Reader: From Romanticism to Ecocriticism.* London: Routledge.

Cronon, William, ed. 1995. *Uncommon Ground: Rethinking the Human Place in Nature.* New York: W. W. Norton.

Eagleton, Terry. 2003. *After Theory.* London: Allen Lane.

Glotfelty, Cheryll, and Harold Fromm, eds. 1996. *The Ecocriticism Reader: Landmarks in Literary Ecology.* Athens: University of Georgia Press.

Hardt, Michael, and Antonio Negri. 2000. *Empire.* Cambridge: Harvard University Press.

"Harvesting Poverty: The Case against King Cotton." 2003. Editorial. *New York Times* December 7. http://www.nytimes.com/2003/12/07/opinion.

Hoberek, Andrew. 2002. Review of William Conlogue, *Working the Garden: American Writers and the Industrialization of Agriculture. Journal of the Midwest Modern Language Association* 35. 2: 105–108.

Hooks, Bell. 1994. *Teaching to Transgress: Education as the Practice of Freedom.* New York: Routledge.

Johnson, Alex. 2004. "Bush Makes Case for Second Term." January 21. MSNBC Online. http://video.msnbc.com/ID/4000590/.

King, Neil Jr. 2004. "The Outlook: Poor Nations Need Trade Talks to Succeed." *Wall Street Journal* August 2, A2.

Kingsolver, Barbara. 2000. *Prodigal Summer: A Novel.* New York: HarperCollins.

Klein, Naomi. 1999. *No Logo: Taking Aim at the Brand Bullies.* New York: Picador USA.

Kolodny, Annette. 1975. *The Lay of the Land: Metaphor as Experience and History in American Life and Letters.* Chapel Hill: University of North Carolina Press.

Lobe, Jim. 2004. "International Groups Denounce World Trade Pact." Common Dreams Newscenter August 2. http://www.commondreams.org/headlines04/0802-01.htm.

Manning, Richard. 2004a. *Against the Grain: How Agriculture Has Hijacked Civilization.* New York: North Point.

———. 2004b. "The Oil We Eat: Following the Food Chain Back to Iraq." *Harper's Magazine,* February, 37–45.

Mazel, David, ed. 2001. *A Century of Early Ecocriticism.* Athens: University of Georgia Press.

Oelschlaeger, Max. 1991. *The Idea of Wilderness: From Prehistory to the Age of Ecology.* New Haven: Yale University Press.

Passavant, Paul A., and Jodi Dean, eds. 2004. *Empire's New Clothes: Reading Hardt and Negri.* London: Routledge.

Phillips, Dana. 2003. *The Truth of Ecology: Nature, Culture, and Literature in America.* Oxford: Oxford University Press.

"Restitution for Black Farmers." 2004. Editorial. *New York Times* July 27. http://www.nytimes.com/2004/07/27/opinion.

Sarver, Stephanie L. 1999. *Uneven Land: Nature and Agriculture in American Writing.* Lincoln: University of Nebraska Press.

Schlosser, Eric. 2001. *Fast Food Nation: The Dark Side of the All-American Meal.* Boston: Houghton Mifflin.

Smith, Valerie. 1998. *Not Just Race, Not Just Gender: Black Feminist Readings.* New York: Routledge.

Sweet, Timothy. 2002. *American Georgics: Economy and Environment in Early American Literature.* Philadelphia: University of Pennsylvania Press.

Wirzba, Norman. 2003. *The Essential Agrarian Reader: The Future of Culture, Community, and the Land.* Lexington: University Press of Kentucky.

Yaeger, Patricia, ed. 1996. *The Geography of Identity.* Ann Arbor: University of Michigan Press.

Youngman, Sam. 2002. "Black Farmers Rally for Relief; USDA Denies Using Unfair Loan Practices." [Memphis] *Commercial-Appeal* July 2, 2002. http://proquest.umi.com/pqdweb?did=131553711&sid=1&Fmt=3&clientId=2335&RQT=309&VName=PQD.

CHAPTER 14

History's Place Markers in Memory: 1954 and 1999

Thadious M. Davis

History, like memory, is fragile. There is little accounting for what gets recorded as history and what gets lost in memory. I was thinking about the difference between the two while watching a transformed Al Sharpton speak at the 2004 Democratic National Convention. His Godfather-of-Soul "do" tamed so that those without personal memory of the 1960s could take him seriously and his rhetoric invigorated so that those with historical memory could identify with his message, Reverend Sharpton ignited the stage with a fast-paced overview of black voting and black access to voting rights from the nineteenth century through the twentieth century. From memory of the promised forty acres and a mule to freed people, he wove a memorial to rights denied, lost, contested, sought, gained, and constricted over more than a century of struggle.

But what prevents that moment from crashing and burning in its very high-voltage incendiary brilliance? It is the ever-present reality of the "rights revolution" as a fact of cultural consciousness.

The Supreme Court decision *Brown v. Board of Education*, 374 U.S. 483 (1954), celebrated a fiftieth anniversary in 2004. That May 17, 1954, decision played in the background of Reverend Sharpton's speech, though he never made specific reference to it. Implicit in calling up the several pieces of voting rights and civil rights legislation, *Brown* is almost synonymous with the overturning of power blocks and political authority through legal strategies and revisionist thinking. It marks the beginning of the "rights revolution," the underlying concept fueling Reverend Sharpton's recounting of the hard-fought and costly struggle for voting rights that African Americans had waged for nearly a century. The *Brown* decision in 1954, according to Mark Tushnet, "shaped Americans' understanding of constitutional law for the rest of the twentieth century" (Tushnet 2002, 160). And, despite the fact that a second *Brown* decision in 1955 included the directive, "with all deliberate speed," allowing for slow compliance or virtual inaction, the case continues to influence constitutional law in the early years of the twenty-first century. The residual impact stems, Waldo Martin suggests, from the applicability of *Brown* to "the marginalized, including other peoples of color, women, gays and lesbians, and the disabled . . . . that is, 'judicial activism' on behalf of human rights, notably the rights of oppressed groups and individuals" (Martin 1998, 34). In *Brown*, the Supreme Court opened a way for judicial activism by aligning liberal social change with the Constitution. By digressing from its own history of preserving the status quo in constitutional law and of obstructing legislative change in matters of liberal politics, the Court initiated a widespread consciousness of rights as an avenue

193

for juridical intervention and legal protections of rights under law (Tushnet 2002, 160). Conservative politicians allied with the political right, however, have in the years since the 1954 decision also adopted the notion of protected rights in efforts to stall social change and activism, so that just as Tushnet, Martin, and other legal historians have observed, the impact of *Brown* on constitutional law has been apparent and evident from every part of the political, interpretive spectrum.

Three texts related to the *Brown* decision can be brought to bear on the issues of memory and history and their fragility: Alice Walker's *Meridian* (1976); Ntozake Shange's *Betsey Brown* (1985); and Thulani Davis's *1959* (1992). Together, these three novels, written in remembrance of the struggle for civil rights during the 1950s and 1960s, form historical place markers for geopolitical awareness and activism. They represent the human face of social change and transformation occurring during the end of the twentieth century, when multiple challenges to discriminatory practices and to unequal structures shaped their arguments around precedents the Supreme Court established in the *Brown* ruling. These texts, and *1959* in particular, provide a personal narrative for the collective rights revolution and for what is at stake in thinking about both the mid-twentieth-century transformation in the interpretation of laws affecting rights and the regression in the interpretations at the end of the century.

To teach these three novels together is not merely to teach civil rights history in terms of the *Brown* case and school desegregation but also to teach the dismantling of "separate but equal" dogma emanating from the 1896 *Plessy v. Ferguson* case and the emerging of modern public protests and rights activism in the United States. In a very important sense now often forgotten or elided, rights activism and public protests stem from the racial segregationist codes that swept through all of the states in the late nineteenth and early twentieth centuries. Although clearly labor activism and strikes as protest should not be ignored in this account, they shall, for the time being, play only in the background in order to foreground the connection that has been lost between the second half of the 1950s and the second half of the 1990s, culminating in Seattle in November 1999. I use the term "lost," because U.S. policy watchers and political observers have a way of bowing, perhaps unintentionally, to the segregationist strategies of old. They do so not with malice aforethought but with the ease and comfort of the familiar, the always-there and always-accessible fall into hegemonic white thinking and formulation of internal national history and collective memory. External national history functions differently, and as such can come under close scrutiny from a variety of lenses and perspectives, including most recently the corrective lens of imperialism. Internal history, however, is another matter, largely because race rights and racial activism have so conveniently been separated from mainstream concerns with the economy, the environment, privatization, militarization, globalization, downsizing, or outsourcing.

194

Who remembers, for example, that in general sit-ins did not initially occur at court houses or city halls, but rather at stores and places of business, that boycotts occurred where there were buses and public transportation and retail stores and restaurants committed to racial segregation and capitalism?

How many celebrating Martin Luther King Day recall that King was killed in protesting not segregated spaces but rather the economic injustice of the condition of sanitation workers in Memphis, and that support for those striking workers came on the heels of his public outcry against the war in Vietnam?

Who remembers that race riots occurred in urban areas not because of segregation but because of the economic exploitation of people living within the ringed-off areas of cities consciously cordoned off by expressways, highways, and railroad tracks; red-lined by banks and commercial lending institutions; targeted by local and federal policing agencies for surveillance and oppression; used as appropriate sites for dumping by toxic waste companies and garbage disposal and sanitation facilities; with residents rendered unemployed by the removal of jobs to far-flung suburban parks and the withdrawal or reduction of public transportation; and turned into wasteland ghettoes by the elimination of services for cleanup, maintenance, or restoration?

These questions embed pieces of the forgotten. Yet they are also tangible sites of memory. They recall attention to the rationale and necessity of bodies on the line during the marches, protests, and demonstrations. The strategies in the long road to *Brown* and in the 1960s Civil Rights movement were enabled by an awareness of the workings of capital in cultural contexts, by a recognition of the significance of commerce and financial units, and by an understanding of the interconnectedness of business practices and social structures. Underlying these strategies was the fiber of the rights decision that had been handed down in *Brown*.

There is, then, ample reason for taking a fresh look at texts that emerge out of historical memory and racial consciousness of the coming of desegregation in the aftermath of *Brown*. These historical fictions, read through the lens of the present national and international macrocosm, provide a dimension of remembering, of memory with the potential of having future import.

Meridian, the most philosophical of the three texts, interrogates the idea of protest and the forms of protest available to civil rights activists. Although it takes up many of the problematic issues identifiable within organized mid-twentieth-century civil rights movements (gender equity, nonviolent versus violent protest, white involvement, and so on), *Meridian* may be read as a meditation on the evolution of rights consciousness. The protagonist, Meridian Hill, is no simplistic participant in civil rights activism. Instead she is a woman who comes to terms with society's construction of gender roles, with the hegemony of social attitudes around race, with the deficiencies in the expectations for motherhood and maternity, with the burden of sexuality and heterosexual relations. But she is also a woman who in the postcivil-rights era searches for causes in which to enact her faith in expansive rights for all, and most particularly for black people still discriminated against in the South.

At the very beginning of the novel, an emblematic scene establishes Meridian in a social and moral space. She stares down a tank purchased "during the sixties when the townspeople who were white felt under attack from 'outside agitators'—those members of the black community who thought that equal rights for all should extend to blacks" (Walker 1976, 4). The tank, painted white and festooned with red, white, and blue ribbons, stands at the ready in Chicokema's public square alongside "a statue of a Confederate soldier facing north whose right leg, while the tank was being parked, was permanently crushed" (4). The public square holds the power to crush protesters, and the icon, though disabled, is supported by the force resident within the tank and within the white community. Truman Held, Meridian's friend and former lover, arrives just as Meridian challenges the tank by leading a march to protest black children's being denied entry to a traveling show because blacks were only allowed in on a special day. Truman's response to the denial is: "But the Civil Rights Movement changed all that!" (5). His assumption is that the work he, Meridian, and many others performed during the movement has effected change; the reality is that, much like the southern governments who moved slowly in responding to *Brown* "with all deliberate speed," the town has not progressed very far in achieving equal access and equal rights. Described as looking like Che Guevara and a revolutionary (10), Truman has expectations based on his memory of protest marches; he is surprised that the marchers "*are* all black" (6), and that they do not "burst into song" when Meridian steps off the curb leading her band of child protesters, "their heads held high and their feet scraping the pavement" (7). The object of the demonstration is admission to see what Truman immediately terms a "rip-off," a supposedly mummified white woman, "'Marilene O'Shay, One of the Twelve Human Wonders of World: Dead for Twenty-five Years' . . . 'Obedient Daughter,' . . . 'Devoted Wife,' 'Adoring Mother' . . . 'Gone Wrong'" (5). Killed and then commodified by her husband for sexual transgressions, Marilene O'Shay exists as an inert commercial body, a sign of the connection Meridian makes between the civil rights movement, the women's movement, and their challenge to oppressive power.

The stakes in this latter-day march is admission to a sideshow for the children of workers at a guano plant. At stake for Meridian is her unswerving commitment to justice for all and equal treatment for all, but one onlooker remarks, "she thinks *she's* God" (8). No matter the odds, Meridian moves toward the tank, which "seemed to grow larger and whiter than ever and she seemed smaller and blacker than ever. And then, when she reached the tank she stepped lightly, deliberately, right in front of it, rapped smartly on its carapace . . . then raised her arm again. The children pressed onward, through the ranks of the arrayed riflemen and up to the circus car door. The silence, as Meridian kicked open the door, exploded in a mass exhalation of breaths, and the men who were in the tank crawled sheepishly out again to stare" (8). The "victory" is, of course, small, but not as "useless" as Truman believes (12). According to the philosophy of self-sacrifice and selflessness that Meridian has adopted, the incident is part of her volunteering to suffer for rights and in ways that no longer simply mirror the quest for voters' rights or school integration.

In ever-widening spheres following her confrontation with a tank, Meridian's story circles back through her past to reveal how she came to be a woman in overalls, having no possessions, subject to catatonic-like spells, wearing a conductor's cap, and like Harriet Tubman leading fearlessly. The narrative maps Meridian's experiences in exterior spaces (the rural South, a women's college, the civil rights movement, the urban North, a black nationalist organization, "Freedom Schools"), and with equal attention, it charts her interior evolution.

She becomes conscious of her rights as a black, a woman, a citizen, and of her duties as a true revolutionary. With the evolution of her thought, Meridian ascends to positions of greater isolation within the available communities. Outcast for leaving her husband, for abandoning her child, for rejecting the religion of her mother, for questioning the role of violence in the movement, for resisting the sexualization of women, Meridian basically becomes an ascetic, a martyr, and saint. In isolation, however, she reconnects to the geographies of right that have reconfigured the history of the nation and its people.

Meridian responds to the history of structural violence against black and native people within the United States. The narrative strategy in part gestures toward realigning oneself with the past as a continuum and toward understanding how economic structures lead to the mistreatment and abuse of women and children in particular, or those rendered helpless by the overdetermination and overexertion of patriarchal power. Meridian's ancestor Feather Mae is a major presence in her development. Through her example of resisting her husband's efforts to extend his farm over the Sacred Serpent Mound, an Indian burial mound, Feather Mae teaches Meridian to connect poverty, racism, and sexism with economics and to garner strength from the experience of "physical ecstasy," a communion with the earth, and a body "set free in the world" (51). Meridian sees the later destruction of Sacred Serpent Mound for a segregated commercial park as part of the continuing commodification of culture and destruction of the spiritual. Meridian's father is central to her developing consciousness of the human imprint on land, and provides her with the remembered stories of an ancestral past that link the two of them to Feather Mae. He enables her to see how human beings attempt to shape the natural world to match their ideology and their thinking about hierarchy, about property, about justice. Sharing his love of nature, Meridian grieves when after "blacks are finally allowed into Sacred Serpent Park," she cannot recover "her earlier ecstasy and exaltation" in that now commercial place (52).

Economies of power and cultures of wealth will be challenged as Meridian enters her prime intellectually and spiritually in the recognition of rights and justice, even though her physical body remains frail. The missing, the erased, the absent, the lost, all are written on Meridian's very body. The trope of undiagnosed debilitating illness with a concomitant hair loss destabilizes any notion of a clear-cut solution to the problem of conflicting ideologies so highly visible in the multiple struggles for human rights. Yet, like Lazarus, Meridian returns to health and to the world.

In the final section, Truman Held tells Meridian "your ambivalence will always be deplored by people who consider themselves revolutionists, and your unorthodox behavior will cause traditionalists to gnash their teeth" (227). Meridian's response is clear: "But that is my value. . . . Besides, all the people who are as alone as I am will one day gather at the river. We will watch the evening sun go down. And in the darkness maybe we will know the truth" (227). Collective action remains Meridian's best hope for combating and resisting corrupt, false power. She initiates that action by her performance (13), her use of spiritual and moral power poised against economic and political power. Those who had been active in the collective struggle for rights but who had turned their attention to private accumulation of wealth, to individual commercial pursuits, and to unbridled consumerism may eventually find their way back to Meridian's way, as had Truman Held. Her preparedness for struggle includes forgiveness and love, and with them an unwavering, renewable commitment to spiritual revolution as power within a very material world.

In *Betsey Brown*, Ntozake Shange provides an oblique commentary on the necessity of the rights revolution by representing the background story of a progressive doctor and his family in St. Louis. Naming the family "Brown" is emblematic in referencing the *Brown* desegregation decision and the issue of being "colored" in the United States. The school-aged daughter Betsey functions as the central figure in a family drama that may be read as a deliberate reassessment of a preeminent historical moment of cultural transformation. For Betsey, that moment represents a change so profound that it is reflected in nature: "The sun hovered behind a pink haze that engulfed all of St. Louis that Indian summer of 1959. The sun was a singular preoccupation with Betsey. She rose with it at least once a week" (Shange 1985, 13).

While focusing squarely on the present, the narrative inscribes memory of the past and the upward mobility of black people during the long era of segregation. Memories of race-bound living in the South and in the North circulate in the conversation of Betsey's southern-born and bred grandmother, Vida, whose life has been both shaped and disrupted by segregation, racism, and colorism, and in the voice of Betsey's college-educated, sophisticated mother, Jane, whose career as a social worker involves helping psychiatric patients traumatized by racism. Given the prior movement of the family from location to location in an effort to escape the most virulent forms of racial discrimination, there is no nostalgia for the past, despite the current racial constraints placed upon the family. Greer, the father and a physician, observes that "poor colored people didn't get decent treatment at the clinic" where he works (50). Jane, a wife and mother maintaining a full-time career, feels helpless when her children ask questions about the treatment of black people: "Jane hugged her daughter, hoping Betsey didn't know all she could do about the Negro problem was set the table for dinner" (47). The extended family as a structure responding to the racial tensions of ordinary life in the United States allows for a nuanced examination of the dream of racial equality and a new social order following the *Brown* decision.

Betsey expresses the fears and anxieties associated with segregation and the coming of integration. From her vantage point in the tree growing next to the family's upstairs porch, she is safe from the outside world and free to reflect on race matters. After a particularly difficult day for the family, when two of the children are brought home by the police for "trespassing" on a "whites only" school playground, Betsey observes: "White folks and money seemed to go hand in hand. Whenever a Negro mentioned one, he mentioned the other. Like the white folks had took up all the money and were hiding it from the Negroes, like they kept all the nice houses for themselves, and the good schools, and the restaurants and motels. Just for themselves" (51). Though young, she understands the economics of segregation. She also listens as her father reads "the news to her every night bout the Negroes and the whites and the boycotts and standing up for the race" (42). She knows, for instance, "That's what they were doing in Montgomery, boycotting the white folks till they came round" (42). In the aftermath of the *Brown* decision, Betsey learns of boycotts and marches to end segregation. But her insight into a racially divided world also involves personal comfort and safety: "Grown-ups started driving back up into their driveways and the children came from every direction to greet their parents who'd been off all day working somewhere they let colored work. Next door they was [sic] speaking French and down two house they were Hindi. . . . The nice thing about segregation was the colored could all be together, where the air and the blossoms were their own, as clear as it was impossible for white folks to put a veil over the sun" (43). She comes to this reassuring thought after becoming physically ill and throwing up the first time she "saw the soldiers and the mothers . . . screaming at nine little black children . . . . she couldn't hold food down. Betsey thought on those thoughts and bout what she'd do if a crowd of crackers came cursing her and throwing eggs on her pressed clothes. She thought and tears came to her eyes. She be 'fraid is what, but papa said a struggle makes you not afraid, yet Betsey's tree and she weren't assured of that" (43).

When the Brown family prepares for Betsey and her siblings' entrance into white schools, desegregation in St. Louis becomes a complex reality. The entire family knew that "their lives would never be the same" (92). The impending change entered into the children's thoughts, because they "knew the morning brought a new way of living, another realm into their lives, one they'd been taught was dangerous and hostile. The white people. A classroom full of white people" (92). Jane worried over her children's safety: "Would there be ugly crowds of thin-lipped rednecks throwing tomatoes and bottles at her children? Would she have to go up to the school every day on account of some poor racist child who didn't know niggah is not the same as Negro?" (90). For Jane, though she herself had grown up in an integrated environment in New York, her world is rich as it is: "There was enough of it. From Langston Hughes to Sojourner Truth, her children's worlds were hardly deprived" (90). Jane fears what will be lost to her children in their integrated schools. On the other hand, Greer, who wakes the children every morning with drumming and leads them in recitations of black history, believes that their children will be "paving the way for those yet to come. . . . There's thousands of lives that depend on our children having the courage to go somewhere they've never been accepted, or wanted, when they have a right to go and a right to the best education our taxes pay" (91). His point involves both a race consciousness, making a better social world for black people in the future, and a rights consciousness, having full access to all of their rights as citizens now in the present.

In tracing the movement of the Brown children into a different world, Ntozake Shange writing in 1985 champions the necessity of the rights revolution while questioning the losses for children like Betsey. She understands in retrospect what Betsey could not: "why they weren't good enough already. Why did she [Betsey] have to take three buses to learn the same things with white children that she'd been learning with colored children? . . . Why didn't the white children come to her school? Let *them* get up at dawn and take a trillion different trolleys. Why did the Negroes have to do everything the hard way?

199

Why weren't they good enough already?" (92). These are the very questions that recurred when, fifty years after *Brown*, school integration had not come about although the acceptance of equal rights and rights protection had.

Thulani Davis centers *1959*, her first novel, squarely on the transformations in a community made possible by the struggle for equal access to public education, to public places, and to voting rights. The site of struggle is Turner, Virginia, during a year-long drive that begins with coalitions for integrating the white schools and quickly moves to public demonstrations against segregated facilities, beginning with the lunch counter at the local Woolworth's. Katherine "Willie" Tarrant, a precocious narrator in the tradition of Harper Lee's Scout in *To Kill A Mockingbird*, is a witness to the sea change enacted in her community by the power of individual courage and collective acts. Willie's voice establishes the contemplative, reflexive tone with the opening sentences of the first chapter, "Billie Holiday died and I turned twelve on the same hot July day. The saddest singing in the world was coming out of the radio, race radio that is, the radio of race" (Davis 1993, 7). Race and racial politics resound in the "shattering tones" of Billie's singing and the explicit vocal hierarchy of "white radio" stations in the South (7). But Willie's ear is also attuned to worlds far from rural Virginia: "I hadn't missed Cuba, no one could, because the white folks were so upset about it. It made them crazy, like Little Rock. Cuba broke all the rules" (9). Willie draws a direct connection between school desegregation in Little Rock, Arkansas, and revolution in Cuba, but Cuba more so than Little Rock fires her imagination: "I really didn't know anything about what it was like there. What I heard about was cha-chas, conga lines, glass-shiny dance floors, and swarming ship docks piled high with bales no man could carry—sugarcane, tobacco, coffee, cocoa. A mixture of Xavier Cugat and geography class. When I tried to envision the place now, in 1959, it was still a huge emporium, a roiling market of raw goods and battering rhythmic tongues, blown up from the drawings of slavery in my schoolbooks, except that the raggedy devils lazing on bales had cut machetes loose on the fancy suits. As I saw it, there were no cartoon Negroes in Cuba. And besides that, every time I thought about President Eisenhower, Fidel Castro was like Marlon Brando" (9–10). Willie locates Cuba as marketplace and revolutionary site alongside the popular cultural images of Cuban music and dance.

At twelve years old, Willie pursues a mainly solitary life of immersion in her familial and regional past, though she hardly remembers her mother, Leigh, who died suddenly when Willie was eight. Leigh Stanley Tarrant was a "free-thinking" outsider, who within a week of arriving at Turner College was "upsetting the school" because she "thought the Negroes running the college were stuck in the past, and she was a believer in all things modern" (25). Willie learns little of her mother from her father, Dixon Douglas Tarrant, a college teacher and "basically a nineteenth-century character who was lucky enough to be young in the 1920s" (25). Following his wife's death, Dixon becomes an ironic observer, parenting his teenaged son, Preston, and his adolescent daughter, but emotionally distant from them.

When Willie's ninety-year-old paternal grandmother, Louise Tarrant, dies during 1959, she bequeaths the diary of her only daughter to Willie. That diary links Willie directly to the life, longings, and frustrations of her Aunt Fanny who, before she could achieve her dream of leaving Turner and becoming a nurse, died of tuberculosis at the age of twenty-six. Fannie's secret excursions to traveling black shows and her involvement with a railroad man manifest both her commitment to the full extent of black life and her desire for transcending her closed community.

The deaths of the women in her family animate Willie's imagination and her quest to know life fully even within the restricted territory of segregated Virginia. However, the three deaths also propel her to embrace change because she recognizes the discrimination, gendered and racial, that made the desires of Fanny impossible to achieve, that motivated her grandmother to lash out against the physical landscape when she became pregnant with a tenth child, and that caused her mother to promote the welfare of black rural families. An active seer, Willie ultimately recognizes the transformation that rights activism has wrought not merely within her town but also within her own self and within her widowed father.

In taking up the registration of black voters in the poorer, rural, and less accessible areas adjacent to Turner, she continues the activist work begun as marching on picket lines with her father. In the process, Willie learns of her identification with her mother and an inherited connection to the community beyond the class-defined structures in which she functions in Turner. In a "newspaper-walled parlor," Evelyn Turner, a woman with two small children, immediately signs Willie's voting rights papers and then identifies Willie: "'You must be Leigh Tarrant's daughter,' she said matter-of-factly. . . . 'You got the very face of her on your face'" (281). Willie, who "never thought I had anything of her on my face," discovers that her mother had made a connection with the community based on the work of organizing and combating institutionalized racism. "But yes, yes indeedy I knew her. She was out here a lot. I'll do anything you want, chile, anything. I'll get everybody out here to go down to the courthouse if that's what y'all want. It's no problem. . . . I knew yo' mama. She tried to do something for the kids out here. Course the white folk wouldn't let her but she came out here and we all got organized 'cause she wanted to get a Boys Club started" (281). Willie has never heard of her mother's activism, because within her community Leigh was "the oddball everybody talked about as if she were a saint but for no reason in particular" (281).

The exploits of Leigh Tarrant in the past anticipate the work of her daughter Willie in apprehending the multiple meanings of rights and in attempting to effect the school desegregation decreed in *Brown*. Evelyn Turner's recollections restore a lost mother to her daughter:

Well, you mama was out here, but the white folks wouldn't give her a charter for no Boys Club. Then she said we ought to go down to the City Hall and we went. And she was a mess, too, wouldn't let nobody ride the bus 'cause she said it was wrong to be riding in the back. She was from someplace else, of course, so we just humored her on that one, but look at us now. It's funny, ain't it? We tried to get lights when they put lights out on the county road. We tried to get the road tarred, and named. . . . Then they run the railroad right t'ru like we wadn't even here. It's a whole nother bunch of folks over beyond the trees 'cross the tracks. She come out here and got some children that was left when the father disappear one time. The mother took sick and passed and I guess he couldn't handle it. (Davis, 281–282)

Evelyn Turner's account of Willie's mother trails off into a scenario that resembles what happened to Dixon when Leigh died. Dixon had disappeared emotionally from his children precisely because he could not handle his wife's death. That resemblance is not lost on Willie: "It was easy too to see what the old man [Dixon] had been up against, trying to give what a woman had taken with her to the grave" (282). That insight, coupled with more details of her mother's exploits (laying out a softball field still in use, identifying with the black underclass, taking her young daughter with her everywhere she worked among the poor), allows Willie not only to forgive her father for contemplating giving her up when his wife died but also to remember her mother's face and with that memory to recover the repressed face of a black boy whom she, as a child in the company of her mother, had seen killed by a train that refused to stop. Willie names him and the destruction that decimated an already impoverished community.

Evelyn Turner's words, "Leigh walked to her own drummer" (282), reverberate in Willie's completion of the narrative. It is not a story of triumphant marches in Turner and elsewhere in the South. Neither is it the successful desegregation of schools or stores nor the breaking of economic strangleholds over the black community. It is, instead, a reckoning of the cost of walking in the rights revolution. Willie concludes, "School integration did not come till after I finished high school. It took six more years" (295). She reveals that the boycott went on for several years during which businesses died, and in an act of retribution two years into the boycott, the authorities sent in the wrecking balls after declaring Turner "in need of urban renewal" (296). The people of Turner eventually shopped at the Buena Vista shopping mall, where the first restaurant opened after the passage of the Civil Rights Act in 1964.

During the summer after the demonstrations began, Willie and her best friend Marian continued the work of registering voters, but the town is different: "We passed Walters' department store and the others, nearly empty stores where only white people now shopped. There were no more pickets, because they were totally unnecessary. Ever since the police sicced dogs on people's mamas on the picket line nobody would go in there, not even people who didn't approve of the boycott. The store owners were regarded as animals for going along with the animals that brought out other animals. People didn't do business with animals. However closed off we might have been from the world other people knew, we regarded our ways as the ways of people" (290). Willie puts it in simple terms: "People didn't do business with animals." She continues with a clear delineation between the people and animals: "But the whites' ignorance that the people were the people and that the highest good was to wish another life had them up against the will of the humans to live as people. . . . We never questioned if the way of the people could survive our own actions. . . . And we never questioned if the way of the people could survive if we lived among the others, because it was the way of the people. . . . And the other way was the way of animals who sicced dogs on people's mamas and children. It was not the way" (291).

Of particular importance in *1959*'s denouement are the geopolitical connections made between the aftermath of *Brown* in one Virginia town and the impact of persistent racist practices on a generation of young people and on a global dispersal of those same practices. Willie persists in her activism, but sees herself moving with the others displaced from the razed Turner, "like nomads, scattered to the invisible perimeter" (297). Her brother Preston prepares for entering Howard University, while contemplating going further south to Nashville and other "places where the sit-ins still needed bodies; he'd gotten interested in a new organization called the Student Non-violent Coordinating Committee" (292). Preston's best friend Cole eschews college to enlist in the Army's Airborne Division in order to take a more activist stance than his father, Coleman, a novelist living within his own head.

Cole's military experiences, however, run counter to his expectations of positive interventions such as in Arkansas or Alabama. They signal the coming of covert operations around the globe, and especially in Vietnam. Cole "was dropped out of a helicopter into a fetid jungle without being told its name. In fact, he was told that, technically speaking, he was never there. And he should remember that fact. And when he finally returned to the States it was no longer the fifties and he was utterly mute" (294). Cole has "no way to account for so many places that didn't exist and things that didn't happen, things that 'we' would not do" (294). Dropped in the Alps "to run radio wires across a border to tie on to Russian lines or to undo lines that Russians had run to army communications lines," he disappears with his unit "from that place and all other places the same way, and then they hit the last place. . . . No passports, no visas, no borders. Just a landing strip. A helicopter. We weren't there and we had no problem there. . . . Just jungle" (295).

Secretive and officially nonexistent, his assignments are rife with shots, bullets, wounded and lifeless men doing "just a job" (295). They play out against the extended representation of violence in the attack of dogs on the protesting women and children of Turner who had surrounded Walters' Department Store in a peaceful, nonviolent demonstration. The mayor and town officials behind the attack carefully hide their role in the events, but one small brown woman with the same name as the white mayor challenges him: " 'He's your boy, you got him out here doing your dirty work for you. Him and all his Klan buddies are out here every day calling for blood, itching to get us all killed if they can. Don't think you fooling anybody. You in it too . . . acting like you don't have nothing to do with it. You-all think you still own us. You gonna sic dogs on your own kin, Burleigh?' " (268). On command, the dogs quickly rip into her arm, drawing blood; they also lunge into the women standing in shock and "tore into the women's legs, purses, skirts, arms" (269).

Davis sketches a parallel between the mayor's effort to disguise his part in authorizing and perpetrating the violence against the women and the attempts by the federal government to hide its aggressive moves around the globe. There is, for example, no mistaking Vietnam in Cole's representation of his unit's drop into "the last place": "For a miniature base in the middle of nowhere, it was well supplied with something like a PX, a screening room, mess, American trinkets. They said the French weren't a presence in the country anymore, but the people running the operation were French. Asian soldiers speaking French, American Pathfinders and Rangers, all specialists, training in English. There was no war. No perimeter. The jungle was on his skin like thick hair. The young Asian men squatted close to the ground. What they did there clung close to the ground too, and the vegetation closed in on everything that refused to move. There was no perimeter" (295).

What in 1959 is a warning of tragedies to come is in 1992, the year of the novel's publication, a fate completed, but with the imperialistic consequences still unfolding at the beginning of the twenty-first century, when the covert border crossings have less to do with military units with fire power being secretly dropped into jungles and more to do with multilateral trade agreements and corporate power that, not unlike the earlier militaristic excursions, have as their objective exerting control over nation-states.

In much the same way that Seattle was the enactment of contested borders that might also be read as a new world rights revolution against a corporate globalism and consumerist ideology, *1959*, *Betsey Brown*, and *Meridian* are relational narratives of rights that reference and remember *Brown v. Board* as challenging and contesting the narrow and strict legal confines into which law and custom attempted to place the equal protection clause of the Fourteenth Amendment. At the end of *The Third Life of Grange Copeland* (1970), Alice Walker depicts a carload of black and white youths driving Georgia's back roads to register black voters, and she has one of them connect Grange Copeland's appearance to that of Bayard Rustin, the brilliant organizer of the March on Washington. With that casual reference, Walker links a legendary hero of the Civil Rights movement and a gay rights activist with an uneducated, poor farmer in the segregated South, and in so doing she moves Grange into a realm of political action for rights. That very movement made possible by *Brown* is precisely what ignited a society to accept moral imperatives when faced with injustice and, whether acknowledged or not, it is what lingered in the social memory of the Seattle activists.

Works Cited

Davis, Thulani. [1992] 1993. *1959, A Novel*. New York: HarperPerennial.

Martin, Waldo E. 1998. *Brown v. Board of Education: A Brief History with Documents*. Boston: Bedford.

Shange, Ntozake. 1985. *Betsey Brown, A Novel*. New York: Saint Martin's.

Tushnet, Mark. 2002. "*Brown v. Board of Education*." In *Race on Trial: Law and Justice in American History*, ed. Annette Gordon-Reed, 160–173. New York: Oxford University Press.

Walker, Alice. 1970. *The Third Life of Grange Copeland*. New York: Harcourt Brace Jovanovich.

———. 1976. *Meridian*. New York: Harcourt Brace Jovanovich.

CHAPTER 15

Along the Border

Bill V. Mullen

> Texas prisonz mah home
> (Get treated like a slave)
> All I want is to get out,
> Maybe move to Abu Ghraib
>
> Goin' to Abu Ghraib!
> (A torturous vacation)
> Ten years in Abu Ghraib!
> Do mah time in another nation
> — Tiamat Lam'en'ehar

> At times I fly around and see situations that remind me of the tough times that I went through, some of the poverty. . . . I sometimes see myself in the kids that are out there. It reminds me of our days growing up near Mexico.
> — Lt. General Ricardo S. Sanchez

In hindsight, James Byrd's street-dragging execution by white supremacists in 1997 in Jasper, Texas, seems like the opening salvo of the Bush era in American politics: a jacked-up bit of white road rage in which dark-skinned men are dragged behind the hot rod forces of history—the lynch mob as think tank.[1] That domestic terror is one of only many moments threatened with evisceration in the post-Seattle world. As Amy Kaplan has noted, one impact of 9/11 was the conscious production of new forms of political amnesia meant to eradicate stains on the national record; the reappropriation, for example, of the phrase "ground zero" as a metaphor for the "exceptionalism of American suffering" (Kaplan 2003, 84).

This essay will attempt to counter ethnic cleansing as both dememorialization and political praxis by examining how the U.S.-Mexico border in particular is both a literal and figurative site, a new ground zero, as it were, for marking a historical continuum from Seattle to the current war in Iraq. I will argue first that the border discloses the objective and political conditions that must be confronted by activists who seek to recuperate the political momentum that led to the important insurrection of antiglobalist, antiracist, and prodemocracy organizers in Seattle. Second, I will propose that the border must be understood in the wake of 9/11 as central to the symbolic configuration of contemporary civilizationist discourse that has undergirded U.S. imperialism before and after Seattle. It is a discourse grounded in racism, political disenfranchisement, and hypernationalism, on the one hand, and a culturalist rhetoric that seeks to expropriate the nationalist logic of borders as a primal strategy of political containment, on the other. Third, analysis of the border as physical location and political trope reveals the foundational logic of the U.S. state's war in perpetuity against progressive anticapitalist forces in the United States and globally, dating to the era of the Cold War. This perpetual "border war" demonstrates the significance of "terrorism" as a racialized remaking of capitalism's old foes and the old boss/new boss sameness of the corporate state in drawing hard boundaries around fatal shores. Finally, attention to the unfolding history of the U.S.-Mexico border in the wake of both Seattle and 9/11 reveals, or re-reveals, newly contested sites for possible political struggle that we cannot afford to forget in light of efforts after 9/11 to erase, eradicate, and blur the memories of 1999, before and beyond.

In the spring of 2004, results of the 2003 census disclosed that the state of Texas had become for the first time in recorded U.S. history a nonwhite-majority state. African Americans, Asian Americans, Native Americans, and Latinos, the state's largest ethnic minority, were reported to slightly outnumber "whites" by a 51.5−49.5 ratio ("Whites" 2004, 1). The census also showed that poverty in Texas had jumped a full percentage point between 2000 and 2003 (about 200,000 new poor); that the share of Texas households with incomes under $25,000 increased (as did those with incomes above $150,000), and that Texas ranked dead last among U.S. states in percentage of people without health insurance: 24.6, a full nine points above the national average (Sallee 2004; U.S. Census Bureau 2003, 21, 23). Latinos comprised more than 57 percent of the uninsured. (U.S. Census Bureau 2003, 25). Texas is also home to the three poorest metropolitan areas in the United States: McAllen-Edinburg-Mission, Brownsville-Harlingen-San Benito, and Laredo. All three sit along the U.S.-Mexico border near *colonias*—largely serviceless communities of immigrants. After 9/11, this same border stretch saw a rapid rise in arrests, detainments, and deaths of immigrants when Immigration and Naturalization Service and Border Patrol operations were folded into the Department of Homeland Security.[2]

These post-9/11 security measures along the border were contiguous with Texas's historical disciplining of its demographic majority; a study conducted by the Death Penalty Information Center revealed that in 2003 Texas continued to lead the nation in the execution of nonwhites. Since 1976 Texas has killed more than 35 percent of all the prisoners killed in the United States. Of those 321, nearly half were Black or Latino (Death Penalty Information Center, 1−3).

Before Seattle and after 9/11, the U.S.-Mexico border has also been the nation's most persistent site of the violence against workers that was inaugurated by freefall globalization. In Ciudad Juarez, Mexico, across the border from El Paso, more than 340 women have been murdered since the arrival of foreign-owned assembly factories, or *maquiladores*, in the early 1990s. There are more than 400 *maquiladores* along the Juarez border owned by U.S. corporations such as Ford, Alcoa, RCA, General Motors, and General Electric. They operate in tariff-free zones with endless supplies of cheap labor, and generate as much as $16 billion per year in profit. The vast majority of murdered women are members of the *maquiladora* workforce who ride a bus to work from the country to the city to earn \$3 to \$4 a day. Many of the women killed in Juarez have also been raped, slashed, maimed, or dismembered. Their sexual lynchings articulate their classed, raced, and gendered position at a familiar nexus of north-south capitalism; they are sisters under the skin to New York and Bangkok's textile slaves whose lives disclose the androcentric terror of globalization.

The impossibility of mediating these conditions through traditional democratic means has also been borne out by recent events along the border. In the November 2004 vote in Arizona, for example, a statewide measure easily passed that tightened controls on immigration, required voters to show proof of citizenship, and made it a crime for state workers not to report illegal immigrants seeking benefits such as welfare (*New York Times* 2004). Arizona and Texas have seen a sharp resurgence since 9/11 of border vigilantes who have kidnapped, repatriated, or killed newly arrived immigrants. Indeed, the link between NAFTA, new racial disciplinarity, globalization, and the ideological adjudication of the border in the American imagination of empire was perhaps most sharply articulated in the midst of the 2004 presidential race when Samuel Huntington, past president of the American Political Science Association and former coordinator of security planning for the National Security Council, published his book *Who Are We? The Challenges to America's National Identity*. Huntington argued that unchecked Latino immigration to the United States would have this consequence: "the cultural division between Hispanics and Anglos will replace the racial division between blacks and whites as the most serious cleavage in American society" (Huntington 2004, 28). A form of Manichean border theology, Huntington's brown peril thesis, in the tradition of Madison Grant's *The Passing of the White Race* and Lothrop Stoddard's *The Rising Tide of Color against White World Supremacy*, perilously linked bilingualism and job competition, intermarriage and illegal immigration.

Yet as David Palumbo-Liu has noted, Huntington's book was part of a much longer neoconservative project to deploy democracy as a surrogate strategy for containing dissent against authoritarian capitalism. The book was an update of work Huntington had contributed much earlier to the 1973 Trilateral Commission convened by David Rockefeller. The 1975 publication of the commission, *The Crisis of Democracy: Report on the Governability of Democracies to the Trilateral Commission,* (Crozier 1975), included a section titled "The United States," authored by Huntington. In it, Huntington cautioned that "In the United States the strength of democracy poses a problem for the governability of democracy in a way that is not the case everywhere. . . . We have come to recognize that there are potentially desirable limits to the indefinite extension of political democracy. Democracy will have a longer life if it has a more balanced existence." This balance depended, wrote Huntington, "in the basic American value system and the degree of commitment which groups feels toward that system" (Crozier 1975, 115). Huntington later distilled his thesis into his 1996 book *The Clash of Civilizations and the Remaking of World Order,* published during the ascent of the U.S. anti-globalization movement. Huntington argued that in a post-Cold War world the major conflicts "will not occur between nations nor through ideological conflict (capitalism vs. socialism) but through 'civilizational conflict'" (Huntington 1996, 118). In particular, Huntington cited the economic, military, and economic expansion of "Asian civilizations" and the widening demography of Islam as factors in what he called the decline in "relative influence" of the West (305).

It is important to note that the "Battle of Seattle" offered a quite different reading, or antireading, to the Huntington thesis generally: "globalization," not "civilization"; economy, not culture; capitalist process, not racial and ethnic difference was the engine driving history toward some fatal inequality, a post-Third World hegemony that demonstrated not the "jihad versus McWorld" scenario of Huntington's civilization thesis but the terrifying specter of a world totally penetrated by market forces. Yet Huntington's thesis was also meant to anticipate and contain the specter of multiple Seattles. As David Montejano has noted, Huntington's total access to neoconservative inner circles since the 1970s cemented his ideological relationship to both Reagan and Bush Republicanisms, which now occupy five of our last seven presidencies, and to Washington policymakers. Indeed, the Huntington thesis finds sinister echo in both the Hart-Rudman Report on National Security that is the harbinger of the Patriot Act, and the Bush foreign policy statement on global "hegemony" that coincided with his arrival in office. Seen in this light, the 1975 *Trilateral Commission Report* must be understood as an early template for Homeland Security and a recipe for the rise of the carceral/punitive state that has reached its apotheosis on the U.S.-Mexico border. The shadows of both fall across this gloomy assessment by Palumbo-Liu: "The conditions for a participatory democracy are worsening as the imperative to protect our civilization trump all other considerations. In this case, the rights and privileges of minorities of all stripes are at risk. The antidemocratic motif laid down in Huntington's 1975 essay is now reinforced by the current crisis [of 9/11]. American national identity has now been blended with civilizational identity as the United States tries to rally its allies against terrorism" (Palumbo-Liu 2002, 126).

It is this linguistic and political trajectory that likewise interests Nikhil Pal Singh. In his essay "Cold War Redux: On the 'New Totalitarianism,'" published in an important *Radical History Review* special issue on 9/11, Singh argues that "It is almost too obvious that *terrorism* now occupies the place and function that *fascism* held in World War II and communism held within the discourse of the cold war" (Singh 2003, 173). Singh argues that contemporary neoconservatives and members of the Bush regime have gradually recycled a version of Hannah Arendt's influential Cold War totalitarianism thesis. Specifically, Singh writes, the Cold War "Inaugurated an era in which racial terror could be forgotten, repressed, or displaced onto others by the world's dominant powers. The United States in effect mediated the process by attempting to make the story of its own intranational triumph over a history of racial differentiation into a supranational object lesson for the rest of the world — even as it was, in the famous words of U.S. airforce general Curtis LeMay, 'bombing Vietnam back to the Stone Age'" (176).

For Singh, 9/11 was a catalyst for the return of this repressed. Colin Powell's role as secretary of state signifies at once what Singh calls the "disciplining" of Black recalcitrance to the aims of the U.S. Cold War project embodied in a new "military multiculturalism," while Christian Nationalist John Ashcroft "reminds us that in the crisis of fashioning a true Americanism, the resources of *herrenvolk* republicanism remain close at hand" (Singh 2003, 177). Like Palumbo-Liu, Singh is less than sanguine about the consequences of this project. They produce, he writes,

> a world in which democracy becomes less and less relevant as an orienting concept in social and political life, while violence reigns supreme. It means a world in which democracy remains caught between the simulated inclusiveness of multicultural capitalism that vitiates sovereignty from above and the racist ressentiment of nationalist reassertion that truncates it from below. Indeed . . . the historic inability to think the constitution of democratic powers outside the antinomy of ethnic absolutism and capitalist liberalism has led in our own time to a fundamental blurring of the boundaries between war and peace. Warfare and violence, once though to result from the breakdown of normal politics, now appear as the norm rather than the exception. . . . It is now clear that anyone who believed bringing down the Berlin Wall in 1989 would bring a 'peace-dividend' had made a sore mistake. We live in a state of constant warfare and in a warfare state: from the cold war to the War on Poverty to the Vietnam War, to the 'police actions' and proxy wars in Central America, to the War on Drugs to the Gulf War to the culture wars to the War on Terror, war provides the general matrix for social and political life in the postcontemporary United States and in the world that is its open frontier. (Singh 2003, 178)

Singh's description of endless war as "open frontier" implies the deracination of borders — political, economic, military — as fundamental to imperial projects. It is a haunting echo and reiteration of a favored maxim of global theorists: act locally, think globally. This odd conflation presents an opportunity for us to think through something we might call, in the old-fashioned Marxian sense, contradiction. In my final pages, I will explore how this insight may help us determine what exactly, then, has been the "dividend" of Seattle in the face of all that has happened since.

Signs Beyond Borders

"If we want to take up the challenge of the twenty-first century, we must also learn languages." Gayatri Spivak, "Terror: A Speech After 9–11" (Spivak, 110).

In her 2003 essay titled "Homeland Insecurities: Reflections on Language and Space," Amy Kaplan compels our attention in the wake of 9/11 to "the relationship between language and space, how words map, blur, and reconstruct the conceptual, affective, and symbolic borders between spheres once thought of as distinctly separate — as either national or international, domestic or foreign, 'at home' or 'abroad'" (Kaplan 2003, 82). Kaplan reminds us that the acts of writing and reading are themselves constitutive of political maps and political choices. Indeed, thinking of language as delineative of literal borders of political discourse resonates with Singh's argument that the failure to think democracy beyond "the antinomy of ethnic absolutism and capitalist liberalism" has helped to efface a wide range of political categories and choices. Abu Ghraib and Seattle, I want to suggest, may be seen as precise embodiments of this antinomy, and thus urgent signposts for thinking and *signing* our way to a different world. How we do we get there from here?

First, I think, we need to hold the language of critical reflection on the Left to more careful scrutiny. "Globalization" and "neoliberalism," for example, favorite terms of both Seattle anarchists and academic Marxists, have been exposed by events since 9/11 to be inadequate descriptors of what might be called the objective conditions in our time. Neither comes close to capturing the synergy of domestic repression, new racism, and xenophobia post-9/11, and the specific anti-Islamic genocidal fervor of the U.S. invasion of Iraq. "Empire," the term for example favored by Michael Hardt and Antonio Negri to describe the current American project of spatial and military remapping, comes closer, but as Singh again astutely points out, "By privileging the imperial over the republican side of U.S. power, it overlooks the ways in which different U.S. racial interests and racial imageries continued to play to different audiences, and in doing so help to mediate the contradictions between the empire and the republic" (177). Empire, that is, provides analysis of American expansion divorced from its internal mechanizations. We might return then to the old favorite imperialism, or neoimperialism, with its vestigial "internal colonization" thesis, to describe the racial terrors of life in the homeland as an inevitable stage of capitalist expansion. Yet this term is also limited as a descriptor of how processes like "military multiculturalism," diasporic population movement, transnational citizenship, and particularly local formations of capital — like, say, the border *maquiladores*—challenge stable models of settler colonialism and neocolonialism. Finally, there is "democracy" itself, a word which, if I am correct, has reached a kind of interpretive aporia that is metonymic of its abusive political applications.

To help resolve the problem of conceptual and political borders, we might also turn collectively to the language of borderlands theory. Writers from and of the border, after all, particularly U.S. Chicana/o writers, have provided numerous frameworks for evaluating the place of the border in the theory and practice of Cold War and post-Cold War capitalism. These frameworks have carefully delineated the border as both a space for lived racial and ethnic experience and a marker of mixed or double consciousness. "La Frontera," in the words of Gloria Anzaldua, literally the U.S.-Mexico border, is a place that marks the mind and body of migrant workers, women, lesbians, and mestizas. Anzaluda's "new mestiza consciousness" is also an effort to produce a *dialectical* border consciousness that can resolve numerous the antimonies of life under racist empires of capital.[3]

Indeed, it is toward a new theory and language of this experience that Marcial Gonzalez points us in his own powerful formulation of a Chicano/a cultural criticism. Gonzalez, too, acknowledges the importance of borderlands theory as a means of articulating the powerful contradictions of lived experience in the contact zone between nations and cultures. Yet, he cautions: "I hold . . . that the social contradictions of class exploitation, racism, and sexism cannot be solved by constructing a cultural identity in the image of the most repressive and racist symbol of demarcation and exclusion produced by capitalism, nationalism, and imperialism—namely, the border. Ideological ambivalence becomes significant only through the meticulous critique of the social and historical determinants of that ambivalence, and only through a praxis aimed at undoing the very structures of power that lie at the root of ambivalence" (Gonzalez 2003, 295).

Gonzalez offers a challenge to identify border histories and border narratives that may help us develop a critical realism that seeks to dismantle racism and exploitation as it seeks to dismantle borders. As space is limited, I will offer a single but I think revealing example of a place to begin thinking on that challenge. In the wake of 9/11, the U.S. Phelps Dodge mining company, a pioneer of nineteenth-century U.S. capital expansion, struck a deal with New Mexico Institute of Mining and Technology, or New Mexico Tech, a small engineering school in Playas, New Mexico, to sell the entire town. Playas, located about fifty miles from the U.S. border with Hiladgo, Mexico, was originally "constructed" by Phelps Dodge in the 1970s as a bedroom community for its mining company employees. In the 1990s, the town went belly up, and as the town boarded up and the population declined, Phelps went shopping. Salvation came in the form of $5 million from the Department of Homeland Security, which channeled the money through New Mexico Tech to turn the college into a school for antiterrorism training. The school will be used to train security, medical, and military personnel to prevent and respond to terrorist attacks (Romero 2004, 20).

Playas sits in the shadow of the White Sands Missile Range and Trinity Site, where the first atomic weapons tests in the United States were conducted prior to the August 1945 annihilation of Hiroshima and Nagasaki. As it happens, Playas is also located near where General John J. Pershing once searched for Pancho Villa, who attacked the nearby bordertown of Columbus, New Mexico, in 1916 in retaliation for U.S. support for the anti-revolutionist Carranza regime in Mexico. In that very same year, Phelps Dodge, according to Barbara Kingsolver, earned more than a 200 percent increase in profits owing to the demand for communications cable and copper shell jackets manufactured for use in World War I. In 1917, "rankled" by the meagerness of their wages against corporate profits, miners in Bisbee, Arizona, went on strike. A preponderance of Mexican miners led the strike. In July of that year, Kingsolver writes, "a posse of vigilantes rode into the streets of Bisbee, arrested some two thousand striking miners and sympathizers, forced them into waiting boxcars of the El Paso and Southwestern (a Phelps Dodge subsidiary), and hauled them over 173 miles of desert to a detention camp in central New Mexico, from which few ever returned to Bisbee" (Kingsolver 1989, 9).

Yet out of the 1917 Bisbee strike came impetus for the formation of the International Union of Mine, Mill, and Smelter Workers. "Mine Mill" became one of American labor's safe homes for Mexicans, women, Communist and radical workers, and labor organizers until well into the twentieth century, and acted as *agent provocateur* of some of its most memorable strikes, perhaps best commemorated in the classic 1954 film *Salt of the Earth*. Today, Mine Mill is gone from Playa, as Playa has gone Homeland Security. Phelps Dodge, meanwhile, is getting more than 60 percent of what it originally sought for the "sale" of Playas, while its workers await direction from Homeland Security. Says Van Romero, vice president for research and economic development at New Mexico

Tech, based in nearby Socorro, "We figure about 200 jobs should be created by our transformation of Playas, and some of those opportunities should to the people living there. We're going to make it as safe as possible for them" (Romero 2004, 20).

Playas, New Mexico, offers a fresh political and semantic marker along what I have been calling the border from Seattle to Abu Ghraib. That is, as a site for recognizing racist, nationalist, and capitalist assault on workers and campaigns of internalized "terror" for that fundamental and fundamentalist American project of making the world safe for democracy. Seeing these signposts along the border may help move us past the antimony of ethnic absolutism and liberal capitalism suggested by Singh. Indeed, Playas discloses in uncanny historical detail that "globalization" is the terror of life lived in the in-between of this antinomy. "We are everywhere," the rallying cry of Seattle and the antiglobalization movement, was meant to express the possibilities of life beyond it. In this respect, Playas may also help us recognize and recover a critical realism that is both pre-Seattle and post-9/11: a dialectical voice of labored, gendered, multiracial, and Communist protest that can still emerge from the zero-sum logic that comprises the U.S. response to "terror" from McAllen to Najaf. It is time, that is, to think and speak again the language of new worlds rising from the ashes of the old. We have nothing to lose but our borders and our chains!

Notes

1. Sanchez, a native of Rio Grande, Texas, is former commander of U.S. ground forces in Iraq; quoted in Limon 2004, 30.

2. Approximately 43,000 persons were deported "without judicial review" from the United States in 2003. On August 10, 2004, the Department of Homeland Security announced that it would expand its use of "expedited removal," whereby immigrants are deported without first going before a trained immigration judge *Yoland Chavez* (Leyva 2004).

3. See Gloria Anzaluda, *Borderlands/La Frontera* (1999). See also Sonia Saldivar-Hull, *Feminism on the Border* (2000) and Ramon Saldivar, *Chicano Narratives* (1990).

Works Cited

Anzaluda, Gloria. 1999. *Borderlands/La Frontera: Towards a New Mestiza Consciousness.* San Francisco: Aunt Lute Books.

Crozier, Michel. 1975. *The Crisis of Democracy: Report on the Governability of Democracies to the Trilateral Commission.* New York: New York University Press.

Death Penalty Information Center. www://deathpenaltyinfo.org.

Gonzalez, Marcial. 2003. "A Marxist Critique of Borderlands Postmodernism: Adorno's Negative Dialectics and Chicano Cultural Criticism." In Bill V. Mullen and James Smethurst, eds., *Left of the Color Line: Race, Radicalism and Modern Literatures of the United States,* 279–298. Chapel Hill: University of North Carolina Press.

Huntington, Samuel. 1996. *The Clash of Civilizations and the Remaking of World Order.* New York: Simon and Schuster.

———. 2004. *Who Are We?: The Challenges to America's National Identity.* New York: Simon and Schuster.

Kaplan, Amy. 2003. "Homeland Insecurities: Reflections on Language and Space." *Radical History Review* 85 (Winter): 82–93.

Kingsolver, Barbara. 1989. *Holding the Line: Women in the Great Arizona Mine Strike of 1983.* Ithaca, N.Y.: ILR Press.

Leyva, Yoland Chavez. 2004. "Expedited Removal Threatens Human Rights." *La Voz de Esporanza* 17.6 (October) 13.

Limon, José. 2004. "Translating Empire: The Border Homeland of Rio Grande City, Texas." *American Quarterly* 56.1 (March): 30.

Montejano, David. 2004. "Who Is Samuel P. Huntington? Patriotic Reading for Anglo Protestants Who Live in Fear of the Reconquista." *Texas Observer* 96.16 (August 13). http://www.texasobserver.org.

New York Times. 2004. November 14, A14.

Palumbo-Liu. 2002. "Multiculturalism Now: Civilization, National Identity, and Difference before and after September 11th." *Boundary 2* 29.2: 110–127.

Perkinson, Robert. 2004. "The Banality of Abu Ghraib." *Daily Times* (June 2), *www.dailytimes.com.*

Romero, Simon. 2004. "In Dying Desert Town, Residents Eagerly Await 'Terror Attacks.'" *New York Times,* September 26, 1, 20.

Salle, Rad. 2004. "Poverty in Texas Climbs Steadily." *Houston Chronicle,* August 27.

Salvidar, Ramon. 1990. *Chicano Narratives: The Dialectics of Difference.* Madison: University of Wisconsin Press.

Salvidar-Hull, Sonia. 2000. *Feminism on The Border.* Berkely: University of California Press.

Singh, Nikhil Pal. 2003 "Cold War Redux: On the 'New Totalitarianism'." *Radical History Review* 85 (Winter): 171–181.

Spivak, Gayatri Chakravorty. 2004. "Terror: A Speech after 9/11." *Boundary 2* 31.2: 82–111.

Tiamat Lam'en'ehar. 2004. "The Abu Ghraib Jam." *www.thesocialistparty.org/spo/archive/songs/abu_ghraib.html.*

U.S. Census Bureau. 2003. "Income, Poverty and Health Insurance Coverage in the United States." Washington, D.C.

"Whites No Longer the Majority in Texas." 2004. *Houston Chronicle,* August 27.

CHAPTER 16

On Behalf of Tomato Pickers Everywhere

Judith Scot-Smith Girgus

On a warm day in late April, a day when the humidity is low and breezes waft through open classroom windows, a day designed to distract students, making them wish for the indolent days of summer — on this day, as on all days, I booted up my computer to send in my absence report and to check my email. The first email I opened came from a freshman, Becky, whose curly hair was never quite kempt and whose uniform skirt was always a bit twisted. Her email read, "There are workers in Florida who harvest tomatoes for the tacos at Taco Bell. These workers pick all day for 42 and a half-cents (not dollars) for each 30 pound bucket of tomatoes. This is less than a tenth of the minimum wage and therefore illegal in the United States. I have the address of the President of Taco Bell, and I have made a petition for all of us to sign! Can I bring it to class?"

Students at this private single-gender school where I have been teaching for fifteen years have laptops, books that come with CDs, tutors when needed, opportunities to travel during a three-week period in January, a student-teacher ration of 14 to 1. They have also internalized the charge that "Great privilege requires great responsibility." Becky was acting on her sense of responsibility. Ultimately, her epiphany served to connect her to those who suffered unjustly. I asked Becky how she had heard of the picker's plight. "On my computer," she replied.[1]

Although I had worried about my students surfing questionable sites and spending inordinate amounts of time viewing gender-demeaning online catalogs, here was evidence that students were also accessing sites that broadened their sense of the world. At school as well as at home, students with technology at hand move into and through a global world. Kevin Leaderer, assistant professor of education at Vanderbilt University, spent a great deal of time observing my students' use of their laptops during the spring of 2003, noting that while technology puts students in touch with many facets of the culture we wish they would avoid, it also serves to dismantle the walls of the classroom, leaving students like Becky, as well as teachers, to travel the world over discovering for themselves, as Becky had, the harsh realities of life for so many in our world.[2] Becky's petition became a metaphor for her freshman English class of the responsibilities they were challenged to embrace.

In the years before I came to this private institution, I had taught for sixteen years in public schools in New Mexico and Oregon. Often my students were children whose parents were migrant workers like those whom Becky so earnestly sought to help. These students needed no computers to understand the economics of tomato picking, fruit picking, and migrant work. In those early years of my teaching career in New Mexico, I noted that students would be in my class for a period of time and then disappear. I learned too that they would very often, weeks or months later, return. Their return was based on the seasonal work whose labor pool their parents were part of. I developed a system of making folders for all students where they could keep their papers, tests, quizzes, and handouts. Once I realized that many of the vanishing students would return, I saved their folders, adding handouts and other materials that marked the passing of the year. Thus, if students did resurface, I could return their folders to them, hoping that in some way this collection of odds and ends would make them feel as if someone had remembered who they were and had counted on them to return.

For these public-school students, unlike the students at the private girl's school, there was no privilege but only a great deal of responsibility. Helping feed the family was at the top of the list. Often this involved absence from school or moving to another location to join with family members in an attempt to keep the family solvent. These youngsters did not need laptops to know how much a bushel of picked tomatoes or peaches would bring — or would not bring. They were intimately familiar with the value of these labors. Although the school district was large, with more than thirty elementary schools, eighteen middle schools, and twelve high schools, no program was in place to help these young people; they shifted from one school to another. Sometimes their records would follow them — sometimes not. At best, if and when they returned to a school, they were given their previous class schedule. Thus, my folder system was for many one of the few constants in their educational experience.

The sense of flux for these students was exacerbated by the loosely monitored curriculum guidelines. For overburdened administrators, quelling behavioral difficulties was inherently more pressing than monitoring what was being taught. Eventually, the school system made two major efforts. In both cases, however, the chasm between theory and practice rendered the efforts ineffective. First, funds were allocated to provide textbooks for every student. Texas book companies profited enormously by this sale; yet, in language arts no curriculum was developed for using these books.[3] Thus, teachers taught a short story here, a skill lesson there. They used these basal readers without training or guidance on how to accommodate individual learner differences. Money became available for textbook companies but not for classroom curriculum development.

Second, specialists were engaged to help classroom teachers with reading programs and to aid non-English–speaking students through pull-out programs designed to enable them to acquire English as a second language. Although the theoretical plan appeared to have merit, in reality an occasional visit to a classroom by a reading specialist for two sessions of thirty minutes per week in a pull-out program for language acquisition did not lessen the challenges in reading and language that impoverished students faced. Indeed, these measures were superficial, merely masking the indifference of the system to low-income students. The programs looked good on paper and in grant applications, but the reality is that disabled readers need more than a weekly visit from the reading specialist, and English-as-a-second-language learners need more than an hour a week in a pull-out program. These ventures did not create educational equality, for they were no match for the unseen power broker, money. In this large school district, socioeconomic conditions created segregated schools. Then as now, schools located in affluent neighborhoods have parents who make their voices heard and become advocates for their children. Parents of the affluent understood the system, could travel to Santa Fe to lobby for educational benefits, could in many invisible ways create privileges for schools in economically solvent neighborhoods. Students from disadvantaged areas of the city whose parents cannot speak English or are working two jobs go without advocates.

By 1986, in New Mexico, another program designed with good intentions served only to disempower further those whom it was meant to help. Work-study programs for low-achieving/low-income students placed high school students in classes for half the day and in businesses like Wendy's or McDonald's for the other half. These youngsters received credit for the hours they worked. Ironically, in many ways, they also received a life sentence. Their chances to improve reading and writing skills were minimized because they were at school on a limited basis. They received little or no college counseling, no information on Pell grants and SAT testing, and were not tracked into Advanced Placement (AP) courses. They were tracked into a service economy which more often than not would be theirs for life. Toward the end of my tenure in this school district, I stopped for gasoline at the end of my teaching day. There was Rudy, a young man I had taught several years before when he was in seventh grade. At that time, Rudy was known for his baseball prowess: he had talent. However, he had gone on to become part of the work-study program and now at nineteen was married, had one child, and worked at the gas station. He never took an AP class; he never took the ACT or the SAT; he knew nothing of Pell grants; and he did not have a baseball scholarship, as probably he should have had, to the University of New Mexico.[4]

Although the years have passed, inequities continue to plague the educational system. Thus, in the first half of my teaching career, I found my students on dead-end paths. Teaching under these conditions, I could empathize with their plight. Where could they go from this world of work-study, from a world where a folder with an odd assortment of papers was all that separated them from anonymity? In the second half of my career, an additional fifteen years, I have encountered another conundrum, different yet equally disturbing. In 1990, when I began teaching at a single-gender preparatory school, I found inequities ranging from administrators who wear blinders, to parents who believe that their hefty tuition payments give them power over the curriculum, to gender and sexual orientation discrimination.[5] These imperfections obstruct the ability of a teacher to use literature as a window into worlds where social and economic injustices prevail.

When I first came to the school, I found a language arts curriculum almost totally absent of women and minority representation, since school policy was to teach "the canon." At that time, literature and the teaching of it in any high school found itself in a stranglehold created by Jacques Lacan and Jacques Derrida, theorists of the later half of the twentieth century. The abstract and impenetrable nature of the work by such intellectuals and literary critics left the high school teacher with very few places to go for literary criticism and analysis that could be applied to the classroom. Stranded, many sought safety in prosaic topics, topics manageable for the teenage mind: the use of color in Fitzgerald's

The Great Gatsby; the significance of the hunt in Faulkner's *Go Down, Moses.* These predictable topics were wedded to a static, unchanging, and unchallenged canon of literature. Thus, the literary works of the first half of the century remained the staple of the 1960s and 1970s. No avenue was open that connected literature to social injustice and educational inequities. An alternative to the reduction of texts to incomprehensible theory appeared on the educational horizon when the boat people began arriving from Vietnam after Saigon fell; when Caesar Chavez made us aware of the desperation of migrant workers; when Betty Friedan exposed us to the *Feminine Mystique.* And when Martin Luther King expressed a dream, his dream included whites and blacks and even garbage workers in Memphis.

These political and social upheavals inspired classroom teachers to look past the established curriculum and toward using trade books and anthologies that reflected the diversity of the country and the brilliance of many who had been invisible and unheard. Both the trade books and the new editions of anthologies like the *Norton Anthology of American Literature* reflected more accurately the world as both teachers and students experienced it.[6] With the backing of the changing definition of appropriate literature, I found that the curriculum committee could be persuaded to include more diversity in the language arts curriculum for grades five through twelve. The content of the curriculum for these young women began to be reshaped and newly envisioned.

The *English Journal,* the established publication of the National Council of Teachers of English, provided a ready venue for teachers and educators to present new perspectives on America. In addition to gender, issues would be devoted to racial and ethnic diversity. Articles would advance literature that highlighted socioeconomic disparity. The journal proffered ideas for broadening the curriculum so that it became a reflection of the wider world. Thus, during the 1990s, issues appeared with themes focused on "Genderizing the Curriculum." One issue included articles on "Why Do We Need to Genderize?" and "Women's Literature in High School." Another issue, "A Classroom Kaleidoscope," carried articles on postcolonial literature, multicultural challenges, and cross-cultural connections in the classroom. Still another issue touted "New Voices: The Canon of the Future."[7] Novels such as Amy Tan's *Joy Luck Club,* Sandra Cisneros's *House on Mango Street,* and Leslie Silko's *Ceremony* were added to reading lists. These works not only offered windows to the worlds of ethnic minorities but also gave voice to socioeconomic experiences not often heard by students of privilege. Anthologies of American literature, too, began to revise the choice of selections, presenting a portrait that was not just white, Christian, male, and monied. Revised editions included works by Toni Cade Bambera, Maxine Hong Kinston, Simon Ortiz, Joy Harjo, and Denise Chavez.[8] Subsequent editions included an even broader representation.[9] During the last decade of the twentieth century, classroom teachers helped America redefine itself by creating a new literary realism for their students. Perhaps the impact was greatest and most valuable in affluent, privileged private schools like the one I teach in; but I was to learn that still waters could be deceptive and deep.

Clearly, administrators and the educational bureaucracy were sensitive to these changes. A review of the themes and articles in established journals like

Educational Leadership, the premier publication of the Association for Supervision and Curriculum Development (ASCD), indicates interest in the reinvention of the American self. Articles on gender and class studies, ethnicity, multicultural education, global perspectives, and economic diversity suggested that those in administrative positions supported the revision of the curriculum.[10]

And then 9/11 happened and the war on terror began. The strike by al Quaeda's jihadists and the war on terror instantly quieted the movement toward inclusivity. Almost overnight the themes of the *English Journal* returned to the safe and noncontroversial. For example: January 2001, "The Lure of Young Adult Literature"; January 2002, "Teaching and Writing Poetry"; November 2003, "Being and Becoming a Teacher"; March 2004, "Teaching the Many Conventions of Language."[11] Like the soccer moms who ensconced themselves in SUVs and the families who found reassurance in McMansions and Faux Chateaux, teachers in their writings immediately returned to the prosaic.[12] Those who had given voice and support for almost twenty years to the groundswell movement celebrating an ethnically and economically diverse America sounded retreat.

As the war on terror found its way into the American consciousness, one would assume that a similar review of ASCD's *Educational Leadership* would mirror the *English Journal's* return to conventional themes and articles. Curiously, it does not, and one would assume that at the administrative level, educators were holding steady. ASCD articles remain forward looking. Seemingly, for those on the administrative level, there is no turning back; thus, the stated position remains one that seemingly embraces literary realism. At the school with which I am familiar, however, a close examination of policies and procedures uncovers a regression to the staid and an entrenchment in the traditional. Reaction at the administrative level is more complicated because it is discreet, disguised; it is difficult to challenge because it exists behind a smokescreen.

What I discern from the vantage of the classroom is that a chasm exists between what actually obtains and what is set forth in the journals and stated as policy. At this school, just as in the public school system, a gap prevails at the administrative level between theory and practice, presenting a way for an administration to appear progressive while actually maintaining or returning to a conservative position. While the announced agenda might be in line with the view reflected in administrative journals, the practice of these theories is quelled in subtle ways and with subtle acts that indicate support for a conventional framework.

Thus it is that I faced again this division between what is announced and what is practiced. For example, the administration will hold that the "new" block schedule is designed to encourage alternative strategies for teaching, learning, and assessment. An examination of the course offerings over the last years, however, reveals that an increasing number of advanced-placement (AP) courses, courses that are at variance with the block-schedule concept, have been listed. AP courses encourage cover-to-cover exposure to specific, traditional material, leaving little room for the voices that found representation in the revised canon. The problem with the dictates of advanced-placement courses is not what is taught but rather what must be left behind. Literary realism and the works of diverse ethnic and economic minorities are cut from the curriculum, leaving a level of regimentation, a closed curriculum, a canon, that passes for excellence when in fact it denies students access to the rich world of diverse literary works and styles.

At the same time that an emphasis on AP courses precludes student exposure to a literary tradition that reflects the world around them, the emphasis on SAT and ACT scores also impacts the vibrancy of literary studies. Unlike Rudy's work-study experience in New Mexico, private schools encourage students to take both the SAT and the ACT multiple times. The cost of these tests is significant, certainly out of the question for the students I taught in New Mexico. It does not stop there, however, for the school has made room in its schedule for SAT practice during the school day and is in the process of revising the SAT preparation course we offer on weekends. New plans will allow students to avail themselves of four weeks of specialized tutoring, while those who are earmarked as potential Merit Scholars will receive twice-weekly, one-on-one tutorials designed to enhance their scores in areas where an analysis of previous scores indicates a weakness in test performance. The ramifications of this are many. For private-school students, SAT preparation time precludes a student's being able to engage in a wider variety of electives and interests. With time invested so heavily in these standardized tests, a great deal is being left unlearned and undiscovered. In many respects, the privileged students lose opportunities to learn about others and experience vicariously worlds outside their own. In addition, this reverence for and investment in the SAT and ACT emphasizes the economic divisions among young people. Not only do the elevated scores produced by coaching and retesting give private-school or affluent students easier access to the coveted openings at prestigious schools but these students also become top contenders for academically based scholarships. The sons and daughters of tomato pickers have little or no way to compete with systems so cunningly devised.

Money and means affect the curriculum in even more ways, since parents in a private-school setting have great power to influence the administration simply by virtue of economics. Tuition, not including books and uniforms, is approximately $15,000 a year. In subtle ways and in overt actions, parents have sought to preserve the homogenous past. Seventh graders read Maya Angelou's *I Know Why the Caged Bird Sings*. Half-way through the book, when Angelou is ten, she describes being sexually compromised by an uncle with whom she is staying. The day after this section was assigned, the head's office was flooded with some 250 phone calls protesting my use of the book. At the same time, all fax machines on campus began to rattle and spew copies of the two-page description of the abuse. Like high-schoolers who pass around lurid descriptions from literary sources, the parents were sending these pages to each other and to the school. I eventually learned that the campaign was spearheaded by a religious fundamentalist who had a telephone tree that included more than one-third of the school's families. While the head maintained that our curriculum could not be dictated by special interest groups, Angelou's book was not approved for use as required reading again.

When next I confronted this watchdog parent group, it was over the assignment of Gloria Naylor's *Brewster Place* for the ninth-grade curriculum. Again

219

the fax machines tumbled out pages, in this case the rape scene and sometimes the pages that deal with the lesbian couple. As I processed the source and content of the objections, I came to suspect that the problem rests in the fact that these books were by African American authors writing about sexual situations involving African Americans. Later, when an assembly that was to feature youngsters from a gay and lesbian group garnered the same barrage of parental protests, I amended the list of forbidden topics to include homosexuality. In a school of five hundred girls, discussion of homosexuality would seem a relevant issue to them as they grow and develop. Rather than provide the young women of the student body with reliable information, the administration succumbed to the pressure of the parents by canceling the assembly. Having directly experienced parental ability to control racial and ethnic texts as well as literary experiences dealing with sexual identity, championing a curriculum that includes economic, racial, and ethnic diversity becomes mandatory for the teacher committed to social justice.

The jijadist terrorists and the subsequent war on terror affected the culture and conscience of this country in many ways, including the life of our classrooms. In the future issues of *English Journal*, strategies to counter this damage need to be articulated. Teachers, again, must insist on a canon of inclusivity, must find ways to counter the pressure placed on administrations from parental voices so that all students, privileged or not, will have the opportunity to know the world in its vastness and variety. In the public-school arena, teachers must become the voice for those students whose parents cannot speak for them. Teachers must work to reflect what Mariama Ba, a Senegalese school teacher, writes in her memoir *So Long a Letter:* "Teachers — at kindergarten level, as at university level — form a noble army accomplishing daily feats, never praised, never decorated, an army forever on the move, forever vigilant, an army without drums, without gleaming uniforms. This army, thwarting traps and snares, everywhere plants the flag of knowledge and morality."[13]

Young men and women from the schools in New Mexico where I taught must be given the intellectual tools and information that will enable them to take charge of their lives. Students from schools of privilege must act on behalf of those less fortunate. Becky's petition did not rock the foundations of the school, but it did illustrate for her class that they have commitments to honor to those whose lives are very different from theirs. For students of privilege it becomes a moral imperative to act on behalf of the tomato pickers.

Notes

1. Becky Hill, interview and conversation with author, Nashville, Tenn., March 1, 2004.

2. Kevin Leaderer, interview with author, Nashville, Tenn., May 13, 2004.

3. As I recall, acquiring basal readers in 1980 for all students in seventh grade language arts across the school district involved the purchase of approximately 8,500 books at approximately $25 a book. Textbook acquisition was mandated for students in grades six through twelve. Profit margins for the book companies were enormous. Many teachers questioned the motivation of central administration in requiring these purchases when students needed so much more in terms of an appropriate curriculum and language training, and when teachers often had to purchase their own paper for use in the copy machine.

4. Consider the students in the movie *Stand and Deliver* who, under the tutelage of Jaime Escalante, do well on their AP exams only to find themselves suspected of cheating and made to retake the exam. This equation seems to read "no money equals cheating while privilege equals academic ability." It must also be noted that to register for an AP class is costly, with a fee of approximately $80 per test.

5. In the interest of fairness, the myriad positive elements in this teaching environment cannot go unmarked. The student-teacher ration is 14 to 1; the college counseling ration is 30 to 1, as opposed to 200 to 1 in many public schools; an advisory program pairs each student with an adult who is both advocate and advisor; a preponderance of teachers hold advanced degrees; the curriculum is laced with opportunities for the athlete, the artist, the scholar; travel opportunities and internships with professionals from doctors to senators are available through a three-week alternative educational program; all students have laptops; all students have access to an exemplary library and media and videography labs; students can involve themselves in any number of clubs and in activities dedicated to service to the community. And these are only a few of the advantages. However, it is not a perfect school, and the anomalies are the focus of this article, for how can a system change and better itself if attention is not paid to the flaws of the design, especially when the weaknesses impact curriculum and the opportunities students have to become knowledgeable, ethical members of society?

6. Nina Baym, general editor, *The Norton Anthology of American Literature*, shorter fourth edition (New York: W. W. Norton, 1995).

7. National Council of Teachers of English, *English Journal* online, http://www.ncte.org/pubs/journals/ej.

8. Nina Baym, general editor, *The Norton Anthology of American Literature*, shorter fifth edition (New York: W. W. Norton, 1999).

9. Nina Baym, general editor, *The Norton Anthology of American Literature*, shorter sixth edition (New York: W. W. Norton, 2003).

10. ASCD, *Educational Leadership* online, http://www.ascd.org/portal/site/ascd/menuitem.

11. National Council of Teachers of English, *English Journal* online, http://www.ncte.org/pubs/journals/ej/contents.

12. Rebecca Bell Metereau, University of Texas (San Marcos), posited in a conversation with the author that both the SUVs and the penchant for overly large, pretentious houses signify a need for protection and means to isolate oneself and one's family from the demons of the outside world.

13. Mariama Ba, *So Long a Letter* Portsmouth, N.H.: Heinemann, 1989.

CHAPTER 17

Langston Hughes
on the Historically White Campus

Joanne M. Braxton

'He is immortal, not because he alone among creatures has an inexhaustible voice, but because he has a soul, a spirit capable of compassion and sacrifice and endurance. The poet's, the writer's, duty is to write about these things. It is his privilege to help man endure by lifting his heart, by reminding him of the courage and pride and sacrifice which have been the glory of his past. The poet's voice need not merely be the record of man, it can be one of the props, the pillars to help him endure and prevail.'
— William Faulkner, Nobel Prize acceptance speech, Stockholm, December 10, 1950

'But here all of us are part of a democracy. By taking an interest in our government, and by treating our neighbors as we would like to be treated, each of us can help make our country the most wonderful country in the world.'
— Langston Hughes, *The First Book of Negroes* (1952)

The College of William and Mary, founded in 1693 in Williamsburg, Virginia, excluded women for two centuries, and African Americans for more than two and a half. Ours is a beautiful campus, filled with magnolia trees and hundred-year-old live oaks, and boasts the oldest academic building in continuous usage in the United States. Gains have been made for both blacks and whites on a campus where black women reign as homecoming queens and white men are welcomed into the African American Male Coalition. Yet the progress of the last four decades maintains a fragile truce with the ghosts of the not-so-distant past.

Although the identity of every African American is constantly under siege, the black student on the white campus quickly learns that acceptance is conditional—learns "not to take things personally." A black student at Columbia or William and Mary or Kent State or the California Polytechnical State University, for example, is more likely to have to deal with the "in your face" variety of racism than a student at Howard or Morgan or Fisk. Students at Cal Poly, for example, were recently greeted with flyers announcing a talk by Mason Weaver, author of *It's O.K. to Leave the Plantation,* and around the country a vocal movement mobilizes potential donors to close their checkbooks to racially affirming institutions.

On July 31, 2003, a white William and Mary student, then an intern at the conservative Heritage Foundation, published a deliberately misleading editorial in the *Washington Times* (www.realdemocracy.com/edupdate.htm). She criticized STP, the Summer Transitional and Enrichment Program, created by the college in 1983, and funded by the Virginia General Assembly as part of a plan to bring about and help maintain a balance of ethnic diversity on thirteen Virginia public campuses. Falsely implying that she had been excluded from this program, she had, in fact, not applied. She also failed to note that the program has had white participants, and that not every black student is invited to apply. Nonetheless, her words, copyrighted in the name of the foundation, were distributed nationally. In response to the wayward editorial, cartoonist Bruce Tinsley took the deception one step further. Using the subject for his September 24 and 25, 2003, nationally syndicated "Mallard Fillmore" comic, Tinsley lampooned the college, suggesting that it "discriminates against whites and insults the intelligence of blacks."

Further destabilizing the environment in which our students live and work, on November 8, 2003, a group of white male students, the self-proclaimed "Sons of Liberty," held an antiaffirmative-action bake sale where prices went down progressively for Asians, African Americans, and Hispanics; whites could purchase four cookies for one dollar, Asians four for seventy five cents, blacks and Hispanics, four for fifty cents, and Native Americans four for a quarter. SOL members also publicly played Ghettopoly, a game that stereotypes blacks, Jews, and Italians. Progressive students and faculty, black and white, reacted immediately, forming SCOPE, the Student Coalition of Peer Education, and organizing an evening program that featured informational presentations by members of the sociology faculty. "Shame on all of us," said one white senior senator, expressing his disapproval that some senators would not join him in censoring SOL. Eventually, SOL was censured by the Student Assembly, the faculty of the Department of History, and the dean of students. Even so, much damage was done, and several black students have since left the college, finding themselves unsuited to the William and Mary experience. Before leaving, Chris Outlaw penned a guest editorial called "A Letter of Apology" to the *Dog Street Journal*, an online student publication. His "Apology," appearing on November 19, 2003, reads, in part:

I'm sorry the world said that you were better than me, and now finally we vocally can say we are equal. I'm sorry I have to prove to W&M that I belong here just because I catch a ball as well as excel academically. I'm sorry that we (minorities) have to depend on each other just to make it through one semester, and that without the Office of Multicultural Affairs the student body would be even less than 13% minorities (or 6% black). . . .

I'm sorry girls still freeze up before getting into the elevator in Morton Hall, when they see me on first and scare the hell out of me and make me check behind myself to unveil the threat. I'm sorry you think I have something against you because of a past our ancestors shared. I'm sorry that we both have to suffer because of something we had absolutely no hand in. . . .

I'm sorry that you think that I don't want white allies. I'm sorry your indirect approval and assistance is needed. I guess we were under the impression that we could all do it collectively, with the assistance of a few laws a few years to close a 400 year long gap. (www.dogstreethournal .com/story/1109)

There is every reason to believe that these conditions present themselves not only on the campus that has been my own academic home for the last quarter century, but on other campuses as well. Thus, nearly four hundred years after the first Africans landed at Jamestown—a mere twenty miles away from where the College of William and Mary would be built seventy-four years afterward—the descendants of the original Jamestown Africans still find themselves unable to taste without bitterness the freedom and liberty that the descendants of more recent (and usually white) immigrants take for granted.

As Jamestown prepares to celebrate its quadricentennial, the poems of Langston Hughes assume an intensely political purpose, offering analysis, comfort, and direction. A substantial number of Hughes's poems address the conditions faced by African American people in historical context, revisiting sites of memory to remind us of the origins of our displacement, our collective grief, our "American Heartbreak." Recalling "the great mistake" of Jamestown, Hughes proclaims:

> I am the American heartbreak—
> Rock on which Freedom
> Stumps its toe—
> The great mistake
> That Jamestown made long ago. (9)

This poem confronts the pain of being excluded from the American dream that the forebears of today's black students helped make a reality in this country for others—not as metaphor but as palpable experience. The black student who chooses to be an American scholar in the Emersonian sense remains intellectually vigilant and true to himself in analyzing the nature of his perceived experience. Hughes's poetry both authorizes and sustains such "inner vision."

What is it like to be a refugee in the country of one's birth? In this country, that experience is often reserved for Native Americans and persons of African descent. Like "American Heartbreak," Hughes's "Refugee in America" speaks once more to the pain of displacement, dislocation, and exclusion. While aesthetically satisfying, the poem cuts with razor sharpness, addressing a profound paradox inherent in the politics of the black experience: In "Refugee in America," Hughes writes:

> There are words like Freedom
> Sweet and wonderful to say. . . .

In the same poem, Hughes recounts our collective sorrow and the somber ambivalence of the wish to forget:

> There are words like Liberty
> That almost make me cry
> If you knew what I knew
> You would know why. (290)

"If you knew what I knew," says the speaker of the poem. What is it that the speaker knows? He knows how it feels to be excluded from the prosperity he has helped to create. He knows the guilt of being the survivor, the one who stands in Freedom's shadow, the paradox of homesickness, and the inability to go back—either to Jamestown or that earlier place, Africa. When neither place can be recognized or remembered as home, profound identity confusion can result. Erik Erikson saw a similar "dis-ease" in Native Americans. Expensive attempts at Native American reeducation, as he pointed out, "only made them fatalistically aware of the fact that they were denied both the right to remain themselves and the right to join America" (Erikson 1975, 45.)

Still valuable today are Erikson's observations that all graduations, "while they establish a reciprocity of obligations and privileges, also threaten with an element of mutilation and exile—if not in the crude form of surgical covenants, then in the insistence that a person's final identity be cut down to . . . the size of a conventional type of adult who knows his place and likes it" (Erikson 1975, 223.) Particularly complex, then, is the matriculation of the black scholar at the white alma mater, where "in loco parentis" is established and the "soul mother" chooses which child to feed first. Mutilation, exile, starvation: these are the threats Hughes accepted in defining himself as a poet, a scholar, and a cultural outlaw.

Young Hughes spent the 1921–22 academic year at Columbia University. One of about a dozen black men in the class of 1925, Hughes, the only black man in his dorm, Hartley Hall, had made his housing arrangements from Mexico by writing in advance, and without any reference to his race. Bored in classes, alienated from most of his racist classmates, and estranged from his father, Hughes lived like a refugee at Columbia, too (see Rampersad 1986, 51–55). "Theme for English B" speaks to the Columbia experience. When given the assignment to: "Go home and write a page tonight / and let it come out of you / Then, it will be true," Hughes's student avatar performs his own exploratory surgery, looking inward to affirm the value of his own black struggle for identity and meaning:

> I guess being colored doesn't make me not like
> the same things other folks like who are other races.
> So will my page be colored that I write?
> Being me, it will not be white. (247–248)

Clearly, Langston Hughes made his own place, and defied all encroachments upon his self-definition. Some years following the Columbia experience, after restorative wanderings that would take him to Africa and elsewhere, Hughes matriculated at Lincoln University, one of the oldest historically black universities, and he graduated from that institution.

In "Theme for English B," the poet escapes cultural annihilation and the looming threat of suicide the same way that Frederick Douglass escaped enslavement and that Viktor Frankl, a Jewish physician-psychiatrist and psychotherapist who lived in Vienna, escaped the Holocaust—by creating meaningful work, by defining his own attitude toward unavoidable suffering, and by maintaining a spiritual or inner life.[1] Today, after the Civil Rights movement and decades of affirmative action, the black scholar, whether on the historically white campus or elsewhere, can increase her or his chances for survival as a whole person by following Hughes's model and embracing the inner struggle to name one's own identity and experience.

In "Song for Billie Holiday," the struggle for transcendence continues. Here Hughes asks:

> What can purge my heart
>   Of the song
>   And the sadness?
> What can purge my heart
>   But the song
>   Of the sadness? (102)

The answer, of course, is the song itself. In short, the poet, like the singer, does his own "logotherapy," to borrow Frankl's term.[2] Having heard, he answers "the call of a potential meaning waiting to be fulfilled by him (Frankl 1963, 166). This is what every black artist must do in this white America, no matter whether she finds herself seated in a classroom or a prison cell, riding in a Lexus or sleeping under a bridge. Write a poem. Do the deed.[3]

Like cultural annihilation or metaphoric death, actual physical suicide is a theme in Hughes's poetry, too, as in "Suicide's Note":

> The calm,
> Cool face of the river
> Asked me for a kiss. (85)

For when the entire thrust of the dominant culture is to obliterate, reeducate, and remake one in an image that does not love him, how can the poet resist the river's seductive embrace—the reflection of his own authentic dark self? And beneath the paradox of being the bastard child of a forced cultural mating in a nation that requires him to eat scraps in the kitchen when company comes, lies yet another paradox as old as human life. None of us, black or white, asks to be born into this existence or if we want to be here. If we have to die, then why do we live, and what do we have to do to get "home"?

> I went down in the valley
> And I crossed an icy stream.
> Then I stood out on a prairie
> And as far as I could see
> Wasn't nobody on that prairie
> Looked like me.
> It was that lonely day, folks,
> I walked all by myself. (138)

Finally, each of us stands alone in that lonesome valley, but a poet who can write a poem about death, suicide, or self-annihilation—or a student who can read such poems with sensitivity and understanding—is more likely to live another day.

Going beyond the paradox, the poet offers not only comfort and analysis but also a remedy. In the long memory of "The Negro Mother," Hughes's weary refugee returns to Africa, the source of human life. Were Langston himself to come back today, he might again address us in this voice, speaking symbolically as both father and mother, revisiting both slave ship and the cotton field as sites of logos and emotion to remind us, once more, of the origins of our grief and suffering:

I am the child they stole from the sand.
Three hundred years ago in Africa's land.
I am the dark girl who crossed the wide sea
Carrying in my body the seed of the free.
I am the woman who worked in the field
Bringing the cotton and corn to yield. (288–289)

Decades after they were written, these are "working words" and props of identity, something for every dark child to lean against when weary. Hughes's outraged mother is one of his own personae, and she claims the refugee, "seed of the free," as her own, steeling the wretched and girding the weary for battle.

But march ever upward, breaking down bars.
Look ever upward at the moon and the stars.
Oh my dark children, may my dreams and my prayers
Impel you forever up the great stairs—
For I will be with you till no white brother
Dares keep down the children of the Negro mother. (288–289)

In this poem, Langston Hughes—father, mother, warrior and griot—recites the generations to console, direct, and, most important, to inspire us to lead.

There is a danger in reading the poetry of Langston Hughes solely as art for art's sake. Hughes would not have countenanced the teaching of his work in the university classroom if an exchange of privilege in any way diminished our appreciation of the radically humanizing potential of his work. Clearly, these are poems for classes in English, American studies, Black and ethnic studies, but they should also be found in the bedroom and the boardroom, in the kitchen and the sanctuary, at our weekends for prospective freshmen, at our orientations, our Homecomings and Homegoings—or on a note to a loved one at Kwanzaa or Valentine's Day.

Were Father Langston permitted to revisit us today, he might have fresh instructions regarding our present conditions—including some words for his own "crossed" seed—the white American scholars of all ages who affirm their allegiance to humanity by standing solidly beside the children of the dark mother, though mutilation, exile, and starvation threaten them as well. In the meanwhile, and until "no white brother / Dares keep down the children of the Negro mother," Langston Hughes has given us, our students, and all his kith and kin, a blueprint for saving our own lives (288–289).

Notes

1. Frankl 1963. Frankl argued that "the meaning of our is existence is not invented by ourselves, but rather detected" (157). By "(1) doing a deed; (2) by experiencing a value; and (3) by suffering," one discovers this meaning. As a self-conscious black poet and activist, Hughes did all three.

2. In *Man's Search for Meaning*, Viktor Frankl wrote: "Logotherapy . . . considers man as a being whose main concern consists in fulfilling a meaning and actualizing values, rather than in the mere gratification and satisfaction of drives and instincts" (164).

3. Frankl advocates a particular approach to the discovery of meaning through the practice of "logotherapy." In his words, "We needed to stop asking ourselves about the meaning of life, and instead to think of ourselves as those who were being questioned by life—daily and hourly. Our answer must consist, not in talk and meditation, but in right action and in right conduct" (122). I am grateful to Barbara C. Swarzenski, M.D., whose grandfather Dr. Georg Swarzenski, fled Nazi Germany in 1939, for introducing me to Frankl's work.

Works Cited

Erikson, Erik. 1975. *Life History and the Historical Moment*. New York: W. W. Norton.

Frankl, Viktor. 1963. *Man's Search for Meaning*. New York: Washington Square Press, Simon and Schuster.

Hughes, Langston. 1959. *Selected Poems of Langston Hughes*. New York: Vintage.

Rampersad, Arnold. 1986. *The Life of Langston Hughes*. Volume One, 1902–1941. New York: Oxford University Press.

PART IV: Art and Activism

This brief section of *What Democracy Looks Like* stands as an essential reminder that writers, too, inhabit a post-Seattle world; that novelists, poets, dramatists, and journalists all produce social and political critique in the language and forms of their respective genres. What follows is a sampling of the voices of those writers who have, often well in advance of literary critics, taken up the urgent issues particular to our time. They ask how legitimate community is to be defended against commercial interests; how the writer addresses threats to democracy without falling into polemic; how information can be presented in a form that spurs the public, including the young, to civic action.

CHAPTER 18

Where the Language Discovers Itself

Carolyn Forché

CAROLYN FORCHÉ: The American poetry community is in some ways a deeply conservative community. It participates in its art as if its art were a profession and as if its work were a commodity in some ways. I mean not everyone of course. But there's a pervasive and prevailing sensibility that seems to project itself that way.

DAVID WRIGHT: And I think even those who don't want to participate in that commodity exchange have to, to some degree. I mean, we all have to go to Wal-Mart at some point.

CF: Yes, we all find ourselves institutionalized in such a way. But you know, I'm going to be misread. What I mean is that I've tried to come to a place that more resembles the place I inhabited in my younger years as a poet. Which is a place that does not attend to the concerns of that artificial world.

DW: At least not in any primary way?

CF: Right. Not in any primary way.

DW: Do you have a community that sustains you? Do you have other writers, or family? Or who are those people for you?

CF: Oh yes. Other writers, other artists. I have very deep friendships. My friends are quite varied in the universe. We're all together but I have friends who are working as rural doctors and friends who are digging sewers in remote areas for people. I have friends who are, most of them, are doing something. Environmentalists, activists.

DW: So this is another one of these assembled communities.

CF: Oh yeah. They're assembled communities and they're environmentalists, and activists, and Native Americans, and others[,] people who are working on the World Trade Organization. And I have a few experimental poet friends. My community of friends is scattered all over the world. We don't see each other very often. We write letters. We make trips. We are on e-mail a lot.

DW: Do you ever wish for the more settled community of your youth?

CF: I won't have it again. I mean, yes, I live in a place. I know my neighbors, I have my son, my husband, and my sisters are around me. I have family in that city. I have a place, a community. But in terms of my work in the world and my spiritual calling and my artistic calling—that community is an assembled international community, and I take heart in their existence.

DW: Couldn't you say that *the Angel of History* is an assembled, historic, international community?

CF: And some of them are dead, but that doesn't matter. I'm friends with a lot of dead people. You know what I mean? And sometimes it bothers me that they left me alone here. But a lot of my friends are dead, and I'm still friends with them.

231

DW: What I think becomes important though is the difference between assembling that community in a generous way that looks in the other's face with faith, versus the sort of way we have global corporations assembling communities.

CF: It's not a community they're assembling.

DW: Well, they claim they are; and they play it off that way.

CF: They borrow the language, but what they're doing . . .

DW: They're homogenizing.

CF: That, and they are commodifying all natural and human resources. They are usurping the democratic right of all peoples to enact laws protective of themselves and their communities. What the WTO actually circumvents is all national, federal, local, municipal, provincial, and state laws if they interfere with one fact, and that is free trade. And the free trade barrier is invoked to override or, what is the word for this, to circumvent?

DW: To supercede?

CF: To supercede all laws that might interfere with global trade. And that includes laws governing labor rights, environmental protection, and so on. So my real concern right now is that usurpation.

DW: The disassembling of settled communities.

CF: What these corporations or the WTO have effectively done is dismantled or usurped the power of whatever participatory democracy we had on the earth. The countries that are going to suffer more are the countries of the undeveloped world. So I've got a big concern there. My community is made up of people who are trying to think through this problem and think through what sort of agency is capable of opposing it, and think through what's going to happen and what we can do.

DW: So let me ask you the question that my wife asks me: If you're concerned about all these kinds of things, why write a dissertation on poetry? Why write poetry, why not become a sociologist or a doctor or a politician? You've already talked about how poetry is not primarily utilitarian.

CF: No, but poetry's part of that world. And poetry's this sort of spiritual expression of it. Poetry arises out of . . . you know, poetry is where the language discovers itself and where language enables us to experience experience. Poetry is what maintains our capacity for contemplation and difficulty. Poetry is where that contemplation and difficulty converses with itself. Poetry is a very important endeavor. It's so important, it's so sacred a practice that the way in which it's been commodified is an angering problem for me. I don't want it to be that way. I'll continue to write it out of joy and longing to do so.

CHAPTER 19

Deep Water, No Life Rafts

George Saunders

AMY LANG: You've alluded to a desire among writers, including younger novelists, to move away from rite-of-passage fiction and fiction concerned mainly with the personal and psychological. What is it about the social and literary moment that prompts this desire?

GEORGE SAUNDERS: Speaking only for myself here, I'd say that, though I've never been particularly interested in rite-of-passage fiction, or straight-on psychological writing, I've noticed in myself, especially since 9/11 (and maybe associated with my approaching middle age) a dissatisfaction with certain aspects of my writing that feel habitual or too tightly culturally constructed. I've found myself asking questions that, for all their *USA Today* ambiance ("We're knitting more socks — and loving it!") do seem to be in the air around the contemporary fiction scene, questions such as: Is our fiction adequate for our time? Ambitious enough? Big-hearted enough? Skeptical enough? Is our fiction too squeamish around political issues? Is our fiction self-limited by certain automatically assumed tonalities? Does our fiction reflexively veer toward the negative ("Life, and particularly life in the U.S.A., sucks") thus failing to credit the real wonder and complexity of life? That is, does our fiction properly account for life, or is it, for stylistic or cultural or evolutionary reasons, every bit as conservative as the realistic or mainstream modes we (some of us) eschew? How can fiction command a larger audience? Is this desirable? Is fiction a dead-end pursuit which has been supplanted by TV, movies? Is fiction, perhaps, our last best hope to sidestep the same-mindedness of even the hippest Big Media Product? Etc., etc.

These are the kinds of questions I've noticed coming up in the work of, and conversations with, writers I admire (Ben Marcus, Brian Evenson, Jonathan Franzen, David Foster Wallace, Jon Ames) — an ongoing struggle with certain conventions of contemporary literary writing that are beginning to feel self-limiting. Or maybe it's just a matter of trying, as we get older and become more respectable, to come to grips with the actual blessings and curses of being alive — that is, to write bigger.

AL: Your own work locates itself in a contemporary, corporatized America. Do you situate your fiction in a lineage of recent social critics such as Thomas Pynchon, Joan Didion, or Don DeLillo?

GS: Well, I'd like to think so. But the main reasons I put my work in that kind of setting is that I find it's funnier. That is, trying to make that kind of world leads to language that is more interesting to me than if I'm trying to make, say, a hunting camp full of stiff-upper-lipped Brits. Or a "realistic" suburban-domestic setting. It just produces odd, charged language and, in some weird way I can't explain, actually makes it easier to get to the kinds of moral/spiritual crises that I think are at the center of our "real" lives.

If, as Chekhov said, art's purpose is not to solve problems but to formulate them correctly, then I think it's an exciting and valid thing for a fiction writer in contemporary America to be looking at the corporation, both in its negative manifestations (oppressive, monolithic, faceless, cruel) and positive (a source of financial stability for the individual, an incredible machine to accomplish tasks, arguably a source of bounty and richness, a way of lifting the tide for all, etc.). But I also find stories involving corporate life (especially where the corporate mission is a quasi entertainment one) to be a rich source of comedy and comedic language. I find myself thinking often of Orwell's idea that bloated or indirect or nonsensical language indicates the presence of a hidden agenda.

AL: As in other moments of dramatic social and economic change, there seems to be a trend — especially among certain poets (such as Carolyn Forché) and playwrights (such as, August Wilson, Suzan-Lori Parks, Tony Kushner) — toward more politically engaged work. Is this where your fiction and the work of other writers of your generation is moving?

GS: I hope not. Only because the phrase "politically engaged work" scares me. What does it mean? What it usually means these days is: Work that reifies an existing leftist agenda. The fact that this agenda is one I happen to agree with doesn't assuage my fears. (Imagine what "our" reaction would be to a novel that had as its stated purpose to advance the antiabortion movement or advocate tax cuts for the wealthy, etc.) In my opinion, art is supposed to do something more. It's supposed to rip the existing categories up and reveal them for what they are: fearful quaking placeholders. Art, in my view, is supposed to remind us that all dualities are false, and potentially dangerous. An "oppressive capitalist" also has an inner "sensitive artist." And vice versa. It's like seeing the word Montana on a map, and reading a bunch of encyclopedia generalities about Montana — art is the thing that puts you down on the ground.

Art is where the most profound part of ourself functions — beyond linear thought, analytical thoughts, or conceptualizing. It's the best chance we have to surprise ourselves with a solution or worldview that never would have occurred to us before. It's deep water and no life rafts are allowed; not the life raft of Belief, not the life raft of Concepts. You have to dive in and see what's actually true. (I should point out that all four writers you mention above do exactly this, in my opinion).

Fiction and poetry and drama have always been essential in rescuing us from whatever duality may be dominant (left-right, Red-Blue, oppressor-victim), the quagmire we find ourselves locked into, where so much energy is being spent constructing straw men and knocking them down. Art is what is allows us to cut through the stereotypes and projections and remake America (or ourselves) along new vectors.

Duality, in its rush to create an Us and a Them, denies commonality. It denies that there might be such a thing as a common set of, say, American ideals. And the more we solidify around our political identities, the less chance there is of working through to some new arrangement.

It's not the case, of course, that these dualities are complete fabrications, or come out of nowhere — it's just that they are of limited usefulness, especially if the goal is transcendence, or a truly new solution.

AL: We note an increasingly globalized fiction in which the United States and its international power shape the plot (*Poisonwood Bible*, Robert Newman's *The Fountain at the Center of the World*, and Barry Lopez's *Resistance*). Some see this fiction as didactic, over-determined, propagandistic. How might one think about "politicized" fiction in this historical moment?

GS: I haven't read these books, I'm embarrassed to admit. But I think I understand what you're asking.

To my way of thinking, if saying a story is "political" means it advocates a preexisting political stance, then political writing is bad. Because there is no mystery or discovery involved. It is all just Proof. That's math but it's not art. The problem with some art that considers itself "political" is that it is incurious. It already knows what it thinks. That kind of art does no work except to dig deeper trenches for the entrenched to stand in while they hurl invective back and forth. A bunch of people with the same view go into the museum, get stroked, and come out even more convinced than they were when they went in. Since we all know where we stand, we can get right down to Rooting For Our Side. Thought? Not necessary. Change? Let them change, I'm not budging. It's actually an incredibly reactionary arrangement. How can a new arrangement be imagined? Real art.

However, if saying a story is "political" means that it takes into account the fact that the world is a complicated interactive whole, and that these days the individual life can't occur uninfluenced by greater forces, then I'd say every great story is a "political" story.

Take the beautiful Chekhov story "Misery." A cabbie whose son has just died looks in vain for someone with whom he can share his loss. In the end, ignored by everyone, he talks to his horse. The story, to me, is completely "political" in the best and truest sense: It shows us loneliness and hints at the causes of loneliness, and its consequences. It wakes us up to the moment. It makes us want to "work against" loneliness. It makes us, maybe, more aware of loneliness and maybe the next time we have occasion to console someone, we see that moment in a larger context. The moment has more to it — we treat it with more respect. And on the grosser level, I'd say the whole coming Russian Revolution is presaged in that story, in the way the man's upper-class fares ignore and mistreat him, in the way he blocks out this mistreatment, but the way that this mistreatment hangs over the story like a dark cloud. Today he talks to his horse, tomorrow he may (he will) do something more violent.

In this sense, "political" just means: This piece of art reflects, with no fear or a priori assumptions, upon what it means to be human. Or: It holds up a mirror. We see how we are. A feeling of discontent wells up, we change.

So for me, no matter how complex or crazed or passionate the political moment is, it still makes sense to try and abide with a human moment, with the human mind, with the human being in action: All answers lie there.

Is there such a thing as nonpolitical, or antipolitical, or apolitical fiction? Sure. The Guy, who we understand to be roughly equivalent to The Author on

235

some level, divorces The Girl. There is, throughout, a metaphor of Dying Foliage. The story is riddled with references to, say, the movie *Casablanca*. This is boring and "apolitical" because it behaves as if there is no outer world on which this suburban world is dependent. It behaves as if the level of affluence shown in the story is a given. It is dull because it pretends that My Carnal Relationship is the most important thing in the world. It is slothful because it does not bother to look beyond the surface of the story, for timeless human tendencies.

I'm not saying, by the way, that the above story could be saved by introducing a Long-Suffering Salvadoran Housecleaner. What I am saying is that, if the story is only about Ralph and Jennifer, it's going to fail to really move us. If it's about, however, some deeper tendencies that are ruining Ralph and Jennifer's marriage (narcissism, self-centeredness, constant discontent, greed, sloth, hubris) then it becomes about all of us, and about the whole world, and is sort of de facto "political."

I once read, in a Zen Buddhist text, a beautiful riff on abortion. This teacher said (I'm paraphrasing here) that the condition of having an unwanted pregnancy contains its own "punishment"—its own inherent karma. It is not good to kill a fetus and it is not good to have a baby you don't want. The problem comes when we try to pretend that one way (abortion) or the other (have the kid) is totally free from consequences. Recognition that there is loss and karma both ways is the correct approach. There is something in this that is relevant to art. A story that "proves" that abortion is 1. totally right, or 2. totally wrong, is a flawed story. As Chekhov said, art doesn't have to solve a problem, it just has to formulate it correctly. That is, it has to account for the real complexity of the situation. And that's enough. We come away from such a work with a renewed sense of respect for life. We come away less certain. Maybe we come away more observant. Or more resolved to be aware. That in itself would be plenty, I think.

Art, in my view, should exist as a form of ritual humility. "For the love of God, man, think it possible that you may be mistaken," said Thomas Moore. Imagine existing in that state all the time, the state of feeling deeply uncertain, awed by one's own uncertainty, and being okay with this uncertainty. A good story can induce that kind of comfort with uncertainty that I think is the key to leading a truly "political" life. Art, then, can be seen as a series of statements or moments that begin with: "On the other hand . . .".

So, winding up this long, confusing answer to a short, precise question: If there could be said to be a deficiency in American art, it is simply that it is not good enough. It has become too conceptual and too idea-based to be truly dangerous. When we go into a museum and see a "work of art" that consists of a picture of George Bush and the word "Liar" painted under it, no one is challenged or flummoxed. No one's deeper nature is engaged. No one goes out dizzy or confused. They only go out Reconfirmed. Or, if they are Republicans, they go out Disgusted and Dismissive. So what's the point? Or maybe American art is not good enough because it has become too personal, to enamored of itself and its maker. The dominant riff seems to be: I Found This Interesting. That kind of work is depressing because the artist just skims her own surface and hands us the residue. Somebody makes a collage of the covers of all the CDs she listened to during July. So what? Will this speak to me on the last day of my life?

My experience of art is that one has to immerse oneself in the craft of it for a very long time and then, with luck, on the rare day, it may be possible to do something new, something that is, inexplicably and irreducibly, greater than the sum of its parts. But the newness is not separable from the doing of it. That's all there is, the doing of it. All newness and political content and greatness is contained in the line-by-line or brushstroke-by-brushstroke doing of it. And this newness comes from the subconscious, not from the conscious, conceptual, mind. Likewise the benefit: Art works on the underconsciousness. What we think about it is not what it did to us, any more than after-sex nostalgic bragging is the sex experience itself. So it requires a great deal of confidence to make or receive a true work of art. We have to kick off from the side of the pool (which is labeled My Beloved Ideas) and get into the water, which is not labeled at all.

Note

Interview questions were posed in writing by Amy Schrager Lang and Cecelia Tichi, 2004.

CHAPTER 20

Not Yet Global Citizens

Laurie Garrett

CECELIA TICHI: Let's talk about *Betrayal of Trust.* Do you think the U.S. citizenry is ready to hear your message about public health?

LAURIE GARRETT: I would say it's just mixed. I think Americans are among the most personally generous people on earth, and they certainly give more on a personal level than, say, their European counterparts, who basically don't understand the concept of charity.

But politically, Americans are completely off the wall. They have no sense of engagement in the world. When you compare, for example, your average Norwegian or your average Brit or your average Italian and their level of engagement in the world to the Americans', it's quite embarrassing. And I would say that if I have a major area of frustration, it's in trying to get Americans to be willing to read about people other than their own neighbors, and realize that that's part of their world, and they have to expand their sense of world.

CT: To see people of the world as their neighbors.

LG: Well, especially if they are people of color. I mean I've had so many speaking engagements where somebody in the audience says, "Yeah, but that's Africa. What do you expect from the Africans?"

CT: We are not very well helped, are we, by our news media these days? Three BBC guys came to talk to me about two weeks ago, and they expressed shock at the news content in the United States, how dangerous it is for Americans to be so uniformed about what's going on.

LG: They're right. It's all about cost-cutting.

CT: I want to ask you about a topic specific to public health. We've been reading a lot about the privatization of water with enormous public-health implications —

LG: [*Nods.*] One of the things I do when I'm giving a public lecture is to always request that there be water at the table. I will always hit some juncture where I'm trying to explain the difference between how Americans approach public health and how the rest of the world does. And I'll hold up the little commercial water bottle, and I'll say, "This is really absurd when you think about it. Everybody is this room has already paid with their taxes to have tap water that is adequately purified and is safe for you to drink. And if it's not adequate, you can vote the whole health board out of business. You can do a Freedom of Information Act request and see all the chemical and microbial composition of the drinking water. If you're of the middle class, you worry about your children's health.

But if you're an American, you take an individualistic approach, and instead of insisting on analysis of the public tap water, you spend three times drop for drop more than it would cost to put unleaded gasoline in your car to buy this

238

water. And where is this water from? Tap water. This happens to be tap water from France or Maine, but it's tap water. And not only that, in order to sell it in bottled form, they've put more chlorine in it, so it's actually got more chlorinated subcompounds than you would get from tap water.

CT: I want to read a paragraph from [p. 201 of] *Betrayal of Trust* and ask about a related issue on the relations between the middle class and upper class and public health. You're talking in this passage about the late 1860s:

> This theme of public health — the need for support from a sizable middle class — would resonate throughout the future history of America. In the absence of a middle class, the rich simply lived separate and unequal lives, maintaining spacious homes along clean, tree-lined boulevards and raising their families through private systems of health, education, and cultural training. That a city might starve, politically and economically, in the absence of the elite's interest and finances seemed of little but occasional Christian concern to them. And the poor lacked the education, money, and skills to choose and run an effective government.

My question is whether increasingly the American middle class, once again in this twenty-first century, has come to identify itself in what you call an individualistic way and have therefore abandoned their citizenly role in the community support for public health that benefits everybody and is vital to the survival of the whole community across lines of class and income. So I'm really asking you, has there been a kind of class Balkanization in America in which this statement you make about the late twentieth and twenty-first centuries, when the word "public" becomes a pejorative term, whether it's school, beach, public health? It's synonymous with riff-raff, and in consequence it guts the broad-based support of the very healthy community activism we need.

LG: Well, there's a bundle there for you.

CT: Yeah.

LG: Well, later in *Betrayal* I talk about the effect of white flight from the cities, and the rise of suburbia. I think that was the first stage. Today, I would say the real problem is — the threat is a global one — it's no longer restricted by the towns or suburbs. Most Americans are middle class. Most Americans have enough financial wherewithal to deal with this on a personal level, though many would argue that since the collapse in the stock market [in 2000], that's less the case today than it was five years ago.

CT: A lot of people have lost jobs. A million people in 2002 between January and August lost their jobs.

LG: That's right, so that, obviously, decreases the size of the middle class, but they still have middle-class values. And it means that, if you look right now at how our administration is dealing with bioterrorism, Secretary Tommy Thompson [of the Department of Health and Human Services] has been mobilized. He is seeking a budget of 5.9 billion dollars for 2003, 1.75 billion which would be for basic research, more than a billion of which would be for basic research, more than a billion of which would be steered to local-level public health. But he has not requested in that budget any significant amount to go

239

to the World Health Organization. Even as Senator Patrick Leahy yesterday says on the floor of the Senate, "Maybe West Nile virus is the result of biological warfare." Even as Leahy says that, you have to ask the question, If you're concerned about the West Nile virus, why weren't some of our resources given to Sudan and Uganda, and Somalia and Egypt, where the virus is?

So, I think that where we are now is that Americans are the global upper-middle class and upper class. There are six Americans whose combined new wealth in the 1990s exceeded the combined new wealth of the 43 poorest nations. And I think they are the super rich, plus your Bill Gates, your Warren Buffet, your Wal-Mart family. But as you get down the food chain here in the United States, most Americans have, still, a sense of personal economy and of community, which is very much defined by ten or fifteen best friends in the immediate neighborhood. They have not yet become global citizens.

CHAPTER 21

The Antitribalist Identity-Based Movement for Pluralist Democracy

Tony Kushner

I am a very old-fashioned kind of homosexual, or rather sexual minoritarian, I am the kind of homosexual sexual minoritarian who believes that sexual minoritarian liberation is inextricable from the grand project of advancing Federally protected civil rights, and cannot be separated from the liberation struggles of other oppressed populations, cannot be achieved isolated from the global struggle for the abolition of the legacy of colonialism, cannot be achieved isolated from the global resistance movement against militarism and imperialism and racism and fundamentalisms of all sorts, the global movement for the furtherance of social and economic justice, the global multiculturalist, anti-tribalist identity-based movement for pluralist democracy, I am the kind of homosexual who believes that all liberation has an inexpugeable aspect that is collective, communitarian, and also millenarian, utopian, which is to say rooted in principle, theory, dream, imagination, in the absolute non-existence of the Absolute and in the eternal existence of the Alternative, of the Other, in the insistently unceasingly mutable character of our character. . . .

WHAT AM I DOING HERE . . . is a good question to ask in a commencement speech. WHAT AM I DOING HERE, or perhaps another way of putting it, WHY ME? . . . .

Having some answer to the WHY ME question . . . is useful as you try to answer the other question, WHAT AM I DOING HERE, a question which vast forces of reaction, otherwise known as the devil, the Republican Party, the petro-chemical industry, Dick and Lynn Cheney, call them what you will, vast and nearly-ineluctably persuasive and pervasive forces of reaction will seek to answer for you: you are here to consume and to surrender. You are here to comply, to be in agreement. You are not, these agents of sin and of Satan will tell you, here to do anything, or rather you are not here to ask what to do, or why. The only action, the only agency permissible is the secret compact of compliance you are expected to make with an order so vast it is nearly invisible, the secret surrender you are expected to have made of your own specificity in the name of an anti-human unjust anti-egalitarian anti-democratic ideology that masks its brutality in the guise of an Individualism that enforces conformity and a Freedom that exists within a desperately circumscribed arena of economic terror, scarcity and selfishness. What you are doing here is knowing never to ask the question WHAT AM I DOING HERE in such a way that your perilous security is imperiled, in such a way that your civilization's failure to provide for you anything like a civilized security, safety, luxury, home, is exposed through your asking and answering. This has always been true, as I'm sure you have learned in your

241

classes, and in your lives, there have always been these forces, these imps and demons, this terror. But you graduate into a world in which the terror has become exponentially greater, though its aim is essentially unchanged, its aim remains the preservation of the global economy of violence and oligarchy, the preservation of grotesquely unequal distribution of the world's wealth and the human services and societal and cultural infrastructures that go with wealth, its aim remains the perpetuation of the tragedies of unequal development, its aim remains injustice, and though it doesn't even know it itself, it is one of the four horsemen of the apocalypse.

The answers you provide for yourself to the question WHY ME will be of great consequence to the way you answer WHAT AM I DOING HERE, but if I may succumb to the immemorial nasty habit of commencement speakers since back in the days when the robes you are wearing were street clothes, and offer you advice: one of the answers to the WHAT question ought to be: I am here to organize. I am here to be political. I am here to be a citizen in a pluralist democracy. I am here to be effective, to have agency, to make a claim on power, to spread it around, to rearrange it, to democratize it, to legislate it into justice. Why you? Because the world will end if you don't act. You are the citizen of a flawed but actual democracy. Citizens are not actually capable of not acting, it is not given to a citizen that she doesn't act, this is the price you pay for being a citizen of a democracy, your life is married to the political beyond the possibility of divorcement. You are always an agent. When you don't act, you act. When you don't vote, you vote. When you accept the loony logic of some of the left that there is no political value in supporting the lesser of two evils, you open the door to the greater evil. That's what happens when you despair, you open the door to evil, and evil is always happy to enter, sit down, abolish the Clean Air Act and the Kyoto accords and refuse to participate in the World Court or the ban on landmines, evil is happy refusing funds to American clinics overseas that counsel abortion and evil is happy drilling for oil in Alaska, evil is happy pinching pennies while 40 million people worldwide suffer and perish from AIDS; and evil will sit there, carefully chewing pretzels and fondly flipping through the scrapbook reminiscing about the 131 people he executed when he was governor, while his wife reads Dostoevsky in the corner, evil has a brother in Florida and a whole bunch of relatives, evil settles in and it's the devil of a time getting him to vacate. Look at The White House. Look at France, look at Italy, Austria, The Netherlands. Look at Israel. See what despair and inaction on the part of citizens produces. Act! Organize. It's boring but do it, the world ends if you don't.

PART V: Another World Is Possible

"Another World Is Possible" comprises four reflections on the problem of democracy in the present moment. Different in scale and focus, they nonetheless all investigate historical and present limits on intellectual inquiry and on political and social activism in the United States. And they all, as well, explore the opportunities to be found in new forms and understandings of democratic society. These essays urge an understanding, vital to the formulation of another world, of the distinction between political and social democracy and recognition of the value for our time of the liberatory social movements of the past. They call for an acknowledgment of the insidious constraints within which "free" inquiry takes place in a putatively democratic academy in league with governmental, corporate, and philanthropic interests. They propose that another world depends our on fully knowing this one. Eloquently summing up the purposes of this volume, these essays argue for a change in the ways we practice and think about resistance.

243

CHAPTER 22

Neither Capitalist nor American: The Democracy as Social Movement

Michael Denning

Democracy is a difficult subject, in part because it has become a universal value: we are all democrats now. In a sense, this has been true for half a century: in 1951, a UNESCO report noted that "for the first time in the history of the world, no doctrines are advanced as antidemocratic. . . . practical politicians and political theorists agree in stressing the democratic element in the institutions they defend and the theories they advocate." And for Americans, this is hard to resist: the United States, we are regularly told, was the first democratic state. "The Revolution created American democracy," the historian Gordon Wood writes, and "made Americans . . . the first people in the modern world to possess a truly democratic government and society." As a result Americans often think of democracy as they think of Coke: invented in the United States and exported to a grateful world. It is a fundamental part of the American ideology. One might be forgiven for thinking that the title of Tocqueville's famous book was "democracy *is* America," even though Tocqueville himself warned against confusing "what is democratic with what is only American": "we should therefore give up looking at all democratic peoples through American spectacles and try at last to see them as they actually are." It is worth recalling that for Tocqueville, with all his limitations, democracy was not simply about elections: it was about the equality of conditions. The US was a democracy, he argued, because it had no proletarians and no tenant farmers; and he explicitly said that his account of democracy only pertained to "the parts of the country where there is no slavery."[1]

Tocqueville himself stands in a long tradition of antidemocrats defining democracy, a tradition that goes back to the early American federalists like Madison and Hamilton and continues in the twentieth century with figures like Joseph Schumpeter and Samuel Huntington. What does it mean when antidemocrats like Huntington, who twenty-five years ago was warning against the excesses of democracy, is now seen as the champion of a "third wave" of world democratization in the last quarter of the twentieth century? What do we make of the fact that the rise of political democracy around the world—celebrated in an enormous scholarly literature on the "transition to democracy"—has been accompanied by a global collapse of social democracy: the savaging of social safety nets, welfare systems and price subsidies, and the global privatization of public lands, public industries, and public services —a new round of enclosures?

Our latter-day democrats have dropped equality of condition from their definitions. The theoretical accomplishment of Schumpeter was simply to redefine democracy as the free market in votes: democracies are states not where the people rule, nor where there is equality of condition, but simply where ruling elites compete for votes in the market-place of elections. It is not surprising that democracy and capitalism emerge as virtual synonyms, and democratic capitalism appears to be the global consensus.

American and capitalist: it's almost enough to make you give up the term. But is that democracy? What do we mean by democracy? Is it the name of a type of political regime? Much of what counts as the debate over democracy pits "utopian" theorists, who tell us what democracy should look like, against "tough-minded" realists who use minimal definitions of democracy to describe what we might call "actually existing democracy." In this chapter, I would like to cut across this debate by reflecting on the history of democracy, arguing that democracy is neither American nor capitalist, but is the social movement that fought for and created the democratic institutions of the state and civil society that we have. Indeed one of the earliest names for that social movement was "the Democracy." Moreover, since every democratic victory is threatened by powerful forces opposed to democracy, the democracy remains the social movements that fight to preserve and extend those democratic institutions. We are *not* all democrats.

The Democracy
In the years between the 1820s and the 1850s, when the modern social movements were invented, a new use of the word democracy appeared, one that seems strange to our ears: "the democracy." "The portion of the people whose injury is the most manifest, have got or taken the title of the 'democracy,'" Thomas Perronet Thompson, one of the philosophical radicals who edited the *Westminster Review*, wrote in 1842. Tocqueville himself, writing in the 1830s, occasionally uses the term in this way: "Is it credible that the democracy which has annihilated the feudal system, and vanquished kings, will respect the citizen and the capitalist?" And John Stuart Mill, in his 1840 review of Tocqueville, writes that "the middle class in this country [England], is as little in danger of being outstripped by the democracy below, as being kept down by the aristocracy above." The *Oxford English Dictionary* places the first use of this meaning of the democracy in 1828, and there are clear analogues in French and German. By the time of the Paris Commune, the *Times* of London was capitalizing the phrase, denouncing the "dangerous sentiment of the Democracy, this conspiracy against civilisation in its so-called capital."[2]

How do we understand this meaning of the democracy? In the eighteenth century, the term democracy was rarely used in a positive sense: educated philosophers and political thinkers, including the American constitutionalists disparaged it. An extensive study of the rhetoric of democracy in North America concludes that, in the eighteenth century, democracy was a term of derogation: "there were very few men willing to call themselves democrats." Even [contemporary historian] Gordon Wood admits that "democracy was commonly used vituperatively"; to find a celebration of democracy, he leaps more than a generation to quote "a renegade Baptist" in 1809.[3]

At the same time, among the sailors, slaves, indentured servants, and dispossessed peasants who lived through the enclosures, impressments, slave trades, and witch hunts of Atlantic capitalism's primitive accumulation, democracy was not a slogan. The "many-headed hydra" of food rioters, slave rebels, pirates, and heretics (whose history has been recovered in the book of that name by Peter Linebaugh and Marcus Rediker) appealed to vernacular hopes and ideals: they spoke of levelling, of the commons, of jubilee, not democracy. Though the struggles for independence in the North American colonies in the 1770s were a key moment in the development of democratic ideas and institutions, they were not unique: as Linebaugh and Rediker argue, they were themselves part of two centuries of insurrection by that "motley crew," ranging from Masaniello's revolt in Naples and the struggles of the Levellers, Diggers, and Ranters in the English Revolution in the 1640s to the wave of eighteenth-century slave rebellions inaugurated by Tacky's Revolt in Jamaica in 1760.[4]

It is into these struggles that democracy—one of those Greek and Latin words, like proletarian, that Renaissance and Enlightenment political theorists with classical education reclaimed from antiquity—begins to filter in the 1790s, as a few Jacobin radicals in France, England, and the United States invoked democracy positively. But after two decades of world war between Napoleon's revolutionary empire and Britain's counterrevolutionary empire, little of democracy—as theory, practice, or even as word—remained in the North Atlantic world. Modern democracy—"the democracy"—emerged in two extraordinary decades (the 1830s and 1840s) when the modern social movements — the labor movement, the women's movement, the abolitionist movement, the anti-imperial national movements, and the new ideologies of socialism and communism — were all born. The most comprehensive historian of the word democracy notes that "broad application" of the word does not occur until the 1830s, and that 1848 "represents the zenith in the application of 'democracy'." In England, it was in these years that the Chartists, the first mass working-class movement in the world, and perhaps the largest mass political activity in any European country during the nineteenth century, came to speak of the Democracy as the movement of the people, often capitalizing the word in their press.[5]

In the early 1840s, the young Germans Friedrich Engels and Karl Marx adopted this usage from the Chartists, as they joined "democrats of all nations" in founding the Society of Fraternal Democrats. In the midst of the German revolution of 1848, they subtitled their newspaper "Organ of the Democracy." "Through their personal connections with the heads of the Democratic party in England, France, Italy, Belgium and North America, the editors," they write, "are in a position to reflect the politico-social movement abroad. . . . In this respect, the *Neue Rheinische Zeitung* is the organ not simply of the German but of the European Democracy."[6] The democracy becomes a synonym for the "social movement," a phrase that also appears first in the 1830s and 1840s, uniting new forms of popular mobilization — marches, rallies, demonstrations, petitions, cheap pamphlets, and newspapers — with new ideologies of emancipation.

In the United States, there are many uses of "the democracy" in this sense in the 1830s and 1840s, though individual instances are tricky to interpret because Andrew Jackson's political alliance successfully appropriated the phrase for its party: what we call in retrospect the Democratic Party was usually referred to as the Democracy. So an address to the democracy, a common subtitle of speeches of the era, sometimes means an address to the followers of Jackson, and sometimes means simply an address to the people, to the social movement. Abolitionist critics of Jackson's Democracy called themselves the "True Democracy," and the working-class opposition to New York's Tammany Hall called itself the "shirtless" Democracy. Transatlantic connections between "the democrats of all nations" abounded: among women's rights activists, among abolitionists — Frederick Douglass, like Friedrich Engels, met with Chartists when he was in England in the 1840s — and among radical artisans.

The revolutionary upheavals that broke out throughout the capitalist world-system in 1848 were seen as an act of "the democracy:" Thomas Carlyle spoke of "this universal revolt of the European populations, which calls itself Democracy" and François Guizot noted that "the chaos today hides itself under a word, Democracy . . . it is the sovereign, universal word." If the democracy was the name of the movement, emancipation was its aim. Emancipation was the great aspiration of the period: with its origins in the abolitionist movement's struggle for the emancipation of the enslaved and in the early nineteenth-century battles for the political emancipation of Jews in Europe and for Catholic emancipation in Ireland, emancipation also became the keyword among early women's rights activists and labor activists: "the emancipation of the working classes must be conquered by the working classes themselves," Marx writes at the formation of the International Working Men's Association.[7]

But within a year or two, the revolutionary republics were defeated, the Chartist leaders were imprisoned, the Fugitive Slave Law had been passed, and the democracy was in tatters. In the wake of the defeats, the democracy began to fragment. As a few elite political figures attempted to claim the banner of the democracy, one sees democrats of the social movement beginning to make a separation between political and social democracy, between bourgeois and popular democracy. As early as 1845, Mike Walsh, the tribune of New York's working-class "subterranean" or "shirtless" Democracy, wrote that "No man can be a good political democrat without he's a good social democrat." In 1851, Marx, now in exile in England, satirized prime minister Lord Russell's claim that "the Democracy of the country . . . has as fair a right to the enjoyment of its rights as monarchy or nobility," because Lord Russell had redefined the Democracy as "the Bourgeoisie, the industrious and commercial middle class," a "king-loving, lords-respecting, bishop-conserving 'Democracy'."[8]

If the "democrats of all nations" of 1848 were the founders of the modern democracy, none of them knew the universal-suffrage parliamentary state that we associate with democracy. The democratic state did not exist anywhere by the middle of the nineteenth century. Where did it come from? What is the relation between the democracy and the democratic state?

The Democratic State

Democratic states are youthful institutions, but most claim more ancient lineages. 1688, 1776, 1789 — it is not only in the United States that we imagine that democracy sprang forth from the rhetoric of a founding bourgeois revolution. In reality, the democratic state — the universal-suffrage parliamentary state, with the freedoms of political opposition — is, as Robert Dahl notes at the beginning of his *On Democracy*, "a product of the twentieth century."[9] Though historians and political scientists argue over the history of particular countries and the criteria of the democratic state — the extent of the franchise, of freedom of opposition, of peaceful alternation of regimes — there is general agreement that the universal suffrage state first emerges in the late nineteenth and early twentieth century, and was well established only after World War II.

Nevertheless, democratic states are often called capitalist or bourgeois, as if they were created, fostered, and supported by capitalists. "No bourgeoisie, no democracy," Barrington Moore wrote in 1966, and few on the left or the right would have disagreed.[10] It was precisely this analysis that had led one tradition of Marxism—that of Lenin—to reject what it called "bourgeois democracy" completely. But a quarter-century of scholarship—going back to a pioneering essay by Göran Therborn—has fundamentally transformed our understanding of the roots of the democratic state. The democratic state may have emerged in capitalist societies, but not because capitalists created it. Rather capitalism creates and strengthens large working classes, and, to quote the major comparative history of democratic states in Europe, North America, and South America, "the working class, not the middle class, was the driving force behind democracy."[11]

This interpretation of the relation between working-class movements — "the democracy"—and the rise of the democratic state illuminates several key aspects of the history of democracy. First, this argument that working-class self-organization was central to democracy makes sense of the timing of the universal-suffrage parliamentary states: they were first decisively, though not irrevocably, won not in the age of Capital, the great boom years of the 1850s and 1860s, but a half-century later, as a result of the organization of workers in the labor movements and socialist parties of the Second International, and the revival of the women's movement in the militant new feminism of the suffrage campaigns. Bourgeois democracy, Therborn rightly notes, was the "principal historical accomplishment" of the Second International. Schumpeter himself recognizes this; his *Capitalism, Socialism and Democracy* concludes with a historical sketch of the socialist parties.

Second, though the success of democratic reforms depended on the strength of working-class organizations — the weakness of Latin American democracy was in part due to its comparatively small working classes — it is clear that workers were not strong enough to win democratic states on their own in Europe, North America, or South America. Democratic victories depended on alliances with middle classes, either urban or rural, and the middle classes were always an ambivalent ally. They also depended on the weakness or defeat of the most consistent opponents of democracy, the large landlords who depended on cheap agricultural labor. Democracy failed where large landlords were strong enough to control the state. Capitalist development and democracy are therefore correlated because "capitalist development weakens the landed upper class and strengthens the working class."[12]

The bourgeoisie, far from being a driving force behind democracy, was rarely even a positive force. Even the contemporary political scientists most impressed with capitalist democracy admit that capitalist elites are not supporters of democracy. Several even suggest that capitalists are so strongly opposed to democracy that political democracy can only exist and thrive if there is a strong party of the right to protect the interest of elites, and if large parts of social and economic life are not subject to political control, if, in other words, issues of social justice are not on the agenda. Without those restrictions, corporate elites support authoritarian attacks on democracy. As Perry Anderson once noted, though we have yet to see a parliamentary transition to socialism, we have seen parliamentary transitions to fascism.[13]

Third, the argument about the relation between working-class mobilization and democracy is not only an historical one; there is strong evidence that the working classes continue to be the driving force in the democratizations of the late twentieth century. Though little of the "transition to democracy" literature has seriously studied late twentieth-century workers, the role of Poland's Solidarity, of the black unions of South Africa's COSATU, of Brazil's Workers' Party, and of the South Korean strikes of the mid-1990s would indicate that the organization and mobilization of working people continues to be fundamental to the establishment of universal-suffrage parliamentary states.[14]

This account also helps us make some sense of the contradictory assessments of US democracy: Samuel Huntington claims that the US was the first democratic country, placing the date at 1828 with suffrage for a bare majority of white men; Therborn, among others, places the US as the last of the core capitalist democracies, dating it from 1970 with the enfranchisement of black Southerners. How do we make sense of this simultaneous originality and belatedness? The extension of the franchise in the early nineteenth-century North did create a kind of democracy of small-holders, that historians have likened to those of Norway and Switzerland at the same time. But the continental United States was hardly akin to Norway and Switzerland, and what looks from one angle like remarkably early democratic institutions looks from another like a brief and regional exception. In most of Europe, after all, opposition to the extension of the franchise came from two sources: labor-repressive landlords who opposed political rights for the peasantry and capitalists who opposed voting rights for workers. "The American peasantry, however, was," as Alexander Keyssar points out in his history of *The Right to Vote*, "peculiar: it was enslaved" and thus not "part of the calculus . . . of suffrage reform."[15] The South was not a democracy but an authoritarian landlord regime. Similarly, as long as industrial workers remained far outnumbered by farmers in the North and West, they were a small part of the calculus of suffrage. In the only state where manufacturing workers outnumbered farmers in the 1840s — Rhode Island — those workers were excluded from political rights. The struggle of Rhode Island workers for the right to vote in 1841–42 resulted in the formation of a People's Convention and a separate, parallel constitution and government that challenged the legitimacy of the state government — a Providence Commune, if you like. An armed confrontation over control of the state arsenal led to the defeat and imprisonment of the suffrage advocates, a history that parallels the struggles of the Chartists across the Atlantic. The spokesman of the Dorr Rebellion, the carpenter Seth Luther, author of *Address on the Right of Free Suffrage*, stands as one of the great plebeian theorists of democracy.[16]

With the end of slavery and the growth of an immigrant working class, the United States witnessed a half-century of disenfranchisement, "a sustained nationwide contraction of suffrage rights."[17] By the early twentieth century, the United States was not a democratic state; the present democratic state in the US was the consequence of the self-organization of industrial workers in the CIO during the 1930s and 1940s and the self-organization of black Americans in the Civil Rights movement of the 1950s and 1960s. From Seth Luther fighting for suffrage in Providence to Robert Moses and Fannie Lou Hamer fighting for voting rights in Mississippi: that has been the line of the Democracy, not the antidemocratic meditations of Hamilton and Madison.

If we understand the close historical tie between the Democracy in the nineteenth-century sense — the social movements of working people — and democratic institutions of universal suffrage and freedom of assembly and speech, we see as well the mistake made by many contemporary scholars of democracy who would artificially separate political democracy from social democracy. For just as there is a close correlation between the strength of democratic politics and that of working-class organization, so there is a close correlation between the strength of welfare states and that of working-class mobilization. As Alexander Hicks notes in his recent study of social democracy and welfare capitalism, "even though democracy did not open the floodgate to demands for mass redistribution, it did function . . . as a sluice gate that permitted an ample flow of income security reforms." This is the case even outside the North Atlantic states. Patrick Heller's recent study of the Indian state of Kerala notes that

> under the impetus of a broad-based working-class movement organized by the Communist Party, successive governments in Kerala have pursued what is arguably the most successful strategy of redistributive development outside the socialist world. Direct redistributive measures have included the most far-reaching land reforms on the subcontinent and labor market interventions, that, combined with extensive unionization, have pushed both rural and informal sector wages well above regional levels. . . . On all indicators of the physical quality of life Kerala far surpasses any Indian state and compares favorably with the more developed nations of Asia.

If the universal suffrage state was the historical accomplishment of the turn of the-century social democracy, the welfare state with its social rights to income security in the face of unemployment, injury, sickness, retirement, and parenting, as well as its rights to universal public education, was the democratic work of social democracy in the age of three worlds. And the role of the social movement in the struggle for feminist democracy is equally clear: if women's suffrage was the historical accomplishment of the first wave of feminist movements, the reproductive rights of divorce, contraception, and abortion have been the democratic victories of the second wave. Democracy depends on "the democracy."[18]

How then can the savaging of social democracy — the enclosure of the commons, the attack on social rights, and the privatization of public goods — that has taken place over the last two decades be seen as a "wave of democratization"? Why do democratic theorists wax lyrical about civil society, that most undemocratic sphere?

The Democratic Society

The irony of the democratic state has been that the extension of citizenship has been accomplished with a devaluation of the political and a restriction of the powers of the public. The political theorist Ellen Meiksins Wood has argued that this was the theoretical accomplishment of the American Federalists: "it was the anti-democratic victors in the USA who gave the modern world their definition of democracy, a definition in which the dilution of popular power is an essential ingredient." The "freeing" of the market from the political realm — particularly the market in those two commodities that had rarely been considered alienable commodities, labor and land — made victories in the political realm often hollow. As labor historian David Montgomery wrote of nineteenth-century America: "the more that active participation in government was opened to the propertyless strata of society, the less capacity elected officials seemed to have to shape the basic contours of social life . . . both the contraction of the domain of governmental activity and the strengthening of government's coercive power contributed to the hegemony of business and professional men."[19]

This is now a fundamental part of the theories of democracy promoted by the "Washington consensus," which insist that economic or social democracy has nothing to do with political democracy. In fact, they argue that economic decision making must be carefully insulated from political power and from popular pressures for a more thoroughgoing democratization of society. As a result, over the last two decades, many of the victories of new democratic states have been undermined by capitalist forces of privatization. Privatization, or what the Midnight Notes group have called the new enclosures, is the devolution of public lands, public industries, public schools, and public services from a realm that is potentially democratic to a realm where democracy rarely exists, a realm euphemistically called "civil society."[20]

"Civil society," we are told by a chorus of its admirers, is the realm of freedom and democracy, the realm of voluntary associations and civic participation, outside the bureaucracies of the state. For Tocqueville, a fundamental part of democracy was freedom of association, and he argued that "Americans of all ages, all stations in life, and all types of disposition are forever forming associations." "If men are to remain civilized or to become civilized," he wrote, "the art of association must develop and improve among them." This was the closest Tocqueville came to the new socialisms of his era, for association was a common synonym for socialism in the 1830s and 1840s. Unfortunately, it was at this point that Tocqueville made a fateful conflation of what he called "intellectual and moral associations" and "manufacturing and trading companies." In Tocqueville and especially in his revivalists, capitalist enterprises are seen as simply one form of "civil association," whose free activity is necessary to the preservation of equality and liberty: this is one source of theories of democratic capitalism. The same slippage can be seen in the German tradition that gave us the concept of civil society: the German word, *bürgerliche Gesellschaft*, means both civil society and bourgeois society.[21]

However, if democracy has its limits even inside the universal-suffrage parliamentary state, rarely penetrating beyond the legislative branch through to the high courts, the bureaucratic apparatuses of the civil services, not to mention the national security state, it hardly exists outside the state. As the Italian political theorist Norberto Bobbio put it, "the present problem of democracy no longer concerns 'who' votes but 'where' we vote." "Today, if you want an indication of the development of democracy in a country, you must consider not just the number of people with the right to vote, but also the number of different places besides the traditional area of politics in which the right to vote is exercised."[22] By this measure, we continue to live in very restricted democracies. One finds little or no democracy in the institutions of civil society, and particularly in manufacturing and trading companies.

There have been struggles to democratize civil society, particularly in the realm of work and economic activity. An important tradition of liberal and socialist thought, going back to John Stuart Mill and including figures like Bertrand Russell, John Dewey, and Robert Dahl, developed notions of "economic democracy" or "industrial democracy," which would extend the procedures of representative democracy into the workplace. But unlike extensions of the franchise, there has been little advance in these rights that the Europeans called "co-determination." It was on the agenda of the European social democratic parties, particularly in Sweden, in the late 1970s, only to fall victim to the counterrevolution against social democracy mounted by Reagan and Thatcher. A quarter century later, these issues — the possibilities for democratic control of the workplace and the labor process, for democratic control of a firm's capital and investment, and for democratic elections of corporate and university boards, — in short, for the democratization of civil society — are hardly visible, though they will be on the agenda of the democracy of the twenty-first century.

Rather, at the present, the counterdemocracy has set the agenda: the privatization of public spheres and the expanding place of the market and civil society in people's lives has had profoundly undemocratic effects. Paradoxically, it is in Tocqueville's realm of association — the civil society of the corporation — that the very right of free association is under threat. In the words of a Human Rights Watch report of 2000, "workers' freedom of association is under sustained attack in the United States, and the government is often failing its responsibility under international human rights standards to deter such attacks and protect workers' rights." The report continues:

Millions of workers are expressly barred from the law's protection of the right to organize. U.S. legal doctrine allowing employers to permanently replace workers who exercise the right to strike effectively nullifies the right. Mutual support among workers and unions recognized in most of the world as legitimate expressions of solidarity is harshly proscribed under U.S. law as illegal secondary boycotts. . . . [There are] millions of part-time, temporary, subcontracted, and otherwise "atypical" or "contingent" workers whose exercise of the right to freedom of association is frustrated by the law's inadequacy.[23']

At the very moment that workers' movements were driving the "third wave" of democratization around the world, the United States experienced two dramatic reversals in workers' rights. First, the 1981 crushing of the air traffic controllers' union by the Reagan administration and the 1980 "Yeshiva" ruling by the Supreme Court which curbed faculty unionism and ended two decades of dramatic labor movement victories in organizing public-sector and white-collar workers. Second, U.S. workers effectively lost the right to strike with the 1983 *Belknap v. Hale* Supreme Court decision that enabled Phelps Dodge to replace striking workers permanently in the midst of the Arizona miners' strike. Over the next decade, striking workers were permanently replaced in several major transport (Greyhound, Continental Airlines, Eastern Airlines) and newspaper (*Chicago Tribune, New York Daily News*) strikes; by the end of the century, strikes had essentially vanished from the United States.[24]

The "United States is almost alone in the world in allowing permanent replacement of workers who exercise the right to strike," the 2000 Human Rights Watch report notes, and it tells the story of the destruction of unions and lives with the permanent replacement of strikers in towns ranging from Pueblo, Colorado, to Jay, Maine. It also finds examples of workers whose right to organize is under attack in all sectors of the economy: from black workers in hog-processing plants in North Carolina to "perma-temps" working for Microsoft in the Northwest, from Mexican-American and Mexican agricultural workers in the orchards of Washington and the fruit and vegetable fields of North Carolina to Asian and Latina immigrant women working in garment sweatshops in New York, from Haitian-American nursing home workers in Florida to shipyard workers in New Orleans.[25]

This attack on the right to organize has also characterized apparently "non-profit" institutions of civil society over the last decade. At Yale University, a battleground for university unionism over more than three decades, graduate teachers and hospital workers attempting to form unions have met vigorous opposition and formal and informal intimidation. As Rebecca Ruquist, a graduate teacher in the French Department and an organizer for the Graduate Employees and Students Organization (GESO), told a Yale audience:

I have taught two semesters of French 115, two semesters of French 130, both of which met five days a week, where I did the teaching, the grading, and all of the work for the course except for syllabus design. When I told the Director of Graduate Studies in my department a year ago that I was going to become GESO's next Chair, he fought with me for an hour about how I was wasting my time, and how ungrateful graduate students were to want a union. When in a meeting I suggested to the current DGS that she advocate for her graduate students with the administration, she pulled me into her office alone to lecture me about keeping graduate school issues out of department meetings. She promised me that she would include a mention of my GESO organizing in a future letter of recommendation.

Both professors have refused to declare their neutrality towards GESO organizing in the department to the French Ph.D. students. This is wrong: it is our right to organize a union here, and faculty need to respect that. The Yale administration should not ask professors to bust their own teaching assistants' union. Yale needs more than to live up to the letter of the law, it needs to live up to the spirit of the law.[26]

Similarly, Peg Tamulevich, a secretary in Medical Records who has worked at the Yale-New Haven Hospital for twenty-three years, said:

I have joined with many of my coworkers at the Hospital to organize a union. We want better patient care, wages and benefits, but more importantly, we want respect. When I was handing out union leaflets outside the hospital, police officers with guns, who are employed by Yale-New Haven, told me that I would be arrested and forced me to stop. This is just one example of intimidation tactics used by the hospital. I care deeply about our democracy in America. At Yale-New Haven Hospital, the fight for democracy is an everyday battle.[27]

Incidents like these are echoed throughout the case studies in the Human Rights Watch report: the one-on-one "meetings" with workers as well as the use of police and security services to harass organizers. Employers regularly walk just inside the law, and just as regularly break it, since there is no punishment for law-breakers. Under US labor law, employers found guilty of violating a worker's rights only have to post a notice saying they will not do it again.

The celebrants of civil society's voluntary associations and democratic deliberations rarely consider civil society's fundamental institution, the workplace. Similarly, economists rarely grapple with the working day: Work and workers only appear in contemporary economics under the guise of the "labor market."[28] In the never-never land of free market economics, we don't work; we sell our weekdays in order to buy our weekends. Economists don't get up in the morning to go to work; they go off to truck and barter their human capital. For most of us, however, capitalism remains what Marx described: "anarchy in the social division of labor, despotism in that of the workshop."[29] The labor market — getting a job — is an anarchic world we try to avoid as much as possible. The reality of capitalism is not the market, but the working day, day after day. Even Tocqueville recognized that "between workman and master there are frequent relations but no true association." The workplace remains the fundamental *unfree* association of civil society, without civil liberties or rights, without freedom of speech and with little freedom of association, assembly or opposition.[30]

And yet, the difficult, exhausting, and often demoralizing struggle by people to organize and mobilize at their place of work, has, as I have tried to suggest, been one of the fundamental driving forces of modern democracy. Unions, like other institutions, have their flaws, but they remain the most democratic institution of civil society, voluntary associations where leaders are elected in contested elections, where oppositions can organize, where ordinary people represent themselves. As a result, vital unions are central to a vital democracy; the decay and collapse of unions, as we have witnessed over the past decades, is a decay and collapse of democracy.

Much has made in recent years about the decline in civic participation among Americans over the last three decades; we're all bowling alone, as Robert Putnam put it. But though Putnam notes the decline in union membership as an aspect of this decline in civic participation, he pays little attention to it, not even noting that the decline was involuntary. There was no organized campaign against people forming bowling leagues; there has been an organized campaign against people forming unions. Across the country, we have seen repeated attacks — informal and formal — on the attempt to organize and associate. The market has efficiently allocated resources to a thriving industry of antiunion managerial consultants. If graduate teachers are not bowling alone, it is because they are striking together.[31]

Moreover, unions are one of the few forms of civic engagement that are not skewed toward wealthier citizens. Critics of the civic-engagement literature have often noted that since those with more time and more money are more likely to participate in politics, civic engagement can have antidemocratic consequences. The historic tendency of the labor movement has been to empower the least powerful, to protect the rights of its members by the practice of what Walt Whitman called the "great word" of democracy: "Solidarity."[32] It is true that unions have often been skewed to workers with more skills and more "market power," especially white workers and male workers. But the labor movement has struggled to reach across the divisions created by the labor market, divisions between "skilled" and "unskilled," "blue-collar" and "white-collar," the "employed" and the "unemployed," "men's work" and "women's work," "white work" and "colored work," to forge alliances where an injury to one is an injury to all. Anyone who reads the Human Rights Watch case studies of black, Latino, and women workers battling for their rights on the job can see why the right to organize is now a crucial civil rights issue.

The right to organize is the fundamental democratic issue of our time. One hundred million Americans working for a living do not have the democratic protections of a union. No democratization of civil society or revival of civic participation will be accomplished without their achieving the right to organize; no change in the inequality of wealth and income will come without that organization. The struggles for union recognition at Yale may seem like a local matter, hardly visible in the distant democratic vista, but the Democracy has always been about the struggles of ordinary people in the here and now.

But this is also a part of a wider struggle against the antidemocratic forces of globalization, of what is called around the world "neoliberalism." The extraordinary proletarianization of millions of the world's peoples on a global assembly line — the world working class has doubled in the last thirty years[33] — may well lead to a renewed Democracy. It has already generated a new social movement unionism, pioneered in the 1980s by Brazilian, South African, and South Korean workers, and now sparking new forms of organization and militancy by the young women in the world's *maquiladoras,* where toys, textiles, and electronics are processed for export. The 1999 protest against the WTO in Seattle by environmentalists and unionists, "turtles and Teamsters," was only the most visible part of the new century's Democracy. The first year of the new century witnessed general strikes against government austerity programs in South Korea, South Africa, Argentina, Uruguay, Nigeria, and India: in India, where twenty million workers went out May 11, 2000, a strike leader said that "the strike was aimed against the surrender of the country's economic sovereignty before the WTO and the IMF,"[34] the surrender of political and social democracy to economic despotism.

It is crucial to reclaim democracy from the antidemocrats, from those who would tell us that democracy is capitalist and American. When we think of democracy, we must remember "the Democracy," the social movements of working people that have been the driving force of the modern democracy around the world. It is working people who must, in the words of that old manifesto, "win the battle of democracy."

Notes

1. Richard McKeon, ed., *Democracy in a World of Tensions: A Symposium Prepared by UNESCO* (Chicago: University of Chicago Press, 1951), 522. Gordon Wood, "Democracy and the American Revolution," in John Dunn, ed., *Democracy: The Unfinished Journey* (Oxford: Oxford University Press, 1992), 91. Tocqueville, *Democracy in America*, translated by George Lawrence (Garden City: Doubledoy, 1969), 454, 456, 238, 580, 620n.

2. Perronet Thompson from the *Oxford English Dictionary;* Tocqueville is quoted in French in Jens Christophersen, *The Meaning of "Democracy" as Used in European Ideologies from the French to the Russian Revolution* (Oslo: Universitetsforlaget, 1966), 80; I quote Tocqueville's nineteenth-century translator, Henry Reeve, in this case because he preserves Tocqueville's use of this meaning of the democracy; Mill is quoted in Christophersen, 160; the *Times* of London is quoted in Francis Wheen, *Karl Marx* (New York: W. W. Norton, 2000), 325.

3. Russell L. Hanson, *The Democratic Imagination in America* (Princeton: Princeton University Press, 1985), 56. Wood, "Democracy and the American Revolution," 98.

4. Peter Linebaugh and Marcus Rediker, *The Many-Headed Hydra: Sailors, Slaves, Commoners, and the Hidden History of the Revolutionary Atlantic* (Boston: Beacon Press, 2000), 211–247.

5. Christophersen, *The Meaning of "Democracy"*, 322, 323. Hal Draper, *Karl Marx's Theory of Revolution*, vol. 2 (New York: Monthly Review Press, 1978), 76.

6. Quoted in Draper, *Karl Marx's Theory of Revolution*, vol. 2, 212n.

7. Carlyle and Guizot quoted in Christophersen, *The Meaning of "Democracy"*, 63, 77. The point about emancipation is made by Bonnie Anderson, *Joyous Greetings: The First International Women's Movement, 1830–1860* (New York: Oxford University Press, 2000), 114. Marx and Engels, *Collected Works*, (New York: International publishers, 1976) vol. 20, 14.

8. Walsh quoted in Sean Wilentz, *Chants Democratic: New York City and the Rise of the American Working Class, 1788–1850* (New York: Oxford University Press, 1984), 331. Marx and Engels, *Collected Works*, vol. 11, 374.

9. Robert Dahl, *On Democracy* (New Haven: Yale University Press, 1998), 3.

10. Barrington Moore, *The Social Origins of Dictatorship and Democracy* (Boston: Beacon Press, 1966), 418.

11. Göran Therborn, "The Rule of Capital and the Rise of Democracy," *New Left Review* 103 (January–April 1977): 38–57. Dietrich Rueschemeyer, John D. Stephens, and Evelyne Huber Stephens, *Capitalist Development and Democracy* (Chicago: University of Chicago Press, 1992), 98; see also 270.

12. Rueschemeyer, Stephens, and Stephens, *Capitalist Development and Democracy*, 271.

13. Perry Anderson, "The Affinities of Norberto Bobbio," in his *A Zone of Engagement* (London: Verso, 1992), 124.

14. See, in particular, Ruth Berins Collier, *Paths toward Democracy: The Working Class and Elites in Western Europe and South America* (Cambridge: Cambridge University Press, 1999).

15. Alexander Keyssar, *The Right to Vote: The Contested History of Democracy in the United States* (New York: Basic Books, 2000), 70.

16. See David Montgomery, *Citizen Worker: The Experience of Workers in the United States with Democracy and the Free Market During the Nineteenth Century* (Cambridge: Cambridge University Press, 1993).

17. Keyssar, *The Right to Vote*, 169.

18. Alexander Hicks, *Social Democracy and Welfare Capitalism: A Century of Income Security Politics* (Ithaca: Cornell University Press, 1999), 20. Patrick Heller, *The Labor of Development: Workers and the Transformation of Capitalism in Kerala, India* (Ithaca: Cornell University Press, 1999), 6–7.

19. Ellen Meiksins Wood, *Democracy against Capitalism: Renewing Historical Materialism* (Cambridge: Cambridge University Press, 1995), 214. Montgomery, *Citizen Worker*, 2, 12.

20. *Midnight Notes, Midnight Oil: Work, Energy, War, 1973–1992* (New York: Autonomedia, 1992).

21. Tocqueville, *Democracy in America*, 513, 517, 521.

22. Bobbio quoted in Anderson, "The Affinities of Norberto Bobbio," 116. Norberto Bobbio, *Democracy and Dictatorship* (Minneapolis: University of Minnesota Press, 1989), 157.

23. *Unfair Advantage: Workers' Freedom of Association in the United States under International Human Rights Standards* (New York: Human Rights Watch, 2000), 8, 10.

24. Jonathan D. Rosenblum, *Copper Crucible: How the Arizona Miners' Strike of 1983 Recast Labor-Management Relations in America* (Ithaca, N.Y.: ILR Press, 1995), 123, 224.

25. *Unfair Advantage*, 196.

26. Rebecca Ruquist, statement made in conjunction with my DeVane Tercentennial Lecture, Yale University, February 13, 2001.

27. Peg Tamulevich, statement made in conjunction with my DeVane Tercentennial Lecture, Yale University, February 13, 2001.

28. When I was first approached about delivering the lecture this chapter was based on — a lecture in a series on democracy — I was asked to address democracy and the labor market.

29. Karl Marx, *Capital*, vol. 1, in Marx and Engels, *Collected Works*, vol. 35, 362.

30. Tocqueville, *Democracy in America*, 558.

31. Robert Putnam, *Bowling Alone: The Collapse and Revival of American Community* (New York: Simon and Schuster, 2000).

32. Walt Whitman, "Democratic Vistas," in *Leaves of Grass and Selected Prose* (New York: Modern Library, 1950), 477.

33. World Bank, *World Development Report 1995: Workers in an Integrating World* (Oxford: Oxford University Press, 1995), 9.

34. Quoted in Kim Moody, "Global Labor Stands up to Global Capital," *Labor Notes*, no. 256 (July 2000), 9.

CHAPTER 23

Ivory Towers, Velvet Gloves

Daniel Lang/Levitsky

This collection's call for literary studies to participate fully in the convergences of the "post-Seattle world" comes on a particular occasion as well as for a particular purpose. It emerges from, and is addressed to, a U.S. academy that is ever more obviously shaped by the economic and political forces that define that world, these times. This essay is an attempt to sketch the occasion, the situation into which Lang and Tichi's proposal for a "new realism" emerges. I will attempt to map some of the territory in which higher education and academic research happens in the post-Seattle United States, with an eye to the institutional obstacles that stand in the way of this collection's approach to literary study. I hope that this piece can serve in part as a tactical guide that can help locate spaces for our convergence, spaces for action. But I also hope it can illustrate why convergence matters — how the economic and political web binds colleges and universities to other institutions and spheres of life in ways that make it impossible to effectively address any of them in isolation.

Although this essay addresses itself specifically to the post-Seattle world, I am not arguing that "Seattle" is a turning point for the institutions and dynamics I am describing. Seattle does mark a change, but as Lang and Tichi point out, it is a change in how we, in the United States (and particularly those of us privileged by our class, skin, gender, and so on), think about and practice our resistance to long-standing structures and forces — not a change in what we are resisting. This piece thus documents the continuity as much as the development of the ways in which "free" inquiry is channeled, encouraged, restricted, or blocked in the academic institutions of the United States.

The first years of the twenty-first century have seen a number of very visible attacks on scholars' freedom to teach and research as they choose. These attacks emanate from the federal government, university and college administrations, and influential foundations alike. Visiting scholars have been barred from entering the country (most notably Tariq Ramadan, a Swiss scholar of Islam and philosophy who would have taken a tenured post at Notre Dame in 2004); new political tests have been imposed for grant approval (most overtly at the Rockefeller and Ford Foundations); and professors have been denied tenure for opposing their schools' partnerships with corporations (most publicly at the University of California at Berkeley, according to reports by an administration-sponsored evaluation team). Scary as they are, these direct attempts to limit intellectual freedom are only one aspect of an environment in which more subtle curbs on "free" inquiry are far more pervasive. The influences of economic and governance structures guide teaching and research toward approved paths, while attacks like these serve as a looming threat for those who stray. The combination, a "structural adjustment" of the U.S. academy, moves its institutions toward ever-closer ties to corporations and ever-greater oversight by federal and state government agencies.

Walls and Ears

Neither overt political restraints on intellectual freedom nor the deep effects of ties to industry and commerce are new to the U.S. academy. A constellation of commitments and connections emerges from the founding documents of colleges and universities, as well as the very names they bear — Yale, Stanford, Rockefeller, Eckerd — linking higher education to international trade, religious maneuvering, exploitative industries, and unsavory racial politics.[1] As well as the wealth of nations, the national interest — as determined by the ascendant forces in the federal government — has consistently been used to constrain the academy. Many states still require the antisubversive "loyalty oaths" that had such devastating effects during the McCarthy years. Although most remain unused, academic administrations have put them into action as recently as 2000.[2] But dead letters or lively specters, loyalty oaths are nothing more than the best-known episode in the tradition of overt restraint of teaching and research that runs from Puritan religious control through Cold War orthodoxy, down to today's homeland security scares.

The contemporary versions of these strategies of explicit political oversight of scholarly work come from several directions. Some are incorporated into major federal legislation and new programs — the Patriot Act, the Student and Exchange Visitor Information System (SEVIS). Others are changes in the functioning of long-standing government programs — the National Endowment for the Humanities, the Office of Foreign Asset Control. Still others come from foundations and school administrations that follow the government's lead. Many use the language of "counter-terrorism" and "national security," while some are part of a neoconservative strategy of appropriating the language of "diversity" and "academic freedom" to preempt liberal counter-arguments. They tend to operate either by controlling access to funding or by extending surveillance over broader and broader areas of intellectual life. The investigative and monitoring aspects of these efforts are key, because their ultimate results come as much from the calculated chilling effect of a fairly small number of exemplary incidents as from the concrete attacks themselves. The declaration of the policies is in many ways the point at which they have their greatest effect, rather than through the results of the comparatively small number of cases in which they are enforced.

The most public of these experiments in political oversight are those embodied in surveillance legislation passed in late 2001. Best known are the provisions of the USA Patriot Act, which give U.S. government agencies the authority to demand libraries' records of who has checked out what books, and impose a gag rule on institutions whose records have been examined (Carlson and Foster, 2002). Similarly pervasive in its reach is the SEVIS system, under which noncitizen students and the schools they study at must report on their locations and the progress of their studies, on pain of deportation (Arnone, 2004a; Field, 2004d). In a unique wrinkle, it requires students to pay for their own surveillance in order to get visas (Field, 2004b). Both of these surveillance programs exemplify the preemptive functions of political oversight. Students and faculty members may not seek out sources they suspect may be thought controversial for fear of being investigated; scholars from outside the country may be less willing to apply to graduate programs or fellowships in the United States, or be intimidated into restricting themselves to subjects of inquiry that will raise no eyebrows at the Department of Homeland Security or FBI. Similarly, both pieces of legislation recruit educational institutions as informers — schools must report on their students to SEVIS, and libraries cannot even disclose the existence of investigations of their readers.

Similar in their effects, though directed mainly at citizens and institutions rather than noncitizen students, are more traditional forms of surveillance and "investigation." At Iowa's Drake University and the University of Texas at Austin (and doubtless elsewhere) administrations have been asked or ordered to cooperate with investigations of campus events. At Drake, this took the form of subpoenas accompanied by sweeping gag orders relating to a 2003 antiwar conference; at Austin, a request for information about the organizers of a conference on "Islam and the Law." Both administrations cooperated fully, and neither informed the targets of the investigations that they were being sought by officers identifying themselves only as members of intelligence and antiterrorism units. In each case, the precise nature of the investigation remains unclear (Walsh, 2004; Arnone, 2004c). The intent of these efforts, however, is not hard to see: to discourage campuses from hosting events touching on subjects seen as sensitive or drawing conclusions deemed impolitic. If the actions of these two administrations are any guide, such attempts may well succeed.

Other ways of achieving the same chilling effect come through funding. Most explicitly, the Ford and Rockefeller Foundations — which gave over $50 million to U.S. higher education in 2003 — adopted new policies in May 2004 declaring that they will withdraw funding from any institution whose expenditures (regardless of the source of the funds) directly or indirectly promotes or supports groups or individuals engaged in certain political activities. The Ford Foundation's criteria are the promotion of "violence, terrorism, bigotry or the destruction of any state"; the Rockefeller Foundation refers to "terrorist activity." The provisions have drawn criticism from a range of elite universities, with Richard Saller, the provost of the University of Chicago, pointing out in the *Wall Street Journal* that any money given "to any U.S. taxpayer could be construed as violating the [Ford Foundation] policy, because the U.S. itself has been involved in the destruction of regimes overseas." The Rockefeller Foundation's policy, similarly, would have barred any school receiving foundation funds from inviting a speaker from the African National Congress to campus, let alone a Sinn Fein supporter like Massachusetts' Senator Kennedy (Golden, 2004).

Some state legislatures have used public education budget cuts to achieve a similar chilling effect. In Missouri and North Carolina, for instance, the 2002 budgets included cuts and restrictive criteria aimed at specific faculty members and course assignments. The Missouri legislature's action was symbolic, since it does not have the power to micromanage funds away from the particular political science professor whose "thought patterns" and work on sexuality some right-wing politicians considered questionable. In North Carolina, a budget rider responding to the assignment of Michael Sells's *Approaching the Qu'ran: The Early Revelations* for a summer orientation reading program could have far more concrete and sweeping effects (Smith, 2002).

Within the federal government, things have been somewhat less direct, though political second-guessing of the peer-review processes at both the National Endowment for the Humanities and the National Institutes of Health has an effect similar to that of the foundations' open litmus tests. The "flagging" of hundreds of NEH proposals considered not "traditional" enough — that is, concerned with sexuality, gender, or race — parallels the NIH's decision to review 289 already approved projects on a list provided by the far-right Traditional Values Coalition (Borrego, 2004; Brainard, 2003; Kaplan, 2004). In each case, projects that have already passed through an extensive examination by scholars in related fields are held up for reassessment or rejection based on their subject matter. Beyond the problems inherent in this scrutiny, these practices are connected to other forms of restriction and intimidation. The Center for AIDS Prevention Studies at the University of California — San Francisco, like others on the NIH review list, has been targeted for federal audits as well as an NIH site visit (Kaplan, 2004). Similarly, in the wake of the *Chronicle of Higher Education*'s reporting on flagging, the NEH launched an "investigation," threatening a former employee with legal action for discussing the practice, and similarly harassing another person quoted in the article (Field, 2004e).

In the works, though not certain of implementation, is a related form of oversight of the 118 area studies centers funded by the $95 million federal Title VI program. The proposed "International Higher Education Advisory Board" would have broad investigative powers to "study, monitor, appraise and evaluate" the activities of the area studies centers, to ensure that the centers "reflect diverse perspectives and represent the full range of views on world regions, foreign language and international affairs." The board, including representatives of the departments of Defense and Homeland Security and the National Security Agency, would, according to its proponents, enforce the presence of right-wing voices in all area studies centers (Subcommittee on Select Education, n.d.; Solomon, 2004; Cole, 2004). Interestingly, the board seems quite redundant, given the power the Department of Education already holds to oversee Title VI area studies centers and to withhold funding if they do not meet government goals. The announcement of explicit ideological testing of the centers' work seems to be a goal in itself, calculated to have an effect on their actions whether or not the proposal becomes law.

International collaboration and contact is a particular target of the current set of restrictive policies. SEVIS and other new bureaucratic hoops through which noncitizen students must pass have caused an abrupt halt in the growth of the international student population on U.S. campuses. After five years of an average 5 percent yearly growth, in 2002–2003 the rate fell below 1 percent. Almost half of the institutions surveyed by the Institute for International Education reported an overall decline in new enrollments by noncitizen students, and 60 percent said new visa procedures were the cause (Jacobson, 2003; Bollag, 2004b). On top of this, denials of visas for faculty from outside the United States add another layer of difficulty to international contact. The case of Tariq

Ramadan, whose appointment as Notre Dame's Henry R. Luce professor of religion, conflict, and peacebuilding at the Joan B. Kroc Institute for International Peace Studies was vetoed by the Department of Homeland Security, has been a subject of debate because of his status as a major European Muslim public intellectual, and because the Notre Dame administration has stood by him (Bollag, 2004a). In a similar but more extensive case, the Latin American Studies Association's 2004 conference had to cancel one-twelfth of its sessions because all sixty-one participating Cuban scholars were blocked at the border, their attendance deemed "detrimental to the interests of the United States" in some unspecified way (Bernstein, 2004). It is impossible to know how many others have had their visas revoked, or never had them approved, but lacked the prominence or institutional backing to publicize the situation.

More subtle, though potentially most sweeping of all, are the constraints maintained by the Treasury Department's Office of Foreign Assets Control (OFAC) on international collaboration with countries under U.S. sanctions. A partial victory for U.S. researchers and writers came in December 2004, when (in response to a legal challenge) OFAC revised its enforcement policy on collaboration with colleagues in Iran, Cuba, and Sudan (PEN American Center, 2004). The basic principle remains that "when a collaborative interaction takes place between an author in a sanctioned country and one or more U.S. scholars resulting in co-authorship or the equivalent thereof," without prior OFAC permission, the publisher faces a million-dollar fine and a ten-year prison term under the 1988 Berman Amendment (PEN American Center et al., 2004). The new policy does, however, establish "general licenses" for publication of works from these three countries, explicitly allowing all actions "ordinarily incident" to the publication of works by "academic and research facilities and their personnel." Nonetheless, the policy just as explicitly affirms a prohibition on unlicensed publication of "any person acting . . . directly or indirectly on behalf of" any state agency or subdivision of a sanctioned country, with the exception of academic institutions (U.S. Department of the Treasury — Office of Foreign Assets Control, 2004). It is unclear to what extent OFAC will use this very large loophole to affect the work of independent scholars and political figures in these countries. Collaborative work by a U.S. theologian and an Iranian cleric, or an edited collection on the Cuban health care system, for instance, presumably fall outside the general licenses. Similarly, the new rules only apply to Cuba, Iran, and Sudan — all work by scholars in other sanctioned countries must still be approved on a case-by-case basis, according to criteria that OFAC has never revealed (U.S. Department of the Treasury — Office of Public Affairs, 2004). As with the old policy, those working on subjects deemed political or sensitive are presumably most threatened, but all fields are equally affected by the principle of prior approval, which the new rules leave unchanged.

These various efforts and investigations harmonize with each other to create a hovering threat. If your research topics, campus activities, slate of speakers, or course lists stray too far from the officially acceptable, you risk investigation or a loss of funding. The aim is less to squelch dissent than to discourage it from emerging in the first place. "Flagged" NEH applicants are unlikely to apply again (Borrego, 2004); administrations are unlikely to approve events that could jeopardize Title VI, Ford, or Rockefeller Foundation funds; departments are unlikely to hire faculty members whose visas may not be approved. The rhetoric of all these measures has a similar effect. It is already seen as dangerous to risk even the appearance of opposition to "security" measures. The proposed Title VI Advisory Board adds to this an attempt to cast progressive educators as those calling for censorship and exclusion on campuses. As in other political spheres, appeals to "freedom" and "security" set forth restrictions in ways that frame even a mild critique as sedition.

Structural Adjustments

These open attacks on certain areas of research and teaching, and certain viewpoints within the U.S. academy, have to a certain extent diverted attention from a conversation that had taken on new urgency in the late 1990s. That debate was phrased in terms of "corporatization" or "privatization," depending on whether private or public institutions were the immediate subject (Engell and Dangerfield, 1998). Neither rubric seems accurate to me, however, given the long history of industrial and commercial involvement in both parts of the academic sphere. Instead, it seems to me, the past few decades have seen a shift in how that corporate involvement operates, analogous to the shifts that have taken place in multinational corporations' economic involvement in local economies around the world. Thus, borrowing a term from the years of organizing that led up to Seattle, I would like to reframe the subject as the "structural adjustment" of U.S. higher education.[3]

The overall effect of this process has been the greater and greater influence of corporate and military priorities on the academy, from research to teaching to institutional functioning. Some of this is direct and obvious, like university-corporate partnerships that have profit-making as an explicit goal. Some is more subtle: judging programs by criteria imported from the corporate world, or by their usefulness to corporations and the government. This "structural adjustment" has not slowed down since the new century began (nor have conversations about it and efforts to resist it entirely ceased), and in some ways has become more pervasive and picked up speed since "national security" replaced "globalization" as the byword of progress. It remains somewhat difficult to see as a whole, however, because it proceeds unevenly, with different institutions and portions of the academy affected more strongly by different aspects of it at different times.

There are some aspects of this structural adjustment that do touch all institutions of higher education in the United States, so I will start this description with them — changes in government funding and regulatory legislation being the most sweeping of all. Public institutions have seen deep cuts in their state support since the twenty-first century began. State-by-state drops of up to 23 percent between 2002 and 2004 have added up to a nationwide 2.1 percent decrease in funding in 2003–2004, which may be the biggest ever in a single year (Arnone, 2004b).[4] These cuts, and the tuition rises, financial aid reductions, hiring freezes, and other restrictions that have followed them, have in many cases been attributed to the effects of September 11, 2001, or the recession that began in early 2001.

But as William Zumeta has pointed out in a report for the National Education Association, tax-funded state spending on higher education (not including student aid), has been steadily declining in relation to the income of states' populations since the mid-1970s (Zumeta, 2004). Other measures confirm the long-term nature of the trend. From 1980 to 2000, state support fell from 45.6 percent to 35.8 percent of public institutions' revenue, with overall government funding dropping from 62.2 percent to 50.4 percent (National Center for Educational Statistics, 2002). Private institutions have been less directly affected, though federal, state, and local government contributions fell from 17 percent to 9 percent of their income between 1995 and 2000 (*Chronicle of Higher Education*, 1997 and 2003).[5]

Both parts of the academy, however, have felt the effects of the accompanying shifts in how government funds are distributed and what they are available to support. In perhaps the starkest example, the federal government has put forward a new, more restrictive ban on funding for schools that do not allow military recruitment on their campuses (Klein, 2004). The fate of this particular initiative is uncertain, given the recent Third Circuit Court of Appeals ruling in several law schools' case against the Solomon Amendment (which established the original funding ban), but the present administration has made very clear its long-term commitment to the policy's goals (Caruso, 2004). Significantly, the only law school to respond to the ruling by ending campus military recruitment so far is Harvard, the most financially secure in the country (Mangan, 2005).

More typical, however, are new funding programs, like the Community-Based Job Training Initiative for community colleges, constructed to require (or in other cases merely encourage) collaboration with corporations or business associations (White House, 2004; Workforce Strategy Center, 2004). Similarly, recent increases in overall funding for academic research, a 13.6 percent boost in 2002, the largest since 1980 (*Chronicle of Higher Education*, 2004b), have come in selective and targeted ways. The recently announced 2005 spending plan is quite revealing: cuts of 2 percent for the National Science Foundation and 1.5 percent for NASA after years of steady increases (Field, 2004a), and a 7.8 percent boost for military research (Field, 2004c). Strikingly, most of this increase is in the form of earmarked funds that need not pass through a peer-review process like that of the National Science Foundation. Earmarks, carve-outs, and setasides, all ways of evading merit-based review processes, have become increasingly common ways of funding research. Academic earmarks alone passed the $2 billion mark in 2003 — more than six times the 1996 level, and accounting for 8 percent of the total federal spending on academic research (Feller, 2004). This "race to the bottom,"[6] as economist Irwin Feller puts it in the *Chronicle of Higher Education*, is also a race to meet the needs of Chambers of Commerce, of congressional campaign donors, of military contractors.

Stockholm Syndrome

Tied to these shifts in funding is the economic interest that institutions of higher education now have in corporate profitability. The Bayh–Dole Act, passed in 1980, allowed universities to patent the results of research done with federal money. In the years since, according to Eyal Press and Jennifer Washburn's research, numerous other laws and tax breaks have followed in Bayh-Dole's footsteps toward the Business-Higher Education Forum's goal of eliminating the walls that still separate the academy and the marketplace (Press and Washburn, 2000; Noble, 2002). The basic effects have been simple — to expand the commercial side of public and theoretically nonprofit universities and colleges; to encourage closer partnerships between schools and corporations; and to vest control over research results in institutions' patent offices, rather than in the broader scholarly community or the particular researchers involved. All of this was accomplished without Bayh-Dole bringing universities the promised financial windfall. Boston University, for instance, lost nearly a fifth of its endowment in the 1980s and 1990s by sinking it in a Bayh-Dole enterprise called Seragen. The school's agenda was set by its stake in the company and its president and trustees' investments, with predictable, if unfortunate, results for the school (though not for the officials involved, none of whom lost their jobs) (Press and Washburn, 2000). Although B.U.'s case is extreme, Lita Nelsen, director of technology licensing at MIT, told Press and Washburn that very few schools earn substantial amounts from such ventures.

Similarly, universities' increasingly large commitment to the stock market makes corporate profits more central to their financial health. According to the National Association of College and University Business Officers, over 57 percent of the $230 billion held in the endowments of U.S. higher education institutions is now placed in stocks. These investments also mark off the wealthiest institutions, which set the standard for less fortunate schools — the nest eggs of the thirty-nine members of the billion-dollar-endowment club grow mainly from investment returns; the rest grow through gifts. Gifts, too, increasingly often take the form of stocks. Of the ninety-one entries whose form was specified on the *Chronicle of Higher Education*'s list of "Major Private Gifts to Higher Education" from 1967 to 2004, 36 percent consisted wholly or partly of corporate stock. This economic stake in the welfare of corporations has direct effects as well as more subtle implications. More blatantly, and perhaps most predictably, the schools most heavily reliant on the stock market are also the least likely to incorporate social responsibility into their fiscal management policies — 13 percent of the billion-dollar club do, as opposed to 28 percent of institutions with endowments under $25 million (Pulley, 2004).

For public institutions, these processes have led to and been incorporated into several waves of structural adjustment. In the first, which began in the 1960s and 1970s, public universities and colleges began charging tuition — in some cases due to decreasing state funding, in others due to open political pressure. Most notoriously, President Ford made the imposition of tuition at the City University of New York part of his price for releasing federal funding to the city during its mid-seventies economic collapse. The second wave, in the 1980s and 1990s, included an increasing development of sources of income not tied to instruction or merit-reviewed research: creating private fundraising foundations, cultivating wealthy donors, spinning off hospitals and professional schools (Selingo, 2003). Private institutions have followed suit, insisting, for instance, as Yale University has in response to union organizing drives at Yale-New Haven Hospital, that teaching hospitals and the schools that support them must be considered entirely separate entities for collective bargaining purposes (Smallwood, 2003). The past decade or so has also seen other kinds of attempts to remodel the U.S. academy on a corporate model, in particular in relation to so-called intellectual property.

Most institutions of higher education have over the past few years adopted "Intellectual Property Policies" spelling out extremely broad claims to the work done by faculty members, technical staff, and in some cases students, in glaring contradiction of traditional academic practice. Emory University's fairly typical policy, adopted in 2002, asserts that the university may claim any copyrightable materials which are "(a) related to the Emory Personnel's normal duties . . . or (b) made with the use of Emory Support . . . and . . . [d]eveloped with the use of substantially more Emory Support than is usually provided"—leaving the "usual" levels of library, lab, office, and computer usage undefined (Emory University, 2002; see also Brigham Young University, n.d.). It also declares that "Emory Personnel [and visitors and students] are bound by this IP Policy regardless of whether they have signed an IP Rights Agreement Form," and requires all to "promptly disclose the existence of any Intellectual Property (that is, Intellectual Property to which Emory may assert ownership rights pursuant to Section 1)" to the administration. Needless to say, the "Conflict Resolution" section places all final decision-making in the hands of the Provost—hardly a disinterested party—after a nominal appeal process (Emory University, 2002). In every detail, these policies parallel standard corporate claims to complete ownership of "work for hire" (a term that appears in academic policies as well) by contractors and employees. The expansion of this vision of intellectual work as inevitably resulting in a "property" that can be made a source of profit—rather than a contribution to a growing field of knowledge about some particular subject—is a stunningly clear indication of how deeply corporate thinking has been woven into the institutional fabric of U.S. higher education.

Another example worth pursuing is the appearance of such corporate catchphrases as "Value-Centered Management" (VCM) in increasing numbers of university and college contexts. These terms of art, sold to institutions and faculty as ways to solve or smooth budget crunches, essentially describe mechanisms for allocating resources based not on instructional or research needs, but on the profitability of different sections of a school. At the University of South Carolina's Special Called Meeting of the Faculty Senate dealing with a VCM proposal, Provost Jerome Odom, after refusing to answer the first question put to him by the faculty—"what in the world is the virtue of this?"—admitted that the approach would pit programs against each other (University of South Carolina Faculty Senate, 2002). From his other statements, and those of other proponents, it is clear that the sole virtue of VCM, and "Responsibility-Centered Management," "Total Quality Management," and the rest of the crop, is that it brings the U.S. academy closer to a corporate model of "high-performing" and "low-performing" units, assessed by their ability to turn a profit.

The implications for instruction and research are clear. One need look no further than the "Selective Excellence" restructuring model pushed on the academy from the late 1980s on, which called for "abandoning or closing [programs]

267

that are of lesser quality" or deemed less worthy of cultivation (Grassmuck, 1990). At Yale, one of the highest profile schools to adopt the term (*Chronicle of Higher Education*, 1996), "Selective Excellence" called for the gutting of the Sociology Department, which is generally ranked among the better programs in the country (Coughlin, 1992), and the total elimination of Linguistics (*Chronicle of Higher Education*, 1992).

Another area in which this adoption of corporate models of management has had a huge impact is academic labor, and the issues of governance that are so intimately connected to it (Bosquet, 2003). Limited space prevents me from giving this sprawling area the detailed attention it deserves, but a few key points are necessary. The shift (paralleling similar efforts in other industries) from a largely full-time, tenured, or tenure-track workforce toward a system based on primarily part-time adjuncts and graduate instructors is well under way. In 2000, 57 percent of U.S. faculty members worked full time, compared to 66 percent in 1980 and 78 percent in 1970 (Allen, 2004), while the percentage of full-time faculty off the tenure track increased by about 8 percent between 1989 and 2001 (AAUP, 2004a).[7] Institutions seem to be looking to the health sciences for models, perhaps hoping that the absence of tenure at medical schools can be extended into other areas of the U.S. academy, in the path of research and licensing approaches pioneered by collaboration with pharmaceutical companies. Recent unionization drives among adjuncts, graduate employees, and faculty have focused on these shifts and have met with stiff resistance from university administrations. The National Labor Relations Board's recent reversal of its earlier ruling in favor of graduate employee unionization at private institutions makes such efforts more difficult, though adjunct organizing is blossoming (Smallwood, 2004).

Another deeply problematic side of academic labor is the wide range of pay for the same work, coupled with the deep taboo among faculty on discussing their salaries with each other (or even disclosing them). Pay differentials of over $150,000 within a given rank at institutions of the same type (AAUP, 2004b) and nearly $40,000 between faculty of similar age and professional qualifications within a single department (de Nîmes, 2004), amount to one of the more extreme rejections of the idea that similar work should receive similar compensation. In this way, at least, faculty have more in common with low-wage contingent workers dependent on employers' or supervisors' favors to make the difference between a minimum and a living wage than they do with most white-collar workers, who can at least rely on a standardized pay scale within a company or division. This corporate model of purely individual relationships between employer and employee runs counter to the very notion of collegiality and the idea of institutions of higher education as communities of scholars.

For public and private institutions alike, the corporate approach is the guiding star. To some extent, the fact that public universities are both more heavily regulated and somewhat buffered by their state funding against total reliance on private funds has served to slow the expansion of this structural adjustment. But more and more, as state education budgets are cut, the taboo on privatization proposals is being broken, often with the explicit goal of facilitating closer university-corporate relationships and increasing "responsiveness" to the mythic all-knowing "market." In 2003, an array of proposals emerged from the year's budget shortfalls (Selingo, 2003). Colorado suggested a voucher system that could divert state funds to private institutions—an "escape from voter-imposed limits on state spending and restrictions on how much they can raise tuition rates." Wisconsin floated the idea of handing its entire university system over to an independent authority. And South Carolina summed up many tendencies of structural adjustment, suggesting that its schools would be presented with two alternatives: "accept more state control, or go private" (Selingo, 2003; Schmidt, 2003). An alternative model presented by two South Carolina education commission consultants elegantly combines the two directions,[8] proposing "a hybrid public-private board consisting partly of gubernatorial and legislative appointees and partly of business and community leaders, with its finances to be derived from both public and private sources" to replace the commission itself (Schmidt, 2003). This body, clearly, would both facilitate public-private partnerships and eliminate "inefficiency," refitting the entire system to suit corporate needs.

Bedfellows

The conflation of the interests of the academy and those of corporations takes on its most explicit form in the joint ventures spurred by the Bayh-Dole Act and similar legislation. These are often embodied in semi-independent centers and institutes affiliated with universities and colleges but not part of their regular governance structures. The basic model, set early on by trendsetters like the MIT-affiliated Whitehead Institute for Biomedical Research, has remained unshaken: these institutes provide a channel through which corporations pay for early access to new research and for a voice in setting research priorities (Blum, 1991; Press and Washburn, 2000). One current example can stand in for the trend as a whole: the Keck Graduate Institute, housed at the Claremont Colleges, allows companies in its "Corporate Partners Program" to decide the research topics for graduate students' Team Masters Projects—a degree requirement—for a mere $50,000 (Keck Graduate Institute, 2004b). The KGI Advisory Council, composed almost entirely of corporate executives, does the same on an institutional level, "forging partnerships between KGI and industry, and target[ing] potential curricular and research initiatives" (Keck Graduate Institute, 2004a). More explicit than most such "partnerships," it is by no means unique.

Variations of the same structure abound. Some schools prefer to keep such deals in-house: the University of California at Berkeley signed a deal with Novartis in 1998 giving the pharmaceutical company two of the five seats on the Department of Plant and Microbial Biology's research committee and the right of first refusal over licensing of about a third of the department's discoveries (Press and Washburn, 2000). Others cover only one position: the occupant of the Kmart chair at West Virginia University's management school must spend up to a month yearly training assistant store managers (Press and Washburn, 2000). Still others apply to graduate students: Wal-Mart's new scholarship program funds journalism students at schools whose large Latino/a populations echo the demographics of the company's minimum-wage workforce; they are expected to attend annual stockholder meetings—an unprecedented request for journalism scholarships (Hays, 2004). But the most fascinating such collaboration of all is the Mercatus Center at George Mason University, which devotes itself to promoting deregulation — much of which directly or indirectly benefits Koch Industries, the oil and gas company that funds the center. Mercatus, according to the *Wall Street Journal*, was responsible for the choice of fourteen of the twenty-three rules on the Bush administration's 2001 federal regulation "hit list," as compared to zero for the National Association of Manufacturers (Davis, 2004).

The Mercatus Center's success in pushing its agenda points to the broad political effects of these corporate-academic joint endeavors, or rather these mobilizations of academic resources for corporate ends. Their effects on the academy itself are no less sweeping. On the institutional scale, it feeds the shift in faculty advancement from a merit-based to a profit-based model, as seen in Oklahoma state officials' proposal to create "tenure and promotion policies that reward faculty members whose research leads to commercial successes" (*Chronicle of Higher Education*, 2004a). The flip side of this is retaliation against critics of these alliances with corporations. The classic example is MIT's refusal to tenure David Noble in 1984, in part because of his vocal criticism of the Whitehead Institute and the Industrial Liason Program (Blum, 1991). This year, a team of scholars invited to review the Novartis-Berkeley deal concluded that "there is little doubt" that it affected the tenure process of outspoken critic Ignacio Chapela (Blumenstyk, 2004; see also Berkeley Faculty Association, 2005). Brown University went both schools one better, eliminating the position held by David Kern after he discovered a serious lung disease affecting employees at Microfibres, a Brown corporate partner (Press and Washburn, 2000). By contrast, Charles Thomas remains in his criminology position at the University of Florida five years after it was discovered that he had "pocketed $3 million in consulting fees from the private-prison industry, in which he also owned stock" (Press and Washburn, 2000). Tractable academics reap rewards from both corporations and the academy — critics are fired.

As in other areas of academic structural adjustment, the more systemic effects of these joint ventures are hard to quantify, since they consist in large part of research not pursued, graduate programs allowed to stagnate, questions not raised or raised in ways that have little to do with the issues at hand. One comparatively well-examined area, however, is the study of global climate change, where the firmness of the scientific consensus makes it easy to see the effects of corporate interest in promoting discredited ideas, and academic collaboration in that effort. Ross Gelbspan's *The Heat Is On* documents the process of creating this artificial debate — a process duplicated with much less fanfare and scrutiny in fields from criminology to history far more often than we would like to think (Gelbspan, 1998). In all, the "partnerships" that U.S. institutions of higher education have been so eager to forge have been in no way the equal pairings the term implies. They have been ways for corporations to exert direct influence over many aspects of academic work and life, from faculty members' employment to research agendas and beyond. As such, they merge with the abovementioned indirect influence of corporate interests and models to power the ongoing structural adjustment of the U.S. academy.

A Fine Old Conflict

This academic structural adjustment is not an even or straightforward motion, or one that is being directed or managed from a single point. In this it is least like the International Monetary Fund programs whose name I have applied to it. In U.S. higher education, the structural nature of the transformation applies to both sides of the equation — as it often does in most of the processes obscured by the term "globalization." What I have tried to describe here are the many ways in which academic institutions are integrated into the present economic and political structures of the United States, and the effects that these processes have on the ideas of "free inquiry" and scholarship which we have been taught sets the academy apart. This integration, not the myth of an unsullied temple of knowledge, defines the terrain on which we move as we try to make real some of those goals of autonomy and freedom in the intellectual sphere as well as in the rest of our lives. Participating in any convergence and movement toward those ends requires a clear idea of where we are, and how our location connects to other areas of conflict and resistance (Holt, 1976). I hope that this description of the conditions of U.S. academic institutions has made some of the paths out more visible; we will only know how they join others when we begin to walk down them.

Notes

1. Stanford University, for instance, like its railroad-magnate namesake, places government-industrial collaboration at its heart — claiming $400 million in federal research and development aid alone in 2002 (*Chronicle of Higher Education*, 2004b). Its relationship to its founder's agitation against the Chinese immigrants who made his fortune is less clear (see Flatté, n.d.). Similarly, land-grant schools' founding legislation explicitly merges industrial and state interests. "Without excluding other scientific and classical studies, and including military tactics. The Morrill Act mandates that land-grant schools teach such branches of learning as are related to agriculture and the mechanic arts" (Morrill Act of 1862; see also Morrill, 1887).

2. Many loyalty oath requirements were struck down in the Supreme Court's 1966 *Keyishian v. Board of Regents* ruling, but 1974's *Cole v. Richardson* held that an oath could be constitutional if phrased as an "affirmation," not a "disclaimer" (Euben, 2001). See *Chronicle of Higher Education* (2000) for a recent use of such an oath in Mesa, Arizona, and Parks and Recreation Board of the City of Mesa (2003) for its scope and persistence.

3. The term comes from one of the International Monetary Fund's basic tools — the Structural Adjustment Programs that impoverished states are required to adopt in exchange for loans or loan extensions. SAPs typically demand cuts in state funding on education, health, and other human services, while mandating no such restrictions for military spending, tax breaks for corporations, and so on. Thus the paradoxes of states deeply sunk in international debt which prevents them from providing medications to slow the HIV/AIDS epidemic's spread, but not from spending tens of millions of dollars on armaments. For more on the IMF and its fellow structural adjusters at the World Bank, WTO, Inter-American Development Bank, and so on, see the books cited in the editors' introduction.

4. Some of the specific state budget numbers are especially telling. For instance, between 1998 and 2001, New York slashed $615 million from the state university system, while increasing by $761 million money spent on state prisons (Shapiro, 1999).

5. Even discounting the 1994–95 budget line for federally funded "Research and Development Centers," which no longer appears in the fiscal 2000 statistics, there is still a 3.3 percent drop (*Chronicle of Higher Education*, 1997, 2003).

6. The phrase "race to the bottom" comes from the labor movement's critique of the competition among national and local governments to win favor from corporations, in the hope of attracting jobs (generally in low-wage and environmentally unsustainable industries, and generally mobile enough to move again once a better deal for the company comes along).

7. It is worth noting that these percentages mask a deep gender division — 62 percent of men were full-timers in 2000, versus 50.5 percent of women — and racial disparities that would be more frequently noted if there were more than a token number of faculty of color in the U.S. academy (Allen, 2004).

8. From the National Center for Higher Education Management Systems and the Center for Public Higher Education Trusteeship and Governance at the Association of Governing Boards of Universities and Colleges (Schmidt, 2003), two of an array of organizations dedicated to bringing the U.S. academy into conformity with corporate norms.

Works Cited

All quotations are from online sources (as listed below) when available.

AAUP (American Association of University Professors). 2004a. "Changing Composition of Faculty at Public and Private Four-Year Institutions, 1989–2001." *Don't Blame Faculty for High Tuition: The Annual Report on the Economic Status of the Profession 2003–04*. April. http://www.aaup.org/surveys/04z/tableb.pdf.

———. 2004b. "Distribution of Individual Faculty Members." *Don't Blame Faculty for High Tuition: The Annual Report on the Economic Status of the Profession 2003–04*. April. http://www.aaup.org/surveys/04z/surveytab8.pdf.

Allen, Henry Lee. 2004. "Employment at the Margins: Nonstandard Work in Higher Education." *The NEA 2004 Almanac of Higher Education*. http://www.nea.org/he/healma2k4/a04p27.pdf.

Arnone, Michael. 2004a. "Customs Officials Gain Access to Database." *Chronicle of Higher Education*, June 4. http://chronicle.com/prm/weekly/v50/i39/39a01904.htm.

———. 2004b. "State Spending on Colleges Drops for the First Time in 11 Years." *Chronicle of Higher Education*, January 16. http://chronicle.com/prm/weekly/v50/i19/19a02401.htm.

———. 2004c. "Texas Campus Is Puzzled by Federal Agents' Inquiry into Conference on Islam." *Chronicle of Higher Education*, March 5. http://chronicle.com/prm/weekly/v50/i26/26a01001.htm.

Berkeley Faculty Association. 2005. "Ignacio Chapela: Tenure at Berkeley." *California Conference of the American Association of University Professors Web Site*, January 19. http://www.aaup-ca.org/chapela.html.

Bernstein, Nina. 2004. "U.S. Denies Cuban Scholars Entry to Attend a Meeting." *New York Times*, October 1. http://www.nytimes.com/2004/10/01/politics/01scholars.html.

Blum, Debra E. 1991. "An Outspoken Critic Campaigns against Campus Ties to Industry." *Chronicle of Higher Education*, July 17. http://chronicle.com/prm/che-data/articles.dir/articles-37.dir/issue-44.dir/44a01102.htm.

Blumenstyk, Goldie. 2004. "Reviewers Give Thumbs down to Corporate Deal at Berkeley." *Chronicle of Higher Education*. August 6. http://chronicle.com/prm/weekly/v50/i48/48a02501.htm.

Bollag, Burton. 2004a. "U.S. Shuts out Muslim Scholar, Raising Fears for Academic Freedom." *Chronicle of Higher Education*, September 10. http://chronicle.com/prm/weekly/v51/i03/03a00801.htm.

———. 2004b. "Wanted: Foreign Students." *Chronicle of Higher Education*. October 8. http://chronicle.com/prm/weekly/v51/i07/07a03701.htm.

Borrego, Anne Marie. 2004. "Humanities Endowment Returns to 'Flagging' Nontraditional Projects." *Chronicle of Higher Education*, January 16. http://chronicle.com/weekly/v50/i19/19a00101.htm.

Bosquet, Marc. 2003. "The Academic Labor Movement in One Volume." *Workplace* 5. http://www.louisville.edu/journal/workplace/issue5p2/bousquetchalk.htm.

Brainard, Jeffrey. 2003. "NIH Begins Review of Studies That Were Questioned at a Congressional Hearing." *Chronicle of Higher Education*, November 7. http://chronicle.com/weekly/v50/i11/11a02401.htm.

Brigham Young University. n.d. "Brigham Young University Intellectual Property Policy." *BYU Web Site.* http://ipsinfo.byu.edu/ippolicy.htm.

Carlson, Scott, and Andrea L. Foster. 2002. "Colleges Fear Anti-Terrorism Law Could Turn Them into Big Brother." *Chronicle of Higher Education*, March 1. http://chronicle.com/prm/weekly/v48/i25/25a03101.htm.

Caruso, David B. 2004. "Justice to Appeal Recruitment Ruling." *Washington Post*, December 14. http://www.washingtonpost.com/wp-dyn/articles/A11092-2005Jan14.html.

Chronicle of Higher Education. 1992. "Yale Considers Trimming Arts and Sciences." January 22. http://chronicle.com/prm/che-data/articles.dir/articles-38.dir/issue-20.dir/20a00501.htm.

Chronicle of Higher Education. 1996. "Yale Decides to Strive for 'Selective Excellence.'" November 8. http://chronicle.com/prm/che-data/articles.dir/art-43.dir/issue-11.dir/11a03503.htm.

Chronicle of Higher Education. 1997. "Revenues and Expenditures of Colleges and Universities, 1994–5." *Almanac 97–98.* http://chronicle.com/prm/che-data/infobank.dir/almanac.dir/97alm.dir/facts.dir/11funds.htm.

Chronicle of Higher Education. 2000. "Communist Student Makes Arizona College Abandon Loyalty Oath," September 22. http://chronicle.com/prm/weekly/v47/i04/04a04702.htm.

Chronicle of Higher Education. 2003. "Finances of Colleges and Universities, Fiscal Year 2000." *The Chronicle Almanac 2003.* http://chronicle.com/prm/weekly/almanac/2003/nation/0102401.htm.

Chronicle of Higher Education. 2004a. "A Brighter Financial Picture for Colleges." *The Chronicle Almanac, 2004–5.* http://chronicle.com/free/almanac/2004/nation/nation.htm.

Chronicle of Higher Education. 2004b. "Top Institutions in Federal Research-and-Development Expenditures, 2001 and 2002." August 6. http://chronicle.com/prm/weekly/v50/i48/48a02304.htm.

Cole, Juan. 2004. "A Big Brother Plan to Monitor Middle East Studies." *Historians News Network*, March 6. http://hnn.us/roundup/entries/3978.html.

Coughlin, Ellen K. 1992. "Sociologists Confront Questions about Field's Direction." *Chronicle of Higher Education*, August 12. http://chronicle.com/prm/che-data/articles.dir/articles-38.dir/issue-49.dir/49a00601.htm.

Davis, Bob. 2004. "In Washington, Tiny Think-Tank Wields Big Stick on Regulation." *Wall Street Journal*, July 16.

de Nîmes, Susan. 2004. Personal communication, October 6.

Emory University. 2002. "Intellectual Property Policy." *Office of the Provost Home Page*, May 23. http://www.emory.edu/PROVOST/policy_bylaws/IP_policy.htm.

Engell, James, and Anthony Dangerfield. 1998. "The Market-Model University: Humanities in the Age of Money." *Harvard Magazine Online.* http://www.harvard-magazine.com/issues/mj98/forum.html.

Euben, Donna R. 2001. "Academic Freedom, Loyalty Oaths, and Diversity in Academe." *Academe* 87.3. http://www.aaup.org/publications/Academe/2001/01mj/mj01lw.htm.

Feller, Irwin. 2004. "Research Subverted by Academic Greed." *Chronicle of Higher Education*, January 16. http://chronicle.com/prm/weekly/v50/i19/19b00601.htm.

Field, Kelly. 2004a. "Budget Cuts Proposed for 2 Science Agencies." *Chronicle of Higher Education*, August 6. http://chronicle.com/prm/weekly/v50/i48/48a02402.htm.

———. 2004b. "Colleges Won't Collect Foreign-Student Fees." *Chronicle of Higher Education*, July 9. http://chronicle.com/prm/weekly/v50/i44/44a02303.htm.

———. 2004c. "Congress Passes Defense-Spending Bill." *Chronicle of Higher Education*. August 6. http://chronicle.com/prm/weekly/v50/i48/48a02302.htm.

———. 2004d. "FBI Gets Access to Student Databases." *Chronicle of Higher Education*, September 24. http://chronicle.com/prm/weekly/v51/i05/05a02403.htm.

———. 2004e. "Humanities Endowment Opens Inquiry into Alleged Leak to a Reporter." *Chronicle of Higher Education*, May 28. http://chronicle.com/prm/weekly/v50/i38/38a02201.htm.

Flatté, Anne. n.d. "Interview with Gordon Chang." *The "Becoming Stanford" Web Site*. http://becoming.stanford.edu/interview/chang.html.

Gelbspan, Ross. 1998. *The Heat Is On: The Climate Crisis, the Cover-up, the Prescription* (Philadelphia: Perseus Publishing).

Golden, Daniel. 2004. "Colleges Object to New Wording in Ford Grants." *Wall Street Journal*, May 4.

Grassmuck, Karen. 1990. "Clouded Economy Prompts Colleges to Weigh Changes." *Chronicle of Higher Education*, January 31. http://chronicle.com/prm/che-data/articles.dir/articles-36.dir/issue-20.dir/20a00102.htm.

Guterman, Lila, and Peter Monaghan. 2004. "Groups Sue U.S. Agency over International Publishing Rules." *Chronicle of Higher Education*, October 8. http://chronicle.com/prm/weekly/v51/i07/07a01601.htm.

Hays, Constance L. 2004. "Wal-Mart Tries to Shine Its Image by Supporting Public Broadcasting." *New York Times*, August 16.

Holt, John. 1976. *Instead of Education* (New York: Dutton).

Jacobson, Jennifer. 2003. "Foreign-Student Enrollment Stagnates." *Chronicle of Higher Education*, November 7. http://chronicle.com/prm/weekly/v50/i11/11a00101.htm.

Kaplan, Esther. 2004. "Political Science." *POZ*, no. 98. http://www.poz.com/index.

Keck Graduate Institute. 2004a. "Advisory Council." *KGI Web Site*, undated. http://www.kgi.edu/about/advisory.shtml.

———. 2004b. "Corporate Partners Program." *KGI Web Site*. undated. http://www.kgi.edu/industry/partners.shtml.

Klein, Alyson. 2004. "U.S. House Committee Passes Bill to Strengthen Law on Military Recruiters' Access to Colleges." *Chronicle of Higher Education*, March 19. http://chronicle.com/prm/daily/2004/03/2004031901n.htm.

Mangan, Katherine S. 2005. "Affirmative Action and Military Recruiting Spur Debate at Law-School Meeting." *Chronicle of Higher Education*, January 21. http://chronicle.com/weekly/v51/i20/20a01901.htm.

Morrill Act of 1862, sec 4. Cited in Office of Public Affairs of the National Association of State Universities and Land-Grant Colleges. "Development of the Land-Grant System: 1862–1994". *NASULGC Web Site*, undated. http://www.nasulgc.org/publications/Land_Grant/Development.htm.

Morrill, Justin W. 1887. "Address." Cited in Office of Public Affairs of the National Association of State Universities and Land-Grant Colleges. "Development of the Land-Grant System: 1862–1994". *NASULGC Web Site*, undated. http://www.nasulgc.org/publications/Land_Grant/Development.htm.

National Center for Education Statistics. 2002. "Current-fund Revenue of Public Degree-granting Institutions." *Digest of Education Statistics*. http://nces.ed.gov/programs/digest/d02/tables/dt330.asp.

Noble, David. 2002. *Digital Diploma Mills: The Automation of Higher Education* (New York: Monthly Review Press). Excerpts at http://www.monthlyreview.org/0302noble.htm.

Parks and Recreation Board of the City of Mesa. 2003. "Meeting Minutes 2003 Nov 13." *Official Web Site of the City of Mesa, Arizona*, November 13. http://citydoc.cityofmesa.org/stellent/groups/public/documents/meetings/prb_minutes2003nov13.hcsp.

PEN American Center. 2004. "Treasury Department Removes Restrictions on U.S. Publications." *PEN American Center Home Page*, December 17. http://penusa.org/go/news/comments/141/.

PEN American Center, American Association of University Presses, and Association of American Publishers. 2004. "First Amendment Problems Remain in Wake of Latest OFAC Pronouncement." *PEN American Center Home Page*, April 5. http://www.pen.org/freedom/pressrel/ofac_april2004.html.

Press, Eyal, and Jennifer Washburn. 2000. "The Kept University." *Atlantic Monthly* 285.3. http://www.aaas.org/spp/rd/ch26.pdf.

Pulley, John L. 2004. "Endowments Post First Gain in 3 Years, but Some Still Lag." *Chronicle of Higher Education*, January 23. http://chronicle.com/prm/weekly/v50/i20/20a00101.htm.

Schmidt, Peter. 2003. "Accept More State Control or Go Private." *Chronicle of Higher Education*, December 19. http://chronicle.com/prm/weekly/v50/i17/17a02401.htm.

Selingo, Jeffrey. 2003. "The Disappearing State in Public Higher Education." *Chronicle of Higher Education*, February 28. http://chronicle.com/prm/weekly/v49/i25/25a02201.htm.

Shapiro, Walter. 1999. "1.8 Million Reasons for Criminal-Justice Reform." *USA Today*, March 17. Final edition. Lexis-Nexis.

Smallwood, Scott. 2003. "Blue-Collar and Clerical Workers, Joined by Some Graduate Students, Strike at Yale U." *Chronicle of Higher Education*, March 4. http://chronicle.com/prm/daily/2003/03/2003030402n.htm.

———. 2004. "The NLRB's Ruling on Collective Bargaining." *Chronicle of Higher Education*, July 30. http://chronicle.com/prm/weekly/v50/i47/47a01001.htm.

Smith, Mark F. 2002. "Improper Activities." *Academe* 88.6. http://www.aaup.org/publications/Academe/2002/02nd/02ndgr.htm.

Solomon, Alisa. 2004. "The Ideology Police." *Village Voice* no. 408. http://www.villagevoice.com/issues/0408/solomon.php.

Subcommittee on Select Education. n.d. "Subcommittee on Select Education Markup of HR 3077." *Committee on Education and the Workforce Home Page*. http://edworkforce.house.gov/markups/108th/sed/hr3077/917main.htm.

U.S. Department of the Treasury, Office of Foreign Assets Control. 2004. "Final Rule." *Department of the Treasury Press Room*, December 15. http://www.treasury.gov/press/releases/reports/office%20foreign.pdf.

U.S. Department of the Treasury, Office of Public Affairs. 2004. "Treasury Issues General License for Publishing Activities." *Department of the Treasury Press Room*, December 15. http://www.treasury.gov/press/releases/js2152.htm.

University of South Carolina Faculty Senate. 2002. "Special Called Meeting of the Faculty Senate." *USC Web Site*, February 13. http://www.sc.edu/faculty/senate/02/minutes/0213.minutes.html.

Walsh, Sharon. 2004. "The Drake Affair." *Chronicle of Higher Education*, March 5. http://chronicle.com/prm/weekly/v50/i26/26a00801.htm.

White House. 2004. "Jobs for the 21st Century." *The White House Online*, January 21. http://www.whitehouse.gov/infocus/economy/more-20040121.html.

Workforce Strategy Center. 2004. "Policy Brief: Workforce Strategy Center Comments on President Bush's Call for Community-Based Job Training Grants." January 29. http://www.workforcestrategy.org/publications/policy_brief_012904.pdf.

Zumeta, William. 2004. "Higher Education Funding: Stagnation Continues; Financial Restructuring Underway." *The NEA 2004 Almanac of Higher Education*. http://www.nea.org/he/healma2k4/a04p61.pdf.

CHAPTER 24

The Status of Intellectual Authority

Silvio Torres-Saillant

I chose academic work as my trade, lured by the belief that the realm of ideas mattered to the world and that trained intellects had a role to play in the transformation of society. The remark by Argentinean writer Ernesto Sábato to the effect that intellectuals had the duty of improving the human caliber of their rulers resonated with the mind-set that made the world of humanistic learning an irrevocable occupational option. However, a couple of decades of service in academia has brought to the fore the difficulty inherent in my initial expectation. Scanning the landscape of the profession today, I perceive a pervasive sense of political disillusionment and ideological fatigue. The demise of the socialist bloc and the consolidation of the neoliberal phase of capitalism probably dealt a fell blow to the hope of many intellectuals with progressive aspirations. The failure of political utopias in Asian, Latin American, and Caribbean countries that had embraced revolutionary principles in their development models must have also given many intellectuals reason to desist from dreaming of a new society, especially in light of the clamorous pronouncements about the end of ideology that came from the winning side, as epitomized by the contention that capitalist liberal democracy as it already exists in the leading Western nations marked "the end-point of mankind's ideological evolution" and consequently "the end of history" (Fukuyama 1992: xi).

A beneficiary of the legacy of the Civil Rights movement, I entered the university as a student at a very auspicious moment in American history. Open admissions in public higher education institutions, the establishment of bilingual education programs, the emergence of affirmative action to regulate hiring and recruitment, the rise of women's studies, and the creation of ethnic studies units in many colleges and universities nationwide had already taken place. With the incorporation into the academy of new social segments from distinct origins came formerly excluded bodies of knowledge that pertained to their lives. Given their recognition of the circumstances of their arrival in the higher education campus, the newcomers often committed themselves to agendas informed by visions of social justice. Their concern with advancing from the academy the material and spiritual well-being of the less empowered linked the symbolic and concrete political realms, creating an intellectual ambience that challenged the conventional divide between the community and the scholar. But this ambience, which ushered me into the academy as a hopeful student, had eroded considerably by the mid 1980s, when I entered as a faculty member. Many of the scholarly ventures that hoped to transform the university by advocating justice and equality in the society as a whole had begun to show lack of political self-confidence.

Numerous progressive scholars seemed to have given up, their political wings presumably clipped by the ferocious repositioning of the ideological structure in contradistinction to which they had regarded themselves. Abroad, the WTO, the IMF, and the Inter-American Development Bank forged ahead, spreading the geopolitical gospel of the New World Order announced by George Bush père in the 1980s. At home, the resurgence of conservative powers did away with the most cherished policies of the New Deal, recasting Franklin D. Roosevelt's "Bill of Economic Rights" into Newt Gingrich's stern "Contract with America." Public assistance, affirmative action, open admissions, bilingual education, remedial instruction, and several other programs that had come into existence to enhance the life chances of social sectors that endured structural disadvantage fell by the wayside, pitiful casualties of a reconfigured articulation of the duties of the state to its citizens. Influential higher education officials such as University of California Regent Ward Connerly, invigorated by his victory against affirmative action there, eyed the dismantling of ethnic studies initiatives in the university system as a necessary next step. Influential historian of education Diane Ravitch, who served as assistant secretary of education during the Bush administration, and conservative writer Dinesh D'Souza, among others, joined a chorus of voices that repudiated the decline of American education, adducing a grievous loss of value as a result of the "political correctness" introduced by the interest groups that had stampeded into the academy since the 1960s.

As progressive scholars powerlessly witnessed the return of the dragon they thought they had slain, especially given the creature's seemingly superior might, since it came backed by the central government and several key donors, they risked being overcome by despair over their irrelevance. To this political scenario must be added the astonishing growth of entertainment in the daily menu of the citizenry. Sports events, reports on Hollywood releases, stories on the lives of celebrities, and programs on the pop music industry dwarfed the coverage and analysis of economic, social, and political information in the media. Noam Chomsky has for decades insisted on the numbing effect that the constant, voluminous, and thrilling deployment of entertainment messages has on the political consciousness of the population. Educators throughout the country have similarly grieved over their students' widespread apathy toward forms of communication — written, spoken, or visual — that fail to approximate the speed, rhythm, and varied stimulation of the typical mass entertainment message. That the news programs in the major television networks have gradually come to ape the visual language and pacing of entertainment and sports segments perhaps indicates that the producers of "serious" news have had to bend to the influence and power of the entertainment industry.

Perhaps it is in the context of the rise of the entertainment imperative that we can best understand the turn to popular culture, with its stress on pop music, dance, and performance arts, in the human sciences over the last two decades. Almost invariably, studies of popular culture — meaning usually the manufactured expressive forms that reach large audiences through the media — highlight the process of signifying "from below" and stress its resistance against the mores favored by the status quo. Yet the rapacity of the corporations behind the mass media and entertainment offerings that large audiences consume should make us pause before imputing resistive and liberatory qualities to the messages they convey, given the power of market forces to flatten all potentially subversive meaning and to depoliticize most forms of communication.

Regarding the turn to culture in the humanities and the social sciences, Terry Eagleton urges us to remain mindful of "one sober fact," namely, that "the primary problems which we confront in the new millennium — war, famine, poverty, disease, debt, drugs, environmental pollution, the displacement of peoples — are not especially 'cultural' at all. They are not primarily questions of value, symbolism, language, tradition, belonging or identity, least of all the arts. Cultural theorists qua cultural theorists have precious little to contribute to their resolution" (Eagleton 2000: 130). Eagleton decries the extent to which the anticolonialist discourse that characterized the utterances of progressive academics in the 1960s and 1970s has given way to the postcolonial meditation that visits us at present, their former sociopolitical advocacy having transubstantiated into a scrutiny of the subversive implications of cultural expression. In his view, today we content ourselves with an examination of "hybridity, ethnicity, and plurality" whereas formerly we would have aimed for elucidating questions such as "freedom, justice, and emancipation" (85). This is no doubt a dismal scenario for someone who, like me, entered the academy convinced that what distinguished this business from the corporate world was its dedication to challenging the instincts of consumer society. Having been sobered up by the shock of ordinary reality, I now wonder what sound basis I could have had for assuming that the academic industry, located right in the middle of the capitalist economic system, would ever operate entirely outside the sphere of its logic. I perhaps should always have known that the academy and its legions of scholars, not excluding progressive ones who have achieved celebrity as public intellectuals, respond to market pressures and to the dynamics of capitalist competition.

Edward W. Said poignantly outlined the texture of the field as it appeared to him over a decade ago by describing the perceptible loss of a sense of vocation among intellectuals, a value he regarded as being nearly swallowed up by the pervasive "professionalization of intellectual life." The pertinent passage says:

> Policy-oriented intellectuals have internalized the norms of the state, which when it understandably calls them to the capital, in effect becomes their patron. The critical sense is often conveniently jettisoned. As for intellectuals whose charge includes values and principles — literary, philosophical, historical specialists — the American university, with its munificence, utopian sanctuary, and remarkable diversity, has defanged them. Jargons of an almost unimaginable rebarbativeness dominate their styles . . . an astonishing sense of weightlessness with regard to the gravity of history and individual responsibility fritters away attention to public matters and to public discourse. The result is a kind of floundering about without direction or coherence. Racism, poverty, ecological ravages, disease, and an appallingly widespread ignorance: these are left to the media and the odd political candidate during an election campaign. (Said 1993; 303)

As progressive scholars, in their exacerbated "professionalization" and discursive "rebarbativeness," restrict the universe of their intervention to the page of the academic journal or the specialized monograph — their influence reaching no farther than the frequent appearance of their names in doctoral dissertations or in the articles whereby young assistant professors seek to secure permanent employment — conservative spokespersons have a field day using the mass media to disseminate their ideological onslaught. D'Souza's fervent celebration of Western colonial domination of the Third World, after appearing in the *Chronicle of Higher Education*, earned a generous allocation of space in the *San Francisco Chronicle*, whose readers learned from a native of India, who thus could boast the authority of the eyewitness, that Europe essentially humanized the regions it dominated. He says:

> I am a writer, and I write in English. My ability to do this, and to reach a broad market, is entirely thanks to the British. . . . My beliefs in freedom of expression, in self-government, in equality of rights under the law and in the universal principle of human dignity — they are all the product of Western civilization. . . . Colonialism was the transmission belt that brought to Asia, Africa, and South America the blessings of Western civilization. Many of these cultures continue to have serious problems of tyranny, tribal and religious conflict, poverty and underdevelopment, but this is not due to the excess of Western influence but to the fact that those countries are insufficiently Westernized. (D'Souza 2002: D6)

Equally unsavory in its retrograde diction as well as its insidious ability to gain currency in public discourse is the recent pronouncement by Samuel P. Huntington that characterizes Hispanic immigrants, especially Mexican, as posing "the most immediate and most serious challenge to America's traditional identity," given their volume, fertility, and reticence to shed the trappings of their ancestry: "The extent and nature of this immigration differ fundamentally from those of previous immigration, and the assimilation successes of the past are unlikely to be duplicated with the contemporary flood of immigrants from Latin America. This reality poses a fundamental question: Will the United States remain a country with a single national language and a core Anglo-Protestant culture? By ignoring this question, Americans acquiesce to their eventual transformation into two peoples with two cultures (Anglo and Hispanic) and two languages (English and Spanish)" (Huntington 2004: 32).

The superficiality of Huntington's analysis, lacking scholarly rigor and a sense of history, did not deter its impact on public opinion, as illustrated in the numerous commentaries it elicited in major print media venues such as *Newsweek*, the *New York Times*, the *Wall Street Journal*, and the *Economist*. The latter's editorial praised Huntington's intellectual courage for confronting the downside of immigration (March 4, 2004). Apart from ventilating their indignation via fora of limited range, Latino scholars could not alter the fact that Huntington commanded greater power than they to influence national opinion about the representation of their people. Their sense of intellectual powerlessness was hardly assuaged by the definition of Latino/Hispanic given by Univision's anchorman Jorge Ramos to PBS's Charlie Rose on national television. As a celebrity, Ramos can have access to massive audiences in a way that scholars could hardly aspire to. As such, he informed Charlie Rose that people of Latin American descent in the United States prefer the term "Hispanic" over "Latino" to name themselves because the latter sounds too close to "Ladino," which he said means "Ladrón" (thief). Whether the interviewer bothered to look up the word "Ladino" or tried to find out by means of what thaumaturgic radar the Univision anchorman had established the feeling of 35 million people of Latin American descent on the matter of gentilitial designation is not clear. But until now, no disclaimer has been issued to rectify the totally erroneous lesson in Spanish semantics imparted by Ramos.

The authority of media personalities — conferred upon them by their fame rather than by rigorous study — surpasses that of progressive scholars, who usually have their access obstructed to the fora that influence opinion. Whether knowingly or unknowingly, they collaborate with conservative spokespersons of the status quo in reducing the progressive intellectual to political irrelevance. A third foe is no doubt the politician, whose influence has reached spectacular dimensions even within the perimeters of the campus where academics do their work. As the head of the CUNY Dominican Studies Institute, an interdisciplinary research unit of the City University of New York, I received a formal lesson in the tenuousness of scholarly authority when confronted with political power. When in 1997 the Institute released a socioeconomic profile of the Dominican population in the City of New York that showed that group experiencing extreme levels of unemployment and underemployment, placing it at the bottom rung of the city's economy, Mayor Rudolph Giuliani declared our findings false. At the time busy at work creating for himself a reputation as a strong leader who had turned the city around by means of his successful crusade against crime, the mayor offered no data to substantiate his view. Though unfounded, his rejection of the findings sufficed to instill meekness in university officials who, while admitting the scientific validity of the study in question, expressed concern about the possible consequences of our displeasing the mayor.

The incident made evident that truth lacks the ability to prevail if the structure devoted to investigating it — the university — answers to higher powers. The same way that the mayor waged open war on two successive chancellors of the city's public schools system, successfully running them out of their jobs, so he used the power of his office to advance or hinder particular policies, programs, or interests in the city university. Through his appointees to the Board of Trustees, he practically ruled the university from his office in City Hall, removing both a chancellor and a college president; raising the bar on admissions, ostensibly to protect the taxpayer's money; and targeting the support services that students from low-income families largely depended on to succeed academically. Not surprisingly, his policies disproportionately affected minority students. But the mayor made them palatable to the middle class by invoking "standards" and the pursuit of academic excellence (Torres-Saillant 2004: 221–222).

The mayor's declared motivations in the end proved incapable of concealing his intent to run the university as a personal hacienda, often at the service of his political desires. Witness his resorting on more than one occasion to punitive or retaliatory actions against his appointees to the Board of Trustees or his allies in the university administration who deviated from his directives. Much evidence exists to show that the mayor's control of CUNY had more the intent of promoting "his own personal and patronage purposes" than of improving the institution in any significant way (Barret 2001). But the overtness of his manipulative schemes, which included his barring city commissioners from speaking with the press about their respective departments, as he monopolized the disclosure of information in all city agencies, did not lessen the favor he enjoyed with journalists. He retained their favor despite the depravity of publicly attempting to expel his wife from Gracie Mansion to make room for his lover; his refusal to consider the possibility of police brutality, even when unarmed civilians, mostly people of color, lost their lives at the hands of law enforcement agents; his boycotting a march of African-American youths that the courts had authorized; and his barring access to public fora within city property to political competitors during his reelection campaign in 1997 or while he considered running for the U.S. Senate in 2000.

Giuliani's political success, built on the systematic disregard for fair play, participatory democracy, and intellectual authority, stands as a boisterous reminder of the role of the university today as a locus of subservience. When the terrorist planes toppled the World Trade Center on September 11, 2001, the city's government spoke with one voice, the mayor's, and the media expressed no curiosity about the silence of the fire and police commissioners, whose agencies most directly had to confront the disaster and the carnage. They had accepted the arrangement whereby only the mayor could speak, and they applauded his iron-fisted control as a measure of leadership. The ultimate beneficiary of the September 11 horror, Giuliani sought to reap advantage of his anointment as "mayor of the world" and subsequently as *Time* magazine's 2001 "Man of the Year" by seeking to extend his term in office for three months after it ended, offering mayoral candidates his endorsement should they support his wish. The State Assembly did not move to change electoral law to suit Giuliani's desire, but he did, only days before his departure from City Hall, prevail upon mayor-elect Michael Bloomberg to let him retain possession of mayoral papers from his eight years in office. The records went to a private storage facility under the control of the newly created Rudolph W. Giuliani Center for Urban Affairs instead of going to the municipal archives, much to the dismay of archivists and historians who felt the privatization of city records, apart from violating the law, threatened to deny the citizens's right to know what their governments are doing ("Rudy Giuliani" 2002: 4).

The approval enjoyed by the likes of Giuliani, aided by the genuflection of the press, trespasses the walls of the university, the arena where progressive scholars can most confidently wield their moral power, given the ever cozier relationship of higher education institutions with the politicians and the corporations. I left CUNY for Syracuse University in the fall of 1999, looking for a respite from the smothering political climate of the university under the regime of the autocratic New York City mayor. But it was clearly a want of forethought that had caused me to construe the Giuliani phenomenon as local. In May 2002, Syracuse University, my home institution, joined New York City and the rest of the country in furthering the glorification of Giuliani by bringing him to campus as the commencement speaker. Beyond his record of disrespect for the academic community and his trampling upon democratic practices, he enjoyed the celebrity conferred upon him by the legitimizing force of his success and, as such, qualified as a role model whether at my campus in central New York or anywhere else in the rest of the United States. Giuliani's validation at the commencement podium appeared as yet another excruciating detail scoffing at the unclear relevance of progressive scholars who yearn for democratic values. Exacerbating their predicament nationwide, the Patriot Act came to further stifle their ability to exert influence on the course of events even from the classroom pulpit with which their profession had endowed them, and they found it necessary to observe caution in order to avoid the perception of insensitivity to the government's obligation to protect the citizenry from external harm.

Two years ago the Syracuse University administration circulated among the faculty a memorandum that explained the institution's constraint to abide by the terms of the Patriot Act, a charge that included furnishing information on any individual whom the federal government identified as the subject of an investigation. With hair-raising clarity, the memo explained that, depending on the particulars of the case, the institution may be forbidden to inform the individual that a probe is under way, lest the university be found guilty of obstructing a government investigation. I imagine that universities throughout the country must have found their ways of conveying to their instructional personnel the bind that the Patriot Act put them in. But even without the frightful ordeal of an investigation, faculty nationwide have come to realize that the texture of campus life has been changed by the advent of the Patriot Act and the subsequent invasion of Iraq. It came as no surprise to hear at a recent professional conference that many colleagues have generally become self-conscious about their treatment in the classroom of political matters that could be deemed sensitive, with several of those present attesting to their own decision to modify their language so as not to unsettle the ideological sensibility of conservative students, for fear of the ways in which they, emboldened by the present climate, might choose to retaliate. The litigious organization Students for Academic Freedom, whose conservative founder David Horowitz authored the influential Academic Bill of Rights, boasts a loyal following in 130 campuses, having already swayed legislators in several states to urge higher education institutions to put in place mechanisms to ensure the "intellectual" protection of "students whose political views differ from those of their professors" (Marklein 2004).

We have here an undeniably overwhelming landscape. One could even understand the sense of powerlessness that might overcome trained intellects with progressive ideals before the apparently inexpugnable wall of entrenched conservatism in sectors of society that impact directly on the academy. The landscape is of the kind that easily fosters pessimism. Particularly resourceful scholars might pursue individual solutions to the systemic drama by immersing themselves in the playground of the capitalist game, achieving celebrity with a discourse aimed precisely at indicting imperialism, capitalism, and the corporations while collecting high salaries from elite universities and charging large lecture fees for expounding on the evils of the system. A more realistic temptation, since elite institutions will seldom dole out bounteous recompense to more than one dissident intellectual celebrity at a time, would be to seek psychological refuge in reenactments of the ivory tower, as Stanley Fish has done. Recasting Marx's proverbial injunction to philosophers of his generation to concentrate on changing the world rather than merely interpreting it, Fish has stated that in the academy "it is exactly the reverse: our job is not to change the world but to interpret it" (Fish 2004).

I would propose, however, that a more salutary antidote against despair is to remain historical and to remember the ways in which earlier generations dealt with the besiegers of democratic ideals with whom they had to contend. I would offer the second Woodrow Wilson administration (1917–1921) as a useful site of investigation, among other things, because then too the federal government felt compelled to limit liberties at home in order to fight for freedom abroad. A quickly passed sedition bill that criminalized all opposition to the war effort and abridged freedom of the press remains unequaled to this day, the McCarthy "Un-American" tribunals notwithstanding. In a December 12, 1917, letter to the president, Helen Keller poignantly asked "Because the Kaiser is destroying freedom in Europe to preserve autocracy, must we destroy it here to preserve democracy?" Randolph Bourne, who in June of that year decried "the unanimity with which the American intellectuals have thrown their support to the use of war-technique in the crisis in which America found herself," perhaps underestimated the role that voices like his and Keller's were playing in combating the regime of complacency and silence (Bourne 1992: 307). Perhaps we might profitably look into the circumstances that caused a regime that incarcerated its citizens for expressing dissident views to lead in little over a decade to the socialist ideals of the Franklin D. Roosevelt government, and whether progressive intellectuals played a role in the transition.

If cultures beget countercultures, authoritarian regimes also beget counterdiscourses. Even today, amid a sea of conservatism and abridged political options, one can derive hope from vibrant moments of democratic self-assertiveness. The November 1999 protest against the WTO that some have termed "the Battle of Seattle" showed that the conversation about the values that should guide the society's priorities has not come to a close, and many excluded voices want to have their say. Progressive scholars wishing to imagine a post-Seattle world can have at their disposal instances of dissent powerful enough to help ward off despondent pessimism, which, as a friend recently reminded me, is also an ideological stance. I treasure the political complexity of the fact that Syracuse University, which in 2002 had joined the national glorification of Giuliani, in the fall of 2004 featured as a guest speaker none other than Michael Moore, whose films have launched a spirited, unexpurgated condemnation of the conservative values that inform the Bush administration. On closer inspection, the landscape is still complex enough for intellectuals to regain their tarnished authority, but they would have to recover their faith in the power of the word to effect change in the world. They cannot continue to satisfy themselves with merely subverting another Enlightenment idea or deploying yet another cutting-edge paradigm that rereads, challenges, or transcends the formulation of this or that critical theory celebrity. Scholars who care about the advancement of democratic ideals must deign to use language in a manner that enables their communication to reach the minds of civilians, the way such influential voices as those of Lydia Maria Childs, W.E.B. Dubois, William Lloyd Garrison, and Frances Ellen Watkins Harper reached them. The universe of their interlocutors has to be larger than the specialized doctoral students or journal subscribers who understand their jargon. Their interventions have to seek more ambitious goals than to make "a contribution to the field" or to secure for them a place of prestige in the profession. Since the weapon they have chosen is primarily the word, they should use it to reach out, democratically.

Works Cited

Barret, Wayne. 2004. "Academic Outrage." *Village Voice* April 4–10. Online edition: http://www.villagevoice.com.

Bourne, Randolph. 1992. *The Radical Will: Selected Writings, 1911–1918*, edited by Olaf Hansen. Berkeley: University of California Press.

D'Souza, Dinesh. 2002. "Two Cheers for Colonialism." *San Francisco Chronicle*, July 7, D1, D6.

Eagleton, Terry. 2000. *The Idea of Culture*. Madden, Mass.: Blackwell.

Fish, Stanley. 2004. "Why We Built the Ivory Tower." *New York Times*. May 21.

Fukuyama, Francis. 1992. *The End of History and the Last Man*. New York: Free Press.

Huntington, Samuel P. 2004. "The Hispanic Challenge." *Foreign Policy* 141 (March/April): 30–45.

"Rudy Giuliani: The Quintessential Control Freak." 2002. *New York Observer*. Editorial, February 5.

Marklein, Mary Beth. 2004. "Proposed 'Academic Bill of Rights' Makes Inroads." *USA Today*, March 16.

Said, Edward W. 1993. *Culture and Imperialism*. New York: Alfred A. Knopf.

Torres-Saillant, Silvio. 2004. "The Limits of Globalization: Caribbean Higher Education and the Borders That Remain." In *The Challenges of Public Higher Education in the Hispanic Caribbean*, edited by Maria J. Canino and Silvio Torres-Saillant, 211–226. Princeton: Markus Wiener.

CHAPTER 25

Teaching after the Battle in Seattle, This Is What Plutocracy Looks Like

George Lipsitz

On October 6, 2003, exactly two months after her twenty-fifth birthday, slam poet Joy de la Cruz died in a car crash on a Nevada highway. A daughter of Pilipino immigrants whose first language was Tagalog, she took up English with a vengeance. Quiet in the classroom, but loud on the stage, de la Cruz created powerful performance pieces that deployed everyday words and phrases as tools for transformative change. Along with her fellow spoken-word artists in the enormously talented and wonderfully interracial Freedom Writers collective in San Diego, de la Cruz brilliantly articulated the insecurities, idealism, anger, and aspirations of her generation.

For those of us who knew Joy de la Cruz, the pain of losing her is excruciating. She was our spoken word warrior, a funny, feisty, and ferociously honest force field that lit up everything around her. She was our morning star, the one that burns so brightly in the eastern sky that all who see it know that a new day is dawning. She made us happy and gave us heart. Her politics and her name matched perfectly. Her parents named her Elaine, but by using her middle name she turned herself into Joy. Her stationery proclaimed "peace-love-joy" and her Web site advised "Don't Postpone Joy." Then, one day, she was dead.

Writing about the death of his friend Lorraine Hansberry from cancer at the age of thirty-five, James Baldwin observed, "When so bright a light goes out so early, when so gifted an artist goes so soon, we are left with a sorrow and wonder which speculation cannot assuage. One is filled for a long time with a sense of injustice as futile as it is powerful. And the vanished person sometimes fills the mind, in this or that attitude, doing this or that"(Baldwin 1995, xix). The ghostly presence of Joy de la Cruz haunts in precisely that way, not only because of her extraordinary talent but also because both her art and her life resonated so profoundly with the contradictions of our time. "I aspire to be a reflection of those around me," she wrote in one of her pieces, musing that perhaps the things to which she aspired might at the same time inspire others. Observing that the Latin root of *inspire* means to *breathe in*, de la Cruz described her artistry as a process of breathing deeply and letting go, releasing fear and reflecting her surroundings. An overwhelming and irrepressible drive toward connection with others permeated her art and her activism. It enabled her not only to aspire and to inspire but also to conspire with others to contest the inequities and inequalities of our age.

Part of the first truly transnational generation of youth, de la Cruz felt the contradictions of her time deeply. She longed for a more just and joyful existence. It outraged her to learn about her fellow *pinays* in the Philippines, forced by their poverty to become prostitutes to foreign tourists and U.S. military personnel. It angered her to see the largely immigrant Latino/a custodial staff at her college working midnight shifts cleaning classrooms and labs for $6.25 per hour with no medical coverage. She despised the repetitive, demeaning, and trivial clerical jobs that she found herself forced to take in order to pay for her food, rent, and school fees. She earned a dollar or two more per hour at these jobs than the campus custodians, and wondered how they survived on their wages when she found herself left with only enough money to pay for economical rations of Top Ramen noodles for dinner every night.

On June 15, 2001, Joy de la Cruz went to jail. San Diego police officers took her into custody along with nine other demonstrators because of their role in a nonviolent direct action protest blocking traffic at a busy intersection near the University of California, San Diego, campus. The demonstration sought to dramatize and support the efforts of the university's janitors to secure a union contract, medical benefits, and a living wage. Upon her release from incarceration the next morning, de la Cruz sent out an e-mail message thanking people who had come to the demonstration, explaining her reasons for choosing to be arrested. Saluting the veteran student activists who had mentored her when she first came to campus, she delineated the legitimacy of the custodial workers' demands. De la Cruz then turned to the ways in which personal and global concerns intersected for her.

She explained that it was important for her as an Asian American and a Pilipina to stand in solidarity with the largely Latino/a immigrant workers. Support for them was a matter of self-respect for her. It gave her an opportunity to put into practice all the things she had learned from the struggles of her parents and her grandparents with the colonial history of their country, from the joyful solidarity and exuberant interethnic antiracism that she had learned as a woman of color feminist, an ethnic studies major, and a participant in political coalitions to defend affirmative action and to oppose the incarceration of juvenile offenders in adult prisons. De la Cruz confided that it was the marching and chanting together in a large group made up of so many different kinds of people that gave her courage, and emphasized especially the exhilarating sense of collectivity she felt from shouting union slogans in English and Spanish. But the most moving part of the demonstration for her came when her fellow Pilipino/a students started a chant in one of the main languages of their ancestral home. "It was hearing the Tagalog chant that really gave me strength and that almost brought tears to my eyes," she wrote, adding "that might sound corny, but it's true. *Maki ba-ka . . . Huwag ma-ta kot!* (Solidarity . . . Have No Fear). Hearing *aking mga kaibigan at kababayan* (my friends and countrymen/ *la raza*) remind us that the struggle continues . . . don't be afraid — hearing not only Spanish, but MY first language — helped me not be so nervous."

Makibaka was a popular slogan chanted by demonstrators in mobilizations against martial law and the Marcos dictatorship in the Philippines during the 1970s. By voicing those words during the 2001 workers' demonstration in San Diego, de la Cruz and her fellow Pilipino students incorporated the organizing drive by the Latino/a janitors into their own long legacy of struggle. Chanting *Huwag matakut* (do not be afraid) on a San Diego street positions newcomers to trade union mobilization in the United States as something much more than "unorganized" workers. It proclaims that low-wage immigrant workers and their allies are also witnesses to empire, veterans of anti-imperialist struggle, and local manifestations of a conflict taking place all around the world.

The spirit of Seattle 1999 — and the organizing and mobilizing that preceded and followed it — permeate the spirit of de la Cruz's e-mail about her arrest. In her message, she linked the local grievances of people very much unlike herself by virtue of their class status, educational background, and national origin to some of her deepest personal identifications in life as the daughter of immigrants, as part of the Pilipino diaspora, and as a nonnative speaker of English. She constructed families of resemblance that transformed differences into similarities. Through what John Brown Childs calls "shared practical action," her presence on the picket line, in the paddy wagon, and in jail enabled her to remain faithful to herself while creating new affiliations, identifications, and associations at the same time (Childs 2003, 11). Through this quintessentially contemporary model of struggle, de la Cruz, as so many others in her generational cohort around the world have done, eschewed simple solidarities of sameness to embrace instead the dynamics of difference. Her identity as an activist drew on what Childs refers to as diverse "emplacements of affiliation," on deeply rooted and clearly demarcated perspectives that serve as a basis for branching out to others with similar but not identical experiences, anxieties, and aspirations (Childs 2003, 25).

Although she was not a janitor, not poor, not Latina, and not a native speaker of Spanish, de la Cruz could embrace the workers' struggle as her own. She discerned something important about other people by reflecting critically on her own personal history, on her knowledge about colonialism in the Philippines, her experiences as a Tagalog-to-English language learner, her struggles as an immigrant daughter, underpaid clerical worker, and feminist activist, and her personal, aesthetic, and moral commitments. She drew deftly on what she already knew to "breathe deep" to "release fear" and to "reflect those around me." Rather than seeking to promote one ideology, one organization, one form of struggle, or one social goal, de la Cruz followed a path that emphasizes struggle as an end in itself, as a place where new identities are enacted, not merely envisioned.

In the spirit of Seattle, we have come to describe the social struggles waged by Joy de la Cruz's generation as "what democracy looks like." Joy de la Cruz and her generation indeed aspire to teach us what democracy looks like, but their aspirations emerge in the context of something much different, from what plutocracy (rule by the rich) looks like. The increasingly indecent global maldistribution of dignity, opportunity, health, and wealth looms large in forming the consciousness and actions of the generation that came of age in the Battle in Seattle. They have known no other world than this one. In their lives, the most affluent fifth of the world's population have come to control 84.7 percent of global wealth, up from 70 percent in 1960 and nearly doubling the gap between the top quintile and the bottom 20 percent (Flusty 2004, 29). They came of age in a world where more than thirty thousand children under the age of five die every day from malnutrition or completely curable diseases (Millen, Irwin, and Kim 2000, 5).

One million orphaned or abandoned children now live homeless in Africa, fending for themselves on the streets. African children wielding automatic weapons comprise a growing percentage of troops in mercenary armies on a continent where more than two million people have been killed in war during the past twenty years, where deaths from AIDS take place most frequently among the generation most likely to be parents, and where transnational financial institutions have mandated the dismantling of state-sponsored education, health care, and housing (Maxted 2003, 51, 56, 69). Of the 4.4 billion people in the poorest countries in Africa, Asia, and Latin America, 60 percent lack basic sanitation facilities. One billion do not have access to safe and uncontaminated water. Eight hundred and twenty-eight million people in the world are chronically undernourished. Nearly a third of them will die before their fortieth birthday (Schoepf, Schoepf, and Millen 2000, 120–121). Yet African countries have been forced by transnational financial institutions from Europe and North America to spend four times as much every year on debt payments as they spend on the health and educational needs of Africans (Gershman and Irwin 2000, 13, 14, 25).

Global income inequality enables entrepreneurs to profit from "sex tourism," whereby wealthy European and American predators buy sex from desperately poor adults, teens, and children in the Caribbean and Asia (Kempadoo 1999, Law 2000). Undernourished Latin American, Asian, and Caribbean women and children work for starvation wages in sweatshops producing sweatsuits and other exercise paraphernalia for affluent consumers seeking physical fitness while consuming diets laced with sugar and fat (Kernaghen 1998, 18). The twenty-four wealthiest families in Mexico control more wealth than the twenty-four million poorest Mexicans (Fuentes 1997, viii).

These inequalities and injustices do not happen in a vacuum. They are part of a deliberate plan to transfer wealth from the global south to the global north. As George Katsiaficas points out, the central premise of the present global economic system is that the life of someone in Europe or North America is worth more than the life of a person in Asia, Africa, and Latin America (Katsiaficas 2004, 4). The practices that promote pain and misery for most of the people in the world produce unfair gains and unjust enrichments for consumers and investors in Europe and North America. It is not simply that the global north is wealthy and the global south is poor, but rather that the poverty of the global south underwrites the prosperity of the global north. This system increases inequality within nations and regions, as well. Poor people in Asia, Africa, and Latin America suffer from austerity policies that require them to divert spending away from education, health care, housing, and transportation in order to pay back loans defaulted on by wealthy local elites. The enormous profits that accrue from debt servicing in poor countries in turn increase the wealth, influence, and power of investors and owners in advanced industrialized nations, who then pursue policies aimed at allowing well-off communities to hoard their advantages, to use their tax base only for themselves, while displacing onto less wealthy areas the costs of remedying complex social problems.

Since 1980, the wealthiest fifth of the U.S. population has enjoyed a 21 percent growth in its income, while those in the poorest three-fifths have seen their wages, working conditions, and living standards stagnate or fall (Tabb 2001, 21). Nearly 85 percent of the 3 trillion increase in stock market valuation between 1989 and 1997 went to the richest 10 percent of U.S. families (Tabb 2001, 21).

Nearly one-half of the nation's income now goes to the wealthiest fifth of households (Miller 2000, 17, 18). The richest 10 percent of families in the United States owns 94 percent of the business assets, 90 percent of the bonds, 89 percent of the corporate stock, and 78 percent of the real estate in the nation (Plotkin and Scheurman 1994, 29).

Even worse than the economic effects of these policies are their concomitant cultural consequences. The relentless commodification of every human relationship and every human activity elevates the avarice and calculation of the consumer over the conscience and responsibility of the citizen. The evisceration of the social wage and the fragmentation of the polity into antagonists competing for amenities and advantages breed anxiety, envy, and disrespect toward others. The global economy's privileging of the financial sector over manufacturing and consumer services has produced a profitability crisis that promotes efforts to find new sources of profit — to turn social security pensions into private investment accounts and to transform public schools into sites for privatized accumulation.

More than 30 million people in the United States live in common interest developments where private homeowners' associations exercise governing power for the sole aim of improving property values in competition with other neighborhoods (McKenzie 1994, 12). Like their predecessors throughout the long history of suburban development, common interest developments promise prosperity, predictability, and security. Yet in actual practice, these arrangements only exacerbate residential inequalities, increase urban problems, and promote forms of defensive localism and hostile privatism.

As each group of homeowners seeks to maximize rewards and minimize obligations at the expense of other social groups, they defund the economic and social infrastructure required to produce the prosperity, stability, and security they seek. Every subunit of government seeks to pass on obligations to every other subunit. This zero-sum game leads inevitability to disappointment. Disappointment promotes resentment, which grows into righteous indignation and rage, which then function as the modal structures of feeling among homeowners' associations, tax limitation groups, and callers to right-wing talk radio. They make up what is probably the most embittered and disgruntled agglomeration of "haves" in the history of the world.

The economic elites whose free-market fundamentalism compels them to push for an infinite expansion of sites for investment and profit face critical contradictions in the real world. They live in bounded nations, but seek boundless sources of raw materials, markets, and labor. Their political power over the state rests on patriotic ideals of national homogeneity, on the idea that the things that unite the citizens of a nation are much more important than the things that divide them. Yet their economic power depends on the rejection of the nation's interests in favor of the mobility of capital to whatever space will bring the highest return to investors. The rapid mobility of labor, capital, and commodities that they seek for economic reasons undermines the appeals to stability, predictability, and cultural homogeneity on which their political power depends. Immigrants of color and their children serve as particularly astute witnesses to these processes because they experience both the penetration of their home countries by foreign capital and the racism directed against exploited immigrants in the United States.

The free-market fundamentalism at the core of transnational corporate capitalist culture is demoralizing in both senses of the word. It destroys morale by fragmenting communities, eliminating meaningful work, and stoking the fires of personal envy, avarice, and aggression. It destroys morality, as well, by making commodities more valuable than people, by reducing all encounters with other humans to a common denominator of calculated acquisitiveness.

Yet while it undermines both morale and morality, this system produces enormous amounts of moralizing and moral panics. When its promises of personal prosperity lead to collective austerity, when the freedom of mobility required for capital increases constraints on people, the culture of transnational corporate capitalism turns to the language of morality and values, blaming individuals personally for what has been created structurally and systemically. Moral pronouncements about the sanctity of human life obscure the system's reliance on war, arms trading, and withholding medicine, water, and food from those who cannot afford to pay the prices deemed appropriate to secure adequate profits. Moral panics over the alleged misbehavior of deviants allows public anger over the consequences of neoliberal policies to become diverted and deflected onto the system's most devastated victims — members of aggrieved racial groups, immigrants, the unemployed, the incarcerated, and people with nonnormative sexual identities.

The artistry and activism of Joy de la Cruz and her partners in rhyme have emerged in direct response to these conditions, to what plutocracy looks like. Immersed in a demoralizing culture, they turn to art and activism to remoralize themselves and others. Their art takes aim at the hostile privatism, defensive localism, competitive individualism, and the contemptuous dismissal of difference that they have seen firsthand all their lives. They respond enthusiastically to the words of Subcommandante Marcos of the EZLN in Mexico when he writes, "we seek a world in which there is room for many worlds" (Sandoval 2000, ii). They proudly affirm the slogan chanted by protestors at the G8 meeting in Genoa, Italy, in July 2001: "a different world is possible." Yet their politics focus less on envisioning macrosocial political solutions to their problems than on enacting new microsocial identities and relationships through the processes of performance art and political protest. Art and politics function for them as ways of making a world worth living in now, as alternatives to the contexts young people know best: the world of consumer capitalism, low-wage jobs, and oppressive schools.

The spoken word art of Joy de la Cruz exemplified these commitments. An instinctive rebel who resisted even the confines of lined paper by choosing to write sideways, in circles, and, in fact, anywhere but on the lines, de la Cruz filled her Web site with antiwar and anticorporate slogans, poems, and speeches. In high school she crossed a significant gender barrier by becoming the first female student in a previously all-male Catholic school. As a college student, she played a key role in organizing the annual University of California systemwide Women of Color conference. Yet most of her artistic work focused on small things close to home. She composed poems about being bored at work, about crushes on boyfriends, about conversations with girlfriends, about choosing the appropriate Halloween costume. She confessed fears about disappointing her parents, her frustrations about performing below her own expectations in school, and her worries that she spent too much time writing and thinking and not enough time living. Through pieces characterized by personal modesty, honest self-criticism, and self-deprecating humor, she sought to create through art an identity more expansive than those open to her as a student, clerical worker, or family member.

In one of her spoken word pieces, de la Cruz lamented her difficulties at the end of one school term. Faced with having to write a ten-page research paper, perform with the Freedom Writers, and attend to her job as a receptionist at a real estate title company, she complained that "my ten pages" conflicted with the demands of "Saturday's stages," and that both school and spoken word art undermined the time she needed to make "those wages." In frustration, she described herself as one of those "procrastinating trying-to-be activist-imitating students" who "must sprint toward an A but still B able to C that's okay."

Joy de la Cruz worried that she was a disappointment to her teachers. Her busy schedule meant that she did not always do the kind of work she was capable of in class, and it slowed her progress toward getting her degree. The university she attended did not give her grades or course credit for helping to organize the women of color conference, for turning ideas into performances of spoken word art, for going to jail to support low-wage workers. Many of her classmates knew nothing about de la Cruz's intelligence, passion, and creative power. She was not the kind of student who raised her hand to volunteer opinions or to answer the instructor's questions. Unless they knew her outside of class, her teachers generally saw her as just another quiet student who did not always come to class, who did not always complete assignments on time, and whose essays did not always demonstrate close engagement with reading assignments and lectures.

Yet no one got more out of a college education than de la Cruz. In one of her poems, she wrote about what she had learned within and against the grain of her classes:

> *Un* means one
> *Ver* means to see
> Here this *universidad*
>   this university
> posits one way to see the truth
> with a big T *verdad?*
> but Time out
> i became an ethnic studies major
> 'cuz I need to be
> able to articulately argue
> why skin hue should not determine
>   life chances
> how racialized experience does shape
>   political stances
> to build "identity based on politics

291

not politics based on identity"
imprisoned by isms
racism sexism classism heterosexism
capitalism
solidarity means we understand
   each other's struggles
not because we fight for, but
because we stand with them
   at the crossroads
   at intersectionalities
   together recognize realities

These ideas were more than words on paper for Joy de la Cruz. They were the core beliefs by which she lived her life. Despite all of her rebellion, resistance, and refusal of classroom protocol — or perhaps because of them — she learned her lessons perfectly.

In his rumination about the death of Lorraine Hansberry, James Baldwin confessed, "it would be good, selfishly, to have her around now, that small dark girl, with her wit, her wonder, and her eloquent compassion" (Baldwin 1995, xx). Hardly a day goes by when Joy de la Cruz's friends do not think the same about her. They are not alone in their longing. The people who knew twenty-three-year-old Carlo Guiliani, killed by police officers who shot him in the face and ran over him twice with their vehicles during the July 20, 2001, protest against the G8 meeting in Genoa, Italy, feel the same way about him. The loved ones and friends of the thousands dying unnecessarily today around the world feel that way, too. It is too late to help them. But it is not too late to recognize and reckon with those who remain, whose lives have not yet been lived and whose stories have not yet been written.

Joy de la Cruz was a wonderful and unique individual. She was also a product of our times, a powerful force thrown forward by events, circumstances, and solidarities of struggle. There are plenty more where she came from. They will be sitting quietly in our classes, watching us warily, wondering if we really have anything to teach them. It will help them to learn about those who precede them, to teach them that the writers of the American Renaissance emerged from the ferment of the antebellum radical social movements for the abolition of slavery, for women's rights, and for utopian socialism. It will help them to learn that the mobilizations by the labor movement during the 1930s had a cultural corollary in forms of expressive culture that helped spread democratic and egalitarian ideals into every sphere of national life (Denning 1997, 201, 273). It will help them to learn that they have been preceded by kindred spirits, that the kinds of thinking that engages them today about nationalism, identity, power, and subjectivity have progenitors in the writings of Claude McKay, Pietro di Donato, Paule Marshall, Fae Myenne Ng, and Helena Maria Viramontes.

292

Yet people learn best what they see for themselves. In the spirit of the Battle in Seattle, young people around the world today are stepping up and speaking out. They are fashioning new forms of art and activism out of their experiences and aspirations. Their learning is not confined to the classroom and their performances are not limited to the stage. They do not look or sound like the experts who come to us prepackaged in the corporate media or credentialed inside the academy. But they will be the authors of whatever future we have.

The art and activism of young people today throws forth new ways of being and new ways of knowing fabricated from the immanent contradictions of our time. Their aspirations and their actions resonate with a key line in one of Joy de la Cruz's most memorable poems, a line that presents a profound challenge to teachers. Anguished by the distance between her desires and the life she actually leads, de la Cruz chides herself for the extravagance of her aspirations and ambitions. Yet she refuses to give up her hopes. Instead, she tries to find a basis for them in what is already present in her life. "Stop trying so hard to get where you think you want to be," she tells herself, "be present where you are."

Works Cited

Baldwin, James. 1995. "Sweet Lorraine." In Lorraine Hansberry (adapted by Robert Nemiroff), *To Be Young, Gifted, and Black: Lorraine Hansberry in Her Own Words*. New York: Vintage.

Childs, John Brown. 2003. *Transcommunality: From the Politics of Conversion to the Ethics of Respect*. Philadelphia: Temple University Press.

Denning, Michael. 1997. *The Cultural Front*. New York: Verso.

Fuentes, Carlos. 1997. *A New Time for Mexico*. Berkeley: University of California Press.

Flusty, Steven. 2004. *De-Coca-Colonization: Making the Globe from the Inside Out*. New York: Routledge.

Gershman, John, and Alec Irwin. 2000. "Getting a Grip on the Global Economy." In Kim Yong Kim, Joyce V. Millen, Alex Irwin, and John Gershman, eds., *Dying for Growth: Global Inequality and the Health of the Poor*, 11–43. Monroe, M.: Common Courage Press.

Katsiaficas, George. 2004. "Seattle Was Not the Beginning." In Eddie Yuen, Daniel Burton-Rose, and George Katsiaficas, eds., *Confronting Capitalism: Dispatches from a Global Movement*, 3–10. Brooklyn: Soft Skull Press.

Kempadoo, Kemala, ed. 1999. *Sun, Sex, and Gold: Tourism and Sex Work in the Caribbean*. Lanham, Md.: Rowman and Littlefield.

Kernaghen, Charles. 1998. "Sweatshop Blues: Companies Love Misery." *Dollars and Sense* 22: 18.

Law, Lisa. 2000. *Sex Work in Southeast Asia: The Place of Desire in a Time of Aids*. New York: Routledge.

Maxted, Julia. 2003. "Children and Armed Conflict in Africa." *Social Identities* 9.1 (March): 51–73.

McKenzie, Evan. 1994. *Privatopia: Homeowner Associations and the Rise of Residential Private Government*. New Haven: Yale University Press.

Millen, Joyce, Alec Irwin, and Jim Yong Kim. 2000. "Introduction: What Is Growing? What Is Dying?" In Jim Yong Kim, Joyce V. Millen, Alec Irwin, and John Gershman, eds., *Dying for Growth: Global Inequality and the Health of the Poor*, 3–10. Monroe, Me.: Common Courage Press.

Miller, John. 2000. "Economy Sets Records for Longevity and Inequality." *Dollars and Sense* 229: 17–18.

Plotkin, Sidney, and William E. Scheuerman. 1994. *Private Interests, Public Spending: Balanced Budget Conservatism and the Fiscal Crisis*. Boston: South End Press.

Sandoval, Chela. 2000. *The Methodology of the Oppressed*. Minneapolis: University of Minnesota Press.

Schoepf, Brook, Claude Schoepf, and Joyce Millen. 2000. "Theoretical Therapies: Remote Remedies: SAPs and the Political Ecology of Poverty and Health in Africa." In Jim Yong Kim, Joyce V. Millen, Alec Irwin, and John Gershman, eds., *Dying for Growth: Global Inequality and the Health of the Poor*, 91–126. Monroe, Me.: Common Courage Press.

Tabb, William K. 2001. *The Amoral Elephant: Globalization and the Struggle for Social Justice in the Twenty-first Century*. New York: Monthly Review Press.

NOTES ON CONTRIBUTORS

PAULA GUNN-ALLEN is professor emerita at University of California, Los Angeles. A widely published poet and fiction and essay writer, she is the recipient of numerous awards, including the Modern Language Association's Hubbell Medal for Lifetime Achievement (2000) and the Native Writer's Circle Lifetime Achievement Award (2001). Her most recent book is *Pocahontas: Medicine Woman, Spy, Entrepreneur, Diplomat*. Author of the groundbreaking *The Sacred Hoop*, she is recognized as a founder of American Indian literary studies.

JOANNE M. BRAXTON is Cummings Professor of American Studies and English at the College of William and Mary. She is the author of *Black Women Writing Autobiography: A Tradition within a Tradition* and editor of *The Collected Poetry of Paul Laurence Dunbar, Wild Women in the Whirlwind: Afra-American Culture and the Contemporary Literary Renaissance*, and a casebook on Maya Angelou's *I Know Why the Caged Bird Sings*.

THADIOUS M. DAVIS is the Geraldine R. Segal Professor of American Social Thought at the University of Pennsylvania. Her most recent book is *Games of Property: Law, Race, Gender, and Faulkner's "Go Down, Moses."* She is completing a study of race, literature, and social geography.

MICHAEL DENNING is William R. Kenan Professor of American Studies at Yale University. Among his publications are *The Cultural Front: The Laboring of American Culture in the Twentieth Century, Mechanic Accents: Dime Novels and Working-Class Culture in America*, and, most recently, *Culture in the Age of Three Worlds*.

CAROLYN FORCHÉ, who teaches poetry writing in the Master of Fine Arts program at George Mason University, has published *Gathering the Tribes, The Country between Us, Against Forgetting*, and *The Angel of History*. She has won Guggenheim and Lannan Foundation fellowships and received awards from the Poetry Society of America and from the Edita and Ira Morris Hiroshima Foundation for Peace and Culture.

ROSEMARIE GARLAND-THOMSON is associate professor of women's studies at Emory University. She is the author of *Extraordinary Bodies: Figuring Physical Disability in American Literature and Culture*, editor of *Freakery: Cultural Spectacles of the Extraordinary Body*, and coeditor of *Disability Studies: Enabling the Humanities*. She is currently writing a book on the dynamics of staring and another on the cultural logic of euthanasia.

LAURIE GARRETT, a science writer for *New York Newsday*, is the author of *The Coming Plague* and *Betrayal of Trust: The Collapse of Global Public Health* (2000). She has taught in graduate journalism programs at Columbia University

and the University of California, Berkeley, and has been honored by the
Overseas Press Club. Garret lectures nationally and internationally and has
been awarded the Pulitzer Prize, the George C. Polk Award, and the George
Foster Peabody Broadcasting Award.

JUDITH SCOT-SMITH GIRGUS has taught literature, language arts, and writing
for twenty-six years in public and private middle and high schools and has
served as well as curriculum coordinator and department chair. She helped to
design and implement a master's degree program for experienced teachers in
conjunction with the University of New Mexico and the Albuquerque Public Schools. A frequent presenter at national conferences for teachers, she was
awarded the Lulu Hampton Owens Chair for Excellence in Teaching in 1996.

TERESA A. GODDU teaches at Vanderbilt University. She is the author of *Gothic
America: Narrative, History, and Nation* and is currently writing a book on an-
tislavery print culture.

ROGER HALLAS is an assistant professor at Syracuse University, where he
teaches film and media studies. His articles have appeared in *Camera Obscura,
Canadian Journal of Film Studies, Millenium Film Journal,* and *The Scholar and
the Feminist Online.* He is currently completing a book about AIDS, bearing
witness, and the queer moving image.

SCOTT HICKS is a doctoral candidate in American literature at Vanderbilt University. His current research explores intersections of agriculture, ecology,
and globalization in twentieth-century American literature.

FREDRIC JAMESON'S books include *Marxism and Form, The Political Unconscious,
Late Marxism,* and *Postmodernism, or The Cultural Logic of Late Capitalism.* A
recipient of Fulbright and Guggenheim fellowships, he is Distinguished
Professor of Comparative Literature at Duke University, where he directs
the Graduate Program in Literature and the Center for Cultural Theory.

AMY KAPLAN, professor of English at the University of Pennsylvania, is the author of *The Social Construction of American Realism* and *The Anarchy of Empire
in the Making of U.S. Culture.* She is one of several authors of *Postcolonial
Theory and the United States* and coeditor, with Donald Pease, of *Cultures
of United States Imperialism.* She is a past president of the American Studies
Association.

TONY KUSHNER is the author of numerous stage plays, including *Angels in
America: A Gay Fantasia on National Themes, Homebody/Kabul,* and *Caroline, or
Change,* which have been produced widely in the United States and worldwide. He has won numerous prizes, including the Pulitzer Prize for Drama,
two Tony Awards, and the New York Critics Circle Award. He has also received grants from the Whiting Foundation and the National Endowment
for the Arts.

AMY SCHRAGER LANG is professor of English and humanities at Syracuse University. Coeditor of the University of Michigan Press series Class: Culture, she is the author of *Prophetic Woman: Anne Hutchinson and the Problem of Dissent in the Literature of New England* and, more recently, *The Syntax of Class: Writing Inequality in Nineteenth-Century America.* She has received fellowships and grants from the Bunting Institute, the American Council of Learned Societies, and the American Association of University Women.

DANIEL LANG/LEVITSKY is a theater artist and organizer based in New York City active in LESSON/PLAN, Jews against the Occupation/NYC, Black Bridge International, and white picket fences. His writing appears in *Bridges/Brkn/Puentes* and *multikid* as well as in forthcoming collections on *Sacco and Vanzetti,* radical Jewish culture, and cultural recycling.

GEORGE LIPSITZ is professor of American studies at the University of California, Santa Barbara. He has been active in social movements for fair housing and educational equity. His publications include *American Studies in a Moment of Danger, The Possessive Investment in Whiteness, Time Passages, Dangerous Crossroads, Rainbow at Midnight, Sidewalks of St. Louis,* and *A Life in the Struggle: Ivory Perry and the Culture of Opposition.*

BILL MULLEN is professor of English at the University of Texas, San Antonio. Coeditor of the University of Michigan Press series Class: Culture, he is the author of *Afro-Orientalism* and coeditor of *Left of the Color Line: Race, Radicalism, and Twentieth-Century Literature of the United States.*

DANA NELSON teaches English and American studies at Vanderbilt University. Editor of a forthcoming special issue of *South Atlantic Quarterly* entitled "AmBushed, or, the Politics of Machtpolitik," she is working on a book-length project on frontier democracy.

JAMES PHELAN is Humanities Distinguished Professor in English at Ohio State University. The editor of *Narrative* and coeditor of the Ohio State University Press series Theory and Interpretation of Narrative, he is the author of four books of narrative theory, the most recent of which is *Living to Tell about It: A Rhetoric and Ethics of Character Narration,* and of the autobiographical journal, *Beyond the Tenure Track.*

JONATHAN PRUDE teaches history and American studies at Emory University. He has published a variety of investigations into the social and culture history of nineteenth-century American working people, including *The Coming of Industrial Order: Town and Factory life in Rural Massachusetts, 1810–1860* and (as coeditor) *The Countryside in the Age of Capitalist Transformation: Essays in the Social History of Rural America.* He is currently completing a project on "The Appearance of Class: The Visual Presence of American Working People from the Revolution to World War I."

297

GEORGE SAUNDERS teaches creative writing at Syracuse University and is the author of two short story collections, *CivilWarLand in Bad Decline*, a PEN/Hemingway Award finalist and chosen by Esquire as one of the top books of the 1990s, and *Pastoralia*, both of which were named New York Times Notable Books. The screenplay for *CivilWarLand* is currently in development with Red Hour Films. His bestselling children's book, *The Very Persistent Gappers of Frip*, won major awards in Italy and the Netherlands.

CECELIA TICHI is the author, most recently, of *Exposés and Excess: Muckraking in America 1900/2000* and *Embodiment of a Nation: Human Form in American Places*. Past president of the American Studies Association, she has received fellowships and grants from the American Council of Learned Societies and the National Endowment for the Humanities. She is William R. Kenan Professor English at Vanderbilt University.

SILVIO TORRES-SAILLANT, associate professor of English and director of Latino-Latin American Studies at Syracuse University, was the founding director of the City University of New York Dominican Studies Institute. Associated with various national projects and institutes in U.S. Hispanic culture, he is associate editor of *Latino Studies* and a senior editor for the *Oxford Encyclopedia of Latinos and Latinas in the United States*. He is the author of *Caribbean Poetics*, *El Retorno de las Yolas*, and the forthcoming *An Intellectual History of the Caribbean*, and coauthor of *The Dominican Americans*.

JOSEPH URGO is professor and chair of the Department of English at the University of Mississippi. He is the author of *Faulkner's Apocrypha: A Fable, Snopes, and the Spirit of Human Rebellion*, among other books and essays on American literature and culture.

CINDY WEINSTEIN is an associate professor of English at the California Institute of Technology. Her most recent publications include *Family, Kinship, and Sympathy in Nineteenth-Century American Literature* and the *Cambridge Companion to Harrriet Beecher Stowe*, which she edited. Her essay on Crane is part of a larger project on facts in fiction.

JANET ZANDY is professor of language and literature at the Rochester Institute of Technology. She is the editor of *Calling Home: Working-Class Women's Writings*, *Liberating Memory: Our Work and Our Working-Class Consciousness*, and *What We Hold in Common: An Introduction to Working-Class Studies*, as well as the author of *Hands: Physical Labor, Class, and Cultural Work*.